Arbitration Agreements
in a Transport Law Perspective

To NIFS

These have been my nursing years.
I've nursed two sons, one husband back to health and this thesis.
Hard work, but well worth it.
Wouldn't do any of it again soon, though.

Stinna

Kristina Maria Siig

Arbitration Agreements
in a Transport Law Perspective

DJØF Publishing Copenhagen
2003

Arbitration Agreements
– in a Transport Law Perspective

© 2003 by Jurist- og Økonomforbundets Forlag
DJØF Publishing, Copenhagen

Cover: Morten Højmark
Print: Gentofte Tryk

Printed in Denmark 2003
ISBN 87-574-0924-2

DJØF Publishing
17, Lyngbyvej
P.O.B 2702
DK 2100 Copenhagen

Phone: +45 39 13 55 00
Fax: +45 39 13 55 55
e-mail: forlag@djoef.dk
www.djoef-forlag.dk

Preface

This thesis has been written primarily during my employment at the Scandinavian Institute of Maritime Law, Oslo. My most sincere thanks are due there. One could say that it would be wrong to single out particular persons for special thanks, as the Institute is an organic place where the accumulative work and being of the individual staff is the essence. Still, having already designated this book to the Institute, I think I am allowed to give some special thanks as well. First and foremost to Professor Hans Jacob Bull, for getting the idea that I should write a Norwegian Doctorate in the first place, for brilliant advice, for – amazingly – having the stamina to see me through it, but most of all for being a dependable, straightforward and decent person. You are truly something special! But thanks should also be given to librarian Kirsten Al-Araki, for always finding what I needed and checking my bibliography, to Professor Thor Falkanger, for convincing me that I could write, and to Per Vestergaard Pedersen for never failing to turn my argument upside down and being a friend. And to the rest of you!

Other thanks are due at the Institute of Maritime Law in Southampton, providing me with research facilities and English insight for 18 months. Professor Nick Gaskell, lecturer Yvonne Baatz, secretary Rosemary Halloway and scientific assistant Raffaella Bonadies ought to be specifically mentioned, each for different reasons. The same is the case with the Department for Private Law, University of Aarhus, Denmark, who provided me with an office for two years and employed me for the last year. I have acquired both good friends and colleagues there, a few of which ought to be mentioned here, namely lecturer PhD Lisbeth Kjærgaard, for letting me avail myself of her good feeling for Danish contract law and generally being around, lecturer PhD Ana Lopez-Rodriguez for making the sprint with me and for providing a research environment, Andrew George for sincere discussions through bookshelves, and Professor Dr. Jur. Torsten Iversen for finally convincing me that this ought to be written in English.

As regards this book, I would like to thank Cand. Jur. Elin Michaelsen for making indexes and generally slaving for me in the last hectic week.

Finally – my extended family. Thank you mum and dad for babysitting so much, and the rest of you for being your normal spirited selves.

And then the three Butlers back home. Thanks to Niel for daring to seize me and to Mikkel and Alexander for proving to me that this is only the second most important thing in the world.

Materials published after 1 June 2002 have generally not been included in this thesis.

Oslo, 16.8.2002

Kristina Maria Siig

Contents

Table of contents

10

13

14

Abbreviations

A.C.	Appeal Cases
CA	Court of Appeal
DCA	Danish Court of Appeal
DSC	Danish Supreme Court
HL	House of Lords
ICC	International Chamber of Commerce
KFE	Kendelser om Fast Ejendom (Arbitral awards regarding real estate)
LB	Borgating Lagmannsrett (Borgating Court of Appeal)
LE	Eidsivating Lagmannsrett (Eidsivating Court of Appeal)
LF	Frostating Lagmannsrett (Frostating Court of Appeal)
LMCLQ	Lloyd's Maritime and Commercial Law Quarterly
LOF	Lloyd's Open Form (Standard salvage agreement)
MCCC	The Maritime and Commercial Court of Copenhagen (Sø- og Handelsretten)
ND	Nordiske Domme i Sjøfartsanliggender (Scandinavian Maritime Cases)
NMC	Nordic Maritime Code
NOU	Norges Offentlige Utredninger (Norwegian travaux préparatoires)
NSC	Norwegian Supreme Court
Sec.	Section
Secs.	Sections
SOU	Statens offentliga utredningar (Swedish travaux préparatoires)
U	Ugeskrift for Retsvæsen (Danish weekly law reports)
VBA	Voldgiftsnævnet for bygge- og anlægsbranchen (The arbitral tribunal for the building and construction trades)
Para.	Paragraph
Paras.	Paragraphs
QBD	Queen's Bench Division

Chapter I. Approaching the subject

§ 1. The thesis

1. Choosing the subject

This thesis deals with the arbitration agreement seen from a transport lawyer's point of view. It has been written as a result of the writer's own curiosity into mainly what rules governed arbitration agreements nationally and, not the least, internationally, and what the effects of those rules were. Also, being a transport lawyer, it seemed logical to investigate the special features occurring when the arbitration agreement is introduced into the transport chain.

Considering the in-built international quality of the transport trade, a strictly national point of view seemed of little value. The international rules as incorporated had to be discussed, and that discussion would be futile if no comparison to and between different national rules could be made. Thus, certain jurisdictions had to be chosen. The writer chose Danish and English law for obvious, albeit not only legal reasons. Danish law, being the writer's legal home ground, lent an example of the "hands-off" policy. Arbitration agreements have always rendered the Danish Courts incompetent to deal with a subject matter falling within the agreement and, as a rule, a dispute encompassed by an arbitration agreement will be dismissed from the Courts.[1] Danish Courts have never been able to revise the arbitration award on the merits. Furthermore, in principle, no general formal requirements for the conclusion of contracts exist. The condition that arbitration agreements should be in writing, seen in the transport conventions' regulation of arbitration agreements, therefore seemed an interesting peculiarity.

---

[1] See Christian V's Danish Law of 15th April 1683, s. 1-6-1.

Admittedly, the impact of Danish law upon arbitration agreements used in international transport is, at most, slight. The impact of English law, however, can hardly be overestimated. "London arbitration clauses" are hugely popular in some areas of the trade, normally resulting in English law governing the arbitration agreement if not the whole legal relationship between the parties.

Traditionally, the English Courts have adopted a more "hands-on" approach to arbitration. Lawsuits brought to the Courts notwithstanding an arbitration agreement were not dismissed, but stayed, the stay being discretionary (or mandatory if the agreement fell within the New York Convention). Also, appeal to the Courts regarding the merits of the case was possible.[2] However, in the new Arbitration Act 1996, a leap towards the "hands-off" policy was made. Furthermore, although oral arbitration agreements are not invalid, the mandatory stay now available under the 1996 Act only applies to arbitration agreements in writing. In those features alone, the two regulations present interesting possibilities of discussion and comparison.

For a long time, examining the position of the law under these two systems seemed sufficient. However, Danish and English regulations are both rather lax as regards which formal requirements should be satisfied when entering into the arbitration agreement. Therefore, the regulations do not throw light on the implications of stricter regulations. A third set of national rules was needed for that purpose. Fortunately the writer did not have to look far, as Norwegian law offered a brilliant example. Also Norwegian Courts do in principle obey the "hands-off" policy. However, because of a very strict formal requirement in national Norwegian law, arbitration agreements entered into in contracts of adhesion or bills of lading are often deemed null and void, leaving the parties to take their dispute to the Courts. The writer has chosen not to give a full analysis of the regulation of arbitration agreements in Norwegian law. Instead, Norwegian law will be considered to the extent that it offers interesting features, which, when compared to Danish and English law, contribute to the understanding of the subject. Fortunately, Norwegian law often does this, so Norwegian law will be discussed almost to the same extent as Danish and English law.

When originally choosing to include some areas of Norwegian law on arbitration agreements into this thesis, it could not be foreseen that Norwegian law faced a total transformation in the statutory regulation of arbitration agreements. However, in NOU 2001:33, a Draft Norwegian Arbitration Act has been proposed, based on the UNCITRAL Model Law, and purporting to abandon the requirement for writing altogether. Thus, at present it remains uncertain whether the description and discussion

---

[2] See the English Arbitration Act 1950 sec. 21 and the English Arbitration Act 1979 sec. 1.

of Norwegian law is soon to be of historic interest only. As a consequence, when relevant the proposals in the Draft will also be considered.

At this point, the reader should be notified that in the end it turned out that the transport-related issues were fewer than originally expected. The writer started her excursion into the regulation of the arbitration agreement in English law on the subject. The focus on shipping-cases found in English law on the conclusion of arbitration agreements does not repeat itself within Danish and Norwegian law. Therefore, the thesis provides a general picture of the arbitration agreement with certain transport related examples, rather than carrying through a transport related view upon all issues. However, if possible, transport law related examples are preferred, and the general conclusions reached are applied to the arbitration agreements found in transport and transport related agreements.

2. Angle, aim and method

The thesis deals mainly with the formation of arbitration agreements; but also the existence and the effects of the arbitration agreement are considered. The thesis concentrates around the principles of contract law and procedural rules regarding arbitration agreements. It applies a dogmatic rather than a functional approach to arbitration. In this respect the thesis differs from other recent works on international arbitration. However, it is maintained that the more traditionalist view, focusing on the areas of arbitration law where contract law and the law of procedure meet is equally valid. And in any case, the mere existence of new interesting literature on the choice of law and party autonomy aspects of international arbitration seems in itself to be a legitimate reason for not applying that focus.[3]

A work like this should not be a handbook. At the same time, it should not be a work of legal theory devoid of connection to the realities of the trade. It is hoped that it is neither. The thesis provides the practitioner with an emphasis on certain problem areas and a thorough discussion of how they have been dealt with – although not always solved – by national and international law. The scholar might be more interested in the thesis' deliberations upon the correct interpretation of and interaction between the relevant sources of law, and the writer's views de lege ferenda. It is hoped that both target groups will find that a new and sometimes challenging light is thrown upon the subject.

In this work, the methodology follows two routes.

---

[3] An obvious example here is the recently published thesis by Guiditta Cordero Moss, International Commercial Arbitration, Oslo, 1999, *Moss (1999)*.

First of all, it must be established what rules govern a certain question and what the exact contents of those rules are. This must be done regarding the law of both or all jurisdictions considered. The method applied at this stage is inductive and carries strong hermeneutic inspiration. The correct understanding of a given rule is sought out, that understanding being influenced by the factual and/or legal context in which the rule exists. At the same time the overall regulation is pieced together by the rules of which it consists. The circularity is obvious, but unavoidable. The rules are not only described. Guidelines as to their correct application, be that by the parties, the arbitral tribunal or by the Courts, are given when relevant.

The rules being thus described are then compared. Any comparison, including the comparison of legal systems, presupposes a point of reference. This may be a common legal basis, for example a convention text. Alternatively, the point of reference may be a legal problem, for example, what is required to incorporate an arbitration clause from one contract into another.

Finally, the rules are evaluated. Clearly, taking the general context, including the motive of a rule, into consideration when seeking the rule's correct understanding, will to an extent incorporate the writer's evaluations into the description of what is the rule. However, throughout the thesis it is sought clearly to distinguish the conclusion on what is the rule from the writer's view on whether the rule is appropriate, or in case of a comparison, which rule is the most appropriate.

In this thesis comparisons are used for two purposes. Firstly, comparisons are used as a means of describing the rules. For that the point of reference needs only to be loosely defined. One may look upon how a certain question is regulated in jurisdiction A and jurisdiction B and thus see whether, and to what extent, they coincide and differ. The comparison will in that way highlight the specific features of an area of law. Secondly, comparisons provide a tool for the evaluation. For that to be possible, however, one must be sure that what is compared is really the same thing. Thus, the point of reference must be fixed so that irrelevant elements do not affect the discussion. Obviously, it will not always be possible to extract identical situations or problems from the relevant legal systems. In such cases the writer has instead described the different rules and relevant pros and cons, seen from the point of view of the respective legal systems. It will not always be possible to establish which regulation is objectively the better. All the same, the writer will express an opinion on which regulation she prefers.[4]

---

[4] A down to earth example: Comparing an apple to other fruits will give a good impression of what is an apple (comparison used for descriptive purposes). But it will not give any idea of whether the apple is a good one. To establish that the apple must be compared to another apple (comparison used for evaluation).

3. Delimitation

This work concerns the arbitration agreement as opposed to the arbitral procedure and the arbitration award. It focuses on rules relevant to dispute resolution by arbitration in international transport agreements, although also strictly national rules will be deliberated. It does not concern itself with mediation or other means of alternative dispute resolution.

The discussions and the legal sources used have been chosen accordingly. The general problems, which may arise when opting for arbitration as a means of dispute resolution, are thus not considered in full and none of the statutory items used have been the basis of an exhaustive evaluation. Instead, a pick-and-choose approach has been adopted, centring only on the rules and topics directly relevant to the arbitration agreement.

The transport agreements considered are contracts for the carriage of goods by whichever means. Arbitration clauses are normally not allowed in contracts for carriage of passengers,[5] so rules concerning such carriage are only considered when particularly relevant.

Considering that this is a thesis on the arbitration agreement, the main focus is the rules of arbitration law dealing with that issue. However, to a considerable extent, especially within Danish law on the formation of contracts and as regards the arbitration agreement's validity on the substance, the arbitration agreement is governed by the general rules of contract law. Still, this thesis must not be seen as a thesis on contract law. To the extent that it is necessary to investigate general contract law rules, this will be done, but often a mere reference to certain rules on contract law will be considered to suffice. In that case, the reader wishing for more information must seek enlightenment elsewhere.[6]

4. The structure

The thesis consists of six chapters, Chapter II containing the thesis' main discussion, namely the discussion of the requirements for the formation of arbitration agreements. However, first, in Chapter I, the arbitration agreement's use and regulations

---

[5] See e.g. Convention for the Unification of Certain Rules for International Carriage by Air, signed at Warzaw on 12 October 1929, Art. 28, e.c, and Convention for the Unification of Certain Rules for International Carriage by Air, Montreal 28 May 1999, Art. 33 cf. Art. 34.

[6] See e.g. *Andersen/Madsen (2001)*, *Andersen (1998)*, *Chitty (1999)*, *Hov (1998)*, and *Woxholth (2001)*.

when applied in the transport chain is presented, and the reader is introduced to the relevant sources of law. In this way, Chapter I aims at equipping the reader with the knowledge necessary when reading the remaining part of the thesis.

As said, Chapter II is concerned with the rules applicable to the formation of arbitration agreements. It regards the general regulation of arbitration agreements and does not aim specifically at transport related problems. In § 1 the features of the arbitration agreement are described. Then, the rules governing the entering into an arbitration agreement under Danish, English and Norwegian law are discussed in §§ 2-4, followed by a brief conclusion in § 5. Finally, the formal requirements of the New York Convention Art. II are deliberated in § 6. In Chapter III, the substantial validity of the arbitration agreement is considered, whereas the principle of Kompetenz-Kompetenz is discussed in Chapter IV.

The aim of the discussions in Chapter II-IV is two-fold. Firstly, the problems emerging are interesting in themselves. The conflict and interaction between national and international rules trigger quite some discussion, as does the differences and/or similarities of the relevant national legislations. Secondly, laying down the general rules provides a necessary platform for Chapter V, in which the specific transport related issues are discussed.

Chapter V, § 1 concerns certain issues regarding the arbitrability of transport disputes. § 2 discusses the regulation of arbitration agreements and clauses found in the Nordic Maritime Codes chapter 13, and in § 3 the transport documentation and its consistency with the formal requirements laid down in the New York Convention is the main issue.

Conclusions and suggestions are found in Chapter VI. The writer's material is much too widespread and the problems much too diverse for one single conclusion to offer itself. However, general views on the impact of the different legislative methods are presented, and the aptness of the national and international legislation to deal with the problems arising under the present regimes are offered, allowing finally a point at the direction legislation has taken (or is likely to take) to be made.

§ 2. The use of arbitration as a means of dispute resolution

When cut to the core, an arbitration agreement is simply an agreement entered into by two or more parties with the object of having disputes between them resolved by someone else, but not by the Courts. Below, in Chapter II, § 1, the legal features of the arbitration agreement are looked into, so for the present the above definition will suffice.

Then, why would one choose to have a dispute resolved by arbitration? A list of the traditional pros would include the freedom to choose the procedural rules applicable; the freedom to choose the arbitrators; the more liberal regard to the choice of law including the acceptance of lex mercatoria and the possibility of deciding the case according to equity; the confidentiality of the proceedings; the one-instance system, which may provide for a more expeditious and comparatively cheaper dispute resolution procedure; and the fact that arbitration agreements and awards are recognised and enforced in almost all jurisdictions.[7]

Having listed such qualities in support of arbitration, one might imagine that all international agreements contain arbitration clauses. The reason that this is not the case is either that the Courts in certain cases might provide similar services, or the inherent inadequacies of arbitration. For example, as arbitration is based on consensus, consolidation is normally not an option, and when compared to the value of what

---

[7] See e.g. Danish travaux préparatoires, p. 23, *Philip (1995)*, and *Russell (1997)*, para. 1.013-1.018. See also, on the choice between the courts and arbitration, *Franklin (2000)*.

is disputed, arbitration might not be so cheap after all.[8] Using documentation from the carriage of goods by sea as an example, some of these points will be deliberated.

Arbitration has a long tradition within the charter-party trade. In fact, within this trade jurisdiction agreements are almost unheard of. The parties to a charter-party agreement are normally professional players in the market. They are relatively equal, which reduces the need for the Courts' protection of one of the parties. The money involved in the charter-party trade renders the costs of arbitration negligible, while at the same time the importance of a quick solution to the dispute becomes paramount. The parties' rights and obligations under a charter-party are governed by the contract rather than by statute or precedence. That, and the international nature of the trade, provides emphasis on the international custom within the trade. The parties may therefore be interested in having their dispute decided by person(s) with specialist knowledge instead of persons with more general legal skills. Especially if within the time charter trade, the parties may still be conducting business whilst having a dispute regarding certain aspects of the charter-party contract. Maybe, according to the charter-party, their business relations are due to be continuing for several years to come. In those cases, arbitration might seem less harmful to the parties' relations than going to the Courts, and thus not jeopardise their future relations. Also, because of the confidentiality of the proceedings, (in theory) no one need know of the parties' dispute, and the terms of their contract are not necessarily made public. Finally, one of the major assets of the owner, the ship, does per definition travel around the world. From the owner's point of view, the ship in that way makes him vulnerable to law suits in many different jurisdictions. Therefore, the arbitration agreement helps him or her by fixing the point for future dispute resolution. From the charterer's point of view the fact that the arbitration agreement may be enforced in almost all jurisdictions ensures that the owner may not de facto escape satisfying the award by keeping his or her major asset – the fleet – outside the jurisdiction in which the award has been rendered. In effect, the award may be enforced against the owner's fleet no matter where the ships are.

The arbitration agreements in the charter-parties are filtered down to the general cargo and container trades through the issuance of tramp bills of lading. (Bills of lading, which refer to the charter-party's conditions of carriage). The arbitration agreement is transferred via the tramp bill of lading to the receiver of the cargo. If only a few cargo owners are connected with the voyage in question, the arbitration agreement may still be advantageous. However, in the container trade and in liner transport of general cargo, the arbitration agreement is generally not the best option. Firstly, certain jurisdictions do not accept that an arbitration agreement between the

---

[8] See the English Arbitration Act 1996 secs. 89-91.

owner and the consignee may be entered into via the issuance of a tramp bill of lading. Secondly, the whole factual situation does suggest itself to arbitration agreements. The owner may have the same interest in the agreement as when employing the ship on a charter-party, but the numbers and interests of the counter-parties have altered dramatically. There may be several hundred cargo owners regarding each voyage, so if a major accident or delay occurs the administration of setting up an arbitration tribunal fit to deal with it would be immense. Also, the interests of the cargo owners may not be identical, therefore, the cargo owners may not be seen as one counter-party fit to match the bargaining powers of the line. Often, the cargo owners have no real bargaining powers at all; they are left to accept the general conditions of carriage of the line. The legislators have appreciated this and have made mandatory rules for their protection. Finally, a cargo owner may only have a small amount of cargo transported. Setting up ad hoc arbitration or furnishing security for institutionalised arbitration may not be economically sound. Therefore, arbitration agreements are not used in liner bills of lading and other transport documents designed to govern the liner trade.

§ 3. Overview of the sources of law governing the arbitration agreement

1. Why regulate arbitration?

If two parties agree that a third party shall decide a dispute between them according to certain rules and a certain procedure, and this is in fact done, and the parties fulfil the award, no regulation of arbitration is needed. The arbitration agreement in that case may create its own legal space, an area of party autonomy disconnected from any national or international law. And in any case, due to the confidentiality, which is the norm in arbitral proceedings, in theory no one will know about it. However, realism has it that the situation here described will not always materialise. Because the legislators regard arbitration advantageous, they have wanted to be of aid when arbitration meets obstacles. Firstly, one of the parties may want to avoid arbitrating the dispute for one reason or other,[9] or, alternatively, may not want to satisfy the award. Therefore, as the Courts of the national states hold the monopoly on enforcing agreements, regulation to ensure that the Courts may enforce arbitration agreements and awards is required. Secondly, the parties may be in agreement that the dispute should be arbitrated but not on how to carry out the procedure. Regulation to address situations where the arbitration procedure grinds to a standstill is thus also beneficial. Finally, even though the legislators wish to support arbitration as a mode of dispute resolution, they do not wish to endorse arbitration and party autonomy being used to create an area of lawlessness. Regulation has therefore been formulated to ensure

[9] He or she might find that the formal requirements have not been satisfied, that the arbitration agreement is invalid, that the arbitration agreement does not regard the dispute before the Courts, or, maybe, that there is no contract whatsoever between the parties.

that certain safeguards, which are considered indispensable, may be enforced also in situations where arbitration is agreed. For these three reasons, national regulation as to arbitration is required.

The need for international regulation is generated by similar considerations. If the international community wishes, as it does, to encourage the parties to international contracts to arbitrate their differences, they must provide for a similar backing of the process. However, if the international support is only the sum of the rules of the national states, the predictability required in international trade is impaired. The parties cannot forecast, which Court may potentially deal with the question of whether the arbitration agreement is valid and binding. The laws of the national states vary as regards the rules on recognition and enforcement of arbitration agreements and awards. An international state of affairs which bases itself solely on the rules of the lex fori therefore renders it virtually impossible for the parties to predict their legal position as regards forum. As a result, they might opt for a jurisdiction agreement, or indeed not agree upon forum at all, even if, in principle, arbitration would suit the parties better. For arbitration to be maintained as an effective means of dispute resolution in international commerce in general, an amount of international unification must be present. If it is not, arbitration agreements will create uncertainties and lead to forum shopping and opposing Court (and arbitration) decisions, rather than being a way of determining forum.

For arbitration to be a real option in international commerce, international law must provide for at least two things: Firstly, the Courts must, to a certain extent and under certain preconditions, accept the derogatory effects of arbitration agreements. Secondly, the arbitration award must, likewise to a certain extent and under certain preconditions, be respected as a final and enforceable settlement of the parties' dispute. International legislation regarding those points must therefore be provided.

Below, the national and international sources of law regulating arbitration and the arbitration agreement are presented.

2. Legislation

2.1. National legislation – the Arbitration Acts
Agreements to arbitrate may be entered into in many different areas of law, and may consequently be affected by a number of different statutory regulations, e.g. the Danish Contracts Act,[10] the English Unfair Terms in Consumer Contracts Regulation

---

[10] Lov nr. 242 af 8. maj 1917, most recently revised in Lovbekendtgørelse nr. 781 af 26. august 1996.

1994,[11] The Unfair Arbitration Agreements (Specified Amount) Order 1999,[12] the Nordic Maritime Code 1994[13] (as far as not Hague-Visby based), etc. To indulge into any such rules at this stage would be to exceed the purpose of this introduction, instead the general rules on arbitration will be presented.

The Danish Arbitration Act 1972 is a result of the work of a committee established by the Danish Ministry of Justice on 2 February 1962, with view to determining whether a more extensive regulation of arbitration was required. Also, the committee should take into consideration whether the New York Convention of 10 June 1958 on the recognition and enforcement of arbitration awards and the European Convention on International Commercial Arbitration of 21 April 1961 should be ratified by Denmark.[14]

The Danish law on arbitration had developed over centuries through case law connected to DL 1-6-1.[15] The result had been a position of the law that was firm, without being rigid. Satisfied with this aspect of the law, the committee suggested an Act, consisting only of provisions which had so far been lacking[16] and which supported the arbitration process. The Danish Arbitration Act thus only concerns the relationship between arbitration and the Courts. In particular, the law aims at regulating the situations where the arbitration procedure needs the assistance of the Courts.

As regards international arbitration, the committee suggested that Denmark became party to the New York Convention of 1958 and the European Convention of

---

[11] Now in version available to this writer the Unfair Terms in Consumer Contracts Regulations 1999, No. 2083.

[12] The Unfair Arbitration Agreements (Specified Amount) Order 1999, No. 2167.

[13] Latest updated Danish version is Lovbekendtgørelse af lov nr. 39 af 20.1.1998, som ændret ved lov nr. 900 og 910 af 16.12.1998 og lov nr. 106 af 13.2. 2001.

[14] Danish travaux préparatoires 1, p. 5.

[15] Christian V's Danish Law of 15th April 1683, s. 1-6-1. "Dersom Parterne voldgift deris Sag og Tvistighed paa Dannemænd, enten med Opmand, eller uden, da hvad de sige og kiende, saa vit deris Fuldmagt dennem tillader at giøre, det staar fast, og kand ej for nogen Ret til Underkiendelse indstævnis, dog Kongen sin Sag Forbeholden." The 17th century Danish roughly translates as "If the Parties arbitrate their Case and Dispute on Danesmen, either with an Umpire or without, then what they say and rule, as far as their Mandate allows them, that stands fast and cannot be brought before any Court to be overruled, the King's Case apart."

[16] Danish travaux préparatoires 1, p. 30.

1961. The committee could not support the then draft European Convention on a uniform law on arbitration.[17]

In England, before the Arbitration Act 1996, arbitration was governed by the Arbitration Acts of 1950, 1975 and 1979. Thus, the object of the Arbitration Act 1996 was not to legislate where no legislation existed, but to revise the legislation already in place. The need for such a revision had been apparent for some time. The Acts only regulated specific questions. The majority of the regulation of arbitration was found in case law. As put by *Lord Mustill:*

"All this has meant that a user of the process and his foreign or non-specialist adviser cannot quickly hope to ascertain, simply by reading the Arbitration Acts and other statutes which contain individual provisions concerning arbitration, how arbitration in England works in practice, and still less how to confront the kind of problem which is likely to arise if the conduct of the reference goes wrong."[18]

This position of the law was not favourable upon the use of London arbitration clauses, and a general feeling that something had to be done emerged.[19] Thus, in 1989 the Department of Trade and Industry published "A New Arbitration Act",[20] which was the response of the Departmental Advisory Committee to the question of

"[W]hether, and if so to what extent, the provision of the Model Law should be implemented in England and Wales, Scotland or Northern Ireland and upon what measures should be taken for that purpose; ... [and to] examine the operation of the Arbitration Acts 1950-1979 in the light of the Model Law and to recommend to the Secretary of State any legislative or other steps which the Committee considers should be taken to improve the system of arbitration in England and Wales."[21]

The Committee concluded that the Model Law should not be adopted as regarded England, Wales and Northern Ireland, although adoption was recommended (and later carried out) considering Scotland. Instead, the Committee suggested the creation of a new Arbitration Act, which would consolidate the existing principles of arbitration law, whether they derived from the acts or from common law.[22] The first at-

[17] Danish travaux préparatoires 1, p. 22 and p. 31.

[18] *Mustill report,* para. 103, 1st and 2nd sentence.

[19] *Rutherford/Sims (1996),* p. 7 and p. 10.

[20] *Mustill report.*

[21] *Mustill report,* para. 2.

[22] *Mustill report,* para. 108.

tempt was the "Draft of a Bill to consolidate, with amendments, the Arbitration Act 1950, the Arbitration Act 1975, the Arbitration Act 1979 and related enactments" of February 1994.[23] However, the Draft Bill was not found satisfactory,[24] and the Bill was rewritten and presented anew in July 1995, under the preamble "An Act to restate and improve the law relating to arbitration pursuant to an arbitration agreement ... ".[25] This draft was well received, and, with a few amendments, became what is now the Arbitration Act 1996. The Act does not provide a full codification of the English law of arbitration. However, it updates and presents most areas of that law in a logical and accessible manner, incorporating many of the common law rules. Thus, the "foreign or non-specialist adviser" will be able to get a very good grip of what is the law on arbitration by reading the Act, and the ambition of making the law user-friendlier has been achieved.

At present, there is no "Norwegian Arbitration Act", instead the general rules on arbitration are found in Chapter 32 of the Norwegian Code of Procedure 1915. The relevant provisions will be discussed below in Chapter II, § 4.

2.2. International conventions on arbitration

Quite a few regional or international conventions on international arbitration exist. First to be mentioned amongst these is the Geneva Protocol of 24 September 1923 on the recognition of international arbitration agreements.[26] The 1923 Geneva Protocol was in 1927 supplemented by the Geneva Convention of 26 September 1927 on the execution of foreign arbitration awards.[27] The 1923 Geneva Protocol and the 1927

---

[23] See United Kingdom Department of Trade and Industry Consultation Document on Proposed Clauses and Schedules for an Arbitration Bill.

[24] 1996 Report on the Arbitration Bill, para. 2.

[25] 1996 Report on the Arbitration Bill, para. 3.

[26] Protocol on Arbitration Clauses signed on behalf of His Majesty at a Meeting of the Assembly of the League of Nations held on the September 24, 1923 / Bekendtgørelse om Danmarks Ratifikation af den i Genf den 24. September 1923 aabnede Protokol vedrørende Voldgiftsklausuler i Handelskontrakter, Bkg. nr. 167 af 15. maj 1925.

[27] Convention on the Execution of Foreign Arbitral Awards signed at Geneva on behalf of His Majesty on September 26, 1927 / Bekendtgørelse om Danmarks Ratifikation af den i Genève den 26. September aabnede Overenskomst angaaende Eksekution af Voldgiftskendelser afsagt i Udlandet, Bkg. nr. 150 af 28. maj 1929.

Geneva Convention were successful and are adopted by both Denmark and England. However, the regulation of the conventions was not considered satisfactory, consequently they were replaced in 1958 by the New York Convention of 10 June 1958 on the recognition and enforcement of arbitration awards.[28] The convention has been extremely successful, and is adopted by most states including Denmark, Norway and Great Britain. These conventions are what might be called general conventions on international arbitration, dealing mainly with the relationship between international arbitration and national Courts. They aim at dealing with the two main areas mentioned above in point 1, namely the conditions for the recognition of the arbitration agreement and the conditions for the enforcement of arbitral awards. The arbitration procedure is generally not dealt with. In the following the New York Conventions rules on the arbitration agreement will be discussed in detail. The 1923 Geneva Protocol and the 1927 Geneva Convention will not be deliberated on.

Finally, the European Convention on International Commercial Arbitration of 21 April 1961 should be mentioned.[29] The convention is a regional convention. It is intended as a supplement to the New York Convention, designed to promote "… the development of European trade by … removing certain difficulties that may impede the organisation and operation of international commercial arbitration in relations between physical or legal persons of different European countries".[30] In other words, the convention aims at facilitating arbitration in what could in 1961 be perceived as East-West arbitration. The convention deals for the most part with the arbitral proceedings, as the rules on the relationship between the Courts and arbitration are found in the New York Convention. Denmark has adopted the convention, but Norway and Great Britain have not. Below, the convention will only be mentioned when particularly relevant.

Further conventions exist. The Washington Convention of March 18, 1965 regards investment disputes arising between states and nationals of other states. Such disputes are to be settled by The International Centre for the Settlement of Investment Disputes. The convention has been widely

---

[28] The Convention on the Recognition and Enforcement of Foreign Arbitral Awards aadopted by the United Nations Conference on International Commercial Arbitration on June 10, 1958 / New York-konventionen af 10. juni 1958 om anerkendelse og fuldbyrdelse af udenlandske voldgiftkendelser.

[29] The European Convention on International Commercial Arbitration opened for signature on 21st April 1961 / Genève-konventionen af 21. april 1961 om international handelsvoldgift.

[30] Preamble of the European Convention on International Commercial Arbitration.

adopted.[31] The Moscow Convention of 1972 addresses arbitration between economic entities in the former Eastern bloc. After the collapse of the Eastern bloc the importance of and numbers of signatories to the convention has decreased. The Panama Convention of 1975 is a regional, general convention on arbitration. Some Latin American states have chosen to adopt this convention rather than the New York Convention. The rules of the Panama Convention of 1975 are to a large extent similar to the rules of the New York Convention.[32] None of these conventions will be subject to further discussion here.

2.3. International transport conventions

The regulation of arbitration agreements found in international transport conventions ranges from none what so ever to a detailed regulation of the conclusion, contents and legal effects of the agreement. In the first group the Hague[33] and Hague-Visby Rules[34] on bills of lading and the COTIF-CIM Convention[35] on international carriage of goods by rail remain totally silent as to arbitration agreements. In fact, the Hague and Hague-Visby Rules do not contain any provisions on forum. COTIF-CIM Art. 56 regulates the jurisdiction of the Courts as regards actions brought under the rules, but does not mention arbitration. In the second group we find conventions, which do in fact govern the use of arbitration agreements regarding disputes covered by the conventions. The Warsaw Convention on international carriage by air,[36] including its supplementary convention, the Guadalajara Convention,[37] the Montreal Convention

---

[31] The Convention on the settlement of investment disputes between States and nationals of other States, opened for signature in Washington on March 18, 1965. *Hjejle (1987)*, p. 147.

[32] See *van den Berg (1989)*.

[33] The International Convention on Bills of Lading signed at Brussels on 24 August 1924.

[34] The International Convention on Bills of Lading signed at Brussels on 24 August 1924 as amended by the Brussels Protocol 1968.

[35] The Convention Concerning International Carriage by Rail of 9 May 1980, Appendix B, Uniform Rules Concerning the Contract for International Carriage of Goods by Rail.

[36] Convention for the Unification of certain Rules Relating to International Carriage by Air, done at Warsaw on the 12th October 1929. See Art. 32, 2nd sentence.

[37] Guadalajara Supplementary Convention, done at Guadalajara on the 18th of September 1961, Art. IX(3), 2nd sentence.

on international carriage by air,[38] and the CMR-Convention[39] on international carriage of goods by road, all contain a basic regulation of arbitration agreements, acknowledging their validity and use under certain formal or substantial preconditions. The most exhaustive regulations are found in the Hamburg Rules on the carriage of goods by sea[40] and the Multimodal Convention.[41] The conventions hold a thorough regulation of the arbitration agreement, and they even offer a remedy (compensation)[42] if the regulation is not complied with. The conventions here mentioned are special conventions, taking into account the characteristics of the trades, and when overlapping the area governed by the general conventions on arbitration, the special rules should prevail.[43] The general conventions, however, form the framework within which the arbitration agreement works in international transport. Thus, the binding nature of arbitration agreements, their acknowledgement and enforcement is not governed by the transport conventions. Instead, they are governed by especially the New York Convention as incorporated into national law. The regulation on arbitration agreements offered by these special conventions is dealt with below in Chapter V.

2.4. Other international sources of written arbitration law
2.4.1. The UNCITRAL Model Law on International Commercial Arbitration
The United Nations Commission on International Trade Law adopted its Model Law on International Commercial Arbitration (the UNCITRAL Model Law) on June 21, 1985. The UNCITRAL Model Law is not a convention, but a template to

---

[38] Convention for the Unification of certain Rules for International Carriage by Air, done at Montreal on the 28th of May, 1999, Art. 34.

[39] Convention on the Contract for the International Carriage of Goods by Road, done at Geneva 19th of May 1956, Art. 33.

[40] United Nations Convention on the Carriage of Goods by Sea, done at Hamburg on the 21st March, 1978, Art. 22.

[41] United Nations Convention on International Multimodal Transport of Goods, done at Geneva on the 24th May, 1980, Art. 27.

[42] Hamburg Rules Art. 23(4), Multimodal Convention Art. 28(4).

[43] See New York Convention art VII(1): "The provisions of the present Convention shall not affect the validity of multilatereal or bilatereal agreements concerning the recognition and enforcement of arbitral awards entered into by the Contracting States … ".

legislators, and it has since its birth had an immense influence upon the developments in legislation on arbitration. The Model Law was created on the background of the UNCITRAL Arbitration Rules,[44] with view to securing uniformity within international arbitration,[45] and has as such been very successful, even if States giving new legislation on arbitration have not always stayed as close to the Model Law as UNCITRAL would have wished.[46] Quite a few States have adopted the Model Law,[47] and even more States, deciding not to adopt it in full, have been inspired by it, adopting solutions that are similar.[48] Thus, since 1985, legislators, wishing to enact a New Arbitration Act, but not to adopt the Model law have seen it necessary to explain why they chose not to.[49]

2.4.2. Arbitration rules

It is a matter of taste whether arbitration rules should be discussed here, or whether they ought to be described below in point 4 regarding private law making. However, some of these rules are so widespread that they tend to be if not normative, then the norm within international trade and commerce. Therefore, the two central sets of arbitration rules will be briefly presented here.

Arbitration rules are set standards of procedure, that may apply to a given arbitral institution,[50] or rules of general applicability, that may be incorporated into the parties' arbitration agreement by ref-

---

[44] UNCITRAL Arbitration Rules 1976, Resolution 31/98 as adopted by the General assembly on 15 December 1976.

[45] Explanatory Note by the UNCITRAL Secretariat on the Model Law on International Commercial Arbitration, para 1.
Here taken from http://www.sice.oas.org/DISPUTE/comarb/uncitral/icomarbe3.asp.

[46] Explanatory Note by the UNCITRAL Secretariat on the Model Law on International Commercial Arbitration, para 3.
Here taken from http://www.sice.oas.org/DISPUTE/comarb/uncitral/icomarbe3.asp.

[47] E.g. Australia, Canada, Nigeria, Scotland Bermuda. (*Swedish travaux préparatoires,* para. 4.2.)

[48] E.g. Bulgaria, Cyprus, Tunisia, Russia, Mexico and Germany. (*Swedish travaux préparatoires,* para. 4.2.) If the Draft Norwegian Arbitration Act becomes a reality also Norway will fall under this heading.

[49] *Mustill report,* para. 89-90, *Swedish travaux préparatoires,* para. 4.3.4.

[50] E.g. LCIA Arbitration Rules, 01.01. 1998 applying to the London Court of International Arbitration.

erence,[51] and apply to both ad hoc and institutionalised arbitration. Arbitration rules will generally tend to deal with the procedure of the arbitral tribunal, and thus aim at filling the void left by most of the international conventions on arbitration. The two most central arbitration rules are the UNCITRAL Arbitration Rules of 28. April 1976 (Resolution 31/98) and the ICC Arbitration Rules, the latest version being the 1998 version, applicable as of 1st January 1998. Both sets of rules acknowledge the doctrines of Kompetenz-Kompetenz[52] and separability,[53] however apart from that their regulation of areas concerned with the arbitration agreement is sparse. Thus, the UNCITRAL rules state in Art. 1(1) that they apply to situations where the parties have agreed in writing that disputes shall be referred to arbitration under the UNCITRAL rules, thus presupposing a written agreement to arbitrate, whereas the ICC rules recommend that the parties use a standard written ICC arbitration clause.[54] Apart from this the rules do not concern themselves with the arbitration agreement, and they will only rarely be touched upon in the following.

3. Decisions and judgments

The English Arbitration Act 1996 offers quite an exhaustive regulation of arbitration. Still, case law is very important. Firstly, as not all areas of arbitration law are regulated by the Act. On certain questions the position of the law is simply left to the Courts to decide. In doing so, the Courts may preserve the position of the law already established by case law before the 1996 Act, thus making all previous decisions relevant. Also, the English Courts have already dealt with the interpretation of the Arbitration Act 1996 in cases decided since the Act went into force on 1 January 1997. These cases, as far as within the work's scope, are obviously immensely interesting.

The very sparse statutory regulation of the Danish Arbitration Act 1972 leaves many areas of arbitration law to be dealt with by the Courts alone. One should therefore expect Danish case law to take up much space in this thesis. It does, but not as much as one might have thought. In the last 50 years, approximately 150 cases relating to arbitration have been published in Danish law journals. Many of these cases deal with areas of arbitration falling outside the scope of this work, such as statutory arbitration or the appointment of arbitrators. However, to the extent that relevant case law is available, and of course it often is, it will be discussed in detail. A similar picture repeats itself regarding Norwegian case law. Considering this, and that – at least out of principle – Norwegian law is mainly presented in this thesis so as to provide a

[51] See e.g. U 2000.897 DSC and U 1987.945 MCCC.

[52] UNCITRAL Arbitration Rules Art. 21(1) and 21(2), ICC Arbitration Rules Art. 6(2).

[53] UNCITRAL Arbitration Rules Art. 21(2), ICC Arbitration Rules Art. 6(4).

[54] *ICC Arbitration Rules*, p. 8.

mirror for the Danish and English regulations, an even greater extent of selectiveness is exercised when presenting Norwegian case law.

4. Private law-making

In an area of law dominated by party autonomy, the lawmaking powers of private parties are essential. As the term "private lawmaking" has no established legal meaning it may be used as a catch-phrase, covering anything from an ad hoc agreement, via company or trade general conditions to private rulings on disputes. The law on arbitration is supplemented with all these kinds of private law making. For example, the parties to an already existing dispute may choose to have that dispute settled by arbitration. The arbitration agreement in that respect creates a specific regulation of the parties' relationship, as does any agreement. However, the agreement will have little or no impact on the general area of law within which it is used. Instead, the arbitration agreement may be, and often is, inserted as a clause amongst other clauses in a standard form of contract. Some of these forms, for example the BIMCO approved charter-parties or the Lloyd's Open Form on salvage operations are dominant within the trade, thus extensively, and indeed within some trades exclusively, regulating the choice of forum in that area of the trade. Regarding international arbitration, also the rules of the arbitration institutions play an important role. They may provide gap-filling or optional background law, or indeed they may provide obligatory regulation, which will have to be abided to by the parties, if they wish to benefit from the institution's dispute-resolving facilities. Finally, within arbitration law, the private lawmaking taking place when giving an award springs to mind. Obviously, an award needs not always create new law. Often it will simply state what is already the law between the parties. But it may go further than that. The arbitrator may choose to rule according to equity, thus sometimes disregarding written or unwritten existing law and creating new. More importantly, the award may be followed by other tribunals or by the Courts in later cases.[55] The precedence from awards may thereby create new law. However, the confidentiality of arbitral proceedings and awards often prejudices any real impact of the awards as a means of throwing light upon the regulation of arbitration agreements in international transport. Awards may only be published if the parties so agree, or maybe, if this follows from applicable arbitration rules. Some awards are published the Yearbook on Commercial Arbitration, some in journals on arbitration law or journals published by permanent arbitral

---

[55] Regarding the arbitration award's value as a legal source, see *Brækhus (1998)*, p. 185 ff and below, § 4, point 1.4.

tribunals,[56] and others in Nordiske Domme i Sjøfartsanliggender (Nordic Maritime Cases, hereafter ND). Arbitration awards may also be found in published Court judgments and decisions. If one of the parties wishes to have the award enforced by the Courts, he or she must provide the Courts with (a copy of) the award, which may in turn be published.[57] Still, the accessible cases are not as numerous as one might have hoped. Therefore, unfortunately, not as many arbitration awards as the writer wished for have found their way to this thesis.

5. Literature

A source to the illumination of what law governs the arbitration agreement may be found in legal literature. General textbooks exist regarding both Danish and English law. In fact, the mass of English literature has exploded within recent years due to the introduction of the Arbitration Act 1996. One must not overlook that also other textbooks, be that on contract law, procedural law or international private law, holds chapters or paragraphs on arbitration and/or arbitration related subjects. General works on international commercial arbitration also present themselves. Furthermore, arbitration law is discussed in many articles. They may be found in either Law Journals dealing specifically with arbitration and like subjects, or in Law Journals that deal with general subjects. Also, quite a few articles are found in published materials from international meetings or conferences.

---

[56] See for example Kendelser om Fast Ejendom (Findings on real estate), where findings of the Danish permanent arbitral tribunal for the building and construction trades are found.

[57] See for example U 1997.251 H. In the case, dispute had arisen regarding whether or not the Danish Courts should enforce an award given by a Norwegian tribunal. An extract of the award was published with the decision of the Danish Supreme Court.

§ 4. Relevant theories on the sources of law

1. National sources of law

1.1. Introductory anecdote

At least within western societies, the ideas of what is the correct solution to a legal dispute between professionals concerning the law of contracts or the law of obligations are so similar that it will be the argumentative route to a certain result, rather than the result itself that will tend to differ. As a consequence, in this writer's experience, one of the most infallible ways to end a placid mood at a dinner where lawyers from different legal families are present is to embark on a discussion of what is a source of law and what are the basic principles of jurisprudence. The Scandinavian and English lawyers will tend to find the Mediterranean lawyers' argument that the judge is merely the "mouth of the Law"[58] little more than laughable, whereas the Mediterranean lawyer will find the Common Law – and to an extent the Scandinavian law – a jungle of unstructured precedence. Finally, after another bottle of Chablis, the Scandinavian and the Mediterranean lawyers will agree to find the Common Law system barbaric due to its lack of a written Constitution.[59]

---

[58] Montesquieu pronounced in Esprit de Lois, in keeping with his theory of the division of powers, that the Courts should only be "la bouche qui prononce le paroles de la loi". (See *Augdahl (1949)*, p. 83, ft. nt. 1 for reference. (Esprit de lois, liv. XI, chap. VI).

[59] I wish to thank my colleagues PhD Ana Lopez-Rodriguez and Andrew George for – albeit unwillingly – having provided the inspiration to this introductory anecdote through many heated discussions taking place whilst eating packed lunches.

This thesis' main focus is upon the international arbitration agreement. Thus, it could be argued that the different national theories on the sources of law need not be discussed in this work. However, applying a dogmatic rather than a functional approach in the thesis necessitates a discussion of the national sources of law – and in any case, much of the law regarding arbitration agreements, be they international or not, or transport related or not, is found in national law.

This writer will employ her best efforts to make use of the sources of law and basic principles on the sources of law that apply within the respective jurisdictions, when indeed dealing with national law. However, certain reservations have to be made. Firstly, this writer is Danish and therefore her Danish "legal upbringing" may taint the application of sources of law that are not Danish. Realistically, despite the efforts to the contrary, the writer may probably positively warrant that the Danishness (albeit unintentionally) will rob off on non-Danish materials. For this I apologise in advance. Secondly, internal inconsistencies within the different national theories on (what are) sources of law leave the writer some leeway to adhere to the version of national theories on the sources of law that she prefers. Those versions will most likely not be to everyone's taste, but the choices so made will be explained and defended below.

1.2. What is a source of law

The discussion of what are the differences in the theories on legal sources of law presupposes a definition on what is a source of law. *Bell* defines a source of law as "the sources of legal justification".[60] According to *Bell*, when decision-makers claim that their decision is correct, they have to show that it is supported by certain legal sources.[61] The decision-maker should base its finding on what are acceptable *formal* – and not substantial – reasons. A definition of a source of law based on this view would thus focus on what are acknowledged formal principles of law. Such an approach makes it relatively easy to establish, what are the sources of law. A source of law may simply be defined by certain formal criteria, be they statutes, higher ranking case law, etc. *Eckhoff* objects to using the term "legal source" in this way, as it suggests that the law is something you may simply find, as long as you know where to look. Instead, he points out, many of the questions one will encounter as a jurist do not have clear answers. In such cases, what the jurist finds in the sources of law will

---

[60] *Bell (2000),* para. 1.02.

[61] *Bell (2000),* para. 1.01.

just be the raw material for the jurist's own arguments and evaluations.[62] *Bell* realises that the law may not always be established by simply referring to a single source of formal law. In that case the lawyer must employ a "range of authority, formal and substantive reasons".[63] Accepting that a legal problem may not always have a clear answer, *Wegener* chooses a Ross-inspired approach, defining a legal source as all the factors, influencing the authorities applying the law in their choice of which rules should be taken into account in the decision of a specific legal case.[64] In this way, legal sources are the sources consulted when wanting to determine what *is* the law within a given area. *Kinander*[65] takes *Wegener's* and *Eckhoff's* points a step further, as he points out that when accepting that the law is not (always) simply found, establishing what is a legal source at the same time *creates* law. Obviously, accepting such a wide definition of a source of law, aimed at establishing what is the solution to a specific legal problem, makes it very difficult indeed to point out *general* rules as to what is a source of law. In this work an approach to what is a source of law ad modum Wegener's approach will be applied, the focus being on which materials the Courts and/or the arbitral tribunals are likely to take into account when assessing the answer to a legal problem.

1.3. A hierarchy of sources of law?

It follows from the Spanish Civil Code Art. 1, that the sources of law are the statute, custom and principles of natural justice – exclusively and in that order. Obviously, in Scandinavian and Common Law systems, the focus on case law renders such a definition inadequate. That does not entail that a prioritised list cannot be made. *Bell* thus lists the hierarchy of English legal norms such: "(1) European Community law, (2) the European Convention on Human Rights, (3) the Constitution, (4) the common law, … (5) statutes, (6) precedents and (7) customs." Also under Scandinavian law, attempts to list the sources of law have been made, most prominently by the Norwegian scholar *Eckhoff*,[66] the list consisting of 1) statutory texts, 2) travaux préparatoires in the broad sense, 3) case law, 4) legal decisions made of other authorities

---

[62] *Eckhoff (2001)*, p. 23.

[63] *Bell (2000)*, para. 1.04.

[64] *Wegener (2000)*, p. 5.

[65] *Kinander (2000)*, p. 334.

[66] *Eckhoff (2001)*, p. 23.

than the Courts, 5) the practise of private parties, 6) conceptions of law as found in particular in legal literature, and 7) principles of natural justice ("the order of things").[67] The Danish scholar, *von Eyben,* more or less adheres to *Eckhoff's* list, mentioning the act/code, the travaux préparatoires, analogy and deductions ex contrario, precedence, custom legal literature and principles of natural justice. Also *Blume* has a similar list,[68] consisting of statutory rules, preparatory works, legal decisions, legal literature and "soft law", the latter being a term used to describe e.g. guidelines issued or FAQ's, which – even if they do not provide a formal norm – do tend to be normative. Still, no definite formal hierarchy between the legal sources can be shown to exist in Scandinavian law. As put by *Blume,* "[all] sources of law are considered equal with the consequence that they all may be decisive for the answer to a question of law. All sources of law may appear in the legal argument. This, however, is only a starting point as ... there will be a tendency that "hard" sources of law prevail over "soft" sources of law. It continues to be natural to attach particular weight to what is stated in the most formalised sources, such as the [Act or Code], but this does not entail that the rule pronounced in the [Act or Code] will always be applied."[69] Still, if a clear provision in an Act or Code determines a question of law that provision will prevail over any other source of law[70] – given that the provision in question is mandatory. Also, Scandinavian law accepts the principle of *lex superior.* Thus, statutory rules or publicly issued guidelines will have to respect higher-ranking statutory authority. This principle gives guidance to legislators and users of public law,[71] however it does not offer much help to lawyers applying the law of contract and obligations.

Then, if there is no hierarchy, why take the time to present these lists of legal sources? Because, when compared, the lists give an idea as to what is considered to be sources of law within the different jurisdictions. Both similarities and differences spring to attention. Statute and precedence is on both the Scandinavian and the English lists. However, travaux préparatoires and legal literature is not on *Bell's* list,

---

[67] See also *Fleischer (1998),* p. 68 ff.

[68] *Blume (2001),* p. 22 ff.

[69] *Blume (2001),* p. 28. Writer's translation.

[70] *von Eyben (1991),* p. 15.

[71] *Blume (2001),* p. 50.

even if it occurs on all the Scandinavian lists here mentioned.[72] The question is, though, what the de facto difference between the two legal families is. A thorough analysis of this issue falls outside the scope of this thesis, but it is possible, within the ambit of this work, to indulge in certain issues. Thus, in the following the use of case law, travaux préparatoires and legal literature will be further elaborated.

1.4. Case law

The Common Law system, being based on a chain of precedents, rather than on statutory enactments,[73] obviously puts considerable emphasis on precedence. Indeed, under the Common Law system precedence is the means by which the law is maintained or – as the case may be – created. In keeping with this, judges in the Common Law system are obliged to consider the case law, and furthermore, under the doctrine of stare decrisis, bound to follow the rulings of higher Courts in analogous cases.[74]

Conversely, it has not always been clear, whether case law is a source of law in Denmark and Norway.[75] As late as at the beginning of the 20th century, it was assumed under Norwegian law that the only sources of law were statute and custom,[76] whereas under Danish law a prohibition of applying precedence as a source of law was lifted in 1771, and no later than in 1815 it was assumed that at least precedence from the Supreme Court was a source of law.[77] At present, it is accepted both under Danish and Norwegian law that precedence is a source of law. Indeed, according to *Eckhoff*, under Norwegian law precedence is the second-most important source of law, its importance only being supervened by statutory rules.[78] However, there are no set rules as to how and when this source of law should be applied. The rulings of the

---

[72] For a different opinion as to whether legal literature is a source of law in Norway, see *Fleischer (1998)*, on p. 72.

[73] *Zweigert (1998)*, p. 181 ff.

[74] *Bell (2000), p. 30.*

[75] *von Eyben (1991)*, p. 76, *Augdahl (1949)*, p. 266.

[76] *Kinander (2000)*, p. 332.

[77] *Augdahl (1949)*, p. 266.

[78] *Eckhoff (2001)*, p. 192.

Supreme Courts will be considered normative *to an extent*,[79] but there are no strict rules as to what extent they are binding, and furthermore, there is no reason of principle that only the rulings of the Supreme Court may be used as precedence.

The different approaches regarding case law as a source of law are not likely to be problematic in this work. Firstly, when discussing English law, the case law deemed of relevance will simply be applied as precedents. Secondly, much of the Danish and Norwegian law here discussed is actually governed by case law, so the problematic conflict regarding what emphasis should be put on case law when confronted with other sources of law rarely occurs. Also, the method applied in this work is inductive. The writer is attempting to establish whether general rules may be deducted from the multiple sources of law that are of relevance within the thesis' scope. The ambiguity of the Danish and Norwegian approach to precedence as a source of law is more likely to in areas where the statutory regulation is ample, and therefore provides less room for the use of precedence.

Discussing case law in a thesis concerned with arbitration agreements, the question whether rulings of arbitral tribunals may be considered a source of law presents itself. The rulings of arbitral tribunals, or indeed other types of "private law-making" is not on *Bell's* list of English sources of law. *Eckhoff* accepts the "practice of private parties" as a source of law, however, what he aims at when using that term is custom and (standard) contracts.[80] Similarly, *Blume's* reference to legal decisions is meant as a reference to the decisions made by the Courts and the administration.[81] Thus, arbitration awards seem not to be accepted by the scholars in works dealing with the general principles of jurisprudence. However, scholars having the main focus elsewhere might not agree with this. Thus, according to *Brækhus*,[82] one should always be able to claim the rulings of arbitral awards as a source of law "in the wider sense", in the same way as one might refer to case law of the lower Courts. Furthermore, if arbitration is the predominant or exclusive means of dispute resolution within a certain area of law, the case law of the arbitral tribunals becomes a source of law that the lawyer will have to take into consideration. *Brækhus* reasons that this also applies to certain arbitral awards that have either been affirmed by legal literature or by the

---

[79] According to Eckhoff, the rulings of the Supreme Court are "pretty close to binding", for any authority apart from the Supreme Court itself, *Eckhoff (2001)*, p. 160.

[80] *Eckhoff (2001)*, p. 244.

[81] *Blume (2001)*, p. 23.

[82] *Brækhus (1998)*, p. 202.

trade de facto adopting the solutions reached by the tribunal. This approach seems to be accepted by Scandinavian scholars of maritime law. For example, the ruling of *Selvig*, acting as a sole arbitrator in the LINVIK[83] case seems to have been accepted as precedence by legal literature.[84] Also *Brækhus'* ruling, acting as a sole arbitrator in JOBST OLDENDORF[85] has attained a similar standing.[86] Concerning the JOBST OLDENDORF case this is rather noteworthy, as, arguably, a ruling of the Norwegian Supreme Court[87] provides the opposite conclusion to a very similar problem. The two cases may be distinguished. Thus, one needs not conclude that within Scandinavian Maritime Law an arbitral award – a source of law that bases its authority on the standing of the arbitrator and the merit of his or her argument alone – *may* overrule the precedence of Supreme Court. However, given that – at least under Danish law – it cannot be proven, that there is a distinct hierarchy between the different sources of law, the conclusion is tempting.

For the purpose of this work the rulings of arbitral tribunals – when available and relevant – will be discussed to the same extent as Court rulings, and – with the same reservation – they will be considered a "source of law". Often, only discussing the Courts' evaluation of a given problem will simply give an incomplete view of the law.[88]

1.5. Travaux préparatoires

There is a long lasting tradition under English law, according to which the Courts are not allowed the use of the parliamentary debates (the Hansard) as aids in the interpretation or definition of a rule of law. The prohibition is based on the conception that doing so would amount to an infringement of Art. 9 of the Bill of Rights 1689. It follows from Art. 9, that the freedom of speech, debates or proceedings of the parlia-

---

[83] ND 1988.288 (Norwegian Arbitration).

[84] *Falkanger/Bull (1999)*, p. 282.

[85] ND 1979.364 (Norwegian Arbitration).

[86] See most particularly *Michelet (1997)*, p. 409, but also *Falkanger/Bull (1999)*, p. 359 ff.

[87] ND 1961.325 NSC, VESTKYST I.

[88] E.g. discussing the principle of Kompetenz-Kompetenz only from the point of view of the Courts' (and not the arbitral tribunals') application of the principle will not provide the reader with the full picture.

ment should not be impeached or questioned by the Courts. However, this view has in later years been somewhat relaxed. In PEPPER V. HART,[89] it was decided that " … the exclusionary rule should be relaxed so as to permit reference to Parliamentary materials where (a) legislation is ambiguous or obscure, or leads to an absurdity; (b) the material relied upon consists of one or more statements by a Minister or other promoter of the Bill together if necessary with such other Parliamentary material as is necessary to understand such statements and their effect; (c) the statements relied upon are clear."[90] Thus, it is no longer ruled out that travaux préparatoires may be applied in the aid of the interpretation of a statute, in much the same way as it is done under Scandinavian law. At this point the work of the English Law Commission should be mentioned. The reports of the Law Commission are frequently referred to by the Courts.[91] Also in the making of the English Arbitration Act 1996 reports were made. Thus, the Departmental Advisory Committee on Arbitration Law issued several reports during the drafting of the Act. Especially the 1996 Report on the Arbitration Bill has been allocated considerable weight by the English scholars and Courts. The Report has all the characteristics that a Scandinavian lawyer would expect to find in the travaux préparatoires of a new act. Even if the position and importance of the Report is not clear, it is referred to by the Courts. Thus, in THE HALKI[92] the meaning of the 1996 Report on the Arbitration Bill para. 55 is analysed in depth, allowing it to be used as an aid in the correct interpretation of s. 9 of the Act. Further examples of the use of the Report as a support for the Court's ruling may be seen in the ARGO CARRIER[93] and in TRYGG HANSA V. EQUITAS.[94] This writer, being Danish, cannot help but being influenced by *Ross'* idea, that a source of law is a rule or principle, that – given that the rule according to its own content is applicable to a given dispute – may form a part of the judge's ratio decidendi.[95] Therefore, even if travaux

---

[89] [1993] A. C. 593 HL, PEPPER V. HART.

[90] [1993] A. C. 593 HL, PEPPER V. HART, P. 640, B-C.

[91] See *Bell (2000)*, para. 1.105 with footnote 178 for references. Bell seems to consider such reports as doctrinal legal writing – legal literature – and not as preparatory works.

[92] [1998] 1 Lloyd's Law Reports 465 CA / (1998) XXIII ICCA Yearbook 802.

[93] [1997] 2 Lloyd's Law Reports 738 / (1998) XXIII ICCA Yearbook 789.

[94] [1998] 2 Lloyd's Law Reports 439 CA, TRYGG HANSA V. EQUITAS, on p. 446.

[95] *Ross (1953)*, p. 55.

préparatoires may not formally be considered a source of law under English law, the 1996 Report on the Arbitration Bill is used by the Courts to interpret the English Arbitration Act 1996, and this writer will not hesitate to do so as well.

Under Danish and Norwegian law, the travaux préparatoires will generally be considered the first place to look for clarification in case a provision in an Act or Code seems unclear in some way. The travaux will generally state the aim and purpose of the relevant statutory instrument, and thus the travaux may be a valuable aid to the interpretation.[96] The travaux préparatoires are not formulated as strictly as statutory texts and they will often reflect the de facto conditions of the society at the time of the passing of the Act or Code. Therefore, they cannot be used mechanically – one must keep in mind that older travaux may consider a reality that no longer exists. Still, the travaux are a very important tool for the interpretation of Acts or Codes, and when considering Danish and Norwegian law they will be used accordingly.

1.6. Legal literature

It follows from what is said above in point 1.3, that legal literature generally is considered a source of law under Scandinavian law, even if it is a source of law that will not always carry much weight.[97] Indeed, literature is unlikely to be accepted if conflicting with any of the more formalised sources of law. The authorities have no obligation to apply the findings of the scholars to a given dispute, but they often will.[98] The extent that legal writings are applied will depend upon the strength of the scholar's legal argument.[99] In the same way as travaux préparatoires, legal literature is not considered a formal source of law under English law. All the same, legal literature is used in legal argument.[100] Furthermore, certain legal works have been allocated an almost authoritative weight within their respective fields, and are often cited by the Courts in their ratio decidendi. *Mustill and Boyd*'s work; *Commercial Arbitra-*

---

[96] *Eckhoff (2001)*, p. 70 ff, *Wegener (2000)*, p. 88, *Blume (2001)*, p. 23.

[97] *Fleischer* tends to find that scholary writings should not be regarded a real source of law under Norwegian law. See *Fleischer (1998)*, p. 72.

[98] *Wegener (2000)*, p. 130 f.

[99] *von Eyben (1991)*, p. 179.

[100] *Bell (2000)*, para. 1.104.

tion,[101] has over the years and through its different editions achieved such a status. Thus, it is referred to in the ratio decidendi of THE ARGO CARRIER[102] and THE HALKI.[103] Also the Norwegian Courts tend to refer specifically to scholary writings in the ratio decidendi.[104] Reference to doctrinal legal writing may also occur in Danish case law, however, the tradition is such that a direct citation of a specific scholar is uncommon.[105]

1.7. Sources of law when applied to specific disputes

Having reviewed the above it seems to this writer that much of the difference regarding the theory on sources of law is exactly that – a difference in theory. When applied to the cases, the Courts seem to avail themselves of the same sources of law in the determination of what it the solution to a specific problem. This observation might not be relevant within all areas of law, but at least when dealing with international arbitration after the English Arbitration Act 1996, the Courts of both Denmark, England and Norway seem to pay attention to mainly travaux préparatoires and case law, followed by scholary writings. Consequently, in this thesis, when dealing with national sources of law, that tendency will be reflected despite (especially the English) theoretical argument to the contrary.

2. International sources of law

2.1. The theory of dualism

Above, the approach to the theory on sources of law adopted in the thesis when national sources of law are used has been discussed. However, much of the material relevant to this thesis originates from international conventions rather than from national law as such. Here, this writer's use of those sources will be deliberated.

---

[101] *Mustill/Boyd (1989)*.

[102] (1998) XXIII ICCA Yearbook 789, p. 793.

[103] (1998) XXIII ICCA Yearbook 802, p. 816.

[104] See e.g. Rt. 1999.1532 NSC, TINE V. LØKEN for the reference to *Mæland (1988)* p. 65, *Schei (1998)*, p. 1084 and *Skoghøy (1998)*, p. 212.

[105] See for a thorough analysis of the Danish Court's use of legal literature as a source of law, *von Eyben (1991)*, p. 180-204.

Danish, English, and Norwegian law support the dualistic theory as regards international law.[106] International law and national law are regarded as two distinct spheres of law. To make international law applicable, it will have to be incorporated or implemented into national law. It is the convention in the form, which national law gives is that is relevant, and it is the rights and obligations of the national incorporation rather than the international convention as such that can be claimed before the national Courts.[107]

It is national law, as it presents itself according to the national theory on the sources of law that decides how the incorporation should take place. It is presupposed that the incorporation has been done bona fide,[108] and therefore there is an assumption that the contents of the national incorporation correspond to the text of the convention.[109] In doubts, therefore, national law should be interpreted in harmony with the convention text to best reflect the rights and obligations undertaken by the States having signed the convention. However, if, even after such interpretation, the text of the convention and the text of the international incorporation still conflict, it is the absolute starting point of the dualistic systems that national law should apply.

The convention text may be incorporated directly by national law simply stating that such and such a convention is part of national legislature. Apart from problems with translations, this way of incorporating rarely gives rise to discrepancies. However, if the convention text has been implemented instead, that is, has been rewritten into national law, discrepancies may occur. In those cases, the concentration upon national law of the dualistic systems often brings the scholars to neglect the study of the convention text as such. The convention, especially if having been rewritten into national law, is regularly regarded to have no real legal relevance of its own when national law is discussed.

Such methodology, according to which the convention in itself is not relevant, is obviously not appropriate if one wants to discuss the international rules per se and/or the interaction between the national and the international rules. In doing that the international sources themselves cannot be disregarded. However, there being no internationally binding theory on the sources of international law, the writer is left with

---

[106] See for example *Germer (1996)*, p. 59 ff. See also *Fleischer (1994)*, p. 258 ff, and – slightly critical – *Eckhoff (2001)*, p. 301 ff.

[107] *Andenæs (2001)*, p. 254 f, *Knoph (1998)*, p. 57.

[108] See e.g. *Fleischer (1994)*, p. 260.

[109] *Eckhoff (2001)*, p. 302 ff, *Knoph (1998)*, p. 17.

no other choice than to define her own approach for the use of the work. Such a creation will have to be explained and defended rather than just applied.

2.2. Approach to the sources of law relevant to this work

Disregarding national theories on sources of law leaves a theoretical vacuum but not a lack of material, which may throw light upon the international regulation of arbitration agreements in international transport. However, not all materials will be used, and the materials actually used will be allocated different weight.

The relevant convention texts themselves will always provide the starting point. The convention itself forms the legal base for the rights and obligations of the states having signed them. This also follows from the Vienna Convention of 23 May 1969 on the Law of Treaties, article 31.[110]

Vienna Convention on the Law of Treaties, Art. 31(1)
1. A treaty shall be interpreted in good faith in accordance with the ordinary meaning to be given to the terms of the treaty in their context and in the light of its object and purpose.

Only if the text of the convention seen in the light of the convention's objective does not solve a specific problem, other means of interpretation will be used.

The conventions have preparatory works. These consist primarily of opinions given during the negotiations preliminary to the adoption of the convention, and have been produced by the relevant international forum. National travaux préparatoires may also provide means of interpretation. According to the Vienna Convention on the Law of Treaties Art. 32, a convention's preparatory works including the circumstances regarding its conclusion may be taken into account when interpreting the convention. However, such "supplementing means of interpretation" are of subsidiary importance when compared to the convention text and its purpose. Furthermore, according to Art. 32, the use of the travaux préparatoires is optional.

In this thesis, international travaux préparatoires will be used with caution, and generally they will only be discussed when they are particularly to the point. One must bear in mind that most international travaux préparatoires are not, as opposed to what is the case for example in Scandinavia, aimed at serving as an important, independent legal source. Accordingly, neither the form nor the contents of the travaux promotes such use. Furthermore, traditionally, travaux préparatoires do not serve as a

---

[110] Vienna Convention of 23 May 1969 on the Law of Treaties. Both Denmark and United Kingdom are parties to the convention. According to the convention's Art. 85, the English, French, Chinese, Russian and Spanish versions are authentic. The official Danish translation may be found Lovtidende C, 1980 nr. 34. (Bekendtgørelse nr. 34 af 29. april 1980).

legal source in common law jurisdictions. Although English law is currently changing on this point, see above, a reluctance to consider preparatory works as relevant
material must be expected from English judges and arbitrators.

The Courts, both national and foreign, have dealt with the international arbitration
agreement on many occasions. Generally, Danish, English and to an extent Norwegian cases are preferred, but also cases from the Courts of other countries are referred
to, given that they are directly aimed at interpreting a given convention text. The
findings of the Courts will normally be given much weight. Still, they will be critically reviewed, and reservations will be expressed when relevant. Taking foreign
case law into account is generally problematic, considering the sources of law accepted in national law, however as already shown the national theories on the sources
of law do not apply here. If one accepts the contention that international conventions
have a life of their own, which is detached from national law, it will follow that other
case law applying the convention is equally relevant.

Legal theory will be assigned the same weight, as is the case under the Danish
theory on the sources of law. Thus, literature may provide points of view, the weight
of which depends solely on the strength of the respective writer's argument. Such
viewpoints may, as any other viewpoint, be used to either support or attack this
writer's case.[111] Conversely, legal theory will not be allocated the same credence, as
is sometimes the case under English law where certain authors seem to have
achieved an almost authoritative weight and consequently often are cited by the
Courts.

To the extent that other legal sources are considered, their relevance will be discussed independently.

By toning down the importance of both international preparatory works and legal
literature it is intended to apply an approach on the sources of international law that
is neither English nor Danish, but, it is hoped, might be acceptable considering the
criteria on which it is based. Obviously, scholars from both camps may disagree with
the hybrid. However, those scholars should bear in mind that this writer specifically
aims at detaching herself from the national theory on the sources of law, as she finds
it inept to answer the questions raised when dealing with international sources of
law. Critics may instead be assured that the writer will apply her best efforts to respect the national theory on sources of law when actually dealing with those sources
of law.

---

[111] See *Bjarup (1993)*, p. 135.

2.3. The theory of dualism versus this work's approach to the international sources of law

If accepting the dualistic starting point, namely that national and international law are two independent legal spheres, A and B, a theory on the sources of law, which tells you what is inside sphere A is not relevant when wanting to establish what lies within sphere B. Thus, the above approach to the international sources of law is not contrary to the theory of dualism. The question is, however, whether the interaction of national and international rules may effect an adoption, in the national sphere, of the above stated approach on international sources of law – through the back door, so to speak.[112] If that were shown to be the case, it would be problematical, as the theory of dualism as a rule accepts only national theories on the sources of law. Still, in this thesis the position of the law under national law is discussed and defined using national theories on the sources of law. In the same way, the international sources of law are described and discussed applying the above stated approach to the sources of law there available. Merely comparing the two does not introduce other theories on sources of law into the national spheres. Thus, the manner in which this writer employs the international sources of law is not converse to the theory of dualism.

---

[112] For a critical point of view on the application of national theories of law to international materials; see *D'Amato, (1984),* p. 182 f., and *Wegener (2000),* p. 11.

Chapter II. Concluding arbitration agreements

§ 1. The arbitration agreement

1. Characteristics

Essentially, an arbitration agreement is an *agreement* entered into by two or more parties with the object of having *disputes* between them *resolved* by *somebody else, but not by the Courts*.

Neither the Danish nor the English Arbitration Acts contain a real definition of what is arbitration and what is an arbitration agreement. The Departmental Advisory Committee behind the English Arbitration Act 1996 decided not to attempt a general definition of arbitration.[113] Instead it was decided to set up certain principles for the object of arbitration. These principles are found in s. 1(1) and 1(2) of the Act, namely the principles of fairness, impartiality, expediency and party autonomy. The principle of party-autonomy is supported by the principle in s. 1(3), that the Courts should only intervene in accordance with what is set out in the Act. However, under the heading "Definition of arbitration agreement", s. 6(1) states that an arbitration agreement is "... an agreement to submit to arbitration present or future disputes ...". Obviously, the definition is rather void of information for those, who have no prior knowledge of what is arbitration, but then, the definition was not intended to be of universal applicability. It was only intended as a tool for the Arbitration Act 1996 PART I.

The Danish Arbitration Act 1972 does not attempt a definition of what is an arbitration agreement at all. The authors of the travaux préparatoires simply refer to what is called the traditional definition,[114] namely that the parties, instead of going to the

---

[113] 1996 Report on the Arbitration Bill, para. 18.

[114] Danish Arbitration Act 1972 travaux préparatoires 1, p. 6.

Courts, agree to leave the final decision of a legal dispute to one or more third-parties, whom they either choose themselves or regarding the choice of whom they make provisions. It will follow from what is said below that in this writer's view the parties need neither name nor prescribe the appointment procedure of the arbitrators for the agreement to be an arbitration agreement. It will be wise to do so as disputes regarding the appointment may prolong the dispute resolution procedure, but for the purpose of a definition the requirement seems superfluous.

One may wonder why no exhaustive legal definition exists. However, as put by *Russell*,[115] the need for a definition has always been subsidiary to the question of what is the purpose of arbitration. And in any case, the majority of lawyers will have a general idea of what arbitration is and how an agreement to arbitrate may emerge.

Having said that the legal definitions are non-existent or insufficient, still in a thesis like this one, the arbitration agreement must be defined in some way. If it is shown that the parties are bound by an arbitration agreement, the Courts will not deal with the subject matter of the parties' dispute. Therefore, one must know when one speaks of an arbitration agreement and when one does not.[116] Here, the key elements of the agreement will be defined and discussed.

The crucial element of the arbitration agreement is the existence of *consent* and/or *agreement*. The arbitration agreement has its basis in party autonomy and therefore only comes into life if consensus between the parties is established. In this respect arbitration agreements are governed by the law of contract and by the rules of national and/or international arbitration law. Within the area of contract law, however, both English and Danish Courts have developed certain special criteria as regards arbitration agreements, which supplement the written law.[117] All of these rules will have to be considered to ensure that an agreement is in fact entered into. The law may prescribe dispute resolution by arbitration-like fora. However, as long as the submission to the jurisdiction of such forum is not based on the consent of the parties, the term arbitration is not accurate and should be avoided. In this work, the term arbitration will not be used in connection with dispute resolution based on statute rather than on the parties' agreement.

The agreement between the parties must concern *disputes*. These disputes need not have materialised yet. As may be seen later in this work, arbitration agreements

---

[115] *Russell (1997)*, para 1-002.

[116] See *Giersing/Madsen (2000)*, regarding arbitration clauses in accident insurance policies.

[117] One might speak of "the rules of the arbitration contract".

are normally entered into in advance through an arbitration clause in the main contract between the parties.[118]

The agreement should regard having a dispute *resolved*. For example, in a Danish case the agreement to "… transfer further investigation …" of a collision to the Maritime Arbitration Committee of the Moscow Chamber of Commerce was not considered an agreement to arbitrate.[119] Also, it is required that a decision can be given even if the parties cannot be made to agree. The arbitrator(s) may well try to reach a settlement between the parties, but if the arbitrator is not equipped with powers to settle the dispute, in case no voluntary arrangement can be made, the boundaries of what is arbitration have been exceed and the area of mediation has been entered.

The decision reached by the arbitrator or tribunal should be final, or at least as final as permitted by the applicable background law.[120] An agreement to obtain an opinion regarding the parties' dispute will not suffice.

The agreement must concern a dispute of law, however it needs not be the contents of the law that is disputed. On the contrary, ad hoc arbitration is often opted for in disputes where the legal implications of the different potential outcomes are clear, but certain matters of fact need deciding before the correct outcome can be chosen. Still, a distinction must be made to agreements where the parties simply choose to ask a third party for factual information. This applies even if the answer given does in fact settle a dispute between the parties. To use an every day example, imagine that the driver of car A damages a parked car B. It is clear in the case that the accident is solely the driver of car A's fault, and that the driver of car A is liable towards the owner of car B for any damage occurred. However, an argument as to the extent of the damage to car B arises and the owners of the cars involved therefore agree to ask a mechanic to assess the cost of repair. The mechanic will probably not consider himself to have acted as an arbitrator, nor has he in fact done so. One could say that the agreement must require the provider of fact connect this fact to the dispute in some way before one may speak of an arbitration agreement. Surveys and evalua-

---

[118] Although strictly speaking it is not a matter of the definition of an arbitration agreement, it seems proper at this point to emphasise that the dispute(s) must be qualified as to regard a certain legal relationship. An agreement that any future dispute arising for what so ever reason between the parties should be arbitrated may be defined as an arbitration agreement, but is null and void, see below in Chapter III, § 3, point 3.

[119] U 1973.806 MCCC. Writer's emphasis.

[120] Under Danish law no appeal lies on the findings of the arbitrators. Under the English Arbitration Act 1996, s. 69, the Courts are competent to hear an appeal on a point of law. However, the provision is declaratory, and the parties may therefore agree that no appeal shall be allowed.

tions are thus normally excluded from the concept of arbitration. However, grey zones exist.

U 1984.1045 DCA, BØDSTRUP HOVEDGAARD.
In connection with the execution of a will a farm was evaluated. According to the evaluation procedure prescribed, an evaluator was to be appointed by each of the parties involved, and the evaluators in turn were to appoint an umpire. These three persons were to assess the value of the farm and their assessment was binding regarding the execution of the will. The Eastern Court of Appeal found that the form of evaluation stipulated in the will was so similar to arbitration that it rendered the Court unable to judge the findings of the evaluators, unless it could be proven that the evaluation was suffering from serious procedural shortcomings. No such proof was given. The evaluation was therefore binding.

In the BØDSTRUP HOVEDGAARD case, the procedure prescribed included the parties appointing representatives. These representatives were to pick an umpire and then agree upon an assessment of the farm. These features are often found in ad hoc arbitration agreements. It further followed from the stipulation that the value agreed upon by the surveyors was decisive as regards the execution of the will. On that background it seems proper to consider the evaluation equivalent to arbitration.[121]

According to the above definition the agreement should consider having a dispute settled by *somebody else, but not the Courts.* If the parties had agreed for the Courts to settle the dispute, they would have entered into a jurisdiction agreement and thus been outside the scope of what is an agreement to arbitrate.[122]

The parties need not lay down who is to be the arbitrator(s), but they often will. They may choose a permanent arbitral tribunal (institutionalised arbitration). Alternatively, they may point out certain persons or lay down rules as to how appointment should take place if a dispute occurs in the future (ad hoc arbitration). In fact, it suffices to stipulate that the dispute is to be settled by arbitration, so all of these modes are satisfactory.[123] As may be seen from the BØDSTRUP HOVEDGAARD case, under

---

[121] U 1980.737 DSC regarded the evaluation of a farm. The procedure prescribed for the evaluation bore certain similarities to arbitration. However, as it was not necessary for the decision of the case to decide whether the agreement was one of evaluation or arbitration, the Courts did not do so. In U 1970.619 DSC, a stipulation in a will that doubts as to the interpretation of the will was to be settled irrevocably by the estate's executor was not regarded an agreement to arbitrate.

[122] It has been seen in practice, that the parties agree that disputes shall be settled by arbitration, but "with recourse" to the Courts, see [1981] 1 Lloyd's Law Reports 302 CA, PACZY v. HAENDLER, p. 304, col 1. In this writer's view such agreements are best seen as two separate agreements, one arbitration agreement and one jurisdiction agreement.

[123] *Merkin (2000)*, p. 29.

Danish law the agreement does not need to be identified as an arbitration agreement. This is also the case under English law. Thus, in [1993] 1 Lloyd's Law Reports 291 HL, CHANNEL TUNNEL V. BALFOUR BEATTY, an alternative dispute resolution agreement to refer disputes regarding the construction of a cooling system for the Eurotunnel to a panel of three persons "acting as independent experts but not as arbitrators" was entered into. According to the agreements their findings should be given immediate effect "unless and until" the decision was revised by arbitration. Thus, the alternative dispute resolution panel was to act as first instance in a two-tier dispute resolution model. The House of Lords found unanimously that such an agreement had so many arbitration-like features that it was an arbitration agreement for the purpose of the 1975 Act,[124] and thus that the defendant, Balfour Beatty, was entitled to a mandatory stay of proceedings.[125] However, the Court chose instead to stay the case under its inherent discretionary jurisdiction, therefore the findings as to the 1975 Act are, if regarded stringently, obiter dicta.

So: For an agreement to be an arbitration agreement it needs to contain at least these features:

A consent must exist to have a

dispute of law

resolved in a final and binding way by a

third party, who is not the Courts.

An agreement containing only these elements ought to be considered an arbitration agreement by the Courts. However, if the parties want to be sure, they should name the agreement an arbitration agreement. The cases where the Courts have held that an agreement to resolve a dispute is an agreement to arbitrate, although not so named, are special cases. In the BØDSTRUP HOVEDGAARD case, the procedure prescribed was an arbitration procedure in anything but name. In CHANNEL TUNNEL V. BALFOUR BEATTY the procedure prescribed in the agreement presupposed that alternative dispute resolution was carried out before arbitration could be reverted to as a second instance. The case concerns itself with that whole procedure. The case does not support that the Arbitration Act 1975 would have applied if only the agreement to use alternative dispute resolution as a first instance had been tried separately. As both cases are decided with regard to their special circumstances and facts, they do

---

[124]The English Arbitration Act 1975 incorporates the provisions of the New York Convention. It has now been replaced by the Arbitration Act 1996, PART III.

[125] [1993] 1 Lloyd's Law Reports 291 HL, CHANNEL TUNNEL V. BALFOUR BEATTY, per Lord Mustill, p. 302.

not lend themselves to a comparison of the legal position in Denmark and England on this point of law. They only lend themselves as authority that an agreement *may* be regarded as an arbitration agreement although upon its wording alone it is not.

Thus, it should be concluded that the agreement need not (but definitely ought to) be described as an agreement to arbitrate.

Finally, the agreement may well, but need not:

Hold provisions as to the appointment of the arbitrator(s) or arbitral institution, define a seat for the arbitration, and

hold provisions as to the choice of law of the matter or the proceedings or indeed prescribe the arbitral procedure.

2. A gentleman's agreement or a legal obligation?

It is suggested that most lawyers if met with the question of whether or not arbitration agreements are legally binding, (under the precondition of course, that the requirements of the applicable laws are satisfied), would answer in the affirmative. The lawyer would do so confidently with reference to the doctrine of *pacta sunt servanda*. Consequently, the question is seldom considered.[126] However, less confident voices have been heard in legal theory, especially the one of *Dillén*.[127]

Dillén[128] distinguishes between the positive and the negative obligations arising form the arbitration agreement. Positive obligations, according to Dillén, are obligations to do something, namely to aid the expeditious running of the arbitration procedure, whereas the negative are obligations to refrain from doing something, in this case not to seek other means of dispute resolution, especially not the Courts. The distinction is a good working tool, and will be maintained throughout the thesis when relevant. Generally, this writer rejects Dillén's argument, that not all of the obligations arising out of the arbitration agreement are legal ones. However, adopting Dillén's distinction, it is felt that some discussion of his arguments is called for.

As per Dillén, the positive obligations are the essential ones, whereas the negative obligations are secondary.[129] Dillén presumes that the positive obligations are of a legal nature, but reserves himself somewhat as regards the negative.

[126] *Russell (1997)*, para. 7-002 assumes without qualification that an arbitration agreement is a contractual undertaking which may be breached. Often writers do not mention the question at all.

[127] *Dillén (1933)*.

[128] *Dillén (1933)*, p. 142 ff. and 195 ff.

[129] *Dillén (1933)*, p. 195.

According to *Dillén*, a clear answer to the question whether the obligation not to seek a dispute governed by an arbitration agreement settled by the Courts is a legal one, can only be achieved if it is possible to obtain a declaratory judgment from the Courts, that the parties to the arbitration agreement are obliged not to seek their dispute settled by same Courts. Dillén argues, that a party will not be able to establish the *locus standi* necessary to obtain such a declaration,[130] and furthermore, that to give the party the option to do so will entail the possibility of irreconcilable Court decisions regarding the arbitration agreement's negative and positive legal effects respectively.[131]

Dillén's argument, that it will be difficult for a party to establish the *locus standi* required when seeking a declaration as mentioned, seems valid enough. Both in Danish and English law, a declaratory judgment can only be obtained if the question raised bears implications upon a situation which has presented itself, rather than being of a purely hypothetical nature.[132]

It is assumed in Danish law that the *locus standi* for a declaratory judgment regarding the validity and/or scope of the arbitration agreement can be established even before a dispute covered by the arbitration agreement has broken out.[133] However, authors have not maintained that a declaratory judgment regarding only whether the arbitration agreement deters a party from commencing procedures before the Courts may be obtained. Be that as it may, it is not clear to this writer why the possibility of obtaining a declaratory judgment as to the negative effect of the arbitration agreement is the only way to ascertain whether arbitration agreements are in that respect legally binding. Instead, it seems reasonable to argue that the negative duty imposed by the arbitration agreement is a legal one, as opposed to being a duty of morals, if it can be shown that the Courts may enforce it by any means.

The risk of irreconcilable Court decisions does not speak against this. Obtaining a Court's decision recognising the positive legal effects of an arbitration agreement presupposes a binding arbitration agreement being in force between the parties. If the arbitration agreement is not legally binding, then no positive legal obligations will arise from it and vice versa. It is therefore unlikely that a party should be put in a situation where the plea for a declaration that the arbitration agreement prevents the parties from using the ordinary Courts is answered in the negative, but, at the same time, the party is presented with another court-decision obliging him or her to fulfil the positive legal obligations arising from it. Even so, if problems should occur they might in most cases be dealt with by the use of national or international *lis pendens*.

---

[130] *Dillén (1933)*, p. 193.

[131] *Dillén (1933)*, p. 194.

[132] See *Jensen, (1986); Hurwitz, (1940); Sindballe (1917); James (1965)*, p. 29 ff.; *Lawson (1980)*, p. 234 ff, and *Skoghøy (2001)*, p. 293. In [2000] 2 Lloyd's Law Reports 1 QBD, VALE DO RIO V. BAO STEEL the Court found that the Arbitration Act 1996 was not designed to allow a party to seek the determination by declaration of the question whether an arbitration agreement existed. However, the Judge's reasoning is one of Kompetenz-Kompetenz rather than lack of locus standi. The case is further discussed below in Chapter IV, § 3, point 2.

[133] *Gomard (1979)*, p. 27; voldgiftsloven, footnote 1.

Dillén further argues that in some cases no adverse effect, in particular no duty to bear the legal costs, occurs from bringing the case to the Courts despite the arbitration agreement. If a party brings to the Court a dispute, the decision of which presupposes a (preliminary) ruling of an arbitral tribunal the Courts may choose not to dismiss or stay the action as such but instead only stay the part of the case covered by the arbitration agreement awaiting the tribunal's decision.[134] According to Dillén, in such cases it can not be shown that the Court's final distribution of legal costs reflects an enforcement of the arbitration agreement.[135] Dillén continues: "Here one can thus not talk about a legal obligation in any other meaning than that there is an ideal statement ... a fact, which to most people most probably signifies that the talk of an obligation has declined and become a phrase, behind which no legal reality is hidden." [136]

It is not clear to me how one can verify the statement that the Courts in these cases do not bear in mind the arbitration agreement when apportioning the legal costs of the dispute before them. It may be, that the party who brought the action to the Courts is not presented with the full legal costs, but the reasons for this may be plural. Perhaps he or she has simply won the case. Or the counter-party may have acted in a way, which makes it proper that that party should bear his or her own costs.[137] Still, the Courts do in such cases keep the parties to their agreement by staying the action before the Courts pending the outcome of the arbitral procedure. It is hard to see how it can be maintained that an obligation, which is enforced in this way by the Courts, is only an "ideal statement".

It follows from what is said that in this writer's view arbitration agreements impose obligations of a legal nature upon the parties to the agreement if the Courts, regardless of which means are applied, can enforce the agreement. As both the positive and the negative obligations arising out of the arbitration agreement will be recognised and enforced by the Courts when faced with a dispute regarding the obligation in question, it must be concluded that the arbitration agreement is in all respects a legally binding agreement.

---

[134] *Dillén (1933)*, p. 148.

[135] *Dillén (1933)*, p. 194.

[136] *Dillén (1933)*, p. 195: "Här kan man alltså ej tala om någon rättsplikt i annan mening, än att det föreligger ett dylikt ideelt postulat ... något som för många förklarligen är liktydigt därmed, att talet om förpliketelse nedsjunkit till en fras, bakom vilken icke döljer sig någon som helst rättslig realitet". (Writer's translation, which is hoped to be fair to Dillén).

[137] See as an example of this FED 1995.1206, DCA: The plaintiff's property had been damaged by fire. He therefore claimed his insurance. Dispute regarding the claim arose. The plaintiff commenced proceedings before the Østre Landsret (Eastern Court of Appeal), claiming that the insurance company had to pay him DKK 1.35 mill. As the claim was to be settled by arbitration the case was dismissed from the Courts. However, since the insurance company had not participated in the clarification of the case in the proper manner, the plaintiff had had good reason to initiate court-proceedings and each party had to bear his own costs.

3. The legal effects of the arbitration agreement

Having said that the arbitration agreement is a legal, enforceable agreement, the next logical question is what are the obligations arising from it. Dillén only concerns himself with the negative obligation not to seek other means of dispute resolution and the positive obligation to assist the arbitration procedure. However, it seems proper to apply a somewhat wider scope. An overview of the obligations arising out of the arbitration agreement would in this writer's view consist of this:

Chronologically, the first obligation to arise after a dispute within the arbitration agreement has materialised, is the negative obligation not to take a dispute covered by the arbitration agreement to the Courts. Also, the arbitration agreement bars the parties from seeking any other means of dispute resolution, which is not authorised by the agreement. It must be noted that although the Courts may refuse to deal with the subject matter covered by the arbitration agreement, they may not order a party to initiate arbitral proceedings.[138] However, as the Courts, when faced with a binding arbitration agreement, will refuse to deal with the merits of the dispute, a party claiming under the agreement can only enforce his claim through arbitral proceedings. He or she may therefore choose between initiating arbitral proceedings or writing off the claim.

The initiating of the proceedings triggers the positive obligations arising out of the arbitration agreement. The parties must support the proceedings loyally as and when required. The obligations include amongst others the appointment of arbitrators if not already done in the agreement, and the providing of the funds and evidence necessary for the proceedings to be carried out. These obligations persist until the point when the parties either agree to end the proceedings or an award may be granted.

Finally, the arbitration agreement bestows upon the parties the duty to regard an award issued in accordance with the agreement as final and binding.

This entails mainly one positive and one negative obligation, namely the positive obligation to do as ordered by the award and the negative obligation not to seek the same dispute set-tled again by other fora. One may argue that these are obligations arising out of the award rather that the arbitration agreement. In general, however, one cannot regard the arbitral award as independent from the arbitration agreement. The consensus expressed in the agreement is the legal basis for the award, and the validity and binding nature of the arbitration agreement is a necessary precondition

---

[138] [1993] 1 Lloyd's Law Reports 291 HL. CHANNEL TUNNEL V. BALFOUR BEATTY, p. 301 per Lord Mustill: "… the Act [The Arbitration Act 1975] requires and empowers the Court to do no more than stay the action, thereby cutting off the plaintiff's agreed method of enforcing his claim. It is then up to the plaintiff whether he sets an arbitration in motion, but if he chooses not to do so he loses his claim."

for the award being valid and binding. The award may thus be seen as a reflection of the arbitration agreement rather than as an independent legal unit.

Summing up, the arbitration agreement confers four main obligations upon the parties to it. Firstly, the parties may not seek other fora for dispute resolution. Secondly, the parties must loyally aid the arbitration procedure. Thirdly, the parties undertake to do as ordered by the award, and fourthly, the parties are not allowed to seek the same dispute tried again by other fora.

§ 2. Danish case law on the conclusion of arbitration agreements

1. Basic principle: The general rules of contract law apply

Under Danish law there are no formal requirements, which must be satisfied for an arbitration agreement to be concluded. Indeed, the Danish Arbitration Act sec. 1, sub-sec. 1 simply states, that "Legal action regarding disputes, which according to the parties' agreement have to be settled by arbitration … " shall be dismissed from the Court if one of the parties so pleads. The Danish Arbitration Act does not concern itself with the form of the arbitration agreement. Consequently, in theory, the conclusion of arbitration agreements is governed by general rules of contract law. Formal requirements may be found in special legislation, as is the case within certain areas of transport law, but no general rule that arbitration agreements should be in writing exists.

However, due to the fact that an arbitration agreement bars the parties from taking a dispute falling under the agreement to the Courts, arbitration agreements are regarded with some caution, and only when an agreement to arbitrate can be clearly established will it be given effect by the Courts, or indeed the arbitral tribunals. As expressed by the arbitration tribunal for the building and construction trades: "The competence of the ordinary Courts to deal with a dispute is only excluded if it is *clear* that an arbitration agreement has been entered into."[139]

Below, the Danish case law regarding the formation of arbitration agreements will be discussed. In doing that, an obstacle must be tackled: The regulation on the forma-

---

[139] KFE 2002.11 VBA. Writer's translation and emphasis.

tion of contracts is one of the areas where the so-called Scandinavian legal pragmatism becomes most evident. Or, one could say, one of the areas where the concepts are the most muddled.

In theory, one talks about the conclusion, the validity and the interpretation of contracts. In practice, these terms are intertwined. Bearing this in mind, there is no obvious way in which to structure a chapter on the Danish case law on arbitration agreements. *Hjejle[140]* and the travaux préparatoires simply give up, and express themselves in terms of the validity of the arbitration agreement, irrespectively of the problem dealt with. In this work, the traditional distinctions are not maintained either. The writer will offer her best attempt to produce a structured presentation of the cases, but it is openly admitted that some of the cases could easily have fitted under any of the headings given.

This is not a contract law thesis; however, for the benefit of non-Scandinavian readers, a few principles of Danish contract law are outlined: Danish contract law is governed by the Contracts Act 1917[141] and by special statutory legislation. To a great extent, though, the reigning principles are developed through case law rather than statutory law. In the following, the Contracts Act 1917 will provide the starting-point. The regulation of the conclusion of contracts in the Contracts Act 1917 secs. 2-9 only provides the declaratory rules. The parties are free to agree otherwise, and indeed, the custom of the trade will prevail over the Contracts Act, see the Contracts Act 1917 sec. 1, 2nd sentence. According to the Contracts Act 1917 sec. 1, 1st sentence, the declaratory rule of Danish contract law is that offers and replies to offers are binding. Thus, under Danish law, a person putting forward of an offer is bound by the offer. Promises – and not just contracts – are legally binding upon the promisor from the time when they have come to the knowledge of the promisee.[142] A reply to an offer is also binding. An acceptance is binding upon both the promisor and the replying promisee when the acceptance has reached the promisor, whereas a refusal is binding when it has come to the knowledge of the promisor. For an agreement to be concluded, the relationship between the parties must provide an offer given by one party and an acceptance given by the other. There are no distinct requirements regarding how the offer and the acceptance should present themselves. A party may be bound by implied or quasi agreements, by remaining passive towards the other party's claim that an agreement has been formed or what its contents is, or by custom, whether this is a custom of the trade or a custom which has developed between the parties. That an agreement has been concluded may, in case of dispute, be proven by any means. There is no formal hierarchy between different sources of proof in the general rules of

---

[140] *Hjejle (1987)*, p. 33-54; Danish Arbitration Act 1972 travaux préparatoires 1, p. 12.

[141] Lov nr. 242 af 8. maj 1917, as most recently revised in Lovbekendtgørelse nr. 781 af 26. august 1996. For a general presentation of Danish Contract Law see e.g. *Andersen/Madsen (2001)* and *Andersen (1998)*.

[142] Danish Contracts Act, sec. 7, implied.

contract law or procedure. The parties' written contract, if one exists, will often provide the starting-point, but this is due to the fact that its content is easily proven, and not to the fact alone that it is a written document. Proof may still be given as to the parties' negotiations, their expressed or implied intentions, etc. Any written contract is just one type of proof amongst others.

Under Danish contract law, an agreement may be invalid due to forgery, incapacity, error[143] or lack of mandate.[144] Additionally, agreements may be null and void if they are obtained via duress,[145] fraud[146] or misrepresentation.[147] In special cases, an agreement may be declared void if the preconditions on which the agreement is based are no longer present. Agreements which are contra bones mores,[148] unlawful or immoral,[149] are also invalid. Finally, unfair contracts may be declared void or altered by the Courts under the general clause in the Contracts Act 1917 sec. 36. The provision is generally intended to apply to situations where an imbalance in the parties' bargaining power leads to the conclusion of a contract that is inequitable. One should note that the provision applies both to unfairness which is present at the time of the formation of the contract, and to unfairness which arises over time. The Courts have only rarely applied sec. 36 to contracts between professionals, as the provision should not be applied to situations where a calculated risk actually occurs.[150]

When interpreting a contract, the Courts are again free to accept any sort of proof given. However, the starting-point will be the verbatim interpretation of the term or provision in its given context and in consideration of the objective of the parties' contract. The context taken into consideration is both the documentation in the case and any other proof, which may be provided as to the parties' negotiations and intentions. In case this proves fruitless, the Courts may adhere to certain principles of interpretation, e.g. that the interpretation of a contract which upholds the contract should be preferred to an interpretation,[151] which renders the contract void, or that uncertainties or ambiguities in a contracts is generally to the detriment of the party, who could best have avoided them. Thus, both standard documents and other contracts may be interpreted against the drafter.

---

[143] Danish Contracts Act, sec. 32.

[144] Danish Contracts Act, sec. 10, sub-sec. 1 implied and sec. 11.

[145] Danish Contracts Act, secs. 28, 29 and 31.

[146] Danish Contracts Act, sec. 30, sub-sec. 1.

[147] Danish Contracts Act, sec. 30, sub-sec. 2.

[148] Danish Contracts Act 1917, sec. 33.

[149] Danish Law 1683, 5-1-2.

[150] Please note that in consumer contacts § 36 is supplemented by §§ 38a-38d. These sections incorporate the Directive 93/13/EC on unfair terms in consumer contracts.

[151] *Andersen (1998),* p. 264.

2. Focus on knowledge

The formation of the arbitration agreement does not normally give rise to much discussion if the parties enter into an agreement to arbitrate after a dispute has arisen. Instead, it is the arbitration clauses that cause most of the case law. If the arbitration clause is a part of the parties' main contract document, and that document has been made available to all contracting parties before the conclusion of the contract, dispute regarding whether the arbitration clause has been agreed does not normally arise either. Instead, the Courts and arbitral tribunals have in quite a few cases dealt with disputes as to whether arbitration clauses contained in standard forms or general conditions, which are referred to in the parties' main contract without being set out in full, have in fact been agreed to. The question of whether a certain set of standard conditions has been accepted as a part of the parties' contract will therefore be central in the following.

As already mentioned, Danish law contains no general requirement of form which must be fulfilled for an arbitration agreement to be concluded. Out of principle, arbitration agreements may be entered into through oral[152] or implied agreements, by reference, or for example by one of the parties' passiveness. For reasons of securing the level of proof required by the Courts, it must be strongly recommended that the parties enter into a written agreement to arbitrate, but an arbitration agreement may be entered into by any means allowed by the general rules of contract law.

According to Danish literature and case law, there must be a clear agreement to arbitrate.[153] The central issue that the Courts and the arbitral tribunals will be looking to ascertain, is what knowledge the parties had at the time of the formation of the contract. Were they aware, or ought they to have been aware, that an arbitration agreement was part of the contract? An arbitration agreement only exists between the parties if that question may be answered in the affirmative. When seeking to establish what the parties knew or ought to have known, the Danish Courts will examine all the circumstances of the case. One should bear in mind, that as there are no formal requirements as to the arbitration agreement, the documents used will only provide for one type of proof amongst others. A good example of this is given in the SKAGEN HAVN case.

---

[152] Thus, in KFE 2001.193 VBA the fact that the arbitration agreement had not been concluded in writing was not per se a reason for the rejection of the agreement.

[153] *Gomard (1979)*, p. 18, *Hjejle (1987),* p. 42.

2.1. Knowledge or documents – the SKAGEN HAVN case, U 1973.305 DSC

Subcontractor A was hired to provide materials and labour for certain works in connection with a new jetty, being built in Skagen, Denmark. Dispute arose, and A brought a lawsuit against the main contractor, B, claiming the balance of the account and damages due to the fact that B, alleged unjustified, had terminated A's contract; in total a claim for about DKK 0.6 mill. B, on the other hand, contended to have a set off for DKK 1.2 mill. However, primarily, B claimed that the case should be dismissed from the Courts, as the parties had agreed to arbitrate on AB 1951-terms.[154]

It followed from the subcontractor's agreement with the main contractor that the work was based on "… the … client's drawings and conditions, the contents of which are known to you". In turn it followed from the main contractor's contract with the client, Skagen Havn, that AB 1951 applied.

According to B, the agreement between A and B contained a clear reference according to which the drawings and conditions of the client, including the reference to AB 1951, formed part of the parties' contract. A argued that the reference did not provide a sufficiently clear and explicit agreement to arbitrate. Furthermore, the issue of arbitration had not been discussed between the parties. Finally, there was no custom within the trade that disputes were to be settled by arbitration.

The Eastern Court of Appeal found that, according to the proof provided, the question of arbitration had not been specifically discussed in the parties' negotiations. Also, it could not with the necessary certainty be deduced from the reference to the client's "drawings and conditions" that the arbitration clause of AB 1951 was agreed between the parties. Therefore, the case could proceed before the Courts.

These findings were appealed to the Danish Supreme Court. 11 judges heard the case. A majority of six judges found that it had to be concluded from the parties' correspondence that subcontractor A at the time of the conclusion of the contract was aware that AB 1951 was to apply to the parties' contract. Also, A's contention – that this did not necessarily entail that the arbitration clause in § 24 applied – could not be accepted. Consequently, the case was dismissed from the Courts, but the parties were to bear their own costs.

A minority of one judge found that it could not with certainty be established from the parties' original contract that AB 1951 applied to the dispute. However, this was not decisive for the outcome of the case, as A in later correspondence clearly had expressed the opinion that AB 1951 applied to the parties' contract. The judge found with the majority that there was no reason to distinguish between the arbitration clause and the other clauses of that standard document. Accordingly, that judge also voted for the case's dismissal.

Finally, a minority of four judges voted to uphold all the findings of the Eastern Court of Appeal.

Three main points of interest can be deduced from SKAGEN HAVN.

Firstly, as there is no need for the Courts to construct a written arbitration agreement between the parties, the focus will be on the whole situation rather than on the documents. The written documentation may, of course, in itself provide for sufficient proof of the arbitration agreement. However, if it is proved that the party contesting the arbitration agreement did in fact know of it at the time of the conclusion of the

[154] AB 1951: General conditions for works and deliveries in the building and construction trades, 1951-version.

contract – alternatively, that he or she has at a later stage adhered to it – then the written documentation, or lack of it, is of no consequence.

Secondly, it follows from the findings of the Eastern Court of Appeal and from the dicta of the minorities of the Danish Supreme Court that the parties' written contract did not provide for an agreement to arbitrate between the parties. The two-layered reference (a reference to one agreement, which in turn referred to another agreement or form, in which the arbitration agreement was found) used in the case did not in itself satisfy the requirements for clarity set out in Danish arbitration and contract law as regards the conclusion of potentially onerous agreements.

Thirdly, the contention that the arbitration clause in AB-1951 did not necessarily apply even if it was proven that AB-1951 did, was rejected. Thus, under the circumstances in the Skagen Havn case, there was no need to distinguish between the adoption of the standard form, and the adoption of the arbitration clause in it.

2.2. The knowledge of the party in question

As it is the knowledge of the parties to the particular arbitration agreement that is in question, there are no set rules as to what method of incorporation, reference or documentation suffices for an arbitration agreement to be created. For example, in KFE 1982.10A VBA, THE FAMILY HOME, a reference to AB 1972[155] was made in the tender on the building of a family home. The client, who had no knowledge of the trade and who had not had counsel, disputed that any arbitration agreement had been entered into. She did not know the terms of the AB 1972, nor had the builder given her a copy of them. Under those circumstances, the arbitral tribunal hesitated to find that the reference to the AB 1972 in itself barred this client from taking the dispute to the Courts. It was clear that the arbitral tribunal found that *this particular client* was not supposed to know that by accepting a tender on AB 1972-conditions, she also became party to an agreement to arbitrate. This applied although AB 1972 is an agreed document within the building and construction trade.[156] The client was not part of that trade.[157] On the other hand, in cases where both parties are professionals within the same trade, and where common terms or procedures are used, it may be very easy to convince the Courts or tribunals that an arbitration agreement has been

---

[155] AB 1972: General conditions for works and deliveries in the building and construction trades, 1972-version.

[156] *Andersen/Madsen (2001)*, p. 84.

[157] See similarly KFE 2001.193 VBA and U 2002.482 DCA.

entered into. Thus, in KFE 1997.77 VBA, a statement given to the relevant industrial organisation that a supplier was covered by a delivery clause under a contract, obliged the supplier to arbitrate a dispute with the client and the main contractor.

The facts of the case were these: Dispute arose regarding contract work. The client initiated proceedings before the Arbitral Tribunal of the Building and Construction trades against the contractor. The contractor in turn gave third party notice to one of the suppliers. The supplier claimed that there was no arbitration agreement between himself and the contractor, and thus that the tribunal was not competent to hear the case as regards any claims between the contractor and the supplier. The tribunal found in favour of its own competence, as the supplier had given a statement to the relevant industrial organisation that he was covered by the delivery clause governing the deliveries to the contractor. One of the purposes of the statement was to enable the contractor to ascertain, which deliveries were delivered subject to the terms of the delivery clause. This procedure was common in the trade at the time. The statement could be revoked within three months. The supplier had not done so. Taking all that into consideration, it did not relieve the supplier of his duties under the delivery clause, including the duty to arbitrate disputes, that the supplier's information sheets regarding his products had referred to general conditions, which lessened the supplier's obligations compared to what followed from the delivery clause. There might have been a discrepancy regarding the extent of the liability, but there were no conflicting forum agreements.

Finally, in areas where it is common knowledge that arbitration agreements apply, the requisite for the arbitration agreement to be concluded is so lax that it may be hard to construct any real agreement between the actual parties. For example, there is a steady practice that the membership of a trade union in itself entails that any dispute between the employer and the employee regarding the employment shall be dealt with by arbitration. The employee is, by becoming a member of the trade union, regarded as having accepted the rules of the union, including any arbitration agreements which are either provided for there or which have been entered into by the union according to the said rules.[158]

3. Incorrect or insufficient information
Often, disputes regarding both arbitration agreements and other agreements are based on differences in the parties' knowledge at the time of the conclusion of the contract, often combined with the problem that A assumed that B had the same knowledge as A did. The question therefore arises, who bears the risk when these assumptions

---

[158] See for example *implied*, U 1981.530 MCCC, U 1983.730 DSC, U 1985.997 DCA, U 1987.337 DCA, U 1987.406 DCA, U 1993.725 DCA, U 1994.953 DSC, and *directly*, U 1986.314 DSC and U 1986.818 DCA.

prove to be incorrect. Below, it will be ascertained whether or not there is a general rule on the allocation of that risk.

The question, when put thus, might lead the reader to think of the rule of interpretation, which in Scandinavian law is referred to as the rule of unclairty.[159] The rule encompasses the principles that contracts in case of doubt should be interpreted *contra stipulatorem* (or in Anglo-American law *contra præferentem*), *contra venditorem* and *adversus eum*. However, the issue discussed under this heading is what documentation or information has become a part of the parties' contract, rather than how that documentation or information should be interpreted. If it is clear what documentation the parties' agreement consists of, but not what the correct interpretation of that documentation is, then one is outside the scope of what is here deliberated on.

In the following, Danish case law concerning the allocation of the risk for making certain documentation or information a part of the parties' agreement will be discussed.

3.1. The information is in one of the parties' control

3.1.1. The cases

Whether or not there is a general risk allocation is most clearly shown in cases where the parties have an equal position, such as when two professionals within the same trade argue as to the incorporation of standard terms which are customary, or even agreed, within that trade. An example of this may be found in KFE 1984.202 VBA.

KFE 1984.202 VBA

A dispute arose regarding the quality of a delivery of concrete. The builder initiated proceedings against the supplier before the arbitral tribunal. Offers on the delivery contract were to be made according to the builder's tender documents, which included the AB 1972. However, the tender documents had not been enclosed in the builder's letter to the supplier. The supplier therefore claimed that the case should be dismissed from the arbitral tribunal.

The arbitral tribunal found that the reference to the tender documents did not provide certainty that the supplier had agreed that AB 1972 applied to the parties' relationship with the effect that disputes were to be settled by arbitration. Consequently, the case was dismissed from the tribunal.

Generally, AB 1972 was customary as between builders, contractors, sub-contractors and clients, but not as towards suppliers. However, when regarding the supply of concrete, AB 1972 was generally applied.[160] Thus, in the case, the reference in the

---

[159] *Andersen/Madsen (2001)*, p. 385 ff.

[160] Vagner (2001), p. 18.

tender documents to AB 1972 could not have been unexpected by the supplier. Still, the arbitral tribunal found against its own competence. The only thing in the case that can explain why AB 1972 was not agreed was that the supplier was not provided with the tender documents. The builder could have made the documents available to the supplier but he did not. The uncertainty caused by this worked against the builder, so as to make the supplier's challenge of the arbitration agreement successful.

It may seem that the arbitral tribunal was a bit too cautious when deciding against its own competence. However, the incorporation of arbitration clauses through a two-layered reference in itself has been rejected by the Danish Supreme Court in U 1963.488 DSC, KLINTEMARKEN,[161] and was also rejected by the Eastern Court of Appeal and the minority of the Danish Supreme Court in the SKAGEN HAVN case.[162]

The ruling of the tribunal provides a good example of how the risk of non-information is allocated. The builder had the information in his control. He could have given that information to the supplier. He chose not to. Even if the supplier knew that some sort of terms and conditions applied, he did not know which. That lack of knowledge worked to the detriment of the person in control of the information, namely the builder.

The question of who controls the information was also an issue in a case before the Maritime and Commercial Court of Copenhagen, regarding the import of audio equipment from Japan. In that case, however, the risk allocation worked so as to create an arbitration agreement between parties who, it could be argued, strictly speaking had not entered into one.

U 1980.847 MCCC, AUDIO-GROUP OF DENMARK V. YAGI ENTERPRISES
Otkjær's Radio & TV A/S (O) had entered into an agency contract with Yagi Enterprises, Japan (Yagi). O was to act as the sole agent of Yagi's audio products in Denmark. The agency contract held a provision according to which "All dispute or claims resulting from or in connection with this agreement shall be settled through the mediation of the JAPAN COMMERCIAL ARBITRATION ASSOCIATION, located TOKYO, JAPAN."

The owner of O, Gert Otkjær, was also one of the founders of the company Audio-Group of Denmark (AG). Gert Otkjær was the director of AG, and AG's postal address was the same as the one used by O.

In May 1978, Gert Otkjær and the chairman of the board of AG negotiated a contract with Yagi in Tokyo, regarding the delivery of 3350 radios and tape-recorders. Dispute arose regarding the quality of the delivery. AG initiated proceedings before the Courts, claiming damages from Yagi. Yagi

---

[161] See below in point 4.2.1.

[162] U 1973.305 DSC, discussed above in point 2.1.

claimed that the case should be dismissed from the Courts on the grounds that the agreement was between Yagi and O, and, therefore, that the arbitration clause applied.

The Maritime and Commercial Court of Copenhagen found firstly, that the arbitration agreement between O and Yagi was sufficiently clear and unequivocal to bind the parties to the agency contract. Secondly, Yagi had had no reason to understand that the intended contract partner was not O, but AG. On the contrary, Yagi had been legitimate in assuming that O was the party to the contract with the consequence that the provisions of the agency contract, including the arbitration clause, applied. Under these circumstances, AG, on whose behalf director Gert Otkjær acted, was bound by the arbitration clause in the agency contract, and the case was dismissed from the Courts.

Gert Otkjær could have made it clear to Yagi that he was not negotiating the contract on behalf of O but on behalf of AG. Indeed, as by contracting with AG Yagi would be in breach of the agency contract with O, it would have been natural for Gert Otkjær to specify the matter.

Gert Otkjær could easily have provided the necessary information. He did not. Yagi on the other hand was not supposed to have known that the contract partner was not O. In that situation the lack of information worked against the party who had it in his control to provide it, namely Gert Otkjær, so as to create an arbitration agreement between AG and Yagi.

Finally, an example of the allocation of the risk for providing information is provided in the Western Court of Appeal's decision in a case regarding horse insurance.

U 1987.178 DCA, THE USELESS HORSE

A insured a horse with an insurance union. The horse proved to be useless and A initiated proceedings before the Town Court of Århus claiming DKK 20,000 under the insurance. The insurance union claimed that the case should be dismissed due to an arbitration clause in the insurance policy.

The proposal form contained an extract of the insurance terms. It followed from the extract that "... total uselessness shall be evident from the statement of two veterinarians and be approved by the [insurance company's] veterinary consultant, who decides the issue in case of doubt. This decision may be brought before an arbitration tribunal." It also followed from the form that A applied for membership of the insurance union "... according to the [insurance union's] regulations and conditions of insurance, the contents of which I explicitly declare to be familiar with."

The full set of insurance terms was posted to A with the bill. The insurance terms consisted of two closely printed pages, from which it followed in clause 14 that "... Any dispute that might arise between the union and a member ... shall ... be finally determined by arbitration in Århus according to [the Danish Arbitration Act 1972] ...".

The insurance union explained that the union regarded the insurance terms to be accepted in full if the client paid the insurance premium without any objections. The insurance union did not contend that A had been made aware of clause 14 before the insurance policy was issued.

The Western Court of Appeal found that the arbitration agreement in clause 14, according to which the policy holder is deprived of access to the Courts, was so essential, that it could not be considered agreed to by the policy holder by the fact alone that the policy holder had paid the insurance premiums without making any objections as to the insurance terms.

On those grounds, which differed slightly form the grounds set out by the Town Court of Århus,[163] the Western Court of Appeal upheld the Town Court's decision to let the case proceed before the Courts.

It should be noted that the arbitration clause in the horse insurance was typical.[164] As disputes regarding the evaluation of an animal are generally best and most cheaply dealt with by a forum that holds expertise upon that special subject, arbitration clauses *ad modum* the one discussed in the case are common in insurance policies of that kind. Despite this, the starting point of the Court of Appeal is clear. The insurance union had the documentation in its control, and it did not make it available to the counter party until after the conclusion of the contract. Thus, at the time of the filing of the insurance application, A did not have that information. The fact that the insurance union sent the conditions to A with the union's acceptance of the insurance did not make the arbitration clause part of the parties' contract.

The parties may agree to arbitrate at any point of their relationship. The question therefore arose whether A, by paying the premium without protesting the insurance terms, had acceded to the arbitration clause in those terms. The Court of Appeal found that the payment of premium did not provide a clear indication that the arbitration clause had been agreed to by the insured party. As long as an agreement could not clearly be established, the risk of non-information rested upon the party who possessed the information in question.

3.1.2. The rule

The three cases here presented show, that in cases where one of the parties posseses certain information, which includes the arbitration clause or agreement, the onus is upon that party to provide that information. If he or she does not, the information is not part of the parties' contractual relationship. Thus, the risk of incorrect or insufficient information lies upon the party who has the information in his control. This may seem rather self-evident. However, the question is what weight the allocation of the risk of incorrect of insufficient information has when compared to the other

---

[163] It seems from the transcript that clause 14 of the insurance terms had not been presented to the Town Court Judge. Only the extract of the insurance terms had. The clause that "... total uselessness shall be evident from the statement of two veterinarians' statements and be approved by the [insurance company's] veterinary consultant, who decides the issue in case of doubt. This decision may be brought before an arbitration tribunal ..." was not worded so that it in itself could bar A from taking the dispute to the Courts.

[164] *Andersen/Madsen (2001)*, p. 86.

party's general obligation to ascertain him- or herself of the contents of the contract he or she has entered into. For example, in both U 1987.178 DCA THE USELESS HORSE and KFE 1984.202 VBA direct references to certain terms were made in the relevant documentation. Still, in none of the cases did the party who did not have the terms ask for them. Also, in U 1980.847 MCCC AUDIO-GROUP OF DENMARK V. YAGI ENTERPRISES, the letter of credit had been set up on behalf of AG, and AG (not O) was the consignee according to the relevant documentation. Yagi had not made inquiries in that connection. Still, in all three cases the Courts found for the party claiming that he or she had not been properly informed.

This considered, it must be concluded that the obligation of a party to make certain information available to the other party, in case the first party wants an arbitration agreement contained in that information to be a part of the parties' contractual relationship, weighs heavily on the party controlling the information. Indeed, in the cases here discussed the duty to part with the information prevailed over the obligation of the other party to ascertain what the terms of the contract actually were.

As long as the documentation or information is solely in one of the parties' control, the risk allocation is more or less absolute. Only if the counter-party ought to have known, or has given the party controlling the information good reason to assume that he knew, of the disputed information may the risk allocation be reversed. Even if the counter-party may rightfully be blamed for having been careless in ascertaining the contents of the contract, that carelessness will not prevail over the fact that the other party possessed the information but did not provide it. The reason for that simply being, that the information has still not been communicated.

3.2. The information is not solely in one of the parties' control

Even if the relevant documentation is not solely in one of the parties' control, one may still talk of the allocation the risk for incorrect or insufficient information. In this case, the risk is upon the party who could most easily have provided the information, or who had the most reason to do so. Thus, outside the situations where one party controls the information, the line of argument is totally analogous to the line of argument used to explain the so-called rule of unclarity.[165] In the above-mentioned cases, where one of the parties controlled the information, the risk allocation alone decided the case. However, when both parties could have obtained the information or documentation, the risk allocation principle cannot decide the outcome of the dispute, but will be regarded as one argument amongst others. An example of this may be seen in a ruling of the Arbitral Tribunal for the Building and Construction Trades.

[165] *Andersen/Madsen (2001)*, p. 385 ff.

KFE 1996.5 VBA, The Nürnberg Jurisdiction Clause

A German contractor's invitation for tenders held a jurisdiction clause to the benefit of the Courts of Nürnberg. A Danish sub-contractor had in his tender referred to the AB 1972. During the negotiations a pre-printed form was used. The relevant box regarding general conditions had not been ticked, however "AB 72 § 30 + 31" had been added to the box.

After the meeting, the German contractor sent an acknowledgement of the contract, again referring to the Courts of Nürnberg. Dispute regarding extra works arose, and the sub-contractor brought the case to the Arbitral Tribunal for the Building and Construction Trades.

Having heard witnesses, the tribunal found that the issue of arbitration according to the AB 1972 conditions had been raised at the negotiations. However, it remained unclear what had in fact been said at the negotiations and it seemed that no German version of the AB 1972 had been presented at the meeting. Considering also that the relevant box in the form had not been ticked, and that both the tender documents and the confirmation of the contract held explicit jurisdiction clauses making the Courts of Nürnberg the relevant forum, the tribunal found that no arbitration agreement had been entered into. The case was dismissed from the tribunal.

The Danish negotiators could easily have provided their German counter-party with a German version of the AB 1972-conditions, but they did not. This worked against the Danish sub-contractor's claim that the dispute should be arbitrated. However, the case was not decided on that issue alone. Indeed, both the ambiguities in the way the form had been filled and the explicit jurisdiction clauses to the contrary strengthened the German contractor's contention that the Arbitral Tribunal for the Building and Construction Trades was not competent. Due to the ambiguities of the parties' contract, the conclusion in The Nürnberg Jurisdiction Clause case might be explained as an example of the use of the *adversus eum* principle. Indeed, it is probably a matter of temper rather than argument how to regard the case. This writer, however, chooses to regard it as a case, which discusses how to establish what is a part of the parties' contract rather than how that contract should be interpreted. Still, the conclusion of the tribunal does rest heavily on the fact that there were clear provisions in the contract against the application of the arbitration clause of AB 1972.

An example of a case that is more clear-cut on that point is KFE 1982.10A VBA, The Family Home,[166] mentioned above under point 2.2. In that case it was only an issue whether the AB 1972 conditions applied or not. The client based her argument that the arbitration clause did not apply on the fact that she did not know of the AB 1972 conditions and that the builder had not provided her with a copy of the conditions either. In the tender an explicit reference to AB 1972 was made, which would generally have sufficed[167] so as to incorporate those terms including their arbitration

---

[166] The findings of the arbitral tribunal for the building and construction trades in that case was later repeated almost verbatim in a parallel situation, see KFE 2001.193 VBA.
[167] See below, point 4.2.1 regarding U 1973.128 DSC, Vedbæk Strandvej.

clause into the parties' contract; still the tribunal found itself to be incompetent to hear the case. The ruling of the tribunal is rather laconic. It only states that the tribunal had misgivings as to the conclusion that the reference to AB 1972 in itself barred that particular client from taking the disputes to the Courts, and hence, that the tribunal found for the case's dismissal. However, the *de facto* effect of that conclusion was that the risk of non-information was placed with the builder. The AB 1972 conditions could quite easily have been acquired by the client, but the builder bore the risk for her not doing so.

In both the above cases, the party claiming the application of AB 1972 – and hence the competence of the tribunal – would have had less difficulty in providing the counter-party with the necessary information than the counter-party would have had trying to obtain it him- or herself. Also, the party, who wished a certain set of standard conditions to apply, had the stronger cause to ensure that these conditions were known to the counter-party. However, in both cases the conclusion was supported by other circumstances, respectively the ambiguity of the contract and the difference of the parties' knowledge of the trade.

3.3. Conclusion

The cases here discussed support, that there is in fact a risk allocation connected to the providing of information when entering into arbitration agreements. This is not solely a feature of the arbitration agreement, but the weight, the risk allocation carries, is likely to be influenced by the requirement for a clear agreement to arbitrate, which is a general feature of Danish arbitration law.

The use of a risk allocation line of thought can be defended both within and outside areas where one of the parties controls the information. However, out of principle, one must distinguish between the two situations. Outside areas where one of the parties control the information-flow, the risk allocation cannot in itself be expected to decide the outcome of a dispute, but must be supported by other circumstances.

In none of the above cases was it argued that the lack of information/documentation meant that the parties had not contracted at all, or that provisions as to the subject matter of the dispute had not been agreed to. This was due to the fact, that in none of the cases doing so would be in the parties' best interest.

Thus, the cases do not facilitate a conclusion on whether the risk allocation weighed against the parties' duty to ascertain themselves of the terms of the contract they have entered into differs dependent on whether it is an arbitration agreement or an other contractual provision, which is in dispute.

It may very well be argued that the cases dealt with below could have found their conclusion without resorting to the allocation of a risk on one of the parties. However, this writer finds that regarding the issue as a question of the allocation of a risk provides a good tool – or a shortcut even – to understanding of some of the Danish case law on arbitration agreements.

4. Further case law on the necessary requisites for the conclusion of arbitration agreements

4.1. Arbitration clauses – Has the main agreement been concluded?

The parties may have agreed to arbitrate, even if they do not have a "main agreement" in force between them. For example, the parties might agree to arbitrate a dispute in tort, or the parties may agree to arbitrate the compensation, which is to be paid after an agreement has been deemed invalid. However, arbitration agreements entered into after a dispute has arisen seldom give rise to case law. Instead, quite a few cases exist, where the dispute as to the agreement to arbitrate is a reflection of a dispute as to whether the parties' main agreement has been concluded. The general rule in those cases is that where a contract was never concluded, an arbitration clause or provision, which form part of that intended contract, is not concluded either. However, the outcome of the cases will depend on both the correct interpretation of the arbitration clause and on the contentions of the parties. Clear-cut rulings from the Courts or tribunals should not be expected.

This is not a thesis on contract law, nor should it be, so for a thorough investigation of the general rules on the formation of contracts under Danish law one must look to other writers. Here, instead, a few snapshots will be provided, through three rulings on the tribunal's own competence, made by The Arbitral Tribunal of the Building and Construction Trades, touching upon this question.

KFE 1991.14 VBA

The tender documents concerning contract work provided that AB 1972 applied to the contract. Contractor A offered a tender on part of the works. A's tender was the lowest regarding that part of the contract. However, the builder chose to award the contract to B, who had given the lowest bid for the complete contract. A brought proceedings before the arbitral tribunal claiming damages, contending he should have been awarded the contract for the relevant part of the work. The builder disputed the tribunal's competence. According to the builder, AB 1972 only applied if the parties had in fact contracted. As the builder had refused, A's offer this was not the case.

The tribunal found that the provision in the tender documents, according to which offers were to be given on AB 1972 conditions, only provided information to the potential contractors that if their offer was in fact accepted AB 1972, including the arbitration clause contained therein, should apply to the contract. The provision did not provide an agreement between the parties, neither explicit nor implied, that a dispute regarding unjustified refusal of a tender should be arbitrated.

KFE 1992.60 VBA

Sub-contractor B tendered an offer on certain works to A, the main contractor, who had given an invitation for offers with a reference to the AB 1972 general conditions. B's tender referred to certain standard clauses, which in turn referred to AB 1972. After giving the tender, B discovered that there were several calculation errors. If B were to carry out the contract, he would suffer a loss. B sought to be relieved from the offer. A refused and informed B that in case B maintained his position A would give the contract to the next best tender and claim the price difference from B. B then conceded to stand by his offer.

A sent a draft contract to B. The draft contract, however, was not in accordance with the offer given by B, especially as the reference to the standard clauses contained in B's tender was not repeated in the contract. B's counsel asked that they were inserted but A refused. As the proposed contract was not in accordance with B's offer, B's counsel informed A, that B was no longer bound by the tender.[168] A's counsel replied that the draft contract should be signed, and that any dispute regarding the standard clauses should be referred to arbitration. However, B still refused, and consequently A, having advised B beforehand, accepted the next best tender. A then initiated proceedings before the arbitral tribunal, claiming the price differential of 0.5 million Danish Kroner.

Held by the arbitral tribunal: A had not given a written acceptance of the offer. As the case had been presented to the tribunal, no other form of acceptance had been given, nor had B had reason to understand that an acceptance was intended. This was strengthened by the fact that the proposed contract had not been in accordance with the tender offered by B. In fact, the draft contract differed from B's tender in such a way, that B had been justified in regarding the proposed contract as a refusal of the tender, given in connection with A offering to contract on other terms. (Non-conforming acceptance according to the Danish Contracts Act sec. 6, sub-sec. 1).[169] Accordingly, there was no agreement between the parties. The reference to AB 1972 made by B in the tender applied in case a contract was concluded between the parties. That had not been done. B's claim, that the case be dismissed from the arbitral tribunal, was therefore followed.

In KFE 1991.14 VBA and KFE 1992.60 VBA both tribunals reached the conclusion that as no contract had been concluded between the parties, no arbitration agreement had been made either. However, as the facts of the cases differ, so does the reasoning applied by the tribunals. In KFE 1991.14 VBA it was clear that no contract had been concluded. Indeed, the reason for the dispute was A's claim that the builder had been unjustified in not concluding a contract with A. In the case, the tribunal first stated that in general, when tenders were to be given according to certain standard conditions, then the applicability of those conditions presupposed the formation of a contract. Furthermore, the arbitration clause did not, in itself or in the context of the facts of the case, cover a dispute like the one before the tribunal.

---

[168] In accordance with the Danish Contracts Act 1917 § 6, sub-sec. 1.

[169] See regarding the notion of non-conforming acceptance U 1994.344 DSC (commented in U 1994 B 433 ff.) and *Vagner (2001),* p. 29.

In KFE 1992.60 VBA on the other hand, the existence of a contract was at the centre of the dispute. According to A, a contract had been concluded and B was unjustified in refusing to carry out his obligations under that contract. B was therefore liable in damages for the price differential between B's offer and the next best offer. The tribunal found that the main agreement had not been concluded. The reference to the standard conditions presupposed such a contract; thus, the standard conditions did not apply.

Neither KFE 1991.14 VBA nor KFE 1992.60 VBA provide a totally definite rule that when an arbitration clause is a part of the parties' main contract, but the latter contract has not been concluded, then the arbitration clause has not been concluded either. The reason for this is that the parties are ad liberty to enter into an agreement that disputes as to whether or not the main contract has been concluded should be arbitrated. Consequently, the tribunals cannot deduce from the fact that the main agreement has not come into existence to the fact that no arbitration agreement has. For that conclusion to be reached the tribunals must interpret the parties' whole contractual relationship and decide whether the arbitration clauses do in fact cover the actual disputes, as was seen in both cases, but particularly in KFE 1991.14 VBA.

Dependent on the contentions of the parties, the discussion may be more straightforward in the cases where the tribunal finds that an agreement has indeed been concluded on a set of well-known standard terms. In fact, if it follows from the circumstances and proof provided that a contract has prima facie been concluded, the starting point is the dispute should be referred to arbitration. According to the principle of Kompetenz-Kompetenz[170] this is the case even if the acceptance of the offer is in dispute.

KFE 1994.145 VBA, THE MILLWORK

A sub-contractor initiated proceedings before the tribunal, claiming that the builder had wrongfully terminated their contract. The owner claimed that the case should be dismissed as no binding agreement had been entered into between the parties, and thus, that no binding arbitration agreement had been entered into either.

The facts of the case were these: Danish sub-contractor C responded to an invitation for tenders given by the contractor, A, on behalf of "the owner and the operator" of a hotel being built. C was to install the millwork and furnishing of the hotel. The offer was sent to A on August 5th 1992. C also sent a draft contract to A, providing i.a.: "Documents valid for this Contract Agreement: General Conditions – AB 1972 (English translation enclosed)." The offer was negotiated at a meeting in London on August 11th. The minutes of the meeting were signed by C and by representatives of the owner and A. The minutes held:

"Present: …

---

[170] See below, Chapter IV.

An offer for producing and installing the Millwork as detailed on C's offer of 22.06.92 with revisions of 11.08.92 for public areas together with C's offer of 05.08.92 for guest rooms for the sum of 'Seven Hundred and Eighty Thousand Pounds Sterling' (£ 780,000) ... This offer was accepted by [the owner] on behalf of ... subject to C's compliance with [the specifications given].

It is the intention of [...] and C to enter into a Contract of Sale for the above. The contract will be administered by A."

A few points remained unsettled after this meeting. Further communications were made during the next six weeks, however details were still missing. During this period C also crafted a test guest-room.

The real work could not be initiated before the final details were agreed between the parties. However, the time schedule was quite strict. C, therefore, on 13th October 1992, informed A that as the negotiations had lasted so long, C was no longer in a position to keep the delivery schedule originally set out in the offer. On the same day, A sent a letter to the owner with a copy to C, stating: " ... Millwork. We enclose Contract Agreements 5.01 and 5.02 with [C]. The contract has been worked out after a series of meetings and exchange of letters between the parties involved. The latest step was a meeting between C and A 1992-10-05 and the follow-up letter from C of 1992-10-06. ... Please inform C and A about the next step." In the enclosed Contract Agreements 5.01 and 5.02 C was referred to as the sub-contractor and the owner as contractor; a reference to AB 1972 was also made.

On 14th October, the owner sent a fax message in response to C's letter of 13th October. The owner regretted to inform C, that as he (the owner) could not accept the now proposed delivery time, the owner did not wish to enter into a contract with C, and had instead given the tender to another contractor. C immediately disputed that a contract was not yet concluded. However, the owner maintained his position. According to him, the "Contract Agreements" were only to be regarded as letters of intent.

The tribunal held:

Before the meeting of August 11th the owner had been provided with a copy of the draft contract made by C, in which reference to AB 1972 was made. Considering the contents of the minutes of that meeting, which had been signed by representatives of all parties, and considering the witness statements given before the tribunal, the tribunal found that the contract, as revised on the meeting, had been accepted by the owner. Under those circumstances the owner, who in the final draft was named as C's contract party, was obliged to let the dispute regarding the termination of the contract be dealt with by arbitration according to AB 1972, sec. 31, sub-sec. 1. Accordingly, the claim for dismissal was refused.

From the transcript of THE MILLWORK, it seems that the owner did not argue in the alternative. Thus, there was no claim from the owner that even if a contract had been concluded, AB 1972 and/or its arbitration clause did not apply. This enabled the tribunal to give the clear conclusion that as the parties *had* contracted, AB 1972 applied and the tribunal could hear the case.

So, as a rule, when one offers to contract on certain terms, which include a provision that disputes should be arbitrated, the arbitration agreement only becomes effective if the contract is concluded. On the other hand, if one offers to contract on certain terms, which include a provision that disputes should be arbitrated, and the offer is accepted, then the starting point is that so is the arbitration agreement.

These are only points of departure, though. The arbitration clause in itself may not fulfil the requirements set out by statute and case law. Or, the arbitration clause may be worded so as to apply also to disputes as to whether the parties have contracted or not. In that case, an obvious circularity presents itself. However, the circularity is no greater than the, now long accepted, circularity of the doctrine of separability.

4.2. Arbitration clauses – Has the arbitration clause become part of the parties' contract?

The cases discussed above are cases, where the existence of any contractual relationship between the parties has been disputed. Those cases, however, are not the bulk of the case law. Normally, it is quite clear that some sort of contract has been established, but instead it is disputed whether or not the arbitration agreement is a part of that contractual relationship. Such cases are dealt with here. The cases have been divided into groups according to what is their most central issue, namely incorporation techniques, third party conflicts, passivity and competing forms and clauses. In the following, the relevant cases will be discussed. Also, any directions as to how the Courts or tribunals might be expected to deal with similar cases in the future will be given – to the extent that existing case law offers such directions!

4.2.1. Incorporation techniques

There is no general rule of Danish arbitration law that arbitration clauses contained in a standard document or general conditions can only be incorporated through direct reference to the arbitration clause itself. This may be seen from the Danish Supreme Court's ruling in the VEDBÆK STRANDVEJ case.

U 1973.128 DSC, VEDBÆK STRANDVEJ

A sub-contractor initiated proceedings before the Courts against the main contractor regarding the balance of the account in connection to certain works, which the sub-contractor had carried out under a contract with the main contractor. The main contractor claimed that the case should be dismissed from the Courts as the parties had entered into an agreement to arbitrate on AB 1951-terms. It followed from the parties' contract that the basis of the contract was, amongst other things, the specifications, the drawings and AB 1951.

The main contractor pleaded that the parties hereby had entered into a quite clear agreement to arbitrate. According to the sub-contractor, on the other hand, there was, under Danish law, a presumption that the ordinary Courts were competent to hear a dispute. This presumption required that an explicit agreement to arbitrate had been entered into. If it was not, the Courts would not be deprived of their competence. A mere reference to general conditions, which only really regarded the relationship between the client and the main contractor, did not suffice.

The Eastern Court of Appeal found that as the contract held an explicit reference to AB 1951, which had been drafted as an independent point, and upon the wording of which AB 1951 applied between the parties, the agreement to arbitrate was sufficiently clear. The parties' dispute should be arbitrated under AB 1951 § 24.

On appeal the Danish Supreme Court upheld all findings of the Eastern Court of Appeal. The case was dismissed from the Courts.

The contention that an "explicit agreement to arbitrate" had to be entered into was not approved by the Courts. Conversely, the Court accepted that a distinct reference to a set of standard conditions could incorporate the arbitration clause in those conditions into the parties' relationship. The documentation used in the case may be sketched like this:

U 1973.128 DSC, VEDBÆK STRANDVEJ

Accordingly, the Danish Supreme Court in the VEDBÆK STRANDVEJ case approved the following technique of incorporation, "a one-layered reference":

Contract:
This contract is according to / incorporates
Conditions A

↓

Conditions A:
Disputes under these conditions should be
arbitrated

However, one should note that the VEDBÆK STRANDVEJ case is only evidence of two things. 1) That there is no need for an explicit agreement to arbitrate, e.g. through an explicit reference to the arbitration clause sought incorporated, and 2) That arbitration agreements *might* be concluded through a direct reference to the standard document, which contains the disputed clause.

Considering again that the knowledge the parties had or ought to have had is at the centre of attention, one cannot deduce from the Danish Supreme Court's ruling in the VEDBÆK STRANDVEJ case that a direct reference to a set of standard conditions will always suffice. KFE 1982.10A VBA, THE FAMILY HOME,[171] referred to above in point 2.2, provides a clear example of that. In the case, the contract for building a family home contained a direct reference to the standard conditions AB 1972. However, as the client had no knowledge of the trade or the standard conditions, the client was not obliged to arbitrate a dispute under the contract. Still, it must be expected that in most cases between professionals, where a direct reference to a set of standard conditions, which are agreed documents within that trade has been entered in the parties' contract, an arbitration agreement in those conditions will apply to disputes under the contract. (See for example KFE 1994.134 VBA, THE MILLWORK, referred above in point 4.1).

The fact that there are no set formal requirements for an arbitration agreement to be concluded does not entail that any technique of incorporation will suffice. Indeed, there is clear precedence that the reference in an agreement between A and B to a set of conditions, which in turn refer to another set of standard conditions, containing the now disputed arbitration clause, will not incorporate the arbitration clause into A's and B's agreement.

---

[171] See also KFE 2001.193 VBA.

Contract:
This contract is according to / incorporates
Conditions A

↓

Conditions A:
These conditions incorporate
Conditions B

↓

Conditions B:
Disputes under these conditions should be
arbitrated

Such a "two-layered" reference has been tried by the Danish Supreme Court in the SKAGEN HAVN case, referred above in point 2.1, and in the KLINTEMARKEN case.

U 1963.488 DSC, KLINTEMARKEN

In connection with the construction of a housing estate, the main contractor entered into an agreement with a sub-contractor. It followed from the parties' contract, that the sub-contractor was to perform the work "according to drawings and specifications". Dispute arose regarding the work. The sub-contractor brought the dispute to the Courts, but the main contractor claimed that the case be referred to arbitration. The sub-contractor claimed that there was no arbitration agreement between the parties. According to the main contractor, however, the reference in the main and sub-contractor's agreement to the drawings and specifications agreed between the main contractor and the client, in which a reference to the AB 1951 was made, had incorporated the arbitration clause in AB 1951, § 24, into the parties' contract. Generally, it followed from the whole structure of the main contractor/sub-contractor system, that the main contractor entered into the client's rights and obligations under the arbitration clause, if the client objected to the sub-contractor's carrying out of the work.

The Western Court of Appeal found:

"As it cannot with the *necessary certainty* be deduced from the parties' contract, that the arbitration clause relied on by the [main contractor], which according to its wording only applies to the relationship between the client and the [main] contractor, also shall be applied regarding the settlement of disputes between ... the main contractor and the ... sub-contractor, the [sub-contractor] is not barred from ... [pursuing his claim before the Courts]."

Upon appeal to the Danish Supreme Court it became apparent that a folder had been made, containing all the documents which applied to the work, and from which it was clear that the AB 1951 also was intended to apply to the relationship between the main contractor and any sub-contractors. Furthermore, the main contractor referred to a letter written to him by the sub-contractor, which stated that he was rather confident as to the outcome of any arbitral proceedings the client would initiate (as the client had indeed suggested he would).

The new information did not affect the outcome of the decision, and the ruling of the Western Court of Appeal was upheld.

The reference in the sub- and main contractors' agreement to the drawings and conditions agreed between the main contractor and the client, according to which AB 1951 applied, was not sufficient so as to incorporate the arbitration clause in AB 1951 § 24 into the sub- and main contractor's agreement. The Courts thus rejected the two-layered technique of incorporation applied. This was the case even if it followed from the documentation between the main contractor and the client that AB 1951 was intended to apply to the whole "chain of contracts".[172]

Reverting to the SKAGEN HAVN case,[173] the sub- and main contractor's agreement in that case referred to the client's drawings and conditions. The client's conditions in turn referred to AB 1951. The sub-contractor, A, argued that this was not sufficient to provide a clear agreement to arbitrate. The Eastern Court of Appeal and a minority of 4 out of 11 Supreme Court judges supported these contentions made by A and found against the claim for dismissal. The majority of the Supreme Court found that it had been established that A knew that AB 1951 applied. This sufficed for the arbitration clause in AB 1951 § 24 to apply, and the majority therefore found for dismissing the case from the Courts. However, it should be noted that the Eastern Court of Appeal's finding that it could not from the reference to the client's "drawings and conditions" with the necessary certainty be deduced that the arbitration clause of AB 1951 was agreed between the parties, *was not overruled* by the majority of the Danish Supreme Court. The majority, 6 of the 11 judges, found it proved that A, at the time of the formation of the contract, knew that AB 1951 applied. The technique used for written incorporation was not relevant when considering the knowledge A had. Finally, one of the 11 judges found that it could not be concluded from the written agreement that AB 1951 applied to the contract. However, A's counsel had in later correspondence stated that AB 1951 applied to the contract. As there was no need to distinguish between the acceptance of the AB 1951-terms and of the arbitration clause in it, that judge also held for the dismissal of the case.

---

[172] Compare [1964] 2 Lloyd's Law Reports 527 CA, THE MERAK, see below, § 3, point 3.3.2.

[173] Referred above in point 2.1.

A two-layered reference was also rejected in U 1968.664 DCA, MADSEN V. KON-GERSLEV. Master painter Kongerslev employed painter Madsen regarding a contract to be carried out in Godthåb, Greenland. Kongerslev dismissed Madsen, and Madsen claimed certain amounts (salary, travel costs, diets etc.) before Greenland's Court of Appeal. Kongerslev claimed that the case be referred to arbitration. According to the parties' contract, the conditions for the employment were those agreed between the collective trade unions in Denmark and the Ministry for Greenland. According to Greenland's Court of Appeal this did not provide such a clear and unambiguous agreement to arbitrate that the parties' dispute should be settled by the trade tribunal, rather than by the Courts.

In conclusion to the question of which techniques of incorporation will suffice, the following guidelines may be provided: Firstly, there is no general rule of Danish arbitration law that arbitration agreements should be explicit, or may only be incorporated by direct reference.[174] Such a demand is found in the Danish Maritime Code sec. 311, sub-sec. 3 cf. sec. 310, sub-sec. 3, as regards the incorporation of arbitration clauses in charter-parties into bills of lading issued under the charter-party, but no general rule exists. Secondly, between professionals, a direct reference in a contract to a set of standard conditions containing an arbitration clause will, as a starting point, be effective so as to incorporate the arbitration clause.[175] Thirdly, a two-layered reference, where a direct reference is made to a set of conditions, which in turn refer to another standard form that contains an arbitration clause, will not, even between professionals, be effective.[176] Still, it cannot too strongly be emphasised that these are guidelines. The points may provide support for the drafter of arbitration clauses under Danish law, but they do not offer a template by which to settle a dispute. In the settling of a dispute as to whether an arbitration clause has been incorporated, one must always take into account the knowledge of the parties, and not just the documentation used. E.g. a two-layered reference incorporating the arbitration clause of an agreed document might prove effective between long-term business partners in the trade.

---

[174] See U 1973.128 DSC, VEDBÆK STRANDVEJ.

[175] See U 1973.128 DSC, VEDBÆK STRANDVEJ, KFE 1994.145 VBA, THE MILLWORK AND, implied, KFE 1991.14 VBA and KFE 1992.60 VBA.

[176] U 1963.488 DSC, KLINTEMARKEN, U 1973.305 DSC, SKAGEN HAVN and U 1968.664 DCA.

4.2.2. Third party conflicts

4.2.2.1. In general

It is generally accepted as a point of departure under Danish law that succession in or transfer of a party's rights or obligations under a contract means that the succeeding party or transferee obtains all the original party's rights and obligations under that contract. This principle can be seen in the Instruments of Debts Act,[177] sec. 27, however it is a general unwritten principle of Danish Law. In accordance with this, the starting point is that if a person succeeds in another person's rights and/or obligations under a contract, he will also succeed in an arbitration agreement, which forms a part of that contract.

Having stated the point of departure, modifications follow from special rules. Often the transfer of a right might indeed leave the succeeding party or transferee in a different position regarding the contract than was the original party. An obvious maritime example of this is the transfer of a bill of lading to a third party, but bills of exchange or negotiable promissory notes provide a more general example. Another example is that the estate of a physical or legal person might have another legal position as towards its counter-parties than the person would have had, had he not gone bankrupt or – indeed – died.

The issues here outlined cover different aspects of what is in fact (at least) two different problems, namely 1) Who are parties to the arbitration agreement under the general rules of succession and transfer of obligations, and 2) What are the legal effects of arbitration agreements.

In this section only the first question will be addressed. Thus, questions related to issues of succession and direct action will be discussed. The issues of whether a physical or legal person's estate is bound by arbitration agreements entered into by the person is a question of which legal effects arbitration agreements are equipped with, and are consequently not deliberated here. The special considerations, which must be taken into account under the regulation connected to bankruptcy and the administration of estates, brings that topic outside the scope of a discussion of whether an arbitration agreement has become a part of the parties' contract.

Suppose C succeeds in B's rights and obligations under a contract between A and B, due to for example transfer or subrogation. In that case, it is generally assumed in Danish theory that succession in the rights and/or obligations under the main agreement, which the arbitration agreement is appended to, will generally not bring about

---

[177] Lovbekendtgørelse nr. 699 af 23. september 1986 om gældsbreve, som ændret ved lov nr. 389 af 14. juni 1995.

the termination of the arbitration agreement.[178] According to *Windahl* this means that a reciprocal obligation to arbitrate disputes under the main agreement rests upon A and C.[179]

Still, the rule that C and A have a reciprocal obligation to arbitrate their dispute only applies under certain conditions: C must have succeeded in B's rights and/or obligations *and* the claim must be under the original contract between A and B. If either of those two conditions are not fulfilled, then the principle cannot necessarily be applied. Indeed, one must distinguish between the following three situations:

a) C has succeeded in B's rights and/or obligations, and the claim is under A's and B's contract;

b) C has not succeeded in B's rights and/or obligations, and the claim is not under A's and B's contract;

c) C has not succeeded in B's rights and/or obligations, but the claim is based on A's obligations as towards B under A's and B's contract.

4.2.2.2. Situation a: Succession

The transactions here considered are situations where the rights and/or obligations of B are shifted in some way to C. Generally one may freely transfer the rights one has under a uni- or bilateral contract.[180] However, the transfer of obligations normally presupposes the consent of the creditor.[181] To use an example: The seller of goods may transfer his claim for the purchase price to someone else without the consent of the buyer, but will need the buyer's consent if he (the seller) wants to transfer his obligation to deliver the goods. This construction, however, presupposes that it is possible to separate the parties' contract into rights and obligations. Although the Courts normally regard arbitration agreements as a burden upon the parties, arbitration agreements may not be considered to hold only "an obligation" in the way just described here. As put by *Windahl*, "[f]orum clauses can hardly be split into a 'rights-' and 'obligation-part', which may be clearly separated from each other".[182] Thus, it

---

[178] *Hjejle (1987)*, p. 73. See also *Gomard (1979)*, p. 24.

[179] *Windahl (2001)*, p. 245.

[180] *Gomard (1993)*, p. 67.

[181] *Gomard (1993)*, p. 143.

[182] *Windahl (2001)*, p. 245.

cannot, from the fact that an arbitration agreement obviously bestows obligations upon the parties, be inferred that the rights and obligations under the arbitration agreement may only be transferred etc. if the counter-party consents to it.

It must be maintained that arbitration agreements follow the point of departure outlined above in point 4.2.2.1; namely that if C succeeds in B's rights and obligations under the contract between A and B, and a dispute arises under that contract, then the dispute should be arbitrated. This must apply if B's whole contractual position, i.e. both B's rights and B's obligations, is transferred, but it also applies if C only has succeeded in B's *rights* under the contract. An example of such a situation is given in KFE 1983.73 VBA.

In the case builder B entered into a contract with a City Council, A. In the contract between B and A was an arbitration clause. B went bankrupt, and B's claim under the contract was transferred to builder C instead. Dispute arose, and C brought the case before the arbitral tribunal. A disputed the competence of the tribunal. However, the tribunal found that as the case, despite of the succession, concerned the exact same contract, it did not seem reasonable, nor was it supported by the arbitration agreement, that A, due to the succession alone, was freed from its obligations under the arbitration agreement.

In the case C had succeeded in B's rights and obligations under the contract with the City Council (A). This fact could not in itself effect the termination of the arbitration agreement. Neither was it supported by the wording of the arbitration agreement that this was intended. Disputes under the contract were to be arbitrated. This was not altered by the fact that B's claim now belonged to someone else (C).

The tribunal's ruling – that the arbitration agreement did not support the solution that the agreement would fall in case of transfer – calls for a comment, namely that one should always keep in mind that maybe the arbitration agreement upon its correct construction only applies to the original parties' dispute. For example, it may be of consequence whether the arbitration agreement is worded to apply to "any dispute arising out of the contract", or whether it is worded so as to apply to "disputes arising between A and B concerning this contract". For example in U 1963.488 DSC, KLIN-TEMARKEN,[183] the fact that the arbitration agreement was worded so as to apply only to disputes between the main contractor and the client aided the conclusion that the arbitration agreement had not been incorporated into the contract between the subcontractor and the main contractor. Also, in an unpublished ruling from the Maritime and Commercial Court of Copenhagen of 21 March 2000, referred by *Windahl*,[184] a

---

[183] Referred above in point 4.2.1.

[184] *Windahl (2001)*, p. 244. (Unpublished case before the Maritime and Commercial Court of Copenhagen, no. H-0179-97).

jurisdiction clause in an exclusive sales agreement worded "[any] dispute, which cannot be solved through negotiations between *the parties*[185] shall be referred to the Maritime and Commercial Court of Copenhagen", was considered in-transferable. Therefore it did not apply to a dispute between a factoring bank and the buyer.

4.2.2.3. Situation b: No succession

If C neither claims to have succeeded in B's rights and/or obligations, nor bases his claim on A's rights and obligations towards B under A's and B's contract, then the starting point is also clear: There is no contract and hence no agreement to arbitrate between A and C. The problem for the Courts and tribunals in theses situations is generally to establish whether or not the claim is based on principles of succession.

U 1983.123 DSC, THE COLLAPSED ROOF

In 1969-1970 builder A built an industrial building for B. B went bankrupt in 1975, and the pledgee bank re-possessed the building. In 1977 the bank sold the building to C.

In December 1979 half the building's roof collapsed after a heavy snowfall. In the following investigation it became obvious that the construction of the roof had been faulty, and C claimed damages in tort from A before the Western Court of Appeal. A claimed that the case should be dismissed from the Courts due to an arbitration clause in the building contract, alternatively that he be discharged from C's claim.

According to the builder, A, the arbitration agreement had to be seen as an integrated part of A's and B's whole agreement. The clause had been entered into the parties' contract in accordance with the general distribution of risks taking place when drafting a building contract. The arbitration clause could not be severed from the contract as such, and the transfer of the property could not increase the onus resting upon the builder under the contract.

C, on the other hand, claimed that there was precedence that a builder may be liable due to the general rules on tort as towards later owners of that building. The arbitration agreement between A and B could not bar C from seeking a judgment from the ordinary Courts as to whether such a "direct liability" rested upon the defendant. This was especially so as C's claim was not based upon a succession in B's rights and obligations under the building contract.

According to the Western Court of Appeal, the arbitration agreement formed a part of the building contract between A and B. Nevertheless, the Court found, as a general rule, that such a procedural agreement did not bar a later buyer of the property, who had not acceded to the arbitration agreement, from bringing a claim to the Courts, when that claim was not founded on the building contract.

In the case before the Courts, C had not consented to the arbitration agreement, nor was the claim based on the building contract – C had based his claim in tort. Hence, there was no arbitration agreement between A and C and the claim could proceed before the Courts. On appeal to the Danish Supreme Court all the findings of the Western Court of Appeal were upheld.

---

[185] Writer's emphasis.

The rule that follows from the case is clear: If C's claim is not based on succession, and indeed, not based on A's and B's contract at all, then there is no arbitration agreement between A and C.

In THE COLLAPSED ROOF it was quite easy to establish that no succession had taken place. C had no contract with B, and the only connection to A was C having bought a building originally constructed by A. However, sometimes it can be difficult to establish if some sort of succession has taken place, or if the claim is in tort.

U 1976.730 DCA, FINIPAL HUSE

By a contract of Nov. 13th 1972 builder B and buyer C agreed that B should build a house on a plot C had bought from B on the same occasion. According to the contract, the building should be constructed according to drawings etc. provided by Finipal Huse A/S (A).

In 1975 C initiated proceedings against B before the Town Court of Fredericia, claiming a reduction of DKK 40.000 due to subsidence damage. Also, C gave third party notice to A who, according to a contract with B, had projected and supervised the building of the house. A pleaded that the claim against A should be dismissed due to an arbitration clause in the contract between A and B. (AB 1951, § 24).

The Court found that as the claims against A and B were founded on the assumption that certain errors on the part of both A and B had interacted to create the subsidence damage, the claims ought to be dealt with together. There was no direct reference to AB 1951 in the building contract between B and C. Accordingly the claim should be dealt with by the ordinary Courts. As the case had been initiated in Fredericia, which was B's principal place of business, also the case as against A could be heard there.

A appealed the decision to the Western Court of Appeal. In the meantime B had undergone liquidation. No dividend of any consequence could be expected. Before the Western Court of Appeal, C mainly argued that A's liability towards C was based on an independent liability. A had shown negligence in carrying out its duties and the claim against A was thus based in tort.

According to the Western Court of Appeal, C's case was founded on the claim that B and/or A were liable towards C for the damages to the building. These claims had such a common foundation that they ought to be dealt with together. It was therefore legitimate that C had given third party notice to A. The arbitration clause in the contract between A and B did not bar C from taking a claim against A to the ordinary Courts.

It cannot be seen from the ruling of the Western Court of Appeal whether the Court considered C's claim as against A to be based in tort or on some sort of succession in A's contract with B. However, when reading the case one should probably appreciate that there were two main issues in the case; firstly, whether the preconditions for third party notice were indeed satisfied, secondly, whether the arbitration clause in A's contract with B meant that the application for third party notice should be dismissed. The Court's emphasis was on the conditions for third party notice. Having established that those conditions were present, the arbitration agreement in the agreement between A and B became even less likely to be applied, as it would result in splitting up two cases that was obviously best dealt with together. In any case, as

A had not shown that C was actually claiming under the contract between A and B, the arbitration agreement was unlikely to be upheld.

Concluding on the above, the requirement for a clear agreement to arbitrate generally entails that as long as it has not with certainty been established that C's claim is under A and B's contract, then there cannot be an arbitration agreement between A and C. This applies irrespectively of what legal relationship there is between B and C.

Such a conclusion also explains why the Western Court of Appeal in the FINIPAL HUSE case did not determine whether C's claim was in tort or in succession under the contract. There was simply no need to do so.

4.2.2.4. Situation c: Direct action

The situation here dealt with presupposes: 1) That C has not succeeded in B's position under A's contract; 2) That there is no independent arbitration agreement, for example via incorporation, between A and C; and 3) That it cannot be established that A or C respectively knew or ought to know of the arbitration agreement now claimed to exist by the other party.

It would follow from what has been said so far in this chapter that in such a case the starting point is that A and C are neither ad liberty nor under an obligation to arbitrate their dispute. However, in newer Danish literature it has been argued that this third category exists.[186] It would go far beyond the scope of this work to debate the merits of that discussion.[187] Instead, it will for the sake of the argument be accepted that

1) In certain situations C is legitimate in suing in direct action against A, although C bases his claim on A's obligations towards B under A's and B's contract.

2) In those situations the success of C's action may depend on the division of rights and obligations between A and B under their contract.

The absolute rule in this situation must be that as C is not a party to A's and B's contract, there is no agreement to arbitrate between A and C. Also, if the dispute is *linked* to the original contract, but is not a dispute *under* the contract, then the arbitration agreement's scope will generally have been exceeded, and consequently either party may take the claim to the ordinary Courts.

The question is whether there are exceptions to this rule.

---

[186] See in particular *Nørgaard/Pedersen (1995)*.

[187] See for a reference to other writers on the subject *Vagner (2001)*, p. 200.

The writers show little consensus on this point. *Nørgaard/Pedersen* seem to presume that A, as a compensation for the fact that he has had to accept being sued in conflict with the rules of privity of contract, will be able to apply the provisions of A's and B's contract that may limit or exclude A's liability also as towards C.[188] As an exception, *Nørgaard/Pedersen* mention that the actual amount C may claim from A is not necessarily restricted to the amount B could have claimed from A.[189] However, *Nørgaard/Pedersen* do not take a position on the question of the impact of (jurisdiction or) arbitration clauses in A's and B's contract.

Windahl argues at some length whether the position should be the same as when C has succeeded in B's position under A's and B's contract, thus requiring C to respect the arbitration agreement in A's and B's contract.[190] The rationale for that solution should be that it is the fact that A has incurred a liability towards B under the contract between A and B that has facilitated C's direct action against A. *Windahl* finds that C's interest in having the dispute heard by another forum than the one that follows from the contract, should be taken into consideration, especially when it is open to doubt if C's claim is borne by other consideration than A's breach of his obligations towards B; a position which is, although unnoticed by *Windahl*, partly supported by the ruling of the Western Court of Appeal in U 1976.730 DCA, FINIPAL HUSE. Unfortunately, though, *Windahl* reaches no clear-cut conclusion, but only asserts that a too formalistic approach is not desirable.[191] Thus, he finds that it should not be so that any forum clause in the contract between A and B is precluded from being applied to the dispute between A and C due to the fact *alone* that there are no formal contractual relations between A and C.

Ulfbeck discusses, in her doctoral thesis *Kontrakters Relativitet,*[192] the problems of arbitration agreements in connection to contract work when C sues in direct action against A, but the foundation for C's suit is A's obligations as towards B.[193] She splits the discussion of the effect of arbitration agreements up in two questions, namely 1) When C has the *right* to arbitrate the dispute with A; and 2) When C is

---

[188] *Nørgaard/Pedersen (1995)*, p. 387.

[189] *Nørgaard/Pedersen (1995)*, p. 390.

[190] *Windahl (2001)*, p. 247.

[191] *Windahl (2001)*, p. 248.

[192] Translates as "Privity of Contracts".

[193] *Ulfbeck (2000)*, p. 317 ff. and 342 f.

93

under a *duty* to arbitrate disputes with A. According to *Ulfbeck*, C has the *right* to arbitrate the dispute against A if there is a chain of arbitration agreements, so that A and B, respectively B and C, in their internal relationship have entered into identical arbitration agreements. (As is the case if a chain of sub- and main contractors in their internal relationship incorporate the same standard conditions). In support of that claim she refers to the ruling KFE 1994.16 VBA, THE OIL PUMP SWIVEL. In the case a swivel, being a part of an oil-pumping unit for the discharge of oil from tankers, was not sufficiently tight. The owner, C, initiated proceedings before the Arbitral Tribunal for the Building and Construction Trades, claiming that the contractor (B) and the manufacturer (A) of the swivel were liable for the cost of repair and replacement. C himself had originally obtained an offer from A regarding the swivel, but the contract of delivery was between A and B. In the case, a chain of arbitration agreements was present so that A and B, respectively B and C, had agreed that disputes should be dealt with by the tribunal. However, there was no explicit arbitration agreement as between C and A. A therefore claimed that the dispute between A and C could not be heard by the tribunal. The tribunal gave the following ruling on its own competence:

"[A] was from the outset aware of the fact that [C] was the owner, as [A]'s original offer was given directly to [C], and as [A] later participated in negotiations with [C] and [B].

In the contract between [A] and [B] it is agreed that disputes between these parties shall be settled by arbitration in the Arbitral Tribunal for the Building and Construction Trades. The contract between [C] and [B] contains a corresponding arbitration agreement.

The claims against [A] can thus be heard by the Tribunal when they are submitted through [B]. As [A]'s liability for the swivel is neither increased nor reduced by the claims being put forward directly from [C], the arbitral tribunal cannot accept [A]'s claim for dismissal."[194]

According to *Ulfbeck* it follows from the ruling that if there is an arbitration agreement in all parts of the "chain of contracts", then C is also ad liberty to apply the arbitration agreement in a direct action as against A.[195]

Regarding when C is under a *duty* to arbitrate the dispute *Ulfbeck* argues, and this writer concurs, that no duty to arbitrate the dispute with A lies on C if there is only an arbitration agreement between A or B, alternatively that only B and C have agreed to arbitrate. However, *Ulfbeck* finds that it must be assumed that in cases like "THE OIL PUMP SWIVEL", claims within the "chain of contracts" may not be taken to the

---

[194] Writer's translation.

[195] *Ulfbeck (2000)*, p. 318.

Courts, as there is a form of "three-party-agreement" to arbitrate. Thus, in those cases, C will also be under a *duty* to arbitrate the dispute with A.[196]

It seems to this writer that not much is achieved by splitting the issue into a question of whether C has the *right* to arbitrate the matter, alternatively, whether C is under a *duty* to do so. Under Danish law a dispute may only be arbitrated if a clear agreement to arbitrate the actual dispute between the actual parties may be shown to exist. Whichever conclusion one reaches regarding what impact A's and B's agreement to arbitrate has on the dispute between A and C, that conclusion must apply reciprocally to A and C. The parties, A and C, have either been bound by the agreement to arbitrate, or they have not. Accordingly, the rights and duties under the arbitration agreement will be reciprocal, unless it follows from the specific arbitration agreement that they are not, as, for example, when an arbitration clause is worded so as to apply in one of the parties' option.

In accordance with this, it is this writer's standpoint that chains of arbitration agreements cannot, unless special circumstances prevail, provide for agreements to arbitrate in case one member of the chain sues in direct action against another. That C has agreed to arbitrate a dispute with B, and that B in turn has agreed to arbitrate on the exact same terms any disputes which might occur between him and A, does not provide for an agreement to arbitrate between A and C.[197] The idea of "chains of arbitration agreements" must be rejected, unless it follows from the correct interpretation of those agreements that they are effective within the chain. Finally, there is very little, if any, room for the consolidation of arbitration agreements under Danish law.[198] The question remains whether this position can be maintained in the face of KFE 1994.16 VBA, THE OIL PUMP SWIVEL.

Revisiting the tribunal's ruling on its competence in that case, the first point mentioned by the tribunal was that A had known that C was the actual owner, and that A had participated in the negotiations with both B and C. Then it is mentioned that A and B have agreed to arbitrate, and that the same arbitration agreement is found in the contract between B and C. However, the crucial point as regards the agreement to arbitrate is what follows, namely, that *the claims against A can be heard by the tribunal when they are submitted "through" B.* Thus, on this point the tribunal is expressing itself in terms of succession. Indeed it seems that arguments of succession,

---

[196] *Ulfbeck (2000)*, p. 319.

[197] See in the same direction *Brækhus (1998)*, p. 168, regarding a ruling of the permanent technical arbitral tribunal of Trondheim.

[198] See, implied, *Hjejle (1987)*, p. 108 ff.

supported by A's prior knowledge, established an agreement to arbitrate between A and C. The chain of arbitration agreements was not conclusive in that decision. What was relevant was instead that A and B had agreed to arbitrate, and that C claimed *through* B. Having established that, *prima facie,* the claim against A could be heard by the tribunal, the tribunal examined whether there were regards to A that meant that C should not be able to sue in direct action at all. However, as A's potential liability for the swivel would not be affected by C, and not B, bringing the claim, there were no such regard to be taken, and the case could proceed before the tribunal.

Dealing with the subject matter of C's claim, the tribunal found that C could claim under the warranty given by A to B. Thus, the arguments applied in the case seem closer to the argument of succession than to the traditional reasoning for allowing direct action, which amongst other parameters[199] normally presupposes some sort of clear (but not necessarily gross) negligence upon the party who is sued in direct action. Also, seeing the case as an example that if C sues in direct action against A, due to A's liability towards B, then C must respect A's and B's arbitration clause, is not compatible with the Western Court of Appeal's ruling in U 1976.730 DCA, FINIPAL HUSE. Therefore, THE OIL PUMP SWIVEL case could probably more correctly have been dealt with above under situation a,[200] where the position of the law concerning succession and transfer was deliberated upon. Consequently, KFE 1994.16 VBA, THE OIL PUMP SWIVEL does not speak against this writer's position, namely that de lege lata there is no agreement to arbitrate between the actual parties to the present dispute, A and C, and therefore that either party, A or C, can sue before the ordinary Courts.

That point of view may be seen as formalistic.[201] However, when dealing with arbitration agreements Danish law focuses more stringently on the issue of privity of contracts than otherwise. An arbitration clause in a contract is only effective if it provides for dispute between the *actual* parties to be arbitrated. The fact that A may be able to invoke *other contractual provisions*, such as time bars, limitation and negligence clauses etc. against C does not *create* an agreement to arbitrate between A and C. In trades, such as the building and construction trades, where one can foresee that problems such as the one here discussed might occur, one must draft one's standard conditions and arbitration clauses accordingly.

---

[199] See *Nørgaard/Pedersen (1995),* p. 387 ff.

[200] In point 4.2.2.2.

[201] See *Ulfbeck (2000),* p. 317, and *Windahl (2001),* p. 248.

An attempt to solve problems like the one outlined in KFE 1994.16 VBA, THE OIL PUMP SWIVEL, has been made in the newest edition of the Almindelige Betingelser, AB 1992,[202] § 47, sub-sec. 8. According to the provision, if AB 92 applies to the relationship between the builder and other parties, *i.e.* contractors or suppliers, then the agreement to arbitrate according to the rules set out in § 47 also applies in the internal relationship between contractors and/or suppliers.

4.2.2.5 Summing up on third party conflicts

Summing up the position, one should maybe remind the reader that the discussion under this point presupposes that A and C have not somehow entered into an agreement to arbitrate that is independent of A's and B's agreement to arbitrate. Also, one should remind oneself that the position in bankruptcy and the administration of estates is left out. Having said that, the following may be concluded:

If C succeeds in B's contract with A, then C also succeeds in any arbitration agreement in A's and B's contract, unless the arbitration agreement upon its correct construction only applies to disputes directly between A and B.

If C neither succeeds in B's position towards A nor claims under the contract between A and B in some way, then there is no agreement to arbitrate between A and C.

If C has not succeeded in B's position but C's claim is based upon A's obligations towards B, then different opinions exist. However, it is the conclusion of this writer that in those cases no clear agreement to arbitrate A's and C's dispute exists. Consequently, there is neither a right nor an obligation for A and/or C to arbitrate the dispute. Exceptions to this rule may follow from the special construction and wording of the arbitration agreement. In practice the exception can only be expected to apply if a chain of arbitration agreements are worded so as to apply also to cases of direct action under the main "chain of contracts".

4.2.3. Other

4.2.3.1. Passivity

In U 1987.178 DCA, THE USELESS HORSE, referred above in point 3.1.1, it was argued by the insurance union that the policyholder by paying premium without making reservations had acceded to the insurance terms including the term's arbitration clause. The Western Court of Appeal refused the argument. The legal effects of an arbitration clause are so important that the policyholder could not, by the fact alone

---

[202] AB 1992: General conditions for works and deliveries in the building- and construction trades, 1992-version.

that she had paid the insurance premium without objections, be deprived from taking the dispute to the Courts.

The ruling of the Western Court of Appeal might be seen as an indication that arbitration agreements cannot be entered into by a party's passivity. However, that would be to draw the precedence from the case too far. Until a Supreme Court practice to the contrary presents itself, it must be maintained that no requirement that arbitration agreements should be entered into in a specific *manner* lies in the general rules on the formation of arbitration agreements. Instead, it seems that U 1987.178 DCA offers an example that the requirements for the formation of agreements are stricter in situations where a non-professional and a professional enter into an agreement than where two professionals deal within in the same trade.[203] The Court of Appeal's findings in THE USELESS HORSE should not be considered an argument that professional parties operating within the same trade may not be bound by an arbitration agreement sent by A to B along with A's acceptance of B's offer, even if the arbitration clause was not made available to B before the offer was given. This is especially so in cases, such as the case in THE USELESS HORSE, where the arbitration agreement is common within the trade. Thus, in U 1998.998 DCA, referred below in point 4.3.4, the Eastern Court of Appeal took into account the fact that professional parties over a very long period of time had upheld the now disputed arbitration clause as a part of their contract.

Reality has it that the requirement for a clear agreement will often render the possibility of concluding an arbitration agreement through one of the parties' passivity somewhat academic. Still, the possibility remains; and in any case, the passivity can be used as an argument amongst others in favour of the arbitration clause.

4.2.3.2. Competing forms or clauses

A final type of cases that will be briefly mentioned here, are cases where it seems that the parties have entered into conflicting forum agreements. In those cases it is a question *which* forum agreement has become a part of the parties' contract. Generally the situations arise when the parties refer to different sets of standard conditions. The Courts and/or tribunals must look at the parties' whole relationship and determine which forum agreement has become part of the contract. Often, to do so, they must also engage in an interpretation of the wording of the forum agreements and the other contractual provisions. For example, in KFE 1996.5 VBA, THE NÜRNBERG JURISDICTION CLAUSE, mentioned above in point 3.2, the tribunal took into account that even if "AB 72 § 30 + 31" had been added to the box regarding general conditions, the box had not been ticked. The way in which the form had been filled made

---

[203] See *Andersen/Madsen (2001)*, p. 100.

it unclear what had been meant. Thus, in the end the case was decided with strong regard to whom bore the risk of providing sufficient information.

A clearer example regarding adverse forum agreements is offered in KFE 1983.52 VBA.

In the builder's tender documents a reference was made to AB 1972. A German contractor tendered an offer and referred in the offer to his own attached general conditions. These conditions contained a jurisdiction clause according to which the Courts of Hanover were competent in case of a dispute, and a reference to the German VOB-rules. In accepting the offer, the builder both referred to the contractor's own general conditions and to AB 1972 without given any priority to either. Dispute arose regarding the quality of the contractor's work, and the builder took the dispute to the tribunal. The contractor claimed that the case should be dismissed from the tribunal due to the jurisdiction clause in the contractor's general conditions. The tribunal found that as the builder had explicitly accepted the contractor's own conditions and as the jurisdiction clause contained in those conditions was not unusual and was clearly formulated, the builder was bound by the jurisdiction clause, and the case was dismissed from the arbitral tribunal.

The builder had explicitly accepted the contractor's general conditions. Therefore, as a rule, the builder should be expected to have accepted also the jurisdiction clause in those conditions. However, if the jurisdiction clause was unusual and/or unclear, accepting the general conditions would probably not suffice. Still, the jurisdiction clause was none of these things and consequently bound the builder.

No set rules apply to these situations. It is facts rather than law that separate cases with rival forum agreements from the other cases here dealt with, and therefore, the general principles described in this chapter apply. Still, one should keep in mind that the question before the tribunal or the Court might not only be *if* an arbitration agreement has become a part of the parties' contract. Instead, the question might be *which one.* [204]

4.2.4. Summing up on whether the arbitration clause has become a part of the parties' contract

The issue in this section has been whether the arbitration clause or agreement has become part of the parties' contractual relationship. This question will generally be answered in the affirmative if the arbitration agreement has been specifically drafted along with the parties' main contract, or if a standard arbitration clause is contained in the parties' main contract document, and the documentation is available to the parties at the time of the conclusion of the main contract.

---

[204] See also U 1998.1027 DCA, THE LIMITED PARTNERSHIP.

In this chapter it has been shown that arbitration clauses can also become part of the parties' contract through incorporation by reference and succession. It has been suggested that arbitration agreements under certain preconditions might become part of the parties' contract due to passivity. Finally, it has been noted that the test for Courts or tribunals will sometimes be to establish *which* of several possible forum and/or arbitration agreements that has become a part of the parties' contract.

The legal position under Danish law on this subject may be summarised thus:

The incorporation of arbitration agreements under Danish law may be done through a direct reference to the arbitration clause, but a direct reference in not a necessary requisite.[205] Instead, a "one-layered reference" (a general reference to a set of standard conditions) may suffice so as to incorporate the arbitration clause in the standard conditions into the parties' contract, if the parties are professionals within a trade,[206] but might not suffice otherwise.[207] Finally, "a two-layered reference" (a general references to a set of standard conditions, which in turn make a general reference to another set of standard conditions) will generally not suffice even between professionals.[208]

Regarding succession, if a party, C, succeeds in B's obligations under B's contract with A, then C, according to the principle set out in the Instruments of Debts Act § 27, also succeeds in any arbitration agreement in A's and B's contract.[209] Any dispute between A and C, which falls within A's and B's original contract, should be settled by arbitration. However, if C's claim is not based on succession, no agreement to arbitrate exists between A and C.[210] This applies even if C bases his claim against A on A's obligations towards B under the contract between A and B. This also applies even if a "chain of arbitration agreements" has been made (situations where the A and B respectively B and C have agreed to arbitrate their internal dispute on the exact same terms). The only exception being, if the wording of the arbitration agreements in the chain allow for the arbitration agreement to be

---

[205] U 1973.128 DSC, VEDBÆK STRANDVEJ.

[206] As in U 1973.128 DSC, VEDBÆK STRANDVEJ.

[207] KFE 1982.10a VBA, THE FAMILY HOME, KFE 2001.193 VBA.

[208] U 1963.488 DSC, KLINTEMARKEN, U 1968.664 DCA, MADSEN V. KONGERSLEV AND ALSO U 1973.305 DSC SKAGEN HAVN.

[209] KFE 1983.73 VBA and, it seems, KFE 1994.16 VBA, THE OIL PUMP SWIVEL.

[210] U 1983.123 DSC, THE COLLAPSED ROOF and U 1976.730 DCA, FINIPAL HUSE.

applied in direct action. However, it must be required that the subject matters of the dispute between A and C is within the subject matter of the contract between A and B.

Finally, in theory it is possible to enter into arbitration agreements through one of the parties' passivity. However, even between professionals the requirement for a clear agreement to arbitrate renders the possibility somewhat academic, and towards consumers the possibility must be totally ruled out.

4.3. The interpretation of arbitration agreements
4.3.1. Introduction
The discussion of whether the parties' agreement upon its correct interpretation provides for settling the parties' dispute by arbitration encompasses two issues. *Firstly*, the subject matter of the parties' agreement must be to commit certain disputes to *arbitration*. Thus, the minimum requirements as to what may be characterised as an arbitration agreement should be satisfied. This question finds its answer in much the same cases and principles as are mentioned above in § 1, point 1, regarding the characteristics of arbitration agreements. The discussion of § 1, point 1, will obviously not be repeated in full, but some of the issues must be revisited.

To accept the agreement as an agreement to arbitrate, the Courts and tribunals must establish that the "minimum-requirements" for arbitration agreements are fulfilled. In accordance with § 1, point 1, these requirements are that the parties must have *consented* to have a *dispute* with some legal implication, but not necessarily of law, *resolved* in a final and binding way by a *third party*, but not the Courts. *Secondly*, the parties' dispute should be within the scope of the arbitration agreement. The parties must not only have agreed to arbitrate, they must have agreed to arbitrate *this dispute*. To establish whether that is the case, the Courts – and tribunals – must look upon both the wording of the arbitration agreement and the subject matter of the parties' quarrel. Only if the latter is within the first are the parties obliged to arbitrate the dispute.

Case law on what is an agreement to arbitrate is very sparse, whereas quite a few cases deal with the scope of the arbitration agreement. To deal with the issues separately would result in quite an unbalanced chapter. Also, it seems that the standard of interpretation applied by the Courts is the same in the two situations. Hence both issues will be dealt with together in the following.

4.3.2. The starting point: A stringent verbatim interpretation of the provision

It seems to *Andersen/Madsen*[211] that arbitration clauses to a surprising degree are regarded as a burden upon the parties to the arbitration agreement, resulting in the Danish Courts looking rather strictly upon the clauses. The feeling of surprise is probably due to the fact that in professional relationships dispute resolution by arbitration is generally chosen because it appears to be more attractive than the Court's dispute resolution. Probably, one should regard the caution displayed by the Courts and tribunals a little differently. By entering into an agreement to arbitrate, the parties bar themselves from one of the basic notions of a society based on the rule of law, namely that generally a legal dispute may be taken to the Courts. That does not entail that the Courts should always regard arbitration clauses or agreements as burdens, but it does mean that one must be convinced of the parties' consent to arbitration before one bars them from going to the Courts. According to the committee behind the travaux préparatoires, arbitration agreements are subject to a "restrictive interpretation".[212] According to *Gomard,*[213] only disputes, which are *clearly* encompassed by the agreement to arbitrate, cannot be taken to the Courts. Thus, there is consensus that when determining the scope of the arbitration agreement, one should err on the side of caution and only regard disputes included, which are undoubtedly within the agreement to arbitrate.

Danish case law offers quite a few examples that a liberal interpretation cannot be expected. However, the question is what exact standard of interpretation is applied. In the following, the standard of interpretation will be sought established through examples from case law.

Initially, two examples from recent case law on the interpretation of *the arbitration clause* will be given. The two cases are especially to the point, as in the cases there are no disputes as to whether the clause has been entered into, whether it is valid, or whether other contradictory agreements apply instead. Thus, the whole focus is on the interpretation of the clauses alone.

U 1992.4 DCA, THE PARTNERSHIP RULES

Partner, P, in a windmill partnership initiated proceedings before the Town Court of Århus, claiming that he had been unlawfully excluded from the partnership and that the windmill partnership was to pay him certain moneys, which mainly consisted of P's share of the partnership's assets. The partner-

---

[211] *Andersen/Madsen (2001), p. 83.*

[212] Danish Arbitration Act 1972 travaux préparatoires I, p. 12.

[213] *Gomard (1979), p. 21.*

ship claimed that the case should be dismissed from the Courts due to an arbitration clause in the partnership rules, according to which any dispute between the partnership and the partners should be settled finally by ad hoc arbitration, in case no settlement could be reached through negotiations.

Before the Town Court of Århus, P argued that the settlement of the dispute by arbitration would not provide the necessary safeguards. The Town Court of Århus did not approve of that contention, and dismissed the case from the Courts. On appeal to the Western Court of Appeal, P instead argued that as the windmill partnership had unilaterally terminated the partnership, they had also terminated the partnership rules and the arbitration clause in it. In any case, the arbitration agreement should be interpreted so as to apply only to disputes where the parties were on an equal footing. Finally, P repeated the contention made before the Town Court, that considering that the partnership had unwarrantedly and unilaterally terminated P's contract, dispute resolution by arbitration would not be satisfactory.

The Court of Appeal found that the arbitration clause in the partnership rules was worded so as to apply in general to disputes between the windmill partnership and the respective partners. Bearing in mind that P had been excluded, and thus was no longer a partner, the Court of Appeal did not find that it had been established, with the certainty required, that the arbitration clause in the partnership rules barred P from taking the dispute to the Courts. The Court of Appeal thus found for P, and referred the case to the Town Court of Århus for a ruling on the subject matter.

It may reasonably be assumed that the purpose of the arbitration clause in the partnership rules was to refer all disputes arising within the windmill partnership to arbitration, irrespectively of whether that dispute concerned the parties' on-going relationship or the termination of that relationship. Still, the Western Court of Appeal found that the parties' dispute was not subject to the arbitration clause. Upon its wording the arbitration clause applied to disputes between the windmill partnership and the partners. The whole reason for the dispute before the Court was that P was no longer a partner. The Western Court of Appeal applied a strict, verbatim interpretation of the clause. The parties' dispute was not within that interpretation, accordingly, the certainty required for the clause to bar P from taking his claim to the Courts did not exist.

U 1997.568 DSC, S/P Argonaut

On the 30th of March 1993 RGS fixed the suction dredger, S/P Argonaut, to S on a bare-boat charter-party. On the same occasion S and RGS entered into an agreement that S should deliver sand to RGS on a regular basis. Later, on November 26th 1993, the parties entered into an administration agreement according to which RGS should manage S' finances. It followed from § 7 of the administration agreement that "Disputes arising out of the *present* agreement shall be determined by arbitration ..." according to the general rules on arbitration set out in Danish legislation.[214] A dispute arose regarding certain moneys allegedly due under the bare-boat charter-party and delivery contract of 30 March

---

[214] Writer's emphasis.

1993. S took the dispute to the Courts. RGS claimed that the dispute should be dealt with by arbitration.

The Maritime and Commercial Court of Copenhagen found that the arbitration agreement in the administration agreement did not with the necessary certainty provide that any dispute between the parties, not only under the administration agreement but also under the bare-boat charter and the delivery contract, should be dealt with by arbitration. S' claim was based on moneys due under the contracts of 30th March. Accordingly, RSG's claim for dismissal was unfounded. On appeal the Danish Supreme Court upheld all the findings of the Maritime and Commercial Court of Copenhagen.

The findings of the Maritime and Commercial Court of Copenhagen, as upheld by the Danish Supreme Court, are very brief. However, when applying a strict, verbatim interpretation of the arbitration clause in the administration agreement, the arbitration clause only applied to that agreement. As it would be inconsistent with a strict verbatim interpretation of the clause to apply it to disputes arising out of the bare-boat charter-party and the delivery contract, the Courts found against RSG's claim and the case could proceed before the Courts. Also, concluding, at a later stage, an arbitration agreement purported to encompass also an earlier agreement, which held no such clause, probably requires quite specific wording.

When reading these two cases, it seems that the "restrictive interpretation" applied by the Courts, can be described as a stringent verbatim interpretation. In both cases, the test applied by the Courts was whether the subject matter of the dispute fell within a strict verbatim understanding of the arbitration clause. As this was not so, the contention that the disputes should be arbitrated fell.

Another quite clear-cut example of the standard of interpretation applied is offered by a ruling from the Maritime and Commercial Court of Copenhagen in the case U 1973.806 MCCC, SEMEON DEJNEV. That case is not concerned with the scope of the arbitration agreement. Instead, it is concerned with whether the agreement is an agreement to *arbitrate*.

U 1973.806 MCCC, SEMEON DEJNEV

On 24 October 1970 at about 10 AM the Soviet ship M/S Semeon Dejnev collided with the Danish ship M/T Helena Lupe. The owners of Helena Lupe brought a claim for DKK 233256 before the Maritime and Commercial Court of Copenhagen because of the damage to their ship. The owner of M/S Semeon Dejnev did not appear before the Court, but the Maritime and Commercial Court of Copenhagen had received a letter from the Commercial Corporation Sovrybflot of the Ministry of Fisheries Industry of the USSR. The "Commercial Corporation", on behalf of the owners of Semeon Dejnev, claimed that the case be dismissed, as the Master of Helena Lupe shortly after the collision had signed a hand-written agreement in Russian. It followed from the agreement that "The Masters of the vessels came to the agreement to transfer further investigation of the described accident to the Maritime Arbitration Commission at the Chamber of Commerce in Moscow." Also the Soviet Ministry of Foreign Affairs maintained this position and generally refused that the owners of Semeon Dejnev should enter an appearance.

The owners of Helena Lupe claimed that there was no agreement to arbitrate, firstly as it was not within the mandate of the Master to enter into arbitration agreements on behalf of the Owner, and secondly as the agreement according to its wording did not include the settlement of the dispute.

The Court found for both the contentions of Helena Lupe's owners. It was not within the mandate of the Master to enter into an arbitration agreement on behalf of the owners. Additionally, the wording of the agreement only regarded "further investigations" and thus no agreement to settle the dispute regarding the payment of damages had been entered into. However, as the collision seemed to have taken place outside Danish territorial waters, the Maritime and Commercial Court of Copenhagen could not hear the case. The case was consequently dismissed from the Danish Courts.

The findings of the Maritime and Commercial Court of Copenhagen may strictly speaking be regarded as *obiter*. The Court had to dismiss the case, as no Danish Court was competent to hear the case under the rules of the Danish Code of Procedure.[215] Still, the Court ruled on whether an agreement to arbitrate had been entered into. In doing this, the Court applied a verbatim interpretation of the alleged arbitration agreement. To transfer "further investigations" to a certain forum was not the same as transferring the settlement of a dispute to the forum. Also for this reason the alleged arbitration agreement fell. This is in accordance with the very sparse earlier case law on whether an agreement is an agreement to arbitrate. Thus, in U 1945.1060 DSC a statement by a party according to which he agreed that two named persons should act as *experts* on the case, thereby aiding a *solution* of the parties' difference, was not considered an agreement to arbitrate. However, one should keep in mind that under Danish, and indeed English, law, the parties need not name their agreement an agreement to arbitrate, as long as the agreement contains all the other necessary features. Thus, the BØDSTRUP HOVEDGAARD case, referred above in § 1, point 1,[216] does not speak against the contention that the standard of interpretation of arbitration clauses applied by Danish Courts is that of a strict verbatim interpretation.

Summing up, it is concluded that the standard of interpretation applied by the Courts to arbitration agreements and clauses is that of a strict verbatim interpretation of the relevant provision.

4.3.3. A narrow interpretation under special circumstances?
Having established that the starting point, the question remains whether a narrow interpretation might be applied in special cases. The term of "narrow interpretation" is

---

[215] Danish Code of Procedure sec. 244, now sec. 243.

[216] U 1984.1045 DCA, BØDSTRUP HOVEDGAARD.

here used to describe situations, where the arbitration agreement is taken to encompass less that what would follow from a strict verbatim interpretation.

Possibly, U 2000.897 DSC, THE CHANGING MAT, offers an example of such a case. The case regarded the production of inflatable changing mats, sold by Ikea.

U 2000.897 DSC, THE CHANGING MAT

In 1994 Dane Style and IKEA entered into an agreement that Dane Style were to manufacture inflatable changing mats for the IKEA range. The co-operation ended in 1997, and subsequently Dane Style initiated proceedings before the Maritime and Commercial Court of Copenhagen, claiming damages from IKEA of about 1,3 mill. DKK. IKEA claimed that the case should be dismissed from the Courts due to an arbitration clause in IKEA's "General Purchasing Conditions".

It was not totally clear from the facts of the case, and indeed strongly disputed between the parties, whether or not the arbitration clause had become a part of the parties' contract. Also, it was disputed whether the arbitral agreement covered the actual dispute between the parties.

It followed from the "General Purchasing Conditions for IKEA cl. 1, that " ... the general purchasing conditions shall be applicable to all deliveries to IKEA ... ", and from the same conditions cl. 17.1 that "Disputes with regard to an agreement with application of these purchasing conditions or matters of law arising therefrom shall be resolved [by ICC arbitration in Paris] ... ".

The points of dispute were many. However, as summarised by the Maritime and Commercial Court of Copenhagen, the subject matter of the dispute mainly regarded 1) whether IKEA had neglected to give a timely, but not contract-based, notification that they were going to stop buying the changing mat of Dane Style; 2) whether IKEA had been disloyal in having an identical changing mat manufactured elsewhere, thereby being in breach of The Marketing Act[217] sec 1; 3) whether IKEA had made unauthorised use of classified industrial information in breach of The Marketing Act sec. 10; and finally, whether Dane Style had suffered a loss in connection therewith. Taking that into consideration, the Court found that according to the circumstances of the case, the dispute would, at least to a significant extent, have to be decided on grounds, which were independent of the parties' contract. For that reason alone, the arbitration clause in the general purchasing conditions could not lead to the dismissal of the case. Finally, the Maritime and Commercial Court of Copenhagen emphasised that it had not taken a position on whether the General Purchasing Conditions had been agreed or not.

On appeal, the Danish Supreme Court consented that it had not with the necessary certainty been established that the arbitration clause covered the parties' dispute. Already for that reason, the claim for dismissal could not be followed. Accordingly, the case could proceed before the Maritime and Commercial Court of Copenhagen.

In THE CHANGING MAT there was said to be an agreement to arbitrate disputes regarding deliveries under the contract. However, the Maritime and Commercial Court of Copenhagen found that the claim directed against IKEA was not based on that contract. Instead, it was based on the alleged breach of the Marketing Act and on the alleged breach of unwritten obligations arising out of general rules of contract law.

---

[217] Lovbekendtgørelse nr. 699 af 17.7.2000 om markedsføring.

Accordingly, the Court found that the majority of the dispute lay outside the scope of the arbitration agreement.

The General Purchasing Conditions applied to "… all deliveries to IKEA …". And the arbitration clause applied to "Disputes with regard to an agreement with application of these purchasing conditions or matters of law arising therefrom …". This writer concurs that Dan Style's main arguments were ex contractual – and thus, that Dane Style did generally not claim *under* the contract. Also, it can be argued, Dan Style's claim was not based on *deliveries* to IKEA, but on the termination of such deliveries. Keeping that perspective, one can reason that the Courts did nothing more than apply a stringent, verbatim interpretation of the relevant clauses. Still, it seems that the dispute could quite easily have been fitted within the agreement to arbitrate, as the wording used in the arbitration clause was "[d]isputes *with regard to* an agreement", to which the purchasing conditions applied. It *cannot be argued that the dispute did not* regard *the contract between Dan Style and IKEA.* Did the Courts in fact apply a narrow interpretation?

The fact that it was unclear whether the General Purchasing Conditions had been agreed did certainly not *aid* IKEA's contention that the parties' dispute was within the scope of the arbitration clause. However, no link between the two issues is expressly stated by the Courts, and hence, no certain conclusion may be reached. However, in the case the two issues – the uncertainty regarding the conclusion of the contract and the uncertainty regarding the interpretation – supported the same conclusion.[218] Here the case will simply be used as a reminder that the Courts will regard all the circumstances of the case when deciding if a sufficiently clear agreement to arbitrate has been formed. In that decision, insecurities as to whether the arbitration agreement has been concluded or not may, in itself or in conjunction with other circumstances, result in the conclusion that the agreement to arbitrate is not sufficiently clear.

The contention that an arbitration agreement should be interpreted narrowly was made, but failed, in a case before the Danish Supreme Court, U 1997.751 DSC, THE SPF-SOWS.

U 1997.751 DSC, The SPF-sows

Farmer F bred breeding sows. F was connected to the so-called SPF-system – an entity, which, through regulations and health-inspections aims, at keeping the member's stock free from certain diseases and at hindering that those diseases spread. Being connected to the system, F had entered into a

---

[218] *Andersen/Madsen (2001)*, p. 358, point out that the Courts simply skipped the issue of whether the General Purchasing Conditions had become a part of the parties' agreement as in any case the wording of the purported arbitration clause was not sufficiently clear.

"SPF-contract" with "The SPF-Company", and a "Breeding Contract" with the "Pig Department". In both of these contracts were an arbitration clause, according to which, disputes were to be settled by "SPF-Arbitration", an ad hoc arbitration procedure. The clauses read as follows: In the "SPF-contract": "§ 10: Any dispute that might arise in connection with the present agreement and the related regulations ... shall be settled by the "SPF Arbitral Tribunal ... ". In the "Breeding Contract": "18. *DISPUTES*: 18.1. Disputes between the [Pig-Department] and [the farmer] are settled finally by the SPF Arbitral Tribunal."

F bought both boars and boar-semen for his breeding stock from one farmer. After this farmer's stock in March 1994 had been infected with oedema-disease, the "Pig-Department" directed that F, and any other members of the system who had bought stock or semen from that farm, could not sell any stock for about 6 weeks. After those 6 weeks, the SPF-Company directed that F's stock should be under "conditional status", meaning amongst other things that F would have to inform any prospective buyers of stock that his breeding sows were under suspicion of having contracted oedema-disease. Being under "conditional status" brought F's sale of breeding sows to a halt, and since then he had generally had to sell his sows for slaughtering.

F directed a claim against both the SPF-Company and the "Pig-Department" for his losses, DKK 1,9 mill. As regards the "Pig-Department", F based his claim on the fact alone that F had been forced to stop selling sows for 6 weeks even if in fact no cases of oedema-disease had been documented in his stock. Thereby his stock had lost its good name and clientele. To re-gain his clientele, he would have to replace all of his stock. As towards the SPF-Company F's claim was mainly founded on the fact that the SPF-Company had not, in December 1993, when F had bought two boars and an amount of semen from the later infected farm, informed F that the exact E-coli bacteria, which causes oedema-decease (E-coli 0139) had been found in that stock. Thereby the SPF-Company had neglected its duty of information and diligence as towards the farmers connected to the SPF-system.

The SPF-Company and the "Pig-Department" both argued that the case should be dismissed from the Western Court of Appeal due to the above mentioned arbitration clauses.

F did not dispute that the arbitration agreements were valid, but he contended that his claim for damages due to unwarranted measures and/or breach of duty was so untypical as to be outside the parties' intentions at the time of the formation of the arbitration agreements. In support of this he argued that the core of the whole agreement complex was the regulation of the extent of liability if a stock got infected with disease.

The Western Court of Appeal based its findings on the facts that it was undisputed that the arbitration agreements were valid, and that it was undisputed that F based his claim on the contracts made with the SPF-Company and the "Pig-Department" respectively. Reading together the arbitration agreement and the rules for the SPF Arbitral Tribunal, their wording meant that any dispute arising from the two agreements were subject to arbitration. *There was no reason to interpret the clauses so as to only regard disputes on the limitation of liability and the different risk-classes,* as indeed argued by F. Also, considering that F's claim was based on the special health- and control-issues of the SPF-system, there was no reason to regard the type of case or the evidence, which was to be given, as being outside the scope of the arbitration agreements. Accordingly, the Western Court of Appeal dismissed the case from the Courts. On appeal the Danish Supreme Court upheld the Western Court of Appeal's decision according to the grounds.

It cannot be deduced from THE SPF-SOWS case that arbitration agreements should never be interpreted narrowly, but it may be deduced that in the particular case this should not be done. However, one can conclude from the case that when it is undisputed that an arbitration agreement is concluded and valid, and the subject matter of the parties' dispute falls within a verbatim interpretation of the arbitration agreement, then the party claiming that the agreement should not apply has an uphill struggle. Still, such a conclusion is hardly remarkable.

A more constructive conclusion is probably the following: Arbitration agreements, and other agreements, should generally be construed in accordance with the parties' intentions at the time of the formation of the contract. However, if it cannot be proven what these intentions were, as was the case in THE SPF-SOWS case, then those "intentions" cannot effect a narrow interpretation of the arbitration agreement.

Having read these two cases, no clear conclusion as to whether the arbitration agreements are interpreted narrowly offers itself. The only conclusion one may provide is that generally they will not. However, there is no reason why arbitration agreements should not be interpreted narrowly if so warranted by the circumstances. Such circumstances might be that one of the parties can prove that a narrow interpretation is warranted by the parties' intentions at the time of the formation of the contract (as not proved in THE SPF-SOWS), or, maybe, that there is doubt[219] as to whether the arbitration agreement has become part of the parties' contract (as seen in THE CHANGING MAT case). Still, it must be concluded that such a narrow interpretation will be the exception.

4.3.4. Interpreting the parties' whole contractual relationship

The starting point given, in point 4.3.2, that the standard of interpretation regarding arbitration agreements is that of a strict, verbatim interpretation, only applies to the actual provision itself. To the extent that it is the whole contractual relationship that must be considered, the general rules apply, and a restrictive interpretation should not be expected. Clear examples of this are given in the rulings of the Danish Supreme Court, U 1999.1036 DSC, KOSAN A/S and U 1974.378 DSC, KONGEVEJEN. In both cases, the question was which of two possible agreements applied to the parties' relationship. In U 1999.1036 DSC, KOSAN A/S the issue was whether an original skeleton agreement/letter of intent had been superseded by a shareholder agreement, whereas the question in U 1974.378 DSC, KONGEVEJEN was if the account between the contractor and the buyer of the estate should be settled according to a tender given by the contractor or as per account. In the cases, the Courts applied the

---

[219] Indeed, in U 2002.870 DCA, a plea that an arbitration agreement should be subject to a restrictive interpretation was not even considered by the Western Court of Appeal.

general rules on interpretation of contract without particular regard to the arbitration clauses.

U 1974.378 DSC, KONGEVEJEN

A entered into an oral agreement with B to concrete the basements in a housing estate. At the time of the oral agreement, the final drawings and projecting had not been made. A and B therefore agreed that A, when the drawings and the project was made, should tender an offer on the concrete works. B could choose to take the offer, alternatively he could terminate the contract and pay A as per account according to the guidelines for works per account set out by the Danish Contractor's Association.

After the completion of the projecting, A tendered a bid on the concrete works. In the bid A had referred to "Standard Reservation 1" issued by the Danish Contractor's Association, according to which "… it is a precondition for the offer that [AB 1951] apply in their entity". The negotiations regarding the offer were not completed, as B went into financial problems, resulting in B selling the building under construction to C. C succeeded in B's terms of contract with A. C wished to finish the concrete works himself. A therefore finished the agreed part of the works and presented C with the account. C did not accept the account, and initiated proceedings before the Town Court of Århus. A claimed that the case be dismissed due to the arbitration clause in AB 1951, § 24.

According to A it had been presupposed between the parties from the outset that the contract should be on AB 1951 terms. This was confirmed by A's reference to AB 1951 in the tender. A's continuance of the work despite the fact that his offer was not accepted was also on the basis of AB 1951. The fact that the contract was later terminated did not entail that AB 1951 no longer applied. Alternatively, A argued that the application of AB 1951 was the custom within the trade and that the dispute was so complicated and technical that it was best dealt with by arbitration.

C claimed that a clear agreement on arbitration was required for a party to be barred from taking a dispute to the Courts. In the case there was no such agreement. A and B could have entered into an arbitration agreement, in fact the guidelines for works per account recommended that the parties specifically agreed that AB 1951, including the arbitration clause, should apply, but in the case they had not. It was correct that AB 1951 applied to A's tender. However, the tender was not accepted. Finally, C contended that AB 1951 was not accepted as a custom within the trade so that it applied without being agreed upon between the parties.

The Western Court of Appeal found for C. There was no arbitration agreement between the parties in case the work should be done per account. Furthermore, there was no custom within the trade that AB 1951 applied even without the parties having agreed to it. The case was therefore referred to the Town Court of Århus, for a decision on the merits. The Danish Supreme Court upheld the findings of the Western Court of Appeal according to the grounds.

U 1999.1036 DSC, KOSAN A/S.

For the purpose of making a management buy-out of the mother company, 4 executives of different daughter companies and a bank founded a holding company. The management buy-out took place according to plan in April 1989. In June 1989 the associates of the holding company entered into a shareholder agreement containing an arbitration clause, according to which "any dispute which has its grounds in this shareholder agreement, its formation, completion or termination, shall, if no amicable settlement can be reached, be settled finally by arbitration according to The Danish Arbitration Institute's rules".

Five years later one of the executives, E, initiated proceedings before the Courts claiming that the bank was liable in damages for certain activities in relation to the management buy-out. The subject matter of the executives' claim was connected to a skeleton-agreement/letter of intent, drafted in March 1989, which outlined the parties' intentions, rights and obligations concerning the management buy-out. It was the executives' claim that the bank had disregarded the arbitration agreement in a way that made the bank liable towards the executive. There was no arbitration agreement in the skeleton-agreement/letter of intent, so if that contract governed the parties' relationship, the executive would be free to go to the Courts. The bank on the other hand argued that the skeleton agreement had been superseded by the shareholder agreement, drafted in June 1989. To this E argued that the shareholder agreement was only intended to enter into force after certain external investors had gained a part of the shares. This had not yet happened. Accordingly, the shareholder agreement had not entered into force.

The Eastern Court of Appeal based its findings upon the fact that it followed from the preamble of the shareholder agreement that the agreement was to govern the internal relationship between the shareholders. It could not be concluded from the formation or wording of that agreement that it should only apply after the external investors were found. Also, the Court of Appeal put emphasis on the fact that E only at a relatively late stage had based his claim on the skeleton agreement rather than on the shareholder agreement. In the light of those circumstances it was found to be unobjectionable that the subject matter of the dispute was governed by the shareholder agreement, and thus that the arbitration clause in that agreement applied. The Court of Appeal therefore found for the cases' dismissal from the Courts. On appeal, the Danish Supreme Court upheld the findings of the Eastern Court of Appeal.

4.3.5. Summing up the interpretation of arbitration agreements

The standard of interpretation applied by the Danish Courts as regards agreements to arbitrate depends on whether the subject of interpretation is the arbitration clause or provision in itself, or whether the subject of interpretation is the parties' whole contractual relationship.

As far as the arbitration clause or provision is concerned, the standard of interpretation is that of a *strict verbatim* interpretation.[220] It cannot be ruled out that in certain cases the Danish Courts might apply a narrow interpretation of the arbitration clause or provision, however, *clear* examples of this being done in case law have not been found by this writer. Only U 2000.897 DSC, THE CHANGING MAT, presents features that resemble those of a narrow interpretation.

If instead the subject that must be interpreted is the parties' whole contractual relationship, then no special rules exist. Indeed, in those cases it is the general rules of contract law regarding the interpretation of contracts that apply. (See *in petit*, above in point 1).

[220] U 1992.4 DCA, THE PARTNERSHIP RULES, U 1997.568 DSC, S/P ARGONAUT, U 1973.806 MCCC, SEMEON DEJNEV.

5. Conclusion – a general test?

There is a very simple general test for the formation of arbitration agreements under Danish law: A *clear* agreement to arbitrate must be established. The requirement for a clear agreement to arbitrate reappears throughout the widespread cases here discussed, and the conclusion to this chapter could be left at that. However, such a conclusion renders this chapter a mere arbitration law Odyssey. Instead, the question is *what* is a clear agreement to arbitrate. Unfortunately, no precise answer to that question can be given. As a consequence, English, Norwegian and other lawyers who are accustomed to general formal requirements applying to arbitration agreements, must find that Danish law allows for lawlessness. Having read the above, such lawyers have probably reached the conclusion that lawlessness is not the correct term, but that the term unforeseeability might be fitting.

For a person, whether judge, arbitrator or counsel, trying to establish if the parties to a dispute have agreed to arbitrate, the task may prove cumbersome. The whole contractual relationship must be evaluated (if the dispute is not solely on the – alleged – arbitration clause) and the parties' knowledge must be established. However, in doing that the conclusions offered above in points 2-4 will offer guidance. When viewed thus, the method is the same as when applying the parts of English arbitration law that are still governed by precedence.

For the lawyer wishing to draft an arbitration agreement the lack of formal requirements, and hence statutory guidelines, need not provide any difficulties. If the drafter keeps the agreement in clear words and in writing, only depends on direct or one-layered references, and provides the counter-party with a copy of any standard conditions referred to before the conclusion of the contract, then one may be quite certain that the arbitration agreement will be accepted by the Courts or tribunals, even outside professional relationships. That leaves certain issues unsolved, most particularly the question of arbitration clauses in chains of contracts. Unless all the arbitration clauses have been formed so as to apply throughout the chain, also in direct action, Danish law does not cater for the acceptance of arbitration agreements in chains of contracts. In that way, the lack of formal requirements does not, to the extent that one might expect, provide for a greater extent of "favour arbitrii" than does more formal systems.

Evaluating the position of the law under Danish law, the lack of transparency and foreseeability would be the first points of criticism to present themselves. It is very difficult to establish whether an agreement to arbitrate will be deemed "sufficiently clear" by the Danish Courts or tribunals applying Danish law. For non-Danish lawyers the task must be almost impossible.

In defence of the Danish rules it must be emphasised that the focus on knowledge or "should-be-knowledge", rather than on the documentation applied, has made it possible for the Danish Courts and tribunals applying Danish law to reach the decisions, which were the right ones under the given circumstances, without having to side-step a formal requirement. Two very good examples of this are U 1973.305 DSC, SKAGEN HAVN and KFE 1982.10A VBA THE FAMILY HOME.

In the first case, the focus on knowledge made it possible for the Danish Supreme Court to accept the conclusion of an arbitration agreement in a situation where the documentation alone did not provide a "sufficiently clear agreement to arbitrate". Conversely, in THE FAMILY HOME the focus on knowledge made the tribunal disregard an arbitration clause, although the technique of incorporation applied fulfilled the requirements normally given in the trade.

If politicians, arbitrators or lawyers wish that Denmark should be used more as a forum for (international) arbitration, they face the similar problems as did England under the Arbitration Acts of 1950, 1975 and 1979, and which resulted in the 1996 Act, namely, that the bulk of the law has been developed through case law and therefore is not easy to access. Danish law's approach towards arbitration agreements is a "hands-off" policy, which should provide for a good reason to arbitrate in Denmark, however, the lack of transparency counteracts this. If one wants to promote Denmark as a forum for (international) arbitration, one might consider coupling the "hands-off" policy with a lax requirement for a written agreement to arbitrate, thus providing at least a starting point for the determination of whether an agreement to arbitrate has been formed. However, so far Danish politicians have not expressed such a wish, even if the users of arbitration are starting to stir the issue.[221]

Danish Courts and tribunals have developed a flexible attitude towards the arbitration agreement, where the correct decision in the actual circumstances has been the focal point. A requirement that arbitration agreements should be in writing need not shift the focus from that focal point, but it might, unless it is very lax. And if it is very lax, then one will still need to resort to case law to establish what is Danish law on the formation of arbitration agreements. Consequently, unless one wishes to actively promote dispute resolution before Danish arbitral tribunals on an international scale, little seems to be achieved by formulating a requirement for a written agreement to arbitrate.

---

[221] Thus, at a seminar held at "Børsen" in Copenhagen on 31 October 2002, one of the wishes expressed were that an Arbitration Act based upon the UNCITRAL Model Law be introduced in Danish law. As a consequense an inofficial Draft Arbitration Act has been prepared by the Legal Committee for the General Council of the Bar, see *The Law Society (2003)*.

§ 3. English law on the conclusion of arbitration agreements

1. The formal requirements in sec. 5

It has traditionally been required under the English Arbitration Acts that arbitration agreements should be in writing, see the English Arbitration Act 1950 sec. 32 and the 1975 Act sec. 7(1). Writing is also a requirement under the 1996 Act sec. 5. According to the Departmental Advisory Committee "[an] arbitration agreement has the important effect of contracting out of the right to go to the [C]ourt, *i.e.* it deprives the parties of that basic right. To our minds an agreement of such importance should be in some written form".[222]

Arbitration agreements need not be in writing to be recognised by the English Courts. The English Courts *may,* with reference to the principle of pacta sunt servanda, recognise an arbitration agreement entered into otherwise than in writing, as long as the Courts are sufficiently satisfied that the parties intended to arbitrate their dispute.[223] This common law rule remains unaffected by the 1996 Act, as especially provided for in sec. 81(1)(b). The Arbitration Act 1996, however, only applies to arbitration agreements in writing, see sec. 5(1).[224] If the parties wish to avail them-

---

[222] 1996 Report on the Arbitration Bill, para. 33.

[223] *Merkin (2000),* p. 27.

[224] Literature on the English Arbitration Act sec. 5 see *Chitty (1999),* para. 16-015, *Merkin (2000),* p. 26–28, *Merkin (1991),* Part 1, paras. 2.5-2.11, *Russell (1997)* paras. 2-030 to 2-033 and *Tweeddale/Tweeddale (1999),* p. 71 f.

selves of the obligatory stay under the English Arbitration Act sec. 9, or of the assistance of the Courts provided for in the Act,[225] then they must make sure that the agreement to arbitrate fulfils the requirement for writing set out in sec. 5.

The English Arbitration Act 1996 sec. 5 – Agreements to be in writing

(1) The provisions of this Part apply only where the arbitration agreement is in writing, and any other agreement between the parties as to any matter is effective for the purpose of this Part only if in writing.
The expression 'agreement', 'agree' and 'agreed' shall be construed accordingly.
(2) There is an agreement in writing-
if the agreement is made in writing (whether or not it is signed by the parties),
if the agreement is made by exchange of communications in writing, or
if the agreement is evidenced in writing.
(3) Where parties agree otherwise than in writing by reference to terms which are in writing, they make an agreement in writing.
(4) An agreement is evidenced in writing if an agreement made otherwise than in writing is recorded by one of the parties, or by a third party, with the authority of the parties to the agreement.
(5) An exchange of written submissions in arbitral or legal proceedings in which the existence of an agreement otherwise than in writing is alleged by one party against another party and not denied by the other party in his response constitutes as between those parties an agreement in writing to the effect alleged.
(6) Reference in this Part to anything being written or in writing include its being recorded by any means.

The provision provides a wide definition of what is in writing. The requirement will be fulfilled e.g. if the arbitration agreement is evidenced in writing, cf. sec. 5(2)(c) or if an oral reference is made to a written standard form, cf. sec. 5(3). The provision in sec. 5(3) is designed specifically for solving the problems sometimes encountered in salvage operations, where an oral reference is made to Lloyd's Open Form, but will apply generally.[226]

"In writing" includes being recorded by any means, see sec. 5(6). To qualify under this provision it must be assumed that the arbitration agreement must exist in a form that enables subsequent verification of the agreement's terms. Any data transmission, which is basically a transmission of writing, such as E-mails, should be acceptable, provided that the transmission is saved in some way,[227] and also, as submitted by

---

[225] See *Merkin (2000)*, p. 163 f.

[226] 1996 Report on the Arbitration Bill, para. 36.

[227] *Harris (2000)*, p. 75.

Harris[228] a tape recording of an oral agreement might suffice. Under the English Arbitration Act Part I, the arbitration *agreement or clause* must *exist* in writing or in a sufficiently "recorded" form, but the *consent* to arbitration need not be *given* in writing, as is the case within Norwegian law, see below § 4, point 2.2.1. In this way, the requirement for writing in the English Arbitration Act sec. 5 seems to aim at the securing of proof of the arbitration agreement and its terms, rather than providing a test for whether the parties have truly intended to arbitrate. This also concurs with one of the expressed intentions of the Departmental Advisory Committee when suggesting the provision, namely to "reduce disputes as to whether or not the arbitration agreement was made and as to its terms".

Sec. 5 does not stand alone, but should be read in the context of sec. 6(2).

English Arbitration Act 1996, sec. 6 – Definition of Arbitration Agreement, *in extract*
(2) The reference in an agreement to a written form of arbitration clause or to a document containing an arbitration clause constitutes an arbitration agreement if the reference is such as to make that clause part of the agreement.

This provision requires specifically that arbitration agreements may only be incorporated by reference if the reference makes the arbitration clause part of the parties (main) agreement. Also, the provision points at an important feature, namely that the arbitration agreement, apart from being in writing within the meaning of sec. 5, also must be concluded in a way that satisfies the requirements of general rules of contract law. Thus, sec. 5 does not provide an exhaustive regulation of the formation of arbitration agreements under the English Arbitration Act 1996.

So far, sec. 5 has not given rise to much case law. Generally, the definitions of what constitutes a written agreement under sec. 5 are so wide, that if an agreement cannot be construed as written under sec. 5, it is likely that the agreement has not been concluded at all. Thus, it must be expected that in the future the real issue before the Courts and tribunal will be whether there is any agreement between the parties, and not whether this agreement is in writing. To an extent earlier case law may be relied upon in such cases. Thus, under the 1975 Act sec. 1(1), any party claiming "through or under" a party to an arbitration agreement within the scope of the Act was entitled to a stay of Court proceedings. This provision was accepted as authority that parties, who had succeeded in the position of one of the original parties, e.g. through assignment, were also bound by an arbitration clause in the original parties' contract, as seen in [1984] 2 Lloyd's Law Reports 259 QBD, THE LEAGE, and as presumed in [1982] 1 Lloyd's Law Reports 166 QBD, THE QATAR NATURAL GAS PLANT. There is no evidence in the report on the arbitration bill that this position of

---

[228] *Harris (2000)*, p. 74.

the law is intended to be altered. However, one cannot apply case law before the 1996 Act automatically. It was the intention of the Departmental Advisory Committee that the scope for what is a "written agreement to arbitrate" between the parties should be extended by the new Act.[229] Old case law concluding that there is no written agreement between the parties must therefore be critically reviewed in order to establish whether the rationale for refusing the agreement in that particular case still applies. One the other hand, procedures accepted by case law as an agreement to arbitrate under the 1950 or 1975 Acts will certainly also qualify under the 1996 Act. Thus, the question in [1986] 2 Lloyd's Law Reports 225 CA, ZAMBIA STEEL V. CLARK & EATON, regarding whether or not an agreement to arbitrate concluded partly tacitly and partly in writing satisfied the requirement for writing, should still be answered in the affirmative.[230]

Not all problems are solved under the 1996 Act. Under the Arbitration Act 1996, as under the preceding Acts, the incorporation of arbitration agreements by reference calls for special consideration. Especially, one must establish what is required to make a reference to a standard document, which is not in the possession of both parties to the purported arbitration agreement, effective. This point provides for the most important discussion within English law on the conclusion of arbitration agreements, and will be considered in detail below. The problem is especially interesting from a transport lawyer's point of view, as the rules developed in case law generally consider a transport law problem, namely what is required for the effective incorporation of arbitration clauses in charter-parties into bills of lading issued under that charter-party.

2. The incorporation of arbitration clauses from charter-parties into bills of lading under English law

Obviously, when entering into an agreement the parties may choose to refer to provisions, standard form contracts or general conditions printed elsewhere, rather than writing everything anew. If the parties choose to make a written reference to a specific arbitration agreement, problems will not normally occur. However, when a reference is made to standard form contracts or general conditions that contain an arbitration clause, uncertainties emerge regarding whether the arbitration clause has been effectively incorporated. Hence, the form of reference required for an arbitration clause to be considered incorporated must be established.

---

[229] *Merkin (2000)*, p. 27.

[230] See also [1997] 2 Lloyd's Law Reports 738 QBD, FAHEM & CO. V. MAREB YEMEN INSCE.

The English Courts have mainly dealt with the question of what form of reference is required when concerned with shipping and construction cases. Within the shipping cases the question has normally been what is required to consider the provisions of a charter-party to be incorporated into a (tramp) bill of lading issued under it. Often this has been done specifically with the arbitration agreement in mind, but also other provisions have been discussed.

It seems that these "charter-party cases" have formed the position of the law on the subject. Approaching the issue from a shipping point of view is therefore legitimate. This does not mean that construction or other cases may be totally ignored, but their importance is secondary.

Non-English readers should bear in mind that the English rules on interpreting contracts may differ from their own rules on the interpretation of contracts. English Courts do aim at defining the intention of the parties, but the main rule of interpretation is that of a strict, verbatim interpretation, only concerned with the contents of the contract in question. The document is considered to stand alone, and only if the document itself cannot be interpreted in a meaningful manner, other means of interpretation will be taken into account.[231] The Courts are not barred from departing from the natural meaning of certain words or terms, but they are only likely to do so if the parties' intentions can be proved, and those intentions conflict with that meaning.[232] Therefore, as a starting point, if a document refers to a provision, the provision ought to read naturally into the document. This gives rise to problems in the tramp trade, as provisions in a charter-party deal with the relations between the owner and the charterer and thus rarely are worded in a way that adequately describes the relation between the owner or charterer and the holder of the bill of lading. *Ventris* describes the problem very aptly:

"The difficulty arises from not giving to words their apparently natural meaning and consequently the subject must be very difficult for a foreigner to comprehend."[233]

Below, a more or less chronological approach is applied. Thus, first the case law up to the 1996 Act is considered. Then the relevant provisions of the 1996 Arbitration Act are discussed, and finally, the cases decided under, or relevant to, the 1996 Act will be reviewed. Good reasons for that structure exist, as, in this writer's view, the

---

[231] *Chitty (1999)*, paras. 12-043 and 12-044.

[232] *Chitty (1999)*, paras. 12-070 and 12-053

[233] *Ventris (1986)*, p. 148.

English Arbitration Act 1996 has provided a continuation of, rather than a change in, English law on the subject.

Numerous cases on the incorporation of arbitration clauses under English law exist, and not all of these cases will be discussed. Instead the most important cases are scrutinised. The picture presented is considered to represent a fair view of the law on the subject even if certain less important cases are disregarded.

3. English case law before the Arbitration Act 1996

Above the principle of a strict verbatim interpretation has been mentioned. When applied to the incorporation cases, one should thus not be surprised that as a starting point, verbatim incorporation is required.

3.1. The starting point. Hamilton v. Mackie and Thomas v. Portsea

The leading case regarding the principle of verbatim incorporation is the case HAMILTON V. MACKIE.

(1889) 5 T. L. R. 667 CA, HAMILTON V. MACKIE
Having carried out a transport of timber, the owner directed a claim for freight against the holder of the bill of lading. The bill of lading had been issued according to a charter-party. The charter-party contained, amongst others, provisions to the effect that any dispute, which might arise under the charter, was to be settled by arbitration at the port where the dispute arose. The bill of lading was stamped: "All other terms and conditions as per charter party". Initially the Court stayed the owner's suit for freight, as the case ought to be settled by arbitration. The owner appealed. The Court of Appeal referred themselves to the existing authorities and said: "Where there was in a bill of lading such a condition as this, 'All other conditions as per charter-party', it had been decided[234] that the condition of the charter-party must be read verbatim into the bill of lading as though they were printed *in extenso*. Then, if it was found that any of the conditions of the charter-party on being so read were inconsistent with the bill of lading, they were insensible, and must be disregarded."

The Court of Appeal then applied this principle to the facts of the case. The provision in the charter-party had to be read verbatim into the bill of lading at the place where the reference was made. A provision according to which "All disputes under this charter shall be referred to arbitration ..." did not make sense in a bill of lading, as the clause dealt with a dispute between the parties to the charter-party. Therefore, the reference was irrelevant and the arbitration clause was not incorporated into the bill of lading.

---

[234] The Court of Appeal does not specify the cases referred to.

Hence, when reference is made to provisions in other documents, the reference is to the provision as it stands and not to the principle it expresses. If the provision has to be reworded to fit into the document referred from, the Courts will disregard it.

Obviously, the view upon incorporation by reference expressed in HAMILTON V. MACKIE is too restrictive to adequately fulfil the needs of modern-day trade. Fortunately, as mentioned above, the English Courts are not excluded from disregarding the natural meaning of certain words or phrases if the intentions of the parties are proven to be different from that meaning. However, when a case appears before the Courts, it will be that precise intention which is disputed. It must therefore be established what is required to consider such a mutual intention as proven, in spite of one of the parties' subsequent denial.

To a large extent that question was answered in the case THOMAS V. PORTSEA, which introduced the distinction between provisions which are closely connected to the carrying out of the transport and the payment of freight, and provisions which are not, such as arbitration and other boilerplate clauses. The decision is coming of age but is still central to the issue, and it has been discussed in all subsequent decisions on the question of incorporation by reference.

[1912] A. C. 1 HL, THOMAS V. PORTSEA[235]

During a transport of timber a claim for demurrage accrued. The owner attempted to enforce the claim before the Courts. The owner of the cargo who, according to a cesser-clause, was responsible for demurrage, claimed there was an arbitration agreement between the parties and requested that the lawsuit was stayed.

The charter-party contained an arbitration clause: "Any dispute or claim arising out of any of the conditions of this charter shall be adjusted at port where it occurs, and same shall be settled by arbitration." A bill of lading was issued for the cargo. It contained i.a. a printed clause: "... [freight to be paid] ... for the said goods, with other conditions as per charter party with average accustomed." Furthermore, in the margin of the bill of lading was a clause, written by hand: *"Deck cargo at shipper's risk, and all other terms and conditions and exceptions of charter to be as per charter party, including negligence clause."* Authority already existed according to which "... conditions as per charter party ..." did not incorporate the arbitration clause of the charter-party into the bill of lading. It was therefore the written clause, which gave rise to most of the discussion.

A stay was granted by the County Court and the Division Court, but not by the Court of Appeal. The House of Lords found unanimously that the arbitration clause was not incorporated into the bill of lading, the main argument being: "... when it is sought to introduce into a document like a bill of lading – a negotiable instrument – a clause such as this arbitration clause, *not germane* to the receipt, carriage, or delivery of the cargo or the payment of freight ... this should be done in *distinct and specific words, and not by general words ...*".[236] The Court further based its argument on the authority

---

[235] Appeal of (1911) P. 54 CA, THE PORTSMOUTH.

[236] *per* Lord Atkinson, p. 6, emphasis added.

from HAMILTON V. MACKIE. The bill of lading was the starting point, and the arbitration clause "…
only governs the way of settling disputes between the parties to the charter party, not disputes arising
out of the bill of lading".[237] The arbitration clause was not fit to be read directly into the bill of lading.
It would require " … indeed some modification to make it read even intelligibly in its new connection … [and it] … is difficult to hold that words which require modification to read as part of the
bill of lading and purport to deal only with disputes arising out of a document made between different
persons are quite sufficiently explicit …".[238]

Therefore, the arbitration agreement in the charter-party was not incorporated into the bill of lading, and a stay was refused. The House of Lords consequently upheld the decision of the Court of
Appeal and refused to grant a stay. There was no agreement to arbitrate between the parties.

Clauses that did not concern the main obligations under a bill of lading, such as the
obligation to pay freight or the owner's obligation to take in charge, carry, and deliver the goods according to the parties' agreement, could not be incorporated by a
general reference to the conditions of the charter-party. However, it followed *obiter*
and *ex contrario* from the House of Lords' decision that a reference from a bill of
lading to a charter-party might incorporate the charter-party's arbitration clause if the
reference was "sufficiently explicit".

It thus had to be decided what was needed for the reference to be considered "sufficiently explicit". In THE NJEGOS[239] a reference in a bill of lading was made to "All
the terms, conditions and exceptions of … [the] … charter-party, including the negligence clause …". This provision did not incorporate the arbitration clause of the
charter-party into the bill of lading.

A similar result was reached in THE PHONIZIEN.[240] According to a clause in the
charter-party "Any dispute arising under this Charter Party shall be referred to Arbitration in London." As per the authority of THOMAS V. PORTSEA, the arbitration
clause could not be incorporated into the bill of lading by general words. Hence, a
reference worded "All terms, conditions, liberties, and exceptions of the Charter
Party are … incorporated …" did not include the arbitration clause. Furthermore, in
keeping with HAMILTON V. MACKIE[241] the arbitration clause had to be disregarded,
as it could not be read directly into the bill of lading in its natural meaning. (In THE

---

[237] *per* Lord Loreburn, LJ, p. 6.

[238] *per* Lord Robson, p. 11.

[239] (1935) Lloyd's List Law Reports 286, Adm. Ct. Also published in [1936] P. 90, Admiralty Court.

[240] [1966] 1 Lloyd's Law Reports 150 QBD.

[241] (1889) 5 T. L. R. 667 CA.

PHONIZIEN, it was the owner of the ship who disputed that an arbitration agreement was entered into. The fact that the Court declined to grant a stay most probably referred the consignee to enforce his claim before the Rumanian Courts against the ship owner, the Rumanian State).

3.2. Making way for manipulation – The Annefield

The distinction from THOMAS V. PORTSEA [242] between the provisions which are germane to the obligations described in the bill of lading and the provisions which are not, was upheld in THE ANNEFIELD. Still, for two reasons the case deserves a separate discussion. Firstly, as what could be worded "the principle of manipulation" was put into words, and secondly, since the principle set out in HAMILTON V. MACKIE[243] regarding verbatim incorporation was finally restricted.

[1971] 1 Lloyd's Law Reports 1 CA, THE ANNEFIELD[244]
A Liberian company owned the Annefield. She was fixed on a time charter-party to an Italian company, which in turn fixed her on a voyage charter-party (Centrocon) to the company SA. SA transported a cargo of maize from Argentina to the Mediterranean. The consignee claimed that the cargo was damaged and demanded that the dispute be settled by arbitration. This arbitration was never carried out. Five years later the cargo interests initiated an action *in rem* against the Annefield. Annefield's owner requested a stay because of the arbitration agreement. In the High Court, Admiralty Division, Brandon J refused to stay the case, since the arbitration clause in the charter-party was not incorporated into the bill of lading.[245] The case was appealed.

The documents contained the following relevant clauses: In the voyage charter-party cl. 39: "All disputes from time to time arising out of this contract shall ... be referred to ... [arbitration] ... ". In the bill of lading: "... in accordance with the Charter Party dated in London 1.3.63 all the terms, conditions and exceptions of which Charter Party, including negligence clause are incorporated herewith".

Lord Denning found that "... a clause which is *directly germane* to the subject-matter of the bill of lading ... can and should be incorporated into the bill of lading contract, even though it may involve a degree of *manipulation of the words* in order to fit exactly to the bill of lading. But, if the clause is *not one which is thus directly germane*, it should not be incorporated into the bill of lading contract unless it is done *explicitly in clear words* either in the bill of lading or in the charter-party."[246]

---

[242] [1912] A. C. 1 HL.

[243] (1889) 5 T. L. R. 667 CA.

[244] Appeal of [1970] 2 Lloyd's Law Reports 252.

[245] [1970] 2 Lloyd's Law Reports 252, p. 263, col 2.

[246] Emphasis added.

According to THOMAS V. PORTSEA an arbitration clause was not directly germane to the subject matter of the bill of lading. Incorporation would thus require explicit words either in the bill of lading or in the charter-party. As there was neither such an explicit reference in the bill of lading nor words in the charter-party to the effect that the arbitration clause should also apply under the bill of lading, the arbitration clause had not been incorporated. The appeal was dismissed, and the case could proceed before the High Court.

To arrive at the concept of verbal manipulation, the Court had to limit the authority of HAMILTON V. MACKIE and the theory of verbatim incorporation of the words referred to. According to the Court, this was not "… a rule of interpretation of universal application. It was a useful test in that case. That is all." Instead one should read the documents together and "… take the clauses in the charter-party and apply them to the bill of lading in so far as they are reasonably applicable to it …".[247] Or as Lord Cairns put it: "The rule in HAMILTON V. MACKIE must be applied intelligently and not mechanically."[248]

By thus checking the authority of HAMILTON V. MACKIE, the Court of Appeal cleared the way for a verbal manipulation of the wording of a charter-party, given that the reference in the bill of lading was adequately explicit.

3.3. Establishing the modern view

3.3.1. The Rena K

The verbatim manipulation, suggested by the Court of Appeal in THE ANNEFIELD, was first carried out by Justice Brandon in THE RENA K. Although the case only proceeded before the High Court, the findings in the case have carried great authority. The approach chosen by Brandon J simply seems to be the right one.

[1978] 1 Lloyd's Law Reports 545 QBD, THE RENA K
On April 13th 1977 Rena K was fixed on a voyage charter-party, which contained amongst others the following clause: "All disputes, which may arise under this charter to be settled by Arbitration in London." Two bills of lading were issued for the cargo, both including references to an underlying charter-party and its arbitration clause, but in particular the following clause is interesting: "All terms, clauses, conditions and exceptions *including the Arbitration Clause,*[249] the Negligence Clause and the Cesser Clause of the Charter-Party dated London 13 April 1977 are herewith incorporated."

---

[247] *per* Lord Denning, M. R. , p. 4.

[248] *per* Lord Cairns, p. 5.

[249] Emphasis added.

During the transport, seawater damaged a part of the cargo of sugar. The consignee initiated actions *in rem* and *in personam* against Rena K and her owner respectively. Rena K's owner requested a stay, as the parties had entered into an arbitration agreement.

The consignees put forward an argument based on the authority HAMILTON V. MACKIE. The clause referred to in the bill of lading only considered disputes under the charter-party. Therefore, it could not be read directly into the bill of lading and the clause had to be disregarded. Rena K's owner contested this and claimed that the explicit reference in the bill of lading to the arbitration clause in the charter-party showed that the parties to the bill of lading had intended that any future disputes should be settled by arbitration. In such a case it would be adequate to manipulate the wording of the arbitration clause in the charter-party so that it applied also to disputes arising out of the bill of lading.

Justice Brandon first made it clear that the facts were so to distinguish this case from earlier precedence, as the reference in the bill of lading contained a specific reference to the arbitration clause in the charter-party. This wording had to be understood to mean that the parties to the bill of lading had intended that the arbitration clause in the charter-party should apply to disputes under the bill of lading as well. Brandon J continued: "... if it is necessary, as it obviously is, to manipulate or adapt part of the wording of that clause in order to give effect to that intention, then I am clearly of the opinion, that this should be done".[250] Hence, the parties were considered to have entered into an arbitration agreement and the case before the Court was stayed.

In THE RENA K, an explicit reference in the bill of lading to the arbitration clause in the underlying charter-party was found to effectively incorporate that arbitration agreement into the bill of lading. The effect of this was that the parties under the bill of lading were considered to have agreed to arbitrate on the terms stated in the charter-party.

This could only be done because the explicit reference to the arbitration clause proved that the parties to the bill of lading had in fact intended the arbitration agreement in the charter-party to form part of their contract. This solution to the problem of incorporating special provisions such as arbitration clauses into a document seems balanced and manageable. It must be noted that it is the same solution that is chosen in the Nordic Maritime Code secs. 311 and 310, sub-sec. 3, for cases where the carrier wishes to enforce an arbitration agreement in a charter-party against a holder of the bill of lading, not being the charterer under the charter-party.[251] However, in English law the principle must be seen as being generally applicable when introducing unusual or potentially onerous clauses into a contract by incorporation by reference. Also, the principle must be seen more as a general requirement of contract law than as a feature of maritime law concerned with protecting the presumed weaker party under a tramp bill of lading, as is the case under the Nordic Maritime Code sec. 311.

[250] *per* Brandon, J, p. 551.

[251] See Chapter V, § 2.

3.3.2. Incorporation by general reference – The Merak

After the Rena K, it was clear that the arbitration clause of a charter-party could be incorporated into a bill of lading by a specific reference, even if the arbitration clause was worded in a way that only covered the relationship between the owner and the charterer. Nevertheless, incorporation by specific reference followed by a verbal manipulation is not the only way in which arbitration clauses in charter-parties may be incorporated into bills of lading under English law. This has been clear since THE MERAK.

[1964] 2 Lloyd's Law Reports 527 CA, THE MERAK[252]

On 21 April 1961 the cargo owners and WD entered into a charter-party according to which the cargo owners were to supply the cargo and WD the ship for a voyage from Finland to Newport. On 15 September WD sub-chartered the Merak for the purpose of the transport. Both charters were made using the Nubaltwood form.

The following clauses of the charter-parties are of relevance:

In the charter-party dated 21 May: "The Bills of Lading shall be prepared in the form endorsed upon this Charter and ... freight and all terms, conditions, clauses (including Clause 32), and exceptions as per this Charter ...". Clause 32 was an arbitration clause according to which "Any dispute arising out of this Charter or any Bill of Lading issued hereunder shall be referred to arbitration ...".

In the charter-party dated 15 September "Bills of Lading ... to be signed with reference to Charter-party dated 21st April 1961 ... ".

The master of Merak issued bills of lading " ... as per Charter dated the 21st of April 1961." The bills of lading contained a reference clause: "All terms, conditions, clauses and exceptions including cl. 30 contained in the said charter party apply to this Bill of Lading and are deemed to be incorporated herein."

It was obvious that the reference to clause 30 instead of clause 32 was erroneous. (Clause 30 in the charter-party of 21 April was a substitution clause).

During the carriage a part of the cargo was damaged. Furthermore, a part of the cargo was hauled from Brixham to Newport. The owners of the cargo wanted to recover the loss hereby incurred, and initiated Court proceedings. Merak's owner requested that the suit be stayed since the parties had entered into an arbitration agreement. Queens Bench Division granted a stay. The consignees appealed the decision.

The Court of Appeal was split regarding the question of whether or not the bills of lading should be corrected, so that the reference to clause 30 should be read as a reference to clause 32. However, the Court unanimously found that this was of no consequence, as the arbitration clause (clause 32) was incorporated into the bills of lading even if the reference to clause 30 was considered an error and disregarded as such.

The bills of lading contained a *general reference* to the charter-party. The charter-party itself contained a provision to the effect that disputes, *including disputes arising under bills of lading issued*

[252] Appeal of [1964] 2 Lloyd's Law Reports 283 QBD. Also published in [1965] 2 W.L.R. 250.

under the charter-party, should be referred to arbitration. The arbitration clause was therefore incorporated into the bill of lading. The authority from THOMAS V. PORTSEA did not inhibit this solution as in that case the arbitration clause was only worded to cover disputes under the charter-party. Thus, as the parties had referred their dispute to arbitration, the appeal was dismissed, and the stay granted by Queens Bench Division was upheld.

The bills of lading contained a general reference to all the provisions of the charter-party. One of these provisions was an arbitration clause, which according to its wording also applied to disputes arising out of bills of lading issued under the charter. The arbitration clause in its natural meaning could thus be read verbatim into the bills of lading. In such a case an explicit reference was not necessary and, hence, the erroneous reference to clause 30 was of no consequence to the case. In other words: As verbal manipulation was not necessary, a general reference sufficed.

The findings of the Court of Appeal in THE MERAK are clearly not contrary to the authority of HAMILTON V. MACKIE.[253] The charter-party's arbitration clause could be read verbatim into the bill of lading. However, the findings of the Court of Appeal do strike as being contradictory to the authority of THOMAS V. PORTSEA, and to the principle that only provisions germane to the transport agreement can be incorporated into the bill of lading by a general reference.

The Court of Appeal manages to distinguish the two cases from each other. In both THOMAS V. PORTSEA and THE MERAK a general reference was made. However, in THE MERAK the arbitration clause could be read directly into the bill of lading. This was not the case in THOMAS V. PORTSEA. Therefore, according to the Court of Appeal, the cases were not analogous and the Court was thus not bound by the precedence.

The findings of the Court of Appeal in THOMAS V. PORTSEA: "... when it is sought to introduce into a document like a bill of lading – a negotiable instrument – a clause such as this arbitration clause, not germane to the receipt, carriage, or delivery of the cargo or the payment of freight ... this should be done in distinct and specific words, and not by general words ..." [254] were not *obiter.* Furthermore, they were put in generally applicable and absolute terms. Even though the arbitration clause in THE MERAK was in fact worded to apply to disputes arising out of the bill of lading, it is hard to see why the general reference to the charter-party used in THE MERAK should not be exactly within the scope of application of the principle described in THOMAS

---

[253] (1889) 5 T. L. R. 667 CA.

[254] *per* Lord Atkinson, p. 6, emphasis added.

v. PORTSEA. This is especially so if one regards the problem from the point of view of the holder of the bill of lading.

The explanation of the approach of the Court of Appeal probably lies in the particular facts of the case. As mentioned, WD and the cargo owners entered into a charter-party on 21st April 1961. WD chose to use chartered tonnage to carry out his obligations under the contract of carriage evidenced in the charter-party. Both the main and the sub-charter were made on the Nubaltwood form. Thus, the cargo owners were already acquainted with the arbitration clause in the charter-party, as it formed a part of their initial agreement with WD, even if the legal relationship between the cargo owners and the performing carrier, the owner of THE MERAK, were governed by the bill of lading. The case was thus distinct from the situation where the holder of the bill of lading has acquired it by negotiation, and for that reason is unfamiliar with the terms of the charter-party under which the bill of lading has been issued. Consequently, the Court of Appeal found it necessary to side-step THOMAS V. PORTSEA to reach what was probably the correct result in the case.

Even so, the precedence from THE MERAK should not be restricted. The Court of Appeal expressed itself in general terms, and in any case, it should not be the law that arbitration agreements in charter-parties may never be incorporated into bills of lading by general reference. But readers of the case should bear in mind that in THE MERAK, the holder of the bill of lading was closely connected to, although not party to, the charter-party under which the bill of lading was issued.

3.3.3. Incorporation by general reference – the wording

The reference used in THE MERAK was widely worded, incorporating "All terms, conditions, clauses and exceptions ..." of the charter-party. This was of importance to the outcome of the decision, as became apparent after a few more cases.

[1982] 1 Lloyd's Law Reports 286 QBD, THE EMMANUEL COLOCOTRONIS (No. 2)
The Emmanuel Colocotronis was chartered on a voyage charter for the transport of wheat. According to the charter-party the contract of carriage was to "... be completed and superseded by the signing of Bills of Lading ... which ... shall contain the following clauses ...". After this 19 printed and 18 typed clauses were listed, one of these an arbitration clause. The clauses were not introduced in full into the bills of lading, instead the bills of lading held a clause of reference: "All other conditions, exceptions, demurrage, general average and for disbursements as per above named charter-party."

The carriage was delayed by three months due to the monsoon and the owner of Emmanuel Colocotronis claimed demurrage. The receivers purported to have a counter-claim for damaged cargo. The owner, however, held that the dispute was to be settled by arbitration. The consignees disputed this, and therefore the Court had to decide whether the arbitration clause of the voyage charter-party had been successfully incorporated into the bill of lading.

The arbitration clause could not be classified as a provision regarding "... demurrage, general average [or] ... disbursements ...". Neither was it an exception clause. It followed from this that the clause had not been incorporated into the bill of lading by explicit reference. Hence, it had to be decided if the provision had been incorporated by a general reference, which according to THE MERAK could be done if the provision of the charter-party was worded in such a way that it could be applied to the charter-party.

Staugthon, J. held that the term "condition" according to his view was a general expression.[255] It followed from the wording of the bill of lading that the holder of the bill of lading had to refer himself to the charter-party. Furthermore, in the charter-party it was explicitly stated that the arbitration clause had to be incorporated into the bill of lading. Under these circumstances the general clause of reference had incorporated the arbitration clause of the charter-party into the bill of lading and a stay was granted.

According to Justice Staugthon, the term "condition" in the bill of lading was a general one. Furthermore, according to the charter-party, the charter-party's arbitration clauses should be incorporated into the bill of lading. The precedence from THE MERAK had held this to be sufficient and the clauses were therefore incorporated.

The conclusion of Staugthon, J. that the term "condition" was a general one was problematic. It was contradictory to existing authority according to which the term "condition" should not be given its natural meaning but instead a narrower, legal one, developed through case law. It follows from the legal definition of what is a condition, that only provisions, which bestow upon the parties obligations concerned with the actual carrying out of the transport may be characterised as such. Staugthon J was aware of these authorities but still found that in the specific case the term "condition" was of general connotation. In the VARENNA, The Court of Appeal rejected this view.

[1983] 2 LLOYD'S LAW REPORTS 592 CA, THE VARENNA[256]

A cargo of crude oil was carried on a Fina voyage charter-party from Tartous to Wilhelmshaven. During the voyage a claim for demurrage arose. The charterers failed to pay the demurrage and the owners of Varenna directed the claim against the cargo owners instead. They in turn argued that they had already put the charterer in funds to pay the owner's claim for demurrage. However, before paying, the charterer had gone into liquidation. The carrier initiated proceedings before the Courts. The consignees claimed that an arbitration clause in the charter-party had been incorporated into the bill of lading and requested a stay. If the cargo owners were granted a stay of Court proceedings, a time bar in the arbitration agreement would come into force and bar the owner's claim. Hence, the consignees would not have to pay demurrage twice.

---

[255] Staugthon, J. p. 293.

[256] Appeal of [1983] 1 Lloyd's Law Reports 416 QBD.

The relevant clauses were very similar to the ones discussed in THE EMMANUEL COLOCOTRONIS. It followed from the charter-party that disputes under the charter were to be settled by arbitration. Furthermore it followed that bills of lading issued under the charter-party were to refer to "all terms and conditions ... including ... the Arbitration Clause" of the voyage charter-party. However, the reference clauses in fact entered into the bills of lading only referred to " ... all conditions and exceptions ... including the negligence clause".

The central dispute in the case was whether Staugthon, J.'s findings in THE EMMANUEL COLOCOTRONIS were in fact correct, or whether the findings of Justice Hobhouse in the High Court decision of the Varenna were to be upheld. Hobhouse, J. had based his decision upon the traditional, narrower legal view regarding which provisions were "conditions", and which were not. In accordance with this he had found that the reference to the conditions of the charter-party only incorporated " ... conditions ... to be performed by the consignees on the arrival of the vessel".[257]

The Court of Appeal held, albeit with a slightly varying reasoning, that Justice Staugthon's decision in THE EMMANUEL COLOCOTRONIS was not one to be followed. There was clear authority in case law that the term "condition", when inserted into a charter-party, was to be understood as referring to "... the conditions under which the goods are loaded, stowed, kept, cared for, carried and discharged".[258] Hereafter, the Court considered THOMAS V. PORTSEA[259] and the theory of incorporation of clauses germane to the contract of carriage. The Court also took into account that the legal consensus on the term "condition" had already been acknowledged at the time when THOMAS V. PORTSEA was decided.[260] An understanding of a term that had been long established should only be departed from if this was dictated by compulsive surrounding circumstances or if it was clear from the context that the parties had intended another meaning.[261] In the case before the Court, this was not so. Hence, as the reference to "conditions" did not constitute a general reference to the charter-party, the arbitration clause had not been incorporated into the bill of lading, and there was no reason to grant a stay. The appeal was dismissed.

The Court of Appeal overruled the conclusion reached by Justice Staugthon in THE EMMANUEL COLOCOTRONIS. At the same time the Court of Appeal specified the preconditions required when applying the findings in THE MERAK in future cases. See especially Lord Justice Oliver:

"The incorporating words in [THE MERAK] were ... general words but they were as wide as they could possibly be. ... [They] could not, in the absence of some strong indication to the contrary, be

---

[257] [1983] 1 Lloyd's Law Reports 416 QBD, p. 421, col. 2.

[258] p. 595, column 1.

[259] [1912] A. C. 1 HL. Appeal of (1911) P. 54 CA, THE PORTSMOUTH.

[260] p. 595, column 1 and 597, column 2.

[261] p. 597, column 2.

cut down or restricted. ... All the clauses of the charter-party were to be applied, subject only to the test of consistency, a test clearly passed by the arbitration clause in that case."[262]

The findings of the Court of Appeal in THE VARENNA were endorsed by the Court of Appeal in [1989] 1 Lloyd's Law Reports 103 CA, THE FEDERAL BULKER. The relevant clauses were almost identical[263] to the ones found in THE EMMANUEL COLOCOTRONIS.[264]

The Court found that charter-party's arbitration clause was not incorporated into the bill of lading. The Court based this conclusion partly on THOMAS V. PORTSEA.[265] A general reference, including a reference to "terms and conditions" only incorporated the provisions, which were directly relevant to the carrying out of the transport.[266] Furthermore, the Court emphasised that due to the negotiability of the bill of lading, clear rules regarding incorporation were paramount. There was no reason for changing a long established practice according to which arbitration clauses were not incorporated by referring to the "terms and conditions" of the relevant charter-party.[267]

In that respect THE FEDERAL BULKER does not distinguish itself from THE VARENNA.[268] Instead, what is interesting about the case in hand is its *obiter*. In the case it is stated by both Lord Justice Bingham and Lord Justice Butler-Sloss that the scope of what can be considered a general reference and thus, when used, incorporates any provision of a charter-party into a bill of lading as long as the provision is

---

[262] p. 598, column 2.

[263] In the charter-party: "[This] ... contract shall be completed and superseded by the signing of Bills of Lading ... which ... shall contain the following clauses ... 11. All disputes ... arising out of this contract shall ... be referred to ... arbitration ...".
In the bill of lading: "All terms, conditions and exceptions as per charter-party dated January 20, 1986 ... to be considered as fully incorporated herein as if fully written ...".

[264] [1982] 1 Lloyd's Law Reports 286 QBD. The case is discussed above.

[265] [1912] A. C. 1 HL, appeal of (1911) P. 54 CA, THE PORTSMOUTH.

[266] p. 106, column 1, ff.

[267] p. 105, column 2.

[268] [1983] 2 Lloyd's Law Reports 592 CA.

sensible there, can be found by reading THOMAS V. PORTSEA and THE MERAK together.[269] In THOMAS V. PORTSEA the reference clause was worded thus:

"Deck load at shipper's risk, and all other terms and conditions and exceptions to be as per charter-party, including negligence clause."

Instead, in THE MERAK, a much wider wording was used:

"All the terms, conditions, clauses and exceptions including Clause 30 contained in the said charter party apply to this Bill of Lading and are deemed to be incorporated herein."

The most obvious difference between the wording of the reference clauses is the reference in THE MERAK to all *clauses* of the charter-party. Such a wording will necessarily include the arbitration clause. The other difference concerns the context of the reference clause. In THOMAS V. PORTSEA it seems as if "all other terms and conditions and exceptions" refer back to the proviso that the shipper bears the risk for deck cargo. This suggests that only provisions of similar nature, the provisions germane to the contract of carriage, are intended to be incorporated. This is not the case in THE MERAK. Conversely, in that case the reference appears independent of the other provisions and is worded in a way that clearly aims to incorporate all the charter-party's provisions into the bill of lading.

This is a significant variation in the legal effects of provisions that, according to the natural meaning of the words used, should be analogous; a variation caused by the fact that the expressions "conditions" and "terms" through more than a century have been allocated a legal meaning under English law which differs from their natural one. It is this discrepancy which is at the base of Staugthon J's conclusion in THE EMMANUEL COLOCOTRONIS and which causes Lord Justice Watkin to hesitate in THE VARENNA.[270] If one wishes to incorporate arbitration clauses or other boilerplate

---

[269] As per Bingham, LJ, p. 108, column 1 and per Butler-Schloss on p. 110, column 1.

[270] [1983] 2 Lloyd's Law Reports 592, p. 599, column 2: "When parties to a contract are in dispute about the manner of its performance it is obviously of the utmost importance that any agreement they have made in that contract as to the forum where such a dispute should be resolved be given effect to. Here we have a charter-party which contains a clear provision for reference of disputes to arbitration and a bill of lading to which it is related the terms of which would appear, upon a robust common sense construction of them, in the absence of authority, so it seems to me, to incorporate the charter-party arbitration clause in that bill. Hence I have striven in considering the large accumulation of authority to which we were referred to ascertain whether the view taken of them by Mr. Justice Staugthon in *The Emmanuel Colocotronis*, which continues to have an attraction to me, can be supported. Alas! with no enthusiasm I am obliged to say that I have reached the conclusion, for reasons explained by my Lord, that the weight of authority is opposed to that view."

clauses into a bill of lading by a general reference to the underlying charter-party, one should use terms, which are legally neutral, such as "provisions" or "clauses".

After the Court of Appeal's decision in THE FEDERAL BULKER, the position of the law as regards the incorporation of arbitration clauses from charter-parties into bills of lading seemed clear. Arbitration clauses could be incorporated in two ways. One could make an explicit reference to the arbitration clause. This would incorporate the arbitration clause into the bill of lading even if the clause had to undergo a certain amount of verbal manipulation if it was to read into the bill of lading. Or, one could incorporate arbitration clauses by a general reference provided *that* the reference was wide enough to embrace also the arbitration clause and *that* the clause referred to in the charter-party (*i.e.* the arbitration clause) was worded in a way that made sense under the bill of lading, and, probably, *that* the contents of the clause were not in other ways contrary to the contents of the bill of lading.

Still, uncertainties arose with the decision of the House of Lords in THE MIRAMAR.

3.4. Slight confusion – The Miramar

[1984] 2 LLOYD'S LAW REPORTS 129 HL, THE MIRAMAR[271]

On the 19th of May 1980 The Miramar was fixed on a voyage charter-party to Petrochem. A bill of lading was issued for the cargo of 12000 tonnes of crude oil. The defendant, Holborn, was the consignee. During the transport, a considerable claim for demurrage had accrued under the voyage charter. Miramar's owner directed a claim for demurrage against both Petrochem and Holborn. Petrochem, according to the demurrage clause in the voyage charter-party, and Holborn due to a reference in the bill of lading to the provisions of the charter-party.

The demurrage clause was worded thus, in extract: "DEMURRAGE. Charterer shall pay demurrage per running hour and pro rata hereof at the rate specified in Chapter I ...". According to the bill of lading "... [the] ... shipment is carried under and pursuant to the terms of the Charter dated May 19, 1980 between ... [owner and charterer] ... and all the terms whatsoever of said charter ... apply to and govern the rights of the parties concerned in this shipment".

The owner argued in accordance with the authorities from THE MERAK and THE ANNEFIELD, used *ex contrario*. Since the provision regarded an obligation germane to the contract of carriage, namely the payment of freight, a general reference would incorporate the demurrage clause into the bill of lading, even if the demurrage clause would have to be manipulated to read into the bill of lading. Lord Diplock, speaking for a unanimous House of Lords, did not accept this reasoning, the reasons for that being plural. Firstly, the findings of Russell and Denning in THE MERAK and THE ANNEFIELD

---

[271] Appeal of [1984] A. C. 626 / [1984] 1 Lloyd's Law Reports 142. See also Queens Bench Division in [1983] 2 Lloyd's Law Reports 319.

were, strictly speaking, obiter and as such not binding.[272] Secondly, incorporation presupposed that the words "the charterer" in the voyage charter-party were replaced by the words "the consignee" or alternatively "the bill of lading holder". To manipulate the wording in that way would create a result in the case before the Court, which was commercially unsound. As it was put: "No business man who had not taken leave of his senses would intentionally enter into a contract which exposed him to a potential liability of this kind ... For my part, I can see no business reason for verbal manipulation of that designation."[273] Even if THE MERAK and THE ANNEFIELD did provide for a certain degree of manipulation regarding clauses, which were directly germane to the carriage of the goods, the cases did not create precedence that verbal manipulation should be carried out in a case as THE MIRAMAR.[274]

Hence, as the demurrage clause had not been incorporated into the bill of lading, the holder of the bill of lading was not responsible for the payment of demurrage and the appeal was dismissed.[275]

After the House of Lord's decision, it was uncertain if THE MIRAMAR was a solitary exception to the principle that the provisions germane to the contract of carriage could be incorporated into the bill of lading by a general reference, or if a real change in the law had taken place. If it had, it seemed that only an explicit reference would incorporate provisions of the charter-party into the bill of lading, germane or non-germane alike. This was discussed at quite some length in the cases THE NAI MATTEINI and THE OINOUSSIN PRIDE.

[1988] 1 LLOYD'S LAW REPORTS 452 QBD, THE NAI MATTEINI

The Nai Matteini was fixed on a consecutive voyage charter-party on 13th July 1976. According to the charter-party, any disputes "... which may arise between the owner and the charterer regarding ... this contract ..." were to be settled by arbitration and according to Italian law.

On April 30th 1981 the charterer then fixed Nai Matteini on Asbatankvoy to SAMCO. The vessel was to carry a cargo of oil from the Arabian Gulf. This charter-party contained an arbitration clause in Chapter II, clause 24. "Arbitration. Any and all differences and disputes of whatsoever nature arising out of this Charter shall be put to arbitration ... in the City of London ... pursuant to the laws relating to arbitration there in force ...". Furthermore, it followed from Asbatankvoy Part I that English law governed the charter-party.

---

[272] p. 131, column 2.

[273] p. 132, column 2 and p. 133, column 2.

[274] p. 134, column 2.

[275] Explanatory note: Generally, demurrage accrued during a voyage should be stated on the bill of lading, to be binding upon a holder of the bill of lading in good faith (see for example Hamburg Rules Art. 16(4) or the Nordic Maritime Code sec. 269, sub-sec. 1, and sec. 299, sub-sec. 2, 2nd sentence).

SAMCO, in turn, transferred their rights according to the charter-party to the cargo owners, Svenska Petroleum AB. The owner's agent issued bills of lading for the cargo, Svenska Petroleum AB being the consignees. According to the bills of lading "... all terms, conditions and exceptions (including but not limited to Due Diligence, Negligence, Force Majeure, War Liberties and Arbitration clauses) contained in which Charter Party are herewith incorporated and form a part hereof".

On discharge, 2000 tonnes of oil at a value of USD 0.5 million were missing. The consignees initiated arbitral proceedings. The owner of Nai Matteini disputed that an arbitration agreement was in force between the owner and the consignees, Svenska Petroleum AB. The owner therefore commenced a suit before the Courts for the settlement dispute on jurisdiction.

Justice Gatehouse found that the findings of the House of Lords in THE MIRAMAR were to be seen as generally applicable.[276] THE RENA K had thus been overruled, and verbal manipulation of an arbitration clause should not be carried out even if the charter-party contained an explicit reference. In any case, the case before the Court distinguished itself from THE RENA K. In the latter case, two bills of lading were issued under one charter-party. In THE NAI MATTEINI , one bill of lading was issued under two charter-parties, without it being clear which charter-party was the relevant one. The presumption in these cases was that the bill of lading was issued pursuant to the main charter-party (in this case the consecutive voyage charter-party).[277] In the case, there was no reason to depart from this presumption. As the arbitration clause in the consecutive voyage charter-party could not be applied to disputes arising out of the bill of lading without verbal manipulation, and as verbal manipulation after the House of Lord's decision in the Miramar was no longer permitted, no arbitration agreement was entered into between the parties.

According to Justice Gatehouse, the findings of the House of Lords in THE MIRAMAR had effected a general ban on verbal manipulation. This understanding of THE MIRAMAR was contested by Justice Webster in THE OINOUSSIN PRIDE.

[1991] 2 LLOYD'S LAW REPORTS 126 QBD, THE OINOUSSIN PRIDE

Bills of lading were issued for a cargo of timber. By mistake, the quantity of the cargo had been wrongly stated. Therefore, a new set of bills of lading was issued. These held an exception of liability for deck cargo and a reference to the charter-party, according to which "[all] terms, conditions, provisions and exceptions including the arbitration clause of the relevant charter party dated May 11, 1988 ..." were incorporated into the bills of lading. None of these clauses were found in the first set of bills of lading issued.

The arbitration clause in the charter-party was worded thus: "Should any disputes arise between owners and charterers, the matter in dispute shall be referred to ... [arbitration] ... in London ...". To the clause had been added "English law to apply".

---

[276] p. 459, column 1.

[277] In this respect Justice Gatehouse refers to the precedence of THE SAN NICHOLAS, [1976] 1 Lloyd's Law Reports 8, and to THE SEVONIA TEAM, [1983] 2 Lloyd's Law Reports 640 and Scrutton, p. 65.

The cargo was loaded on deck. During the carriage, the vessel was hit by the typhoon Agnes and a substantial part of the cargo was washed overboard. Under the following dispute, the choice of law of the matter was called into question.

It was found that the second set of bills of lading had substituted the first set issued. It therefore had to be decided if the arbitration clause including its proviso for choice of law had been incorporated into that set of bills of lading. Due to the phrasing used in the charter-party, incorporation required a verbal manipulation.

Webster, J. worded the problem in this way: "... are those words ... [shippers or receivers] ... to be added to cl. 17 of the charter-party, or are some words of incorporation in the bill to be notionally deleted, i.e. the words 'including the arbitration clause'? In the absence of authority I would conclude that, if practical, effect should be given to the expressed intention of the parties to the bills, namely, to incorporate the arbitration clause in them, and that it is not only practical but necessary to do so by adding those words to cl. 17 ...".[278]

However, Webster, J. did not lack authority. Conversely, he found that THE MIRAMAR had not overruled THE RENA K. In THE MIRAMAR, there was only a general reference to the charter-party, and no explicit reference to its arbitration clause. Even if THE MIRAMAR expressed a generally applicable rule according to which general references did not incorporate provisions of a charter-party into a bill of lading issued under it, surely the case did not carry any precedence regarding the legal effects of explicit clauses of reference.

Accodingly, the arbitration clause was incorporated into the bill of lading, and the matter of the case thus governed by English law.

The House of Lords in THE MIRAMAR was only concerned with the question of incorporation of germane provisions by general reference. Therefore, the findings of the Lords were not binding in a case where the incorporation by specific reference was discussed. Justice Webster was consequently free to regard the provisions expressly referred to as incorporated, even if this required verbatim manipulation.

3.5. Certainty – The Nerano

Fortunately, the uncertainties, which arose after the decision of the House of Lords in THE MIRAMAR, were to a large extent dealt with and eliminated by the Court of Appeal in the NERANO case. In this case, a specific reference to the charter-party's arbitration clause was made in the bill of lading. The Court of appeal found, in accordance with the RENA K, that the arbitration agreement had been incorporated into the bill of lading. However, to do so they had to confront THE MIRAMAR.

[1996] 1 LLOYD'S LAW REPORTS 1 CA, THE NERANO
October 26th 1991 the defendant ship owner issued a bill of lading. On the face of the document was this clause: "THE CONDITIONS AS PER RELEVANT CHARTER PARTY DATED 02.07.1990

---

[278] p. 130, column 2.

ARE INCORPORATED IN THIS BILL OF LADING AND HAVE PRECEDENCE IF THERE IS A CONFLICT." On the reverse of the document one could read the following: "All terms and conditions, liberties, exceptions and arbitration clause of the Charter Party, dated as overleaf, are herewith incorporated."

The charter-party was entered into between the ship owner and the co-defendant, the charterer, on the Gencon form. The charter-party contained in clause 36: "... any dispute ... between the Owners and Charterers ... shall be determined in London England according to the Arbitration Acts, 1975 to 1979 and any amendments or modifications thereto and English law to govern".

According to the receivers, the cargo of steel had been damaged by seawater. The receivers took their claim to the Courts. The owner requested a stay due to the arbitration clause in the charter-party.

The case required a discussion of both the correct construction of the bill of lading and the question of the incorporation of the arbitration clause. In addition, the Court discussed the apparent conflict between the findings in THE RENA K and THE MIRAMAR. According to the authority of THE RENA K, the arbitration clause had been incorporated into the bill of lading by explicit reference. This was not inconsistent with the House of Lords' decision in THE MIRAMAR, as the reference in that case was to a provision in the charter-party which was both potentially, and in the case also actually, very onerous. Therefore, strict requirements had to be met to incorporate the provision into another document. This was not the case when concerned with arbitration clauses. Saville, L. J. stated, with a unanimous Court of Appeal behind him, that "... by identifying and specifying the charter-party arbitration clause it seems to me to be clear that the parties to the bill of lading did intend and agree to arbitration, so that to give force to that intention and agreement the words in the clause must be read and constricted as applying to those parties. Indeed it seems to me that it would be an extraordinary result if English law reached a different conclusion".[279]

Furthermore, as the arbitration agreement had not been subsequently altered, the appeal was dismissed, and the stay that was granted by the High Court upheld. The dispute had to be settled by arbitration.

The Court of Appeal found that the ruling in THE MIRAMAR was carried by a special regard to the very onerous nature of the provision sought incorporated. Thus, the case did not lay down a principle of general application.

The Court of Appeal's construction of the findings of the House of Lords in THE MIRAMAR is found to be the correct one. The deciding point in the latter case was not the method of incorporation chosen; rather it was the fact that incorporating the clause in question seemed commercially unsound. A provision should only be verbally manipulated if not doing so would be contrary to the parties' proven intention. When a provision is such that "... no business man who had not taken leave of his senses ..."[280] would want to be bound by it, it will be very difficult to prove that one of the parties has in fact intended to be just that. Hence, verbal manipulation can only

---

[279] p. 4, column 2.

[280] THE MIRAMAR, [1984] 2 Lloyd's Law Reports 129 HL, p. 132, column 2.

rarely be expected to take place when dealing with unusual or unusually burdensome provisions.

In other words: The onus of proof is hard to lift for the party who wishes to show that a potentially arduous provision which, according to its own wording, does not apply to the parties to the dispute is in fact intended to govern their relationship. This was very much the position in THE MIRAMAR since, according to the provision in the charter-party, claims for demurrage had to be directed against the charterer as opposed to the consignee, as was claimed by the owner.

Another weighty argument in THE MIRAMAR was that a general reference to the provisions of the charter-party does not provide the owner with an extra debtor for any claim the owner may have under the charter-party. See here the Court of Appeal in THE NERANO, explaining the findings of the House of Lords in THE MIRAMAR thus:

"... The House of Lords was concerned with demolishing the argument that there was some rule of construction to the effect that general words of incorporation of the terms of the charter-party brought into the bill of lading contract all the obligations imposed on the charterers germane to the shipment, carriage or delivery of the goods and (by changing the language of the charter) imposed those obligations on the bills of lading holders or consignees instead of or in addition to the charterers."[281]

The boundaries of which provisions may be incorporated into a bill of lading by a general reference and which, due to their unusual or burdensome nature, may not, await further decisions. The House of Lords has only stated that provisions, which for business reasons appear to be totally undesirable, may not. Unfortunately, what is 'commercially unsound' or 'undesirable for business reasons' will have to be decided individually in each case, making total certainty illusory. However, when concerning oneself only with arbitration agreements, a conclusion may be reached.

4. Summing up the position of the law before the 1996 Act

The position of the law on incorporating the provisions of one document into another, with special view to the incorporation of the provisions of charterparties into bills of lading may be summarised thus:

---

[281] [1996] 1 Lloyd's Law Reports 1 CA, p. 4, column 2.

4.1. Points of departure

It is primarily the bill of lading that determines which provisions are incorporated. See THOMAS V. PORTSEA: "The bill of lading itself is the primary document to be considered."[282]

The wording of the charter-party provisions referred to should, as a starting point, read verbatim into the bill of lading with a reasonable result. See HAMILTON V. MACKIE: "... the conditions of the charter-party must be read verbatim into the bill of lading as though they were printed in extenso. ... if this was inconsistent with the bill of lading they [the provisions of the charter-party] were insensible, and must be disregarded." However, this principle is only a starting point and should not be applied unthinkingly. See THE ANNEFIELD: "Lord Esher [one of the members of the Court of Appeal deciding HAMILTON V. MACKIE] was not laying down a rule of interpretation of universal application. It was a useful test in that case. That is all. ... The rule in HAMILTON V. MACKIE must be applied intelligently and not mechanically."[283]

4.2. The technicalities of the incorporation

Provisions of a charter-party, which, according to their wording, are applicable to the bill of lading, may be incorporated therein by a general reference to all the provisions of the charter-party. See THE MERAK: "... the incorporating clause is clear and wide and to be understood requires reference to the charter-party ... the holder has to refer to the charter-party and select therefrom the clauses which apply ... It is difficult ... to see ... that parties to a bill of lading, if they use wide enough words of incorporation, cannot ... agree to incorporate into the bill of lading an arbitration clause which expressly applies to disputes arising out of the bill, that is to say, disputes arising out of the shipment, carriage or delivery of the goods."[284]

If, instead, the provisions referred to in the charter-party are not worded in a way, which is appropriate when dealing with a dispute arising out of the bill of lading, two distinct situations exist:

The provisions of the charter-party, which are directly germane to the shipment, carriage or delivery of the cargo, may as a point of departure be incorporated into the bill of lading by a general reference to the charter-party. See THE ANNEFIELD: "... a

---

[282] [1912] A. C. 1 HL, p. 5.

[283] [1971] 1 Lloyd's Law Reports 1 CA, p. 4 column 1 and p. 6, column 1.

[284] [1964] 2 Lloyd's Law Reports 527 CA, p. 531 and 534.

clause which is directly germane to the subject-matter of the bill of lading ... can and should be incorporated into the bill of lading contract, even though it may involve a degree of manipulation of the words in order to fit exactly the bill of lading."[285]

An exception to this can be found regarding provisions, which are unusual and onerous. See THE MIRAMAR: "... no business man who had not taken leave of his senses would intentionally enter into a contract which exposed him to a potential liability of this kind; and this, in itself, I find to be an overwhelming reason for not indulging in verbal manipulation of the actual contractual words used in the charter-party ...".[286] Thus, a general clause of incorporation does not transfer all the obligations of the charterer to the consignee or bill of lading holder. Where one should draw the line regarding which clauses of a charter-party may be incorporated by general reference, will, pending further case law, have to be decided by a review of the facts of the specific case. However, as the parties to international contracts of carriage are normally both professionals, the threshold for disallowing incorporation should be high.

Provisions, which are not directly germane to the shipment, carriage and delivery of the cargo, such as arbitration clauses, may be incorporated into the bill of lading by an explicit reference in the bill of lading to the clause in question. Given that an explicit reference is made, the (arbitration) clause of the charter-party will apply to the bill of lading even if the clause is worded to only apply to the parties to the charter-party. THE RENA K: "... added to the usual words of incorporation ... [are] the further specific words 'including arbitration clause'. The addition of these words must ... mean that the parties to the bills of lading intended the provisions of the arbitration clause in the charter-party to apply in principle to disputes arising under the bills of lading ...".[287] THE OINOUSSIN PRIDE: "... effect should be given to the expressed intention of the parties to the bills ...".[288] THE NERANO: "[The parties] have expressly identified and specified the charter-party as something to be incorporated into their contract ... to give force to that intention and agreement the words in the clause must be read and construed as applying to those parties."[289]

---

[285] [1971] 1 Lloyd's Law Reports 1 CA, p. 4.

[286] [1984] 2 Lloyd's Law Reports 129 HL.

[287] [1978] 1 Lloyd's Law Reports 545 QBD, p. 551.

[288] [1991] 1 Lloyd's Law Reports 126 QBD, p. 130.

[289] [1996] 1 Lloyd's Law Reports 1 CA, p. 4.

5. The Arbitration Act 1996 sec. 6(2)

5.1. A new regulation or a statement of fact?

The English Arbitration Act 1996, as opposed to the 1950 Act[290] and the 1975 Act,[291] specifically mentions the possibility that arbitration agreements are entered into by incorporation. The provision is found in sec. 6(2).

Arbitration Act 1996 sec. 6(2).
"The reference in an agreement to a written form of arbitration clause or to a document containing an arbitration clause constitutes an arbitration agreement if the reference is such as to make that clause part of the agreement."

The provision makes it clear that incorporation of arbitration agreements may be done either by reference to a written arbitration *clause*, or to a *document* containing such a clause. This is only a description of the de facto way in which the incorporation may be carried out, and as such hardly novel. The real problems of the discussion are less distinct in the wording. The first question one may raise is what requirements of form govern the reference itself. This is not regulated by sec. 6(2) but by s. 5, in particular ss. 5(2), 5(3) and 5(4). As is the case with arbitration agreements as such, the reference must fulfil the requirement for the agreement to be in writing for it to fall within Part I of the Act. As already mentioned, an agreement is "in writing" under sec. 5(2) if the agreement is made in writing, if the agreement is made by exchange of communications in writing, or if the agreement is evidenced in writing. Thus, an oral reference to the standard salvage agreement in LOF is made in writing according to sec. 5(3). Likewise, the reference in a bill of lading to an arbitration agreement in a charter-party is made in writing in the bill of lading, and, one might say, evidenced in the charter-party. One must note that sec. 5 is just the starting point. The criteria for a written agreement is just an initial test that the arbitration agreement has to pass if the regulation of the Arbitration Act 1996 Part II is to apply to it, and consequently, in most cases, if the agreement is to be regarded valid. One cannot deduce from the fact that the agreement is in accordance with sec. 5 the conclusion that an arbitration agreement has been entered into between the parties. Contract law and other rules of arbitration law may provide further criteria.

---

[290] See the Arbitration Act 1950 s. 32.

[291] See the Arbitration Act 1975 s. 7.

The criteria of contract law, which have to be fulfilled for the incorporation to be effective, are regulated in sec. 6(2). The incorporation is accepted if "... the reference is such as to make that clause [the arbitration clause] part of the agreement". What is in fact regulated by sec. 6(2) has given rise to different conclusions. Thus, according to *Harris*,[292] the wording of sec. 6(2) must be interpreted so that specific reference to the arbitration clause is no longer required. Also *Rutherford/Sims*[293] seem to find that sec. 6(2) provides some clarity as to whether or not an explicit reference is required, considering the provision an authority that explicit reference is no longer necessary. This writer disagrees with the findings of *Harris* and *Rutherford/Sims*. Instead, it is submitted that sec. 6(2) is void of independent legal content. The provision "... [if] the reference is such as to make that clause ... [a] ... part of the agreement ..." does not give any guidance as to what is required to achieve just that. The provision merely refers the material issues to be dealt with by other rules. Consequently, sec. 6(2) does not regulate what criteria of substance, or of contract law if one likes, that have to be fulfilled for an incorporation to be effective. But then the Departmental Advisory Committee did not intend to regulate that question. See hereto para. 42 of the 1996 Report on the Arbitration Bill:

"42. The second subsection reflects Article 7(2) of the Model Law. In English law there is at present some conflicting authority on the question as to what is required for the effective incorporation of an arbitration clause by reference. Some of those responding to the July 1995 draft Clauses made critical comments of the view of Sir John Megaw in *Augthon* v. *M F Kent Services* (1991) 57 BLR 1 (a construction contract case) and suggested that we should take the opportunity of making clear that the law was as stated in the charterparty cases and as summarised by Ralph Gibson LJ in *Augthon*. ... It seemed to us, however, that although we are of the view that the approach of Ralph Gibson LJ should prevail in all cases, this was really a matter for the Court to decide. The wording we have used certainly leaves room for the adoption of the charterparty rules in all cases, since it refers to references to a document containing an arbitration clause as well as reference to the arbitration clause itself. Thus, the wording is not confined to cases where there is a specific reference to the arbitration clause, which Sir John Megaw (but not Ralph Gibson LJ) considered was a requirement for effective incorporation by reference."

[292] *Harris (2000)*, p. 78 f. "What the subsection resolves is that there need not be a specific reference to the arbitration clause as a pre-requisite to incorporation, as Lord Justice Megaw considered in *Augthon* v. *M F Kent Services* (1991) 57 BLR 1, and as subsequent cases ... have emphasised. Rather, as Lord Justice Ralph Gibson considered in *Augthon*, a more general reference to a document containing such a clause may be sufficient to effect incorporation. However, whether Lord Justice Ralph Gibson's approach is to apply without limitation (as the DAC clearly thought it should) has been left to the courts to decide."

[293] *Rutherford/Sims (1996)*, p. 55.

To fully appreciate the Committee's preference, one must know the dicta of Sir John Megaw LJ and Ralph Gibson, LJ in the AUGTHON case. The case will be discussed in detail below in point 5.2.3. For the present, this summary suffices: The AUGTHON case concerned a sub-sub contract for electrical works. The question was whether an arbitration clause in the sub-contract also applied to the legal relationship between the parties to the sub-sub-contract. Both Judges found that the actual reference did not fulfil the requirement for written agreement in the Arbitration Act 1950, and a stay was refused. However, both Judges expressed views, which were strictly speaking obiter, upon the correct approach to the incorporation of arbitration clauses. Gibson LJ referred to the position of the law as stated by the charter-party cases (see above point 4). Having concluded that there was nothing in the charter-party cases to bar incorporation by general words, he found that the parties had expressed their intention to arbitrate well enough to make it legitimate for the Court to indulge in a verbal manipulation of the arbitration agreement in the sub-contract so that it could also apply to the sub-sub-contract. Megaw LJ's point of departure was the dicta from THOMAS V. PORTSEA. He found that this dicta was of general application and, consequently, that the arbitration clauses, including the one in question, could not be incorporated by general words.

The Committee did express a preference for the view that the charter-party cases should still apply.[294] Especially, the Committee thought it inappropriate to require specific references to the arbitration clause in all cases. The statement of the Departmental Advisory Committee cannot be drawn further than that. Para. 42 of the report does not support that specific reference may no longer be required. Also, the wording of sec. 6(2) particularly points out that incorporation might be achieved by either specific or general reference. It opens up for the assumption that specific references may still be required in certain cases, and after all, it was never the law that a specific reference was always necessary. Even if some change was intended, sec. 6(2) has not been worded sufficiently clear to make the strong precedence discussed above obsolete. This writer is consequently of the opinion that sec. 6(2) effects no change in the law of the incorporation of arbitration agreements. This was also the conclusion of Justice Jack, QC, in TRYGG HANSA V. EQUITAS.[295]

---

[294] *Tweeddale/Tweeddale (1999)*, p. 84.

[295] See also *Merkin (2000)*, p. 31.

Dispute arose regarding several reinsurance contracts entered into between Trygg Hansa and Lloyd's syndicate. Lloyd's and Equitas took four actions to the Courts. The defendant, Trygg Hansa, sought the actions stayed under sec. 9 of the Arbitration Act 1996 as, according to Trygg Hansa, there was an arbitration agreement between the parties.

The arbitration agreements relied on by the defendant were found in the primary insurance contracts. The defendant claimed that the agreements had been validly incorporated into first the excess of loss insurances and then into the reinsurance of the excess of loss insurances. In both cases, general words of incorporation had been used. The question before the Court was whether such incorporation sufficed to make the arbitration agreement in the primary insurance contracts apply to a dispute under the excess of loss reinsurance contract.

According Trygg Hansa, sec. 6(2) of the Arbitration Act 1996 had changed the position of the law on the subject so that the incorporation of arbitration agreements followed the same rules as the incorporation of other provisions. Alternatively, Trygg Hansa claimed that if the existing case law still applied, the references in the excess of loss insurance contracts and in the reinsurance of excess of loss contracts were sufficient to incorporate the arbitration agreements in the primary insurance contracts into the reinsurance contracts. For the support of the latter argument, the defendant relied on the judgment of Ralph Gibson, LJ in AUGTHON LTD. V. M.F. KENT SERVICES LTD., (1991) 57 B.L.R. 1. To deal with the matter, the Court had to decide whether the introduction of sec. 6(2) of the Arbitration Act 1996 had changed the law on incorporation of arbitration clauses by reference. Judge Raymond Jack, QC, found: "Section 6 does not state how it is to be decided whether 'the reference is such as to make that clause part of the agreement'. As there is an existing body of authority relating to the question [of] what is required to incorporate an arbitration clause from another document, unless there is any contrary indication, it would seem that those authorities should be applied."[296] A different approach to the question of incorporation would entail an abandonment of the idea that the arbitration clause differs in species from clauses that deal with the performance of a contract. Maintaining that idea, one had to appreciate that an arbitration clause would not necessarily be incorporated into a contract along with the incorporation of provisions dealing with the contract's performance. When seen in that light it was hard to interpret para. 42 of the 1996 Report on the Arbitration Bill so that it abandoned the rules of incorporation developed in the charter-party cases.[297] Consistent herewith, Justice Jack, QC, held that "... in the absence of special circumstances general words of incorporation would not be treated as effective for the purpose of the 1996 Act".[298]

Jack J, QC, found that even outside the charter-party cases, sec. 6(2) of the Arbitration Act did not effect a change in the law. This strongly supports this writer's conclusion, namely that at least within the charter-party cases, the law has not been

---

[296] p. 446, col. 1.

[297] p. 447, col. 2.

[298] p. 447, col. 2.

changed. The incorporation of arbitration agreements from charter-parties into bills of lading is thus still regulated as sketched above in point 4.

However, it must be considered whether the new provision and the findings of the DAC when put together opens up for a less stringent approach outside bill of lading/charter-party situations.

5.2. The protection of the negotiable bill of lading and the case law

5.2.1. Gibson's findings in the Augthon case

In the AUGTHON case, the High Court had found that the parties' agreement fulfilled the criteria for arbitration agreements to be in writing. However, the arbitration clause sought incorporated concerned the parties to the sub-contract. Thus, if applied to a dispute arising between the parties under the sub-sub-contract, the wording of the clause had to be amended. Stannard J found on the basis of the existing authorities that

"… where terms had been incorporated into a contract by reference to another contract, the terms not being expressly set out, then, as a matter of construction, the only terms which were effectively incorporated were those germane to the subject-matter of the first contract, and did not include an arbitration clause in the latter contract unless the words of incorporation explicitly referred to that clause, or, perhaps, unless the arbitration clause expressly referred to disputes under the former contract".[299]

In the case before the Court, there was neither an explicit reference in the sub-sub-contract to the arbitration clause in the sub-contract, nor was the arbitration clause, clause 61, worded so that it also applied to disputes occurring out of the sub-sub-contract. On that background the Court found that the arbitration agreement had not been incorporated into the sub-sub-contract and a stay was refused.

The High Court's judgment corresponds to the conclusions stated above in point 4 and is not at all controversial. On appeal, the Court of appeal was in agreement that the requirement for written agreement as described in the Arbitration Act 1950 sec. 32 (and as re-enacted by the Arbitration Act 1979, sec. 7(1)(e)) was not satisfied. This was not controversial either. However, the further obiter findings of the Court of Appeal are.

Ralph Gibson LJ took his starting point in the dicta of Brandon J of the High Court in THE ANNEFIELD. Brandon J's findings were upheld by the Court of Appeal,

---

[299] The writer's version of the Augthon case has been downloaded from the internet. Therefore, unfortunately, reference to the relevant page of the case cannot be made.

and concur with the position of the law described above, point 4. However, Gibson LJ restricted the dicta from THE ANNEFIELD:

"The propositions stated by Brandon J were not, in my judgment, as stated by him or as stated in the cases from which they were derived, intended to be a statement of rules applicable to the incorporation of an arbitration clause, from one document or contract into another contract by words of reference, in the case of all or any sorts of contract and in all sorts of circumstances."

Conversely, they were tinted by the factual situation in which the dispute had occurred, namely that of incorporating into a negotiable instrument an arbitration agreement from another document, a document that would frequently not be available to the person acquiring the negotiable instrument. The rule deriving from THE ANNEFIELD, that verbal manipulation of an arbitration clause in a charter-party would only be carried out if there was an explicit reference in the bill of lading to that clause, was, according to Gibson LJ, only applicable to the charter-party cases. In that perspective, there was no *general* rule of construction, preventing the incorporation of an arbitration agreement through the use of general words of incorporation[300] – there was just a specific rule, applicable to the charter-party/bill of lading relation, stating that incorporation could not take place if verbal manipulation was required.

According to the learned judge, instead of blindly applying the charter-party authorities outside their scope, one should use the general rules of construction as developed within the relevant field of the law. This was also what had in fact been done in the charter-party cases:

"Thus, in the House of Lords in Thomas v. Portsea, their Lordships were applying, as I understand their speeches, ordinary principles of construction to the particular contract contained in the bill of lading there under consideration with due regard to the nature of that contract and of the circumstances in which it was made."

Gibson LJ set out to apply the ordinary principles of construction of engineering and construction contracts. Still, some consideration had to be paid to the fact that an arbitration agreement bars the parties from taking a dispute to the Courts. In this respect the learned judge found support in the charter-party cases to the extent that those cases did not rely on the negotiability issue.

"The distinction between conditions of a contract which define the rights and obligations of the parties with reference to the subject matter ... on the one hand, and on the other hand, those which con-

---

[300] p. 21.

trol or affect the rights of the parties to enforce those rights and obligations by proceedings at law was, as stated above, emphasised in Thomas v. Portsea. That distinction is as relevant, in my judgment, in a case of this nature about engineering work as it is in a case of charterparty and bill of lading. It provides good reason for requiring that an alleged intention of the parties to exclude the ordinary right of access to the court by an arbitration agreement, which may well include special terms of limitation, be *clearly demonstrated* from the terms of the contract."[301]

Having established that a clear demonstration of intent was necessary, it remained for Gibson LJ to consider whether that intention had been shown to exist to a degree, which would make the necessary modification of the arbitration agreement legitimate. Here Gibson LJ embraced the argument of the appellants that it would be "… perverse …" if the Court was to consider the parties as having effectively incorporated the conditions of the sub-contract, "… suitably modified …", but not as having incorporated the arbitration clause, although it required no other degree of modification. In the case, common standard forms with well-known provisions were referred to on a back-to-back basis. Augthon had been aware of these terms when entering into the contract. This feature alone made the case distinct from the bill of lading situation, where often the holder of the bill of lading would have had no opportunity to make him or herself acquainted with the terms of the underlying charter-party. Also, within the engineering trade, arbitration clauses were common, which was known to the parties. Taking that into consideration, Gibson LJ found that the parties in the AUGTHON case had expressed their intention to incorporate the arbitration clause so clearly that it would be proper for the Courts to manipulate the wording of the arbitration clause in the sub-contract so that it would also apply to the sub-sub-contract.

It was never the law that arbitration agreements could not be incorporated from one document into another by general reference to the first document. One needs only refer to THE MERAK[302] where the Court of Appeal found that general words of reference had in fact incorporated the arbitration agreement in a charter-party into a bill of lading. Gibson LJ's findings may thus not be criticised for assuming that general reference may suffice. However, Gibson's conclusion rests on the view that the somewhat stringent requirements for incorporation to be effective as developed in case law are caused by the Courts paying considerations to the negotiable nature of the bill of lading. Thus, according to Gibson, outside those situations there is ample

---

[301] Emphasis added.

[302] [1964] 2 Lloyd's Law Reports 527 CA.

room to adopt another approach. As put by Jack J, QC, in TRYGG HANSA V. EQUI-TAS:[303]

"... [It] seems to me that the practical outcome of the approach of Lord Justice Ralph Gibson is that outside the bill of lading/charter-party situation a general reference will be effective and an arbitration clause will be modified as to parties if the field is one where arbitrations are common and there are no contra-indications".[304]

This writer shares that interpretation of Gibson's (obiter) findings. In the following the case law will be consulted with view to ascertaining whether the authorities support that the charter-party cases are just that (special rules for the shipping trade based on negotiability-considerations) or whether the rules developed in the charter-party cases are in fact of general applicability.

5.2.2. The negotiability issue in the charter-party cases – weighty or not?

Obviously, one may regard all the cases where the incorporation of an arbitration agreement from a charter-party into a bill of lading was refused as providing a de facto protection of the bill of lading, and as such, as a de facto regard to negotiability considerations. This approach, however, is erroneous. What must be ascertained is if, and if so to what extent, the regard to the negotiability of the bill of lading has been decisive in any of the above cases.

THOMAS V. PORTSEA[305] was decided by four members of the House of Lords. Two of these, Lord Loreburn and Lord Gorell, decided the case purely on general principles of construction of contracts without regard to the negotiability of the bill of lading. Lord Atkinson concurred with the vota of Lord Loreburn but added his famous speach:

"... when it is sought to introduce into a document like a bill of lading – a negotiable instrument – a clause such as this arbitration clause, not germane to ... the proper subject-matters with which the bill of lading is conversant, - this should be done by distinct and specific words, and not by such general words as those written in the margin of the bill of lading in this case".[306]

---

[303] [1998] 2 Lloyd's Law Reports 439 QBD.

[304] [1998] 2 Lloyd's Law Reports 439 QBD, p. 447, col. 1.

[305] [1912] A. C. 1 HL. Appeal of (1911) P. 54 CA, THE PORTSMOUTH.

[306] p. 6.

Considering that Lord Atkinson agreed with the findings and conclusions of Lord Loreburn, the here cited regard to the negotiability is hardly an indispensable part of Lord Atkinson's reasoning. Rather it must be understood as a further argument for the conclusion already reached by Lord Loreburn. Conversely, the vota of Lord Robson attaches considerable weight to the negotiable nature of the bill of lading. Lord Robson's starting point is that the putative arbitration clauses discussed in the case should not be insensible when incorporated into the bill of lading. In the case, he finds the clauses dealing with disputes arising under the charter-party will need quite some modification so as not to be insensible if introduced into the legal relationship between the parties under the bill of lading. However, Lord Robson does not discard the possibility that incorporation may be effective for that reason alone. Instead, he finds in conclusion that considering that the bill of lading is a negotiable instrument, one must be very explicit and precise if one wishes to enlarge the obligations or re-duce the rights arising out of it. In the case a sufficient clarity had not been achieved, and Lord Robson therefore concluded with the other Lords that the arbitration clause had not been incorporated.[307]

The case thus reviewed it is clear that the protection of the negotiable bill of lading does not *in itself* carry the conclusions of the House. Lords Atkinson and Robson do find that regard should be taken to the negotiability – Lord Robson to the greatest ex-tent. Still, the finding of the House of Lords does not rest upon the issue.

Also in THE FEDERAL BULKER[308] the negotiability of bills of lading and its impact upon the requirements for the incorporation of arbitration clauses in charter-parties into bills of lading became subject to scrutiny. There, it was said by Bingham LJ that:

"Generally speaking, the English law of contract has taken a benevolent view of the use of general words to incorporate by reference standard terms to be found elsewhere. But in the present field a dif-ferent, and stricter, rule has developed, especially where the incorporation of arbitration clauses is concerned. The reason no doubt is that a bill of lading is a negotiable commercial instrument and may come into the hands of a foreign party with no knowledge and no ready means of knowledge of the terms of the charter-party. The cases show that a strict test of incorporation having, for better or worse, been laid down, the Courts have in general defended this rule with some tenacity in the inter-ests of commercial certainty."[309]

---

[307] p. 11.

[308] [1989] 1 Lloyd's Law Reports 103 CA.

[309] p. 105, col. 2.

These findings form a part of the general introduction to Bingham LJ's statement of the law in the case. They are not repeated in the Learned Judge's decision. Thus, it is hard to determine if, and if so to what extent, the regard to the negotiability has affected his conclusion, and indeed the conclusions of the Court of Appeal. What can be determined, though, is that the other judges did not specifically mention the negotiability issue. In any case, the subject matter of THE FEDERAL BULKER is not whether verbal manipulation may or may not be carried out but instead whether a reference to "conditions" is a reference to arbitration and other boilerplate clauses. Bingham LJ's reference to the interest of commercial certainty must be seen in that light. It is this writer's view that the Court of Appeal's conclusion in THE FEDERAL BULKER provides no authority, and indeed no support, for the contention that as a matter of principle, the strict requirements for incorporation found in the charter-party cases do not apply to other circumstances.

The Court of Appeal also kept the negotiability in mind in THE MERAK.[310]

"The bill of lading is a commercial document to be used by commercial people. It is a negotiable instrument which may be acquired by a party who has no knowledge of the charter-party to which it refers, and the Court should be mindful of this circumstance."[311]

However, in the case a clear and wide incorporation clause had been opted for. Therefore, to understand the bill of lading, the holder of the bill of lading had to refer himself to the charter-party, and there select the applicable clauses.[312] Also Davies LJ expresses obiter that, as a general rule, a bill of lading, being a negotiable instrument, had to be construed according to its terms without reference to "… any extrinsic facts or documents."[313] But, the learned judge found that in the case that rule did not apply, since a valid reference to the charter-party was made, and furthermore, since the plaintiffs, contesting the arbitration agreement, were already parties to the same charter-party.[314]

---

[310] [1964] 2 Lloyd's Law Reports 527 CA.

[311] Sellers LJ, p. 521, col. 2.

[312] Sellers LJ, p. 521, col. 2.

[313] Davies LJ. p. 534, col. 1.

[314] See the discussion of THE MERAK above, point 2.3.3.

It is noteworthy, that having taken regard to the negotiability of the bill of lading, a general incorporation clause was still found to be adequate. As mentioned above in point 3.3.2, the facts of THE MERAK are somewhat out of the ordinary. One should therefore be careful not to apply the findings of the Court of Appeal in that case too generally. It would be wrong to deduce from the case that even a party who has acquired a bill of lading by negotiation should put it upon himself to track down the relevant charter-party to ascertain whether any of the non-germane provisions there printed are worded thus that they may apply to the bill of lading.

The House of Lords' judgment in THE MIRAMAR obviously effects a protection of the bill of lading's value as a document of title although the Lords did not express themselves in negotiability terms. Even so, THE MIRAMAR cannot be regarded as an authority that the negotiability question has been paramount in the charter-party cases, and that general incorporation therefore normally will be effective in other cases. Firstly, of course, the conclusion of the House of Lords in THE MIRAMAR is that under the particular circumstances of the case even a provision that was germane to the subject-matter of the contract of carriage was not incorporated into the bill of lading by means of general reference. This is quite the opposite view of the one contended by Gibson LJ in the AUGTHON case. Secondly, as found by both the High Court in THE NAI MATTEINI and the Court of Appeal in THE NERANO, the facts of the case in THE MIRAMAR were so extreme as to preclude any general principle to be deduced from it, except, maybe, the principle that a general reference to other documents will not in all cases and circumstances effect the incorporation of provisions germane to the subject-matter of the parties' contract.

Not all the charter-party cases discuss the negotiability question. The ones that do, do not provide clear guidance as to what regard should be had to the bill of lading as a document of title. However, one thing can be concluded, namely that the charter-party cases thus reviewed hardly support that the stringent requirements found there, especially as far as the question of verbal manipulation is concerned, are due only to the regard to the negotiable nature of the bill of lading, and the general interest in protecting its value as a document of title. Still, if those considerations do not explain the rules, one must ascertain which considerations do, and whether those considerations are generally applicable or not. At this point of the argument it is appropriate to return once again to the Augthon case.

5.2.3. Sir John Megaw's findings in the Augthon case
In the AUGTHON case both Judges found that the requirement for a written arbitration agreement had not been fulfilled. In the relationship between the parties a sufficiently clear written direction to where the arbitration clause could be found was lacking.

Megaw LJ also found against the claim that an arbitration agreement had been entered into for another reason, namely, that the general words of incorporation used did not suffice. The speech of the learned judge strongly suggests that general words of incorporation may never suffice. This seems contrary to the authority from THE MERAK.[315] Also, Megaw seems to reject the possibility of verbal manipulation, even if in the case the incorporation had been sufficient. This corresponds badly to the precedence from THE RENA K[316] (although this was a High Court case and as such not binding on the Court of Appeal) and THE ANNEFIELD.[317] As a consequence, the dictum of Megaw LJ has been largely ignored. Still, though one may differ as to these issues, Megaw's argument is remarkable for other reasons, and will be examined here.

To reach his conclusion that a specific reference was necessary in the construction case, Megaw first had to dispense with the argument that the existing case law was based on negotiability considerations. This he does thus:

"It is, however, important to note that it is implicit in the speeches that other clauses of the charter-party could validly be incorporated into the bill of lading by the use of general words, such … as clauses which governed 'shipment or carriage or delivery or the terms upon which delivery is to be made or taken.' These might obviously include clauses of substantial commercial importance – for example, exception clauses, demurrage clauses, provisions for hire and such like. These, it is clear, are not to be shut out from incorporation merely because the bill of lading is a negotiable instrument, as well as a document evidencing a contract, passing from hand to hand.

Hence, it follows that the reason for excluding an arbitration clause is certainly not confined to the special features of a charter-party/bill of lading relationship, nor to the fact that the bill of lading is a document of title."[318]

If the charter-party cases were founded on the regard to the protection of the negotiable bill of lading, a general rule that other provisions could be incorporated by general reference was illogical. The raison d'être behind the rules had to be found elsewhere.

By entering into arbitration agreements the parties were precluded from taking disputes covered by the agreement to the Courts. The wording used to obtain such a legal effect had to be clear. The requirement in the Arbitration Acts for written

---

[315] [1964] 2 Lloyd's Law Reports 527 CA.

[316] [1978] 1 Lloyd's Law Reports 545 QBD.

[317] [1971] 1 Lloyd's Law Reports 1 CA.

[318] Emphasis added.

agreement also focused on the need for certainty. But the main reason for the conclusions reached in case law was, according to Sir John Megaw LJ, the distinct nature of the arbitration agreement, or in other words, the rules were founded in the doctrine of separability.

"[The] status of a so-called 'arbitration clause' included in a contract of any nature is different from other types of clauses because it constitutes a 'self-contained contract collateral or ancillary to' the substantive contract.[319] ... *This status of 'self-contained contract' exists irrespective of the type of substantive contract.* ... If this self-contained contract is to be incorporated, it must be expressly referred to in the document which is relied on as the incorporating writing. It is not incorporated by a mere reference to the terms and conditions of the contract to which the arbitration clause constitutes a collateral contract. ... *The distinction which Thomas v Portsea drew between the arbitration clause and other clauses of the charter-party applies equally to the arbitration clause of the engineering sub-contract in the present case. That, in my opinion, is decisive of the appeal.*"

According to Megaw LJ, the explanation for the position of the law as put forward in the charter-party cases is that an arbitration clause is an independent "self-contained" contract. This applies to all arbitration agreements regardless of the substantive situation that they are purported to cover. Thus, the charter-party cases do not provide a special aspect of arbitration law. They provide the general rule. Colman J later, in EXCESS INSURANCE V. MANDER,[320] concurs with this point of view, as does Jack J QC in TRYGG HANSA V. EQUITAS.[321] Also, considering the relevant case law, it is supported by this writer.

Having arrived at that conclusion, Megaw LJ found that when wanting to incorporate an arbitration agreement from one document into another, one must refer directly to the arbitration clause itself for it to be incorporated.

Generally, writers have found Megaw's conclusion in the case to indicate that arbitration agreements may only be incorporated by specific reference.[322] As mentioned above this would be in conflict with THE MERAK. However, there is no reason why THE MERAK cannot stand untarnished. Firstly, and most obviously, it could be argued that the findings of Megaw LJ were obiter, and thus could not overrule the authority from THE MERAK. (Megaw had found that the form of reference did not fulfil

---

[319] Here Megan LJ refers to the dicta of Lord Diplock in BREMER VULCAN V. SOUTH INDIA SHIPPING [1981] A. C. 909.

[320] [1995] L.R.L.R. 358.

[321] [1998] 2 Lloyd's Law Reports 439 QBD, p. 447, col. 2.

[322] *Rutherford/Sims (1996),* p. 55; *Merkin (2000),* p. 30; *Harris (2000),* p. 78.

the requirement for writing in the Arbitration Act 1950. The case fell already for that reason). Secondly, and most importantly, the authorities do not necessarily clash. According to Megaw, a reference in a contract to "contract A" (the substantive rules of a contract) would not incorporate "contract B" (the arbitration clause), even if the two contracts were printed in the same document. It does not follow from the logic of that argument that a reference to the document itself, including any provision there printed, cannot be acceptable. That was the case in THE MERAK.

Neither logic nor the regard to commerce requires that the dictum of Megaw LJ should be interpreted so as to preclude incorporation by general reference. In this work, therefore, no such interpretation will be employed.

Instead, the dictum will be used to place the charter-party cases in the right systematic box, namely the box concerned with the general law on arbitration agreements. Apart from that the dictum provides emphasis on the fact that when incorporating arbitration clauses one should make sure that the incorporation one has made or purported to make will in fact include the arbitration clause when that clause is viewed as a separate, separable, self-contained contract. No further effects need be deduced from the learned judge's conclusion.

6. Conclusions and the prospects *de lege ferenda*

It is this writer's conclusion that English law on the incorporation of arbitration agreements and clauses is as described in the charter-party cases. The cases are, as pointed out by Megaw LJ, founded on the regard to the arbitration agreement being a distinct and separable contract. They are also to a degree founded on the regard to certainty in a situation where it is alleged that a party has had the intention of excluding him or herself from going to the Courts with a given dispute. It cannot be shown that the cases, in addition to that, rest on the regard to the protection of the bill of lading as a negotiable instrument and document of title. Instead, the "charter-party cases" present a generally applicable regulation of the question of incorporation. At present there is no room for applying a different, less stringent, approach where other documents and/or legal relations are concerned. Until new case law, which can be seen to overrule the existing, presents itself, the position of the law remains as stated above in point 4.

To this writer there can be no doubt that the doctrine of separability and the protection of a party allegedly having agreed to oust the Courts' jurisdiction in a certain matter do not require that arbitration agreements may only be incorporated by specific reference. The possibility reserved in THE MERAK for incorporation by general reference must be maintained. But even so: Can English law, as described above, cater for the needs of the players in the market or is it too restrictive?

To answer that question one should distinguish between two situations: On the one hand, the situations where reference is made to a standard form of contract, as for example when the salvor and the person in need of assistance agree that the salvage operation should be subject to the regulation in Lloyd's Open Form. In such a situation, THE MERAK provides authority that a general reference should suffice, provided that the reference is worded so as to encompass the standard form in its entirety and not just its rules of substance.

The real difficulty, on the other hand, arises when one refers to a contract already in existence between other parties. If one has not made a specific reference to the arbitration agreement, the sought incorporation will be likely to fail the second test of THE MERAK, namely the requirement that the language used in the clause referred to should encompass, or at least be reasonably applicable to, the dispute to which it is sought introduced. Certainly, arbitration agreements in such contracts may be incorporated by specific reference, but is there a need for the clauses also to be incorporated by a general reference?

There does not seem to be a real need for the possibility of incorporating arbitration clauses by general reference in these situations in the maritime trade. The actual use of tramp bills of lading seems to be decreasing. The construction is not used within the container trade, neither is it the norm within liner transport of general cargo. In charter-party based transport of goods belonging to the charterer, which are not intended for sale, the situation only arises if the carrier has to take in outside tonnage. Thus, generally, it is only in transport of bulk cargo under tramp bills of lading that the problem presents itself. Numerically, one may expect the situations where the problem arises to be comparatively few. Also, one must consider whether there is a general need to introduce the conditions of the charter-party into the bill of lading. Obviously, within free trade the carrier has good reasons for introducing exceptions, disclaimers and limitations of liability into the bill of lading contract. However, transport in free trade is decreasing with the current international trend in legislation where mandatory rules to the benefit of the cargo interests are being introduced, often with a lex fori choice of law provision regarding cargo going in and out of the jurisdiction. Thus, the idea of one regime of liability both as regards the relation owner/charterer, owner/bill of lading holder and charterer/bill of lading holder is generally illusory. When within carriage of goods by sea a genuine demand for change cannot be seen to exist.

In the reinsurance market and in the building and construction trades, contracting on back-to-back conditions is a widespread phenomenon. In the reinsurance market to ensure compatibility between the risks insured in all layers, and in the building and construction trades for reasons of convenience and to avoid incompatible recourse claims. Furthermore, in the building and construction trades a tradition for additional oral agreements exists.

The English law on incorporation of arbitration clauses as presented in the charter-party cases does seem too rigid as to provide a satisfactory regulation within trades where a legitimate need to contract on back-to-back terms exist, and where such contracts are in fact common.

The requirement for specific reference for the incorporation of arbitration agreements into bills of lading in the Nordic Maritime Code sec. 310 (sec. 13:60), as referred to in sec. 311 (sec. 13:61), only applies if the holder of the bill of lading is in good faith as regards the arbitration clause in question.[323] If knowledge of the arbitration agreement already exists there is no need to protect the holder of the bill of lading. The same line of thought lies behind the dictum of Davies JL in THE MERAK. In the case, he found the requirement for specific reference inapplicable as the parties to the bill of lading already were, or ought to have been, aware of the arbitration clause.

It is suggested that in future cases where it may be established that the party challenging the arbitration agreement knew or ought to have known of the agreement, the Courts should take that knowledge into account. In certain cases that knowledge may be considered sufficient to establish an intention to arbitrate as between the parties. If it proves impossible to meet the requirement for written agreement found in the Arbitration Act 1996 s. 5, the arbitration agreement may be accepted under the Court's inherent jurisdiction.

Employing such an approach would mean a shift from focusing mainly on the arbitration agreement as a separate agreement, to focusing on the need to protect parties who contract out of the protection of the Courts via entering into an arbitration agreement. If that shift in focus is carried out, it is obvious that the need to protect a party who already knew of the arbitration agreement is negligible. Also, so far, the English Courts have not differentiated the requirements for entering into arbitration agreements in accordance with the trade in which the arbitration agreement is purported to operate. Good reasons for this may easily be found, as uncertainties are obviously avoided through such a unified approach. However, maybe it is time for a change – especially within trades where back-to-back conditions are legitimate and numerous.

---

[323] See below, Chapter V, § 2, point 4.2.

§ 4. Norwegian law on the conclusion of arbitration agreements

1. Introduction

So far, Norwegian law has provided an example of a stringent approach to arbitration agreements. As mentioned above in Chapter I, § 1, point 1, this writer found that certain excursions into a regime with stringent formal requirements would be beneficial to the work, bearing in mind that the work deals with the law of two regimes with lax requirements as to the form of arbitration agreements. In the following, therefore, the formal conditions that must be fulfilled for arbitration agreements to be recognised under national Norwegian law will be described and discussed.

A discussion of the formal requirements does not provide the full picture of the law on the conclusion of arbitration agreements. The formal requirements exist in symbiosis with the interpretation of the arbitration agreement. It has already been shown, in § 2, that under Danish law the issue of conclusion and the issue of interpretation often merge, this mainly being due to the lack of any formal requirements under Danish law. This chapter, although mainly concentrating on the formal criteria, will therefore also provide a brief overview of the newer Norwegian cases on the interpretation of the arbitration agreement. Lacking that, many aspects of the comparison to Danish and English law will be lost.

Arbitration agreements, procedures and awards are governed by the Norwegian Code of Procedure Chapter 32. The Code was given in 1915 and the language used in the sections bear the mark of age. However, as the legislators opted for a rather modest regulation consisting of only 21 sections mainly dealing with the question of the relationship between arbitration and the ordinary Courts, Chapter 32 has survived relatively untarnished until now. Presently, however, the Norwegian Code of Procedure is undergoing a total revision. The mandate of the legislative committee includes the evaluation of whether a revision of the regulation of arbitration is beneficial.[324] The legislative committee has suggested that in the new Code of Procedure, the regulation of arbitration should be taken out and left to a separate Arbitration Act based on the UNCITRAL Model Law.[325] The committee's suggestions were published on December 20th 2001 in NOU 2001:32, dealing with the draft new Code of Procedure, and NOU 2001:33, presenting the Draft Norwegian Arbitration Act. In the Draft Arbitration Act the committee has abandoned any formal requirements for arbitration agreements, consumer relations apart, thus dramatically altering the position of Norwegian law regarding the formal requirements for arbitration agreements dramatically. At this point, it seems quite certain that the new Norwegian Arbitration Act will become a reality. Therefore, the proposed regulation will be discussed in quite some detail.

Still, in the following the main issues to be discussed are the existing formal conditions for arbitration agreements, as they have been presented in the Norwegian Code of Procedure and case law. This will take place in point 2. In point 3, certain choice of law problems will be discussed, whereas in point 4 the possibility of accepting an arbitration agreement under other rules than the Norwegian Code of Procedure will be touched upon. In point 5, an overview of the way in which the Norwegian Courts have interpreted arbitration agreements will be given, enabling a deliberation upon the pros and cons of a stringent formal requirement to take place in point 6. Finally, the proposed regulation in the Draft Norwegian Arbitration Act will be discussed in point 7.

2. The Norwegian Code of Procedure sec. 452

2.1. The basic rule

The Norwegian Code of Procedure Chapter 32 provides the general, statutory framework for the regulation of arbitration and arbitration agreements under Norwegian Law. The regulation is supervened by special rules such as, for example, the Norwegian Maritime Code sec. 311 and 310 and the Norwegian Carriage of Goods by Road Act sec. 44. Even if the rules on arbitration and arbitration agreements are

---

[324] Se http:///www.tvistemalsutvalget.net/mandat.htm, point 14 in particular. (Printed in NOU 2001:33, p. 19, point 2.3).

[325] NOU 2001:33, p. 20, point 2.8.

placed in the Code of Procedure, Chapter 32 should be regarded as independent of the general rules of the Code. One cannot necessarily apply other provisions of the Code of Procedure by analogy if Chapter 32 is silent. On the contrary, if an issue is not directly regulated in the code, one may assume that it is left open for the parties' agreement or the tribunal's decision, as the case may be.[326]

The basic rule on the validity and legal effects of arbitration agreements under Norwegian law is found in the Norwegian Code of Procedure sec. 452.

The Norwegian Code of Procedure sec. 452[327]

The parties may agree that a dispute of law should be settled by arbitration, when they are free to dispose with the subject matter of the dispute. Under the same condition the parties may agree that future disputes of law, which may arise out of a particular matter of law, should be determined by arbitration.

The arbitration agreement must be concluded in writing. If the parties have submitted themselves to negotiations before the arbitral tribunal, it is nevertheless of no consequence that the agreement has not been concluded in writing.

Without the consent of the counter-party, a dispute of law cannot be brought before the Courts if it, according to an agreement, should have been determined by arbitration.

According to the Norwegian Code of Procedure sec. 452, sub-sec. 3, a dispute that falls within an agreement to arbitrate can only be heard by the Courts if the parties consent to it. Otherwise, a valid agreement to arbitrate is a hindrance for dispute resolution before the Courts. Indeed, the arbitration agreement renders the Courts incompetent to deal with the subject matter of a dispute that is covered by the agreement, and the Court will rule to dismiss the case under the Norwegian Code of Procedure sec. 137, sub-sec. 2.[328] The form of the consent is governed by the Norwegian Code of Procedure sec. 452, sub-sec. 2, 1st sentence. It is the requirements as to the form of the parties' consent that will be at the centre of attention in the following.

The Norwegian Code of Procedure sec. 452, sub-sec. 2, 1st sentence states that arbitration agreements must be concluded in writing. The only exception is if the parties have entered into negotiations before the arbitration tribunal and thereby implicitly accepted the tribunal's competence.

According to the *travaux préparatoires,* the requirement for writing has been inserted into the Code to ensure that arbitration agreements only are accepted as de-

---

[326] *Schei (1998),* p. 1155.

[327] Writer's translation.

[328] By "kjendelse".

rogatory by the Courts if the parties intend to arbitrate their dispute, as opposed to having a survey carried out, for example.[329] This has lead to a stringent interpretation of the requirement for writing both in case law and in most legal literature. As put by *Lindboe:*

"The document [containing the arbitration clause] must be signed, *or* the parties must have acceded to it in writing in such a way that [it provides] entirely convincing proof that the document and its substance is binding upon both parties."[330]

However, sec. 452, sub-sec. 2, 1st sentence only states that the arbitration agreement must be "entered into in writing". It does not offer any directions as to how the requirement for writing may be fulfilled. Thus, to establish what is the real impact of sec. 452 one must turn to the case law that has developed under the provision.

2.2. Case law on the formal requirement

2.2.1. A written consent

Generally, the Courts' interpretation of the Norwegian Code of Procedure sec. 452, sub-sec. 2, 1st sentence has been strict. In a leading case, Rt. 1962.1215 NSC, SKARVØY II, a plea that the case should be dismissed from the Courts due to an arbitration clause was rejected. The facts of the case were these: The owners of the vessel Skarvøy II claimed a salvage award from the owners of M/S Windsor, for assistance given to M/S Windsor during an incident at sea. The owners of M/S Windsor claimed that the case should be dismissed as both vessels were insured in insurance unions, which were members of another insurance union, the so-called "Møreringen". It followed from the rules of the "Møreringen", that members of the union had a duty to aid each other in case of an emergency, and that a committee should determine the compensation due for such aid.

---

[329] Indst. O. XV (1912), p. 157.

[330] *Lindboe (1944),* p. 42: "Dokumentet må være undertegnet eller partene må ha gitt det sin skriftlige tilslutning på en slik måte, at det foreligger et helt utvilsomt bevis for at dokumentet med innhold er forpliktende for begge parter."

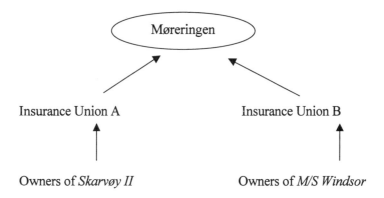

The Norwegian Supreme Court did not find that the rules of the "Mørering", as agreed amongst the mutual insurance unions that were members of it, constituted any *written* consent to arbitration as between persons or entities that were insured in the mutual insurance unions. For further elaboration the Norwegian Supreme Court referred to the minority vota of the Norwegian Court of Appeal. The minority of the Court of Appeal had stated:

"It is … clear that the arbitration provision is inserted both into the rules [of the Mørering] and in the printed text of the [insurance] policy, but as far as I can see … Skarvøy [has not given a] written consent to the clause. The fact that Skarvøy's owner has been invited to [the] general assembly at which the clause was agreed, that he never protested against the clause, and that he by his membership possibly can be said to have agreed to the clause by his actions, is not the deciding factor for me, as the law requires a *written* consent to the agreement."[331]

The agreement to arbitrate had in the case been inserted as a clause in the rules of the Mørering. Thus, the *provision on arbitration* existed in writing. However, the *consent* did not. Interpreting the requirement that "the arbitration agreement must be entered into in writing" in Norwegian Code of Procedure sec. 452, sub-sec. 2, 1st sentence in accordance with the findings of the Norwegian Supreme Court in the SKARVØY II case, one must conclude the following: To satisfy the requirements under Norwegian law, an arbitration agreement must not only *exist* in writing – the consent to arbitration should also be *given* in writing. The most obvious way to give consent in writing is to sign the arbitration agreement, but the findings of the Su-

---

[331] Writer's translation. Judge's own emphasis.

preme Court in the SKARVØY II case cannot be drawn so far as to render a signature indispensable – there are other ways in which one can give consent in writing. Still, the emphasis on writing displayed in SKARVØY II does suggest that cases accepting arbitration agreements on other grounds than signature may be rare. On the other hand, given that the parties have indeed entered into their agreement by signing a document, the ruling of the Norwegian Supreme Court in SKARVØY II does not rule out that arbitration clauses incorporated by reference could be effective.

2.2.2. Incorporating by reference – establishing the parameters

The Norwegian Supreme Court dealt with the issue of incorporation by reference in two cases from 1991. One or both of the cases have been referred to in all subsequent cases on the incorporation of arbitration agreements by reference, making a thorough analysis of the cases proper. Before dealing with those cases, however, two cases from the fifties will be touched upon. In ND 1957.366 NCA, JALNA, the Norwegian Court of Appeal held, *obiter*,[332] that a reference in a bill of lading to a charter-party did not satisfy the requirement for writing in sec. 452, as the issuance of a bill of lading was a unilateral transaction. The Court of Appeal found that entering into an arbitration agreement required the participation of both parties.[333] In the same direction goes the Court of First Instance's finding in the case ND 1953.703 NCA, OSTMARK. In that case the Court of First Instance held that the shippers were not, in a dispute between themselves and the owners, bound by an arbitration clause in the charter-party between the owners and the charterers. The Court of First Instance found that the requirement for writing in sec. 452 presupposed that a written arbitration agreement had been entered into between the parties now in dispute.[334] These rulings have not been overruled.[335] Thus, even when considering the incorporation cases, the writ-

---

[332] ND 1957.366 NCA, JALNA. The findings of the Court of Appeal were *obiter*, as the parties had conceded that the proper law of the arbitration agreement was English law, and that under English law, the reference made in the bill of lading to the charter party ("on payment of Freight and all other conditions as per Charter-Party") was not effective to incorporate the arbitration clause in the charter party into the bill of lading.

[333] ND 1956.366 NCA, JALNA, p. 369.

[334] ND 53.703 NCA, OSTMARK, p. 718. The dispute regarding the arbitration agreement was not appealed to the Court of Appeal. Therefore only the Court of First Instance's ruling is referred to here.

[335] It should be noted, that presently arbitration agreements in tramp bills of lading is governed by the Scandinavian Maritime Code sec. 311, sub-sec. 3 cf. sec. 310 sub-sec. 3. Thus, the actual problem presented in the cases has now been solved.

ten consent of both parties is still required. It is therefore necessary that the main agreement, in which the reference to a set of standard conditions is made, is concluded in a way that fulfils the requirements set out in sec. 452, sub-sec. 2, 1st sentence. Otherwise, incorporation by reference will not be accepted.

Having pointed this out, we will revert to the two 1991-cases.

In both cases, the parties had signed an agreement that referred to a set of standard conditions. Thus, the problems touched upon in the JALNA and OSTMARK cases did not occur. Instead the cases concern the issue of when a reference made in the main document to a set of standard conditions may be effective so as to incorporate the arbitration agreement in those standard conditions into the parties' main agreement. In both cases, the Norwegian Supreme Court stated that such incorporation might satisfy the requirements of the Norwegian Code of Procedure sec. 452, sub-sec. 2, 1st sentence. However, whether this was the case or not should be decided after an examination of the specific facts of the case.

RT. 1991.635 NSC, SITAS V. HØGLUND

Dispute arose between Sitas and Høglund regarding the contract of sales of a machine. Sitas claimed that the contract should be cancelled, and that Høglund was liable in damages towards Sitas for breach of the contract. Høglund, on the other hand, claimed that the case should be dismissed as the sales agreement contained a clause according to which the standard form NLM 71[336] applied. NLM 71 contains general conditions for the sale, delivery and fitting of mechanical and electrical machinery within Denmark, Finland, Norway and Sweden. In article 67, the NLM 71 provides that disputes arising out of the contract shall be arbitrated according to the law on arbitration in force at the place of residence of the seller under the contract of sales.

The contract was dismissed from both the Court of First Instance and the Norwegian Court of Appeal due to the arbitration clause. Sitas appealed the dismissals to the Supreme Court.

The Supreme Court held that the requirement for writing might be satisfied, given certain circumstances, by the parties' signing of an agreement that referred to a set of standard conditions, containing an arbitration clause. However, whether the agreement should be accepted or not depended upon certain parameters, including the whole procedure of acceptance, who the parties were and the extent to which the standard conditions were used in the particular trade.

In the case before the Court the reference to NLM had been highlighted in the last paragraph of the sales contract, immediately above the parties' signatures. Also, both the buyer and the seller were dealing within their trades, and therefore the parties were considered to be on an equal footing as regarded the use of the NLM 71. Finally, the NLM 71 was extensively used regarding deliveries of machinery within

---

[336] General Conditions for the Supply of Machines and other Mechanical, Electrical and Electronic Equipment, issued in 1971 by the organisations for the engineering industries in Denmark, Finland, Norway and Sweden.

Scandinavia, and had been agreed by the Norwegian Workshop's Union. In such a case sec. 452 did not require that the standard conditions should be attached to the sales contract.

Thus, the requirement for written consent in sec. 452, sub-sec. 1 had been fulfilled, and the case was dismissed from the Courts.

RT. 1991.773 NSC, ØSTREM ET AL V. BYGGESERVICE

A building contract held a provision that NS 3401, a standard form often used within contract work, applied to a contract for the construction of an estate of terraced houses. Dispute arose, and the clients (Østrem and others) initiated proceedings before the Court of First Instance. The case was dismissed from the Court according to an arbitration clause in NS 3401. This was also the conclusion of the Court of Appeal. On appeal, Norwegian Supreme Court found, as in SITAS V. HØGLUND, that as a starting point, it might be sufficient to satisfy the requirement for writing in the Norwegian Code of Procedure sec. 452, sub-sec. 2, that a reference was made in the parties' agreement to a standard form containing the arbitration clause in question. Still, one had to take into consideration how the agreement had come about, what the position of the parties' were, and how well known or used the standard document in question was. In the case the clients were in fact a group of consumers, building their respective family homes. However, the NS 3401 standard form was regularly used in contract work, and the Court found that the contract had been entered into after genuine negotiations between the parties, during which the clients had had the opportunity to make themselves acquainted with the contents of NS 3401. Accordingly, the Norwegian Supreme Court found no reason to consider the arbitration clause in NS 3401 void, and the case was dismissed from the Courts.

In the two cases, the Norwegian Supreme Court spells out which parameters should be considered in the determination of whether an arbitration agreement in a standard form had been incorporated into the parties' main agreement by reference. The parameters are:

1. The procedure and circumstances regarding the formation of the agreement,
2. the position of the parties and their knowledge of the trade, and
3. the extent to which the standard form is used within the particular trade.

In both 1991-cases, the standard conditions referred to were widely used within the respective trades. Therefore the Supreme Court concentrated itself upon weight and interrelation of the procedure and circumstances regarding the formation of the agreement vis a vis the parties' position and knowledge of the trade.

In SITAS V. HØGLUND, the reference to NML 71 had been printed immediately above the parties' signatures on the main document. In such a case, the standard document needed not be attached to the main document for the arbitration clause to be effective. This applied even if Sitas was a manufacturing workshop ordering a machine as a one-off occasion, whereas manufacturing and selling machines was Høglund's only business. Equally, in ØSTREM ET AL V. BYGGESERVICE, the Court stressed the fact that real negotiations had taken place between Byggeservice and a group of clients, here named Østrem et al, and that under those negotiations, examples of NS 3401 had been available to the clients. Thus, they could easily have made themselves acquainted with the terms if they had so wished. Under those circumstances, the Court did not pay any attention to the fact that Østrem et al were in fact a group of consumers, building their family homes.

In both cases, it was the circumstances and procedure under which the contract was formed that settled the issue, leaving the position of the parties to play a less significant role. However, in cases where the standard document in question is not commonly used, the position of the parties may be of more importance. Supposing, for example, that Høglund's standard document had referred to a more obscure set of standard conditions, the Court might very well have paid more attention to the fact that Sitas only bought machinery on rare occasions.

Having read SITAS V. HØGLUND and ØSTREM ET AL V. BYGGESERVICE it is clear that there is a two-tier test to be applied when deciding if an arbitration agreement should be considered incorporated by reference. First, the main agreement has to be concluded in a way that fulfils the criteria set out in the Norwegian Code of Procedure sec. 452. Having established that, the three above-mentioned parameters should be evaluated. However, it is not totally clear from the 1991-cases, what the parameters are a test of. In both SITAS V. HØGLUND and ØSTREM ET AL V. BYGGESERVICE it seems that it is the bargaining powers of the parties that are at the centre of the Court's attentions. It was clear, that neither Østrem nor Sitas had been in a position where they were unable to refuse contracting under the conditions now in dispute. In that respect, the standard conditions were not "contracts of adhesion". The cases can thus be read to support that the issue is settled primarily on objective criteria such as the parties' position and the way in which the contract was negotiated and concluded, rather than subjective criteria such as the knowledge the parties had or ought to have had. A purely objective test is nevertheless not workable in all cases. If one disregards the de facto knowledge the parties have and bases oneself purely on objective criteria one will not always get a balanced decision. Fortunately, in Rt. 1999.1532 NSC, TINE V. LØKEN, (considered at length immediately below) the Norwegian Supreme Court gave directions as to the interpretation of the 1991-cases. The Supreme Court held:

"It is obligatory that the parties by the signing of the document have consented to arbitration, see Rt. 1962.1215 NSC [SKARVØY II]. It is however sufficient that the parties have signed a document where reference is made to another document, containing the arbitration clause, cf. Rt. 1991.773 NSC [ØSTREM ET AL V. BYGGESERVICE]. But it is required that the parties knew, ought to have known, or had good reason to make themselves acquainted with the document containing the arbitration clause.

Regarding the question of what the parties ought to have known, it will be of relevance what trades-manship and knowledge of the trade the [first party] had reason to believe [the other party] had."

Thus, it is in fact a subjective criterion that lies at the bottom of the test in the incorporation cases. In ØSTREM ET AL V. BYGGESERVICE, Østrem and the other clients had both good reason and ample opportunity to make themselves acquainted with the document, but they chose not to. Considering also that the standard document referred to was widely used within the trade, the incorporation by reference was accepted. In SITAS V. HØGLUND, Høglund could reasonably expect Sitas to know of the standard conditions. Partly, as the conditions were the most used conditions in Scandinavia, partly as Høglund had referred to the conditions immediately above the signatures on the main document. Taking into account Høglund's expectations, it was proper to find that Sitas ought to have known of the conditions, and the arbitration agreement in them.

The three objective criteria given in the 1991-cases, namely the procedure and circumstances regarding the formation of the agreement, the position of the parties and their general knowledge of the trade, and the extent to which the standard form was used within the particular trade, are thus parameters given to establish the more subjective criteria, namely whether the parties knew, ought to have known, or had good reason to make themselves acquainted with the conditions containing the arbitration clause.

Apart from the initial requirement for a written consent to the main agreement, the test applied to the incorporation of arbitration agreements under Norwegian law does thus not differ much from the test applied when discussing the general rule for accepting arbitration agreements under Danish law.[337] As such, it is just a condensed version of the general rules of contract law that apply when one wants to establish, whether a standard document is a part of the parties' agreement.

2.2.3. Emphasis on signature

Summing up at this point, Norwegian Courts have accepted arbitration agreements as valid under sec. 452, sub-sec. 1, 1st sentence only if *both parties* have given their *written consent* to arbitration. This consent may be given *directly,* for example by signing the agreement that contains the arbitration clause, or *indirectly,* by signing an agreement that incorporates (a standard form containing) the arbitration clause by reference. However, case law after the two 1991-cases does not *necessarily* require, that a signature is given. One can only extract from case law that the agreement must

---

[337] See above § 2, point 4.2.4.

be consented to in writing. Even so, the requirement for a mutual written consent when interpreted this narrowly is not a very workable one and writers of legal literature have attempted to reduce potential undesirable effects of this by devising loopholes in the cases.

Mæland[338] suggests that the Courts may look benevolently upon arbitration agreements within unions. According to *Mæland* the members of a union should be considered to have agreed to any arbitration clauses in the union's rules simply by becoming a member of that union.[339] *Mæland* points out that it is generally accepted that unions have the autonomy to judge themselves in disputes between the union and a member.[340] Dispute resolution by arbitration entails a more extensive protection of the parties due to the notion of audiatur et altera pars and the regulation of bias than does the notion of "self-judging" often found within unions. It therefore seems logical to *Mæland* that also arbitration agreements should be acceptable without both parties' written consent.

More recently, *Røsæg*[341] has suggested that the requirement for writing in sec. 452 should not be seen as a requirement for signature. Firstly, according to both *Røsæg* and this writer, a requirement for signature does not follow from the SKARVØY II case.[342] More importantly, according to *Røsæg*, if a signature is required, Norwegian law will be in breach of Norway's obligations under the New York Convention Art. II(2). It follows from the Norwegian Code of Procedure sec. 36a that the Code applies with the limitations that are recognised within international law or which may follow from international treaties. Thus, it follows from the interpretation of the Norwegian Code of Procedure in itself that sec. 452, sub-sec. 2, 1st sentence should not be interpreted differently from the New York Convention Art. II(2).

Røsæg seems to overlook that there is nothing in the New York Convention to bar the Norwegian legislators from making rules outside the scope of application of the New York Convention that are stricter than what follows from that convention's Art. II. The Norwegian Code of Procedure sec. 36a indicates that the requirement for writing in international arbitration should not be any stricter than what follows from the New York Convention Art. II, but sec. 36a does not imply that national arbitra-

---

[338] *Mæland (1988)*, p. 67 f.

[339] This is the position under Danish law, see above § 2, point 2.2.

[340] "Selvdømme". Translates (verbatim) as "self-judging".

[341] *Røsæg (1999)*, p. 668 ff.

[342] *Røsæg (1999)*, p. 673.

tion agreements can dispense with the stringent formal requirements that follow from the practice of the Norwegian Supreme Court.

A more liberal approach to the Norwegian Code of Procedure sec. 452, sub-sec. 1, 1st sentence is obviously preferable from the point of view of what is the need of international trade, and therefore good reasons for supporting the attempts to push the case law in that direction made in legal literature exist. However, in a Supreme Court ruling from 1999, TINE V. LØKEN, both *Mæland's* argument that the requirement for writing was not as strict within unions and any argument that the requirement for writing in sec. 452 need not be a requirement for signature was rejected.

RT. 1999.1532 NSC, TINE V. LØKEN[343]

Farmer Inge Løken owned a part of the co-operative dairy TINE. He also delivered his production of milk to TINE. In August 1998 Løken initiated proceedings before the Court of First Instance of Trondheim, concerning a dispute regarding the quantity of milk delivered. TINE claimed that the case should be dismissed due to an arbitration clause in the co-operative's rules. The Court of First Instance and, upon appeal, the Court of Appeal, found for Løken. TINE appealed the case to the Norwegian Supreme Court, claiming that the interpretation of the law applied by the Court of Appeal was erroneous.

TINE was a result of a merger, in two stages, of several smaller dairies, one of them Romsdal dairy, of which Løken had been a member and part owner. Although Løken was a part owner, he had not participated actively in the merger. Instead, he had given other members and part owners mandate act on his behalf. However, the rules of TINE had on at least three occasions been sent to Løken.

Counsel for TINE argued that an arbitration clause in a partnership's rules was sufficient so as to make the clause valid. Thus, within unions, there was no need for a specific written agreement to arbitrate as between the particular members and the union. In that way, the Court of Appeal had interpreted the Norwegian Code of Procedure sec. 452, sub-sec. 2, 1st sentence erroneously. Indeed, the counsel argued that sec. 452 did not put down a demand for writing at all as regarded such cases. Alternatively the counsel argued that any requirement for writing that might be deduced from sec. 452, would be fulfilled if a member of the co-operative had given another member mandate to agree to the partnership rules containing the arbitration clause. (Finally the counsel put forward the argument that Løken was bound by the arbitration clause under the rules of succession, but as this argument was new before the Supreme Court the Court had to reject it).

According to the Supreme Court it followed from both the provision itself and the travaux préparatoires that the demand for writing was not only founded on the regard to the securing the proof of the arbitration agreement, but also aimed to ensure that the choice of arbitration as a means of dispute resolution had been reflected upon by the parties. Consequently, it did not suffice that the arbitration agreement was printed in a document. On the contrary, it followed from the SKARVØY II case[344] that the parties must have accepted to arbitrate by signing the document. However, it might suffice for the parties to sign a document that referred to another document containing the arbitration clause,

---

[343] Also published in ND 1999.381. See LF-1998-01052 for the ruling of the Court of Appeal.

[344] Rt. 1962.1215 NSC.

but this would only be so if the parties knew, ought to have known of, or had a reason to make themselves acquainted with the arbitration clause. In deciding what the parties ought to have known, one should take into account what the parties knew regarding each other's level of knowledge of the trade. Here the Supreme Court referred to its own findings in the cases SITAS V. HØGLUND[345] and ØSTREM ET AL V. BYGGERSERVICE.[346] The Supreme Court then quoted the ruling of the Court of Appeal in the TINE case: "As a starting point it must require an indisputable and real agreement between the parties before an arbitration agreement should be considered to exist, that is that both parties have given their written consent to the arbitration agreement. If one has declined ordinary Court proceedings, this is such a far-reaching transaction that one must provide for a stringent requirement for the acceptance [of the agreement]."

The Supreme Court then turned to TINE's claim that arbitration agreements contained in partnership agreements etc. needed not adhere to the strict requirements for writing set out in the Norwegian Code of Procedure sec. 452. The Supreme Court purely rejected this argument. Neither the travaux préparatoires, newer case law nor legal theory supported that the membership of a co-operative or suchlike organisation would suffice as regards sec. 452, sub-sec. 2, 1st sentence so as to bind the members to arbitrate disputes between themselves and the co-op. It was not found, either, that the requirement for writing should be eased when within a union such as the TINE dairy. Even if, to an extent, unions were generally considered to possess a certain amount of autonomy, including the right to decide themselves in disputes between the union and a member, this autonomy did not extend to allowing arbitration without a written agreement. This was particularly the case within unions, such as TINE, which directly affected the livelihood of the farmers delivering their milk for production.

Whether the founders of TINE had bound the members under the mandate they obtained before the merger of the dairies was not clear. However, it had not been shown that Løken had participated at the general meeting where the merger took place, nor had it been shown that he had participated actively in the merger in any other way. The arbitration agreement had thus not been accepted on that ground.

In summing up, there was no reason to set aside the Court of Appeal's findings as erroneous, and the appeal was dismissed, allowing Løken to proceed with his claim before the Court of First Instance of Trondheim.

The Norwegian Supreme Court's decision in TINE V. LØKEN raises several points. The two main points bear direct impact upon the interpretation of the Norwegian Code of Procedure sec. 452, sub-sec. 2, 1st sentence.

Firstly, according to the Norwegian Supreme Court, the ruling of the Court in the SKARVØY II case requires that arbitration agreement must be signed. This finding does not conform to the views expressed by this writer and by *Røsæg*. The part of the ruling of the Norwegian Supreme Court in SKARVØY II that is referred to by the Court in TINE V. LØKEN is this:

[345] Rt. 1991.635 NSC.

[346] Rt. 1991.773 NSC.

168

Held by the Supreme Court: "As an arbitration agreement the provision in the rules of SKARVØY II's insurance company is not valid, as there is no written agreement to arbitrate." The Supreme Court then referred to the minority vota of the Court of Appeal, in the same case stating that: "As said, it is clear that the provision on arbitration has been included in both the company agreement and in the printed text of the insurance policy, but as far as I can see there is not on the part of Skarvøy any written agreement to the clause. That Skarvøy's owner has been summoned to a general assembly where the provision was agreed, that he at no point protested against the provision and that he by his membership and his position as having taken insurance by his actions possibly can be said to have agreed to the provision is not the deciding factor for me, as the law demands not only an agreement but a *written* formation of contract."[347]

This ruling emphasises the requirement for written formation of contract, probably in the form of the written consent of both parties, but it does not demand that a signature is provided. It is maintained that in this respect the Supreme Court drew the findings of the Court in SKARVØY II too far. However, even if the interpretation is found to be open to question, one must suppose that the ruling reflects the Supreme Court's present view upon the law. Thus, irrespectively of how one interprets the vota in SKARVØY II, questions as to whether a signature is indispensable have now been answered in the affirmative.

Secondly, the proposition that arbitration agreements in union's rules need not be agreed to in writing, but should be effective as against a member of a union on the basis of the membership itself was rejected. The Norwegian Supreme Court emphasises this in particular in relation to unions that may make decisions affecting a member's livelihood, but the rejection is aimed at unions in general. *Mæland's* suggestion on this point has thus been firmly overruled.

In the TINE case the Norwegian Supreme Court has expressed a very conservative view upon the formal requirements for arbitration agreements under Norwegian law. This is somewhat surprising as it is divergent to the trend prevailing internationally at this moment, namely the trend that formal requirements should be lax so as to best cater for the needs of international trade.

2.2.4. Summing up

The formal requirement in the Norwegian Code of Procedure sec. 452, sub-sec. 2, 1st sentence, seen in the light of SKARVØY II, SITAS V. HØGLUND, ØSTREM ET AL V. BYGGESERVICE and TINE V. LØKEN, may be summarised as follows:

1. It is required that both parties have signed a document containing the arbitration agreement.

---

[347] Writer's translation.

2. If both parties have signed a document that refers to a document containing an arbitration clause, or refers directly to the arbitration clause itself, such incorporation may be effective. It is however required that both parties knew of, ought to know of, or had good reason to make themselves acquainted with the arbitration agreement. In establishing whether this is the case, the parameters described above in point 2.2.2 should be consulted. Additionally, when considering what a party ought to have known, the reasonable expectations of his counter-party as to the first party's knowledge of the trade should be taken into consideration.

3. Given the clear rejection of acceptance of arbitration agreements due to membership of unions etc. it must as a starting point be expected that the Norwegian Courts will not accept other ways of satisfying the requirement for writing under sec. 452, sub-sec. 2, 1st sentence.

This regulation is obviously too strict as to cater for the needs of parties to international trade transactions that may wish to arbitrate their potential disputes due to regards to neutrality, expediency, expertise and confidentiality. Admittedly, the arbitration agreement will often be signed. Thus, if the subject matter of the transaction is contract work etc. that will normally be the case – at least as between the contractor and his client, if not always between the client and the contractor's sub-contractor. However, in international sale of goods for example, the sales agreement will often be made orally with later reference to a set of standard conditions and solely with unilateral documentation issued, such as invoices, bills of lading and letters of credit as the confirmation. The present Norwegian regulation is not apt to cater for these situations.

3. Choice of law problems

3.1. The problem
The Norwegian Code of Procedure sec. 452 governs the Norwegian Courts' competence to deal with a certain matter. Thus, it may be described as a rule of procedure. Generally, the rules of procedure of the lex fori apply to any case put before the Court. However, there is a general consensus in Norwegian legal literature that the Norwegian Code of Procedure Chapter 32 only applies to Norwegian arbitration agreements and awards.[348] It has been mentioned above in point 2.2.3, that the Nor-

---

[348] *Schei (1998)*, p. 1167, *Mæland (1988)*, p. 40, *Lindboe (1944)*, p. 17. Refer to Eckhoff's travaux préparatoires here.

wegian Code of Procedure sec. 36a provides that the Code only applies insofar as this is consistent with Norway's obligations under international law. "The Code applies with the limitations that are recognised by international law or follow from treaties with foreign states."[349] Such treaties could be the rules of the special transport conventions, discussed below in Chapter V, however generally more important are the rules of the New York Convention, adopted by Norway in the Royal Resolution of 9th December 1960. Considering this, it is somewhat surprising that the Norwegian Supreme Court has been seen to apply the formal requirements of sec. 452 to international arbitration agreements.[350]

The cases are problematic both when seen from a strictly Norwegian point of view, as they seem to stretch the scope of Chapter 32 beyond what is generally accepted, and when seen from the point of view of international law, as the rulings appear to be in conflict with the New York Convention Art. II. The indispensable requirement for arbitration agreements to be in writing is stricter, than what follows from the New York Convention Art. II.[351] It is therefore crucial whether the Norwegian Courts apply the Norwegian Code of Procedure sec. 452, sub-sec. 2, 1st sentence or the New York Convention Art. II(2) to international arbitration agreements. It is this question that will be considered in the following. In the light of sec. 36a, one should expect the rules of the New York Convention to prevail over the Norwegian Code of Procedure sec. 452, sub-sec. 2, 1st sentence. This also seems to be the conclusion reached by case law under the Norwegian Enforcement Act of 26 June 1992, no. 86, sec. 1-4, which is exactly identical to the Norwegian Code of Procedure sec. 36a.

3.2. The Enforcement Act and Norway's obligations under international law

The recognition of arbitration agreements as a reason for declining jurisdiction before Norwegian Courts is dealt with in the Norwegian Code of Procedure. However, the enforcement of arbitration awards is governed by the Norwegian Enforcement Act, especially sec. 4-1(f). According to that provision foreign arbitration awards may provide the basis for Norwegian enforcement if the arbitration award has be-

---

[349] Writer's translation.

[350] SITAS v. HØGLUND, Rt. 1991.635 NSC and FLEKKEFJORD v. CATARPILLAR, HR-2000-01539 NSC.

[351] See for the requirements of the New York Convention, below § 5.

come res judicata in the country of origin, see sec. 4-15, and if it follows from international treaties or conventions that it should be so.

According to the Enforcement Act sec. 1-4 the Act applies with the limitations that are recognised in international law, or which follow from treaties with foreign States. This has already been said to be a verbatim copy of the Norwegian Code of Procedure sec. 36a. Under the Enforcement Act, the provision has been understood to provide that the rules of the New York Convention apply and, in case of discrepancies, prevail over the rules of the Enforcement Act. Thus, in DATEMA V. CRESCO FINANS, LE-1992-02312 CA, it was held that sec. 12 cf. sec. 5 of the then applicable Enforcement Act entailed that the provisions of the New York Convention took precedence over the Enforcement Act. In another case concerning the enforcement of an arbitration award, KRISTIANSEN V. RAISINO, LB-2000-00904 CA, the New York Convention Art. V(1)(a) and V(1)(b) were tried directly before the Court of Appeal, with reference to the Enforcement Act sec. 4-1(f). The rules of the New York Convention were also found to apply in DSI V. VOSTOKTRANSFLOT, ND 1999.322 NCA. In the case, Vostoktransflot requested that execution of an English arbitration award be carried out in assets belonging to the Norwegian company DSI. The Court of Appeal held that the Execution Act sec. 4-1(f) allowed for foreign arbitration awards to be enforced in Norway, if this followed from international treaties. The Court of Appeal continued:

"The New York Convention ... is such a treaty, and it is adopted by Norway and England. According to the Convention Art. II, no. 1, any contracting State shall recognise a written agreement where the parties have referred potential disputes to arbitration. By the expression 'written agreement' is meant, according to the Convention, an arbitration clause in a contract or an arbitration agreement that has been signed by the parties, or which is contained in an exchange of letters and telegrams."[352]

The Court then entered into an evaluation of whether the actual exchange of communication in the case fulfilled these criteria. The Court found that it did not. Consequently, there was no basis for execution and the case was dismissed from the Courts.

Thus, under the Enforcement Act the Norwegian Courts have accepted that the requirements of the New York Convention prevail over the requirements of national law, due to the direct provision to that effect in the Enforcement Act sec. 1-4.

---

[352] Writer's translation.

3.3. The application of the Norwegian Code of Procedure sec. 452

Considering that the Enforcement Act sec. 1-4 and the Norwegian Code of Procedure sec. 36a are a verbatim match, it is unlikely that the provisions should carry a different meaning. Legal literature regard the provisions in the same way, sec. 36a thus allowing for the precedence of the rules of the New York Convention (and indeed other conventions) when applicable. According to *Mæland*,[353] the requirement for writing in sec. 452 is inapplicable to foreign arbitration clauses. This is in accordance with *Lindboe*, who states that chapter 32 of the Norwegian Code of Procedure only applies to Norwegian arbitration agreements and awards.[354]

Nevertheless, the Norwegian Supreme Court have applied the formal requirement in sec. 452, sub-sec.1, 1st sentence to foreign arbitration clauses. In SITAS V. HØGLUND, RT. 1991.635 NSC,[355] sec. 452, sub-sec. 2, 1st sentence was applied to the arbitration agreement, even if the parties had their principal place of business in different countries, and had agreed to arbitration according to Swedish law. Likewise, in FLEKKEFJORD V. CATERPILLAR, HR-2000-01539, a contract of sales of a machine between a German seller and a Norwegian buyer had been entered into with reference to the NLM 92 E form. The arbitration clause in the standard form used in FLEKKEFJORD V. CATERPILLAR is worded thus:

Disputes. Applicable Law.
40. Disputes arising out of or in connection with the contract shall not be brought before the court, but shall be finally settled by arbitration in accordance with the law on arbitration applicable in the Seller's country.
41. All disputes arising out of the contract shall be judged according to the law of the Seller's country.[356]

Nevertheless the Norwegian Supreme Court applied sec. 452, sub-sec. 2, 1st sentence to the clause on the following grounds:

"The Supreme Court, which possess full competence in the case … notes that the requirement for writing in the Code of Procedure sec. 452, sub-sec. 2, is applicable to the case even if the arbitration clause relied on provides for arbitration according to German law, cf. the ruling printed in Rt.

[353] *Mæland (1988),* p. 65.

[354] *Lindboe (1944).*

[355] The case is discussed in detail above, point 2.2.2.

[356] The clause is not printed in the case. Thus, it may be that the parties have made amendments to the clause, but upon the transcript it does not seem that they have.

1991.635 NSC ... [The Court] *sees no reason to make a decision as to the precise contents of Article II, no. 1 and 2 of the New York Convention of 1958.*

The provisions of the Convention establish a duty for the Convention States to recognise arbitration agreements concluded in accordance with the requirement for form given in the Convention. *Apart from that the States are free to determine, which conditions apply to the conclusion of arbitration agreements.*"[357]

At first glance the ruling of the Supreme Court seems totally insensible. The Court seems to have overlooked the obligation arising out of the New York Convention not to impose a requirement stricter than what follows from the New York Convention Art. II(2) upon the parties.[358] The only way in which the ruling can make sense is if the Norwegian Supreme Court did not think that the arbitration agreement was covered by the New York Convention. Below in § 6, point 2, the New York Convention's scope is defined, and that discussion should not be repeated here. However, a short summary of the issue particular in connection to these cases is called for.

The New York Convention Art. I defines, which arbitration awards are covered by the Convention, but the Convention holds no provision governing which arbitration agreements are encompassed by it. Still, there is an overall consensus, that "the Convention regulates ... all arbitration agreements, which have resulted, could result or could have resulted in a foreign award".[359] In short, the Convention applies to all international arbitration agreements.[360] The question then remains what is an international arbitration agreement. This writer maintains, as argued below in § 6, point 2.3, that the New York Convention applies to arbitration agreements that are designed so as to encompass an international dispute, and thus, as a rule that the arbitration agreement is international if the dispute is international. In her thesis on international commercial arbitration, *Moss* defines an "international dispute" thus:

"For the purpose of this work, a dispute is considered as being international if the underlying legal relationship has a foreign element, such as the domicile or habitual residence of one of the parties or the place of performance."[361]

[357] My translation. Emphasis added.

[358] The New York Convention Art. III, 2nd sentence.

[359] Hamm Oberlandesgericht (1997) XXII ICCA Yearbook 707, on p. 708, para. 2, see below § 6, point 2.

[360] Subject to the reservations provided for in Art. I.

[361] *Moss (1999)*, p. 45.

This writer adheres to *Moss'* definition of what is an international dispute. It follows from that that in this writer's view the arbitration agreements in SITAS V. HØGLUND and FLEKKEFJORD V. CATARPILLAR were well within the scope of the New York Convention. It furthermore strikes the writer, that the Norwegian Supreme Court seems to have attached two different legal meanings to the wording "[t]he Code/Act applies with the limitations that are recognised by international law or follow from treaties with foreign states", dependent upon whether the words are found in the Norwegian Code of Procedure or in the Enforcement Act. At present it seems that an arbitration agreement contained in an exchange of telexes, which should fulfil the criteria in the New York Convention Art. II(2), will be accepted under the Enforcement Act as a valid agreement to arbitrate. Thus, an arbitration award given with basis in such an arbitration agreement will be enforced under the Enforcement Act sec. 4-1(f) cf. sec. 4-17, sub-sec. 1. At the same time, a plea for the dismissal of a ruling on the merit of a dispute covered by the arbitration agreement will be disallowed by the Norwegian Courts, as an exchange of telexes does not fulfil the criteria set out in the Norwegian Code of Procedure sec. 452.

It ought to be so that the Norwegian Courts apply the same rules to the arbitration agreement, irrespectively of whether the arbitration agreement is sought enforced directly, due to a plea for the dismissal of a case on the merits, or indirectly through the claim for the enforcement of an award based on the competence bestowed upon the arbitral tribunal in the arbitration agreement. Also, the Norwegian Code of Procedure sec. 36a ought to be taken at face value, and warrant that the provisions of the New York Convention Art. II(2) are indeed applied to arbitration agreements that fall within the Convention's scope.

4. Accepting arbitration agreements under other rules of law

The duty to arbitrate may be imposed on a party due to the general rules of succession in and transfer of rights and obligations. This has been accepted both in Norwegian legal literature[362] and by the Nowegian Courts.[363] Also, the general framework of the Norwegian Code of Procedure sec. 452, sub-sec. 2, 1st sentence should be seen in the context of the special rules of Norwegian law, governing arbitration agreements, the most general of these being the New York Convention Art. II. On a more

---

[362] *Mæland (1988)*, p. 87 f. with footnotes for reference to further literature.

[363] Recognised, albeit obiter, by the Norwegian Supreme Court in Rt. 1999.1532 NSC, TINE V. LØKEN.

specialised level we find the Norwegian Maritime Code sec. 311 cf. sec. 310,[364] the Norwegian Carriage of Goods by Road Act sec. 44,[365] the Package Holiday Act sec. 10-7,[366] the Aviation Code sec. 10-28 (ex contrario),[367] and the Carriage of Goods by Rail Act sec. 5.[368] To the extent that these rules provide an exhaustive regulation of the requirements for arbitration agreements, the Norwegian Code of Procedure chapter 32 – and especially sec. 452, sub-sec. 2, 1st sentence – should not come into play. Still, also provisions of Norwegian law that upon their wording do not directly govern, or exclude, arbitration agreements may come into play. Thus, in the STENA CONQUEST case, the Norwegian Court of Appeal found that a provision in the Norwegian Company Act[369] dealing with the legal effects of a transfer of (a share of) a company was applicable to arbitration agreements.

LE-1992-02124, STENA CONQUEST

In April 1990 the newly formed limited partnership "Wind Conquest" acquired "Stena Conquest." In September 1990 it was discovered that Stena Conquest suffered from severe rust attacks. To repair the damage, 1400 tonnes of steel had to be replaced at a cost of approximately USD 6.5 bio. The repairs necessitated that Wind Conquest called in further guarantee capital. The limited partners did not consider themselves obliged to pay in further amounts. On 22 April 1991, Wind Conquest went bankrupt. The estate of Wind Conquest demanded that the limited partners paid the guarantee capital in full. The partners refused and initiated proceedings before The Oslo Court of First Instance. The estate pleaded that the case should be dismissed due to an arbitration clause in the partnership rules. The Court of First Instance found for the estate and dismissed the case from the Courts. On appeal, the Court of Appeal examined the case thoroughly. The Court distinguished between three situations according to how the partners had acquired their shares.

To the extent that the limited partners had been present at the foundation of the company and had signed the partnership rules, either in person or through mandate, the partnership rules including the arbitration clause bound the partners. On this point, the parties were not in dispute, so those findings of the Court of Appeal were, strictly speaking, obiter.

If the limited partners had signed the limited partner form that referred to the partnership rules of 4 April 1990 and stated that the partner succeeded in all rights and obligations of the transferor, then

---

[364] Law of 24th June 1994, no. 39.

[365] Law of 20th December 1974, no. 68.

[366] Law of 25th August 1995, no. 57.

[367] Law of 11th June 1991, no. 101.

[368] Law of 15th June 1984, no. 74.

[369] Law of 21st June1985, no. 65.

those limited partners too were bound by the arbitration clause, the deciding factor being that the partners had been made aware that the partnership rules existed.

Finally, some of the limited partners had bought their shares in the open market, without any special reference being made to the partnership rules. However, according to the Norwegian Company Act sec. 2-30, the transferee of shares etc. succeeds in all the rights and obligations of the transferor. The Norwegian Court of Appeal found, under considerable doubt, that sec. 2-30 also applied to arbitration agreements.

The Court of Appeal found support for the ruling that arbitration agreements should be considered within the scope of the Company Act sec. 2-30 in the following four grounds:

Firstly, consulting literature, *Mæland* had stated that a transferee, especially in sales, should respect the arbitration agreement, as he should not obtain a better position than had the transferor.

Secondly, keeping in mind the risks connected to buying shares in limited partnerships, the buyers should be diligent in assessing the conditions under which the shares were sold. It was a requirement of the Company Act that a Company Agreement was entered into, and that any such agreement was registered in, and available from, the Company Register. The shareholders had thus had the opportunity to make themselves acquainted with the terms of the Company Agreement, and they ought to have done so.

Thirdly, the shareholders were bound by the arbitration clause insofar as they, subsequently, had received the Company Agreement and remained passive.

Fourthly, all in all, general considerations requested that a person buying the shares of a limited partnership be bound by any arbitration agreement applicable to the shares, which bound the seller of the shares.

The Court of Appeal's findings that partners, who had signed the partnership rules themselves or through mandate as well as partners who had signed a succession agreement referring to the partnership rules were bound by those rules are not controversial. Instead, it is the ruling that arbitration agreements are encompassed by the Norwegian Company Act sec. 2-30 that draws attention. The relevant provisions are these:

The Norwegian Company Act sec. 2-30 in extract[370]
1) By transfer, the transferee acquires all the rights and obligations of the transferor as towards the other partners. He is in the same way as the transferor bound by the decisions and transactions that the company has made before the transfer ...
2) For obligations that lay upon the company at the time of the transfer the transferor and the transferee are jointly and severally liable until the creditor has relieved the transferor of his liability. ...

The Court of Appeal found, even if in doubt, that this wording applied to arbitration agreements. The Court of Appeals conclusion was reached mainly by applying principles of company law, the argument concerning itself with general considerations as

---

[370] Writer's translation.

to what parties buying shares in the open market ought to know or ought to have ascertained. At this particular point the Court does not concern itself with the requirements of the Norwegian Code of Procedure, sec. 452, sub-sec. 2, 1st sentence. For that reason alone, the Court of Appeal's ruling in the STENA CONQUEST case has not been overruled by the Norwegian Supreme Court's ruling in TINE V. LØKEN. Furthermore, in TINE V. LØKEN the Norwegian Supreme Court accepted *obiter*, that the arbitration clause in the co-operative's rules might have been binding upon Løken had it been shown that he had participated actively in the merger of the dairies that lead to the formation of TINE. Thus, the Supreme Court left open the opportunity of being bound by arbitration agreements under the rules of company law even if the strict requirements of the Norwegian Code of Procedure sec. 452, sub-sec. 2, 1st sentence were not met. Consequently it must be concluded that the Court of Appeal's findings in the STENA CONQUEST case have not been overruled, but that the final say on the scope of sec. 2-30 of the Norwegian Company Act awaits the decision of the Norwegian Supreme Court.

Considering the general transferability of the arbitration agreement, it is noteworthy that the Draft Norwegian Arbitration Act proposes as a declaratory rule, that any arbitration agreement governing a legal relationship is transferred with the transfer of the relationship.[371]

5. The interpretation of arbitration agreements. An overview

Having contemplated the Norwegian Court's interpretation of the formal requirements for arbitration agreements in the Norwegian Code of Procedure sec. 452, one might conclude that the Norwegian Courts are exceedingly arbitration hostile. This, however, would be a premature conclusion. Due to the Norwegian doctrine on the sources of law, the Norwegian Courts have considered themselves bound by the wish expressed in the *travaux préparatoires*, namely that it should be ensured that the parties have indeed intended to arbitrate their present dispute. Even if the Courts have been overzealous in the development of the formal criteria, this overzealousness has not been extended to the Norwegian Court's interpretation of the arbitration agreement.

One of the reasons for this may be that – contrary to Danish law – the Norwegian approach to arbitration agreements is generally a very structured one. Leaving aside the situations where the parties to the purported arbitration agreement lack the capacity to contract or where the subject matter cannot be arbitrated, the Courts will first

---

[371] Draft Norwegian Arbitration Act sec. 2-2(2). For English translation of the provision see NOU 2001:33, p. 122.

ascertain that the formal criteria in the Norwegian Code of Procedure sec. 452, sub-sec. 2, 1ˢᵗ sentence have been complied with. Only if this is found to be the case will they consider any further points, such as the scope of the arbitration agreement.

Consequently, for the question of the interpretation of the arbitration agreement to occur, the parties must either agree, alternatively, the Courts must already have established, that the parties have signed an arbitration agreement that, directly or indirectly, seems to require the parties to arbitrate their dispute. This is also at least a part of the explanation why the bulk of the case law on the interpretation of the arbitration agreements is concerned with disputes between the original parties to the contract, and not – as in Danish case law – concerned with whether the arbitration agreement extends to situations where third party has succeeded in, or is otherwise claiming under, the original parties' contract.[372] Such situations will in many cases never make it past the threshold of the Norwegian Code of Procedure sec. 452, and the discussion of the interpretation of the arbitration agreement will thus not arise before the Court, as was the case in Rt. 1994.1024 NSC and Rt. 1990.1031 NSC.[373]

In the following, an overview of the recent Norwegian case law on the interpretation of the arbitration agreement will be given.

5.1. The scope of the arbitration agreement

5.1.1. A claim in tort or a claim in contract?

Often a party seeking compensation after the collapse of a contractual relationship will do so by directing his claim in tort and in damages, alternatively. The question is

---

[372] Above in § 2, point 4.2.2.

[373] In Rt. 1994.1024 NSC, VEIDEKKE V. ULLERÅSEN BORETTSLAG, the client initiated proceedings before the Court against the builders sub-contractor. The sub-contractor claimed that the case should be dismissed from the Courts due to an arbitration clause in the contract between the client and the builder. The Norwegian Supreme Court found, even if in some doubt, that sec. 452 of the Norwegian Code of Procedure required, that the parties to the actual dispute should have consented to arbitration. In the case there was no agreement to arbitrate as between the client (Ulleråsen Borettslag) and the sub-contractor (Veidekke) – indeed there was no direct contractual relationship between them at all. Thus, the client was free to proceed with the case before the ordinary Courts. (Also published in ND 1994.349 NSC). In Rt. 1990.1031 NSC, NORTON & PRODUCTION V. KLAVENESS CHARTERING, dispute arose as to whether the owner or the charterer were liable to pay the shipbroker's fees and commission. The shipbroker initiated proceedings before Oslo Court of First Instance. The owner claimed that the case should be dismissed due to the arbitration clause in the charter-party as between the owner and the charterer, since the shipbroker was claiming his fees and provision under the terms of that charter-party. As the shipbroker was not a party to the charter-party contract he was found to be ad liberty to proceed with his claim before the ordinary Courts.

if this will affect the application of the arbitration agreement. It is questionable whether an arbitration agreement will be applicable to a claim between the parties, if that claim is based in tort and not in contract. The answer to the question depends mainly upon the construction of the arbitration agreement and on the proper classification of the claim. In other words: Does the arbitration agreement cover both claims in tort and claims in contract, and if not, is the party in reality making a claim in contract, or is it definitely based in tort? It should also be borne in mind that the actual type of tort may be of importance. Some types of tort are in effect just another basis for a remedy against the non-fulfilment of a party's obligations, whereas in other cases the tort committed might affect the validity of the whole contractual relationship, including the arbitration agreement, and leave it null and void. The classification of the claim was the main issue in RT. 1996.443 NSC, BRICON V. P&O.[374] The tort allegedly committed in the case would seem to render both the main contract and the arbitration agreement null and void. Establishing whether the claim was in tort or in contract was therefore of utmost importance.

Bricon had entered into a charter-party with P&O. According to the charter-party, any dispute "... under the terms of this Charter Party ..." was to be arbitrated in London according to English law. The Supreme Court stated unanimously that as a starting point this clause encompassed any dispute that arose out of the contractual relationship as such, and not only disputes as to the proper interpretation of the contract, as claimed by Bricon. The Supreme Court was also in agreement that if indeed the whole contractual relationship was null and void, then the arbitration agreement might also fall.[375] However, to achieve that Bricon would have to show that the claim was not made under the contract.

It was not totally clear what was the basis for Bricon's claim. Bricon had claimed both *that* P&O had inveigled Bricon to enter into the charter-party through misrepresentation and *that* P&O had not fulfilled their obligations under the contract. On this issue, the Supreme Court split. The majority found that Bricon had in fact claimed under the contract. In the statement of claims in the writ, Bricon had claimed that P&O were liable as towards Bricon for breach of contract, and the amount claimed was the amount due under the rules of breach of contract. Therefore, the claim was considered to be under the contract and not in tort, and the arbitration agreement would under all circumstances apply to the claim. The minority, on the other hand, found that Bricon had shown that its claim was in tort. The alleged tort would invalidate both the main agreement and the arbitration agreement and consequently the

---

[374] Also published in ND 1996.223 NSC.

[375] See below regarding the discussion of the doctrine of separability, Chapter III, point 2.

claim could be heard by the ordinary Courts. Still, the minority found that there had been so much uncertainty as to the basis of the claim that Bricon had to bear its own costs. Due to the majority's finding – that the claim was under the contract – the dispute was dismissed from the Courts.[376]

In a case from Eidsivating Court of Appeal, the main issue for evaluation was the scope of the arbitration clause. The claimant argued that the claim was in tort, however, the tort was not affecting the validity of the contract, indeed it was just providing the claimant with an alternative remedy for the alleged breach of the contract.

LILLEHAMMER V. MOELVEN, LE-1994-02647, COURT OF APPEAL
The construction-company Moelven contracted with Lillehammer municipality for the building of a school. 16 years later, the roof of the building collapsed. The municipality of Lillehammer claimed damages before Sør-Gudbrandsdal Court of First Instance. Moelven claimed that the case should be dismissed due to an arbitration agreement in the building contract, stating that "… disputes that may arise in relations that concern this contract shall be settled by arbitration …". Lillehammer municipality claimed that since the claim against Moelven had been based in tort and not in contract, there was no agreement to arbitrate the claim. The Court of Appeal found that the claim against Moelven was based on the parties' contract, as the dispute had arisen out of the collapsing of the roof constructed under the contract. It did not matter, whether the claim was actually based in tort or in contract, as long as its factual basis was covered by the contract. The dispute that had arisen did "concern" the contract, and was thus within the wording of the arbitration clause. The case was dismissed from the Courts.[377]

In LILLEHAMMER V. MOELVEN the arbitration clause was worded in wide terms, covering any dispute that concerned the contract. Considering that in the case one of the original parties to the contract directed a claim against the other regarding that other's performance under the contract, that claim concerned the contract, and was covered by the arbitration clause.

The case might remind the reader of the Danish case, U 1983.123 DSC, THE COLLAPSED ROOF, discussed above in § 2, point 4.2.2.3. In that case the buyer, C, of a building built by A for B, directed a claim in tort as towards A after the roof of the building had collapsed. A's contention that the case should be dismissed from the Courts due to an arbitration clause in the building contract between A and B was dismissed, as C was not claiming under the contract, but in tort. Thus, on the face of it, the Danish Supreme Court reached the opposite conclusion to the one given by the

---

[376] A parallel ruling is found in RUUD V. NORION ET AL, (LB-1998-00365). See also above, Chapter III, point 2.

[377] It was also pointed out by the Court of Appeal, that if the case was left to proceed before the Courts, this would be likely to cause problems as regards lis pendens and res judicata.

Norwegian Court of Appeal in LILLEHAMMER V. MOELVEN. However, one must note that in the Danish case it was not the original parties to the contract that were now in dispute, but instead the dispute was between the original party A (the builder) and the latter buyer of the property, C. Furthermore, C had not based his claim on the contract, nor had he in other ways acceded to the arbitration agreement. In such a case, the Courts could hear a dispute regarding C's claim in tort for compensation.

5.1.2. The claim not concerned with the actual contract?

A party may argue, that the parties' present dispute is not within (the part of) the parties' *contractual relationship*, that is governed by the arbitration clause. This may be due to the fact that the arbitration clause or agreement is narrowly worded, designed only to include certain issues or potential disputes, or the fact that the parties' present dispute, although connected with the (main) agreement, which is governed by the arbitration clause, is independent from it. Contentions to this effect were put forward in LE-1992-02674 NCA, ICELANDAIR V. SAS, and in RT. 1994.1489 NSC, M/T LAVENDER.

In the first case, Icelandair and SAS had entered into an agreement that SAS should aid the docking of Icelandair's aircraft. The contract held an arbitration clause according to which "… any dispute or claim arising out of the contract shall be settled by arbitration. This applies equally to disputes regarding the scope and interpretation of the contract." It came to pass that one of Icelandair's aircraft was damaged during docking by a heating pump left at the wrong side of the security line in the docking area. In short Icelandair claimed that the arbitration clause only covered disputes as to the rights and obligations that were *spelt out* in the contract. The use of a heating pump was not a part of the contract, and consequently, a dispute concerning an error in the handling of the heating pump was outside the agreement to arbitrate.

The Court of Appeal found that it was certainly a matter of interpretation of the parties' contract, whether the use of the heating pump fell within that contract or not. Thus, whether SAS' handling of the heating pump during the docking of the Icelandair aircraft had been according to the contract was under all circumstances within the agreement to arbitrate. Consequently the case was dismissed from the Courts.

In RT. 1994.1489 NSC, M/T LAVENDER[378] the partnership Lavender (A) sued the limited partnership Lavender (B) before Oslo Court of First Instance, claiming a settlement of account as regarded certain disbursements that A had had to make under a letter of guarantee issued on behalf of B. B, on the other hand, tried to set off a claim

---

[378] Also published in ND 1994.163 NSC.

for price reduction for a ship sold by A to B, as the ship had failed to meet the agreed classification requirements. A claimed that the claim for set off should be dismissed due to an arbitration clause in the sales agreement: "If any dispute should arise in connection with the *interpretation and fulfilment* of this contract, same shall be decided by arbitration in the city of Oslo ...".[379] B then claimed, that if the set off should be dismissed, so should A's claim, as the disbursements under the guarantee were so closely connected to the sales contract that both claims should be settled by arbitration.

The case was eventually appealed to the Norwegian Supreme Court. The Court found it to be proven that the parties had not, when entering into the sales agreement, foreseen that it would be necessary for A to issue a letter of guarantee on behalf of B. As a consequence, the letter of guarantee was not mentioned in the sales agreement. However, it turned out that B's bank was unwilling to finance B's buying of the ship unless A issued the guarantee. Thus, the sale could not be carried out without the guarantee and therefore the Court found that the guarantee had such close connection to the contract of sales, that it was a dispute within the scope of the "interpretation and fulfilment of the contract." This conclusion was also supported by other considerations: Generally, very good reason existed one forum should settle disputes arising out of one contract. The wording of the arbitration clause also indicated that this had been the parties' intention. Consequently, the parties' whole dispute fell within the agreement to arbitrate, and was dismissed from the Court.

The two cases show that once a dispute is prima facie concerned with the parties' contract, the onus is on the party claiming that the arbitration agreement does not apply to show that it is so. This burden is not easily lifted. The Courts will generally interpret an arbitration clause, purporting to encompass all disputes arising within a certain legal relationship so as to do exactly that. It will not suffice to escape the arbitration clause that the specific event that caused the claim had not been foreseen in the contract – as in ICELANDAIR V. SAS.[380]

---

[379] Writer's emphasis.

[380] LE-1992-02674.

This applies even if the parties have created an additional contractual relationship, as in M/T LAVENDER,[381] provided that that additional contract was necessitated by the endeavour to carry out the parties' original contract.[382]

This principle applies also to contractual relationships that have come to an end, if the fact that support the claim is covered by the contract, normally because the fact incurred before the ending of the contractual relationship. This is especially relevant in connection to partnership contracts etc. where one of the parties directs a claim against the other after the partnership has ended. Thus in LE-1993-00892 NCA, BLANK V. WISLØFF & AASLAND, Blanck left a law-firm driven by Blank, Wisløff and Aasland. Blank sued Wisløff and Aasland before the Oslo Court of First Instance, claiming damages. Wisløff and Aasland claimed that the case be dismissed due to an arbitration clause in the partnership's rules. The Court of Appeal held that as the dispute clearly was rooted in the partnership agreement from 1979 and in the subsequent dissolving of the partnership, the clause was within that agreement's arbitration clause, and consequently the claim was dismissed from the Courts.[383] In LB-1995-02066 NCA NIELSEN V. GJENSIDIGE, NCA, a similar situation arose concerning an agent's claims for damages for wrongful dismissal and further provision. The agency agreement contained an arbitration clause, but the agent made his claim before the Frederiksstad Court of First Instance. On appeal the Court of Appeal held that the issue depended on the interpretation of the arbitration agreement. *However: There was no general principle, that arbitration agreements should be narrowly construed. Indeed, the general principles for the interpretation of contracts applied.* Thus, the starting point was the wording of the provision on arbitration seen in con-

---

[381] Rt. 1994.1489 NSC/ND 1994.163 NSC.

[382] See also ND 1999.425, MAYAN EMPRESS. The General Conditions for repairs of ships and offshore vessels at Norwegian workshops applied to a contract for the repair of the Mayan Empress. According to § 16 of the General Conditions, "[any] dispute arising between the parties in connection [with] this contract shall be settled with final and binding effect for both parties by arbitration in Norway". The workshop brought a suit before Sunnhordland Court of First Instance due to alleged lack of payments under the contract for repairs. The owners of the Mayan Empress, Emerald Empress Holdings Limited claimed that the case should be dismissed due to the arbitration clause in the General Conditions. The workshop claimed that *as* there was no dispute as regarded the *bill* for the repairs, but only as regarded the *payments* made by the owners of the Mayan Empress, there was no dispute under the contract of repairs. The Court found this contention to be phony. In any case the Court found it sufficiently proven that the owners of the Mayan Empress did in fact dispute the claim, and thus, there was clearly a dispute within the scope of § 16 of the General Conditions. As a consequence, the case was dismissed from the Court.

[383] In the same direction see LB-1999-02027 NCA, HELGHEIM & STRØM V. ARNCO CONTAINER VII.

text with the wording of the parties' contract as such, and proof of other agreement or other intentions of the parties would be necessary if this starting point should be departed from. In fact, the Court found no reasons to assume that the parties had intended another meaning than the one following directly from the wording. As the arbitration clause provided that disputes regarding the proper understanding of the contract should be arbitrated in case the parties' negotiations turned out to be unfruitful, the case was dismissed from the Courts.

5.1.3. Disputes based on rights or obligations arising out of mandatory law

It may be, that the parties' dispute arises not out of the contractual relationship as such but instead out of one of the parties' alleged breach of mandatory rules of law, such as trust law, law regarding the protection of intellectual property, marketing law etc. The question then arises whether such a claim is within any arbitration agreement in the parties' contract. The issue borders on the question of arbitrability, and has in that context been discussed on an international level, concerning mainly the arbitrability of the civil effects of anti-trust laws.[384] However, the issue was heard by the Norwegian Supreme Court in Rt. 2000.1312 NSC, regarding claims under the Marketing and Patents Act.

MARITIME WELL V. WELLTEC, RT. 2000.1312 NSC

The Danish company Welltec and the Norwegian company Maritime Well entered into a contract regarding the production of "well-tractors", to be used in maintaining oil and gas wells. The contract contained a re-negotiation and arbitration clause, according to which: "... potential disputes shall be sought solved between the parties by negotiation. If suchlike negotiations do not entail a solution acceptable to the parties, the issue shall be settled by arbitration according to the rules of Norwegian law." During the contract negotiations, Welltec discovered that Maritime Well and another company, Tritec, had started a production of spare parts for Welltec's well-tractors, based on the copying of Welltec's technology. Welltec further learned that Maritime Well and Tritec also had started a production of the well-tractor. Welltec initiated proceedings before Stavanger Court of First Instance, claiming that Maritime Well and Tritec should cease with and refrain from further production of Welltec's products. Furthermore, they claimed damages, NOK 2 mil. Welltec based their claim on provisions in the Norwegian Marketing Act, as well as, potentially, on certain provisions in the Patents Act, should it be found that also patented designs had been copied. On appeal, the Gulating Court of Appeal found that "the legal character of the dispute is based on the Marketing Act ... and [does not have] the parties' earlier contractual relation as legal base". The Court of Appeal did not find that such claim was within the arbitration clause. Due to the Norwegian rules on appeal the Norwegian Supreme Court could not try this finding of the Court of Appeal; the Supreme Court

---

[384] The most prominent case in this respect probably being the so-called Mitsubishi-case, (1986) XI ICCA Yearbook 555. See for a discussion of the case in a Danish perspective, *Lookofsky (1985)*.

could only examine whether the interpretation of the law and the procedure applied by the Court of Appeal was proper.

The Norwegian Supreme Court quoted the Norwegian Code of Procedure sec. 452, sub-sec. 1, according to which arbitration could be agreed for disputes arising out of a particular matter of law. According to the Supreme Court it followed that the legal matter that should be arbitrated must be identified in the arbitration agreement. The interpretation of the provision applied by the Court of Appeal on this point was correct. The Supreme Court continued: "According to the understanding of the arbitration clause, on which the Court of Appeal has based itself, the dispute is thus outside the agreement to arbitrate."[385] The Supreme Court pointed out that it was not ad liberty to try the Court of Appeal's ruling on the interpretation of the arbitration clause, and the appeal was dismissed leaving Welltec free to proceed with the case before the Stavanger Court of First Instance.

The Norwegian Supreme Court emphasised in the case, that it was not ad liberty to evaluate the Court of Appeal's interpretation of the arbitration agreement. Thus, the case does not give guidance as to whether the Norwegian Supreme Court agreed, that disputes under the Marketing Act were outside the scope of the arbitration agreement. One could speculate that the continuous emphasis on the lack of competence shown by the Supreme Court indicates that the Court did in fact not share the Court of Appeal's view, however this would be just that – a speculation. Instead, what may be extracted from the case it that the issue depends upon the interpretation of the arbitration clause. According to the Norwegian Supreme Court's argument, it is perfectly possible to word an arbitration clause so as to encompass disputes regarding the breach of mandatory law. However, contrary to the cases discussed above, the onus of proof is on the party who claims that the arbitration agreement applies.

The ruling coincides with the ruling of the Danish Supreme Court in U 2000.897 DSC, THE CHANGING MAT.[386] None of the cases are clear-cut on the actual interpretation of the arbitration agreement's scope, however they are clear on the fact that an arbitration agreement *may* be worded so as to encompass the dispute.

5.2. The impact of changes in the contractual basis

If the basis of the parties' contractual relationship is altered, the question arises, what impact this has on the application of any arbitration agreements in the contract. The question may be either whether an arbitration agreement in the parties' original contract has ceased to apply, or whether any arbitration agreement in the parties' new contract should also apply to disputes arising out of the original contract. Also this

---

[385] Writer's translation.

[386] Discussed above in § 2, point 4.3.2.

will depend on the interpretation of the arbitration agreement and the interpretation of the parties' contractual relationship as a whole. The Norwegian Courts have intertained the issue on a couple of occasions. In LB-1999-03193 NCA, WIIG V. BEKKE, Wiig and Bekke had, in 1987, formed a limited company. The company agreement clause 6 provided that the conditions, under which one of the shareholders could leave the company, should be dealt with by arbitration. In 1998 Bekke wished to leave the company, and on 29 May 1998 an agreement was made regarding Wiig's purchase of Bekke's shares. The question before the Court of Appeal was, whether the latter agreement entailed that the arbitration agreement in the company agreement had lapsed. As the agreement of 1998 had been very thorough, the Court of Appeal found that it was intended that the latter agreement should replace the agreement from 1987. The new agreement did not contain an arbitration clause and therefore there was no longer any arbitration agreement between the parties. The appeal was dismissed, leaving Bekke free to proceed with the case before the Court of First Instance.

Considering the thoroughness of the agreement regarding Wiig's purchase of Bekke's shares, the Court was convinced that the 1998-agreement was designed to exhaustively regulate Bekke's departure from the company. Thus, the original agreement from 1987 had been replaced by a new one, whereby the arbitration agreement had elapsed.

In LB-1995-01689 NCA, LIMPOX V. SAMHALL, on the other hand, the Court found that the arbitration agreement between the parties had not ceased to apply.

Limpox was the sole agent for Samhall. Their agency agreement contained an arbitration clause. On 31 December 1990, Samhall gave notice to terminate the agency agreement, however, in effect the agency continued until 31 December 1992. After the de facto termination of the agency, Limpox initiated proceedings before the Court of First Instance of Asker and Bærum claiming further payment of commission. Limpox argued before the Court that the arbitration agreement did not apply after 31 December 1990. However, the Court of Appeal found against Limpox on this point. According to the Court, the parties had not seen any need to draft a new agency contract. They had simply continued as hitherto. By thus prolonging the agency contract the parties had also prolonged the arbitration agreement. As the original arbitration agreement fulfilled the requirements set out in the Norwegian Code of Procedure sec. 452, sub-sec. 2, 1st sentence there needed not be a new written arbitration agreement. Interpreting the parties' whole contractual relationship it was obvious that the parties had agreed implicitly that the de facto continuance of their contractual relationship should be governed by their original contract. In such a situation, the prolongation the arbitration agreement needed not be in writing.

The same applies if the parties have made additions to what must be seen to be their original contract. Thus, in RT. 2000.468 NSC, NORSK LUFTAMBULANCE V. ARNULF & VA CONSULTING, the contractual relationship between the parties was construed so as consist of an original contract and appendices to the original contract. Arnulf was the managing director of Norsk Luftambulance (Luftambulance). On 1 February 1996 Arnulf handed in his notice to Luftambulance. An agreement as to the conditions under which the resignation was to take place was made on the same day. On 29 April, before the resignation had become effective, it was agreed that the company VA Consulting, which was owned entirely by Arnulf, should work for Luftambulance on a consultancy basis. It was agreed between the parties that the consultancy agreement should replace the resignation agreement of 1 February. The consultancy agreement contained an arbitration clause.

Dispute arose regarding certain amounts due to the tax authorities. The parties tried to settle the issue in an "agreement of settlement". The agreement declared to respect the consultancy agreement of 29 April. However, eventually, Luftambulance initiated proceedings before the Ytre Follo Court of First Instance, claiming the Arnulf and VA Consulting should reimburse Luftambulance for an amount the latter had paid to the tax authorities.

The agreement of settlement was between Arnulf in personam, VA Consulting and Luftambulance whereas the consultancy agreement of 29 April was between VA Consulting and Luftambulance. Luftambulance therefore claimed that as Arnulf in person was not a party to the consultancy agreement there was no agreement to arbitrate between Arnulf and Luftambulance wherefore the Courts could hear the dispute between those parties.

The Norwegian Supreme Court stated that when the parties originally had agreed that disputes between them should be settled by arbitration, then that arbitration agreement also applied to additional agreements made between the parties, unless facts that supported the opposite solution were shown to exist. The Supreme Court then evaluated the facts of the case. It was not totally clear whether Arnulf himself was actually a party to the consultancy agreement or not. However, the consultancy agreement governed Arnulf's own legal position and he had signed it. The agreement of settlement, which Arnulf was indeed a party to, also had a clear connection to the consultancy agreement. Furthermore, Arnulf himself did not oppose the application of the arbitration agreement. Taking that into account, the agreement of settlement had to be seen as an appendix to the overall contractual relationship between the parties. Considering the degree of connection between the agreements and the connection between the consultancy agreement and Arnulf's earlier contract of employment with Luftambulance, the arbitration agreement in the consultancy agreement applied to disputes arising out of the agreement of settlement.

188

Thus, if the parties' original contractual relationship has been replaced altogether by another, an arbitration agreement in the original contract will not survive. However, if there has been no *replacement* of the original contract, but instead the contract has either continued implicitly or been added to, then the arbitration agreement will, as a starting point, continue to apply.

5.3. Conclusion – the Norwegian Court's interpretation of agreements to arbitrate

The Norwegian case law here deliberated upon seems to allow for the distillation of the following rules of thumb.

1. The Norwegian Courts will not interpret the agreement to arbitrate narrowly. Conversely, they will apply the general rules on the interpretation of contract to the interpretation of arbitration agreements, see NIELSEN V. GJENSIDIGE, LB-1995-02066 CA.

2. Both claims in contract, in tort and claims due to breach of mandatory rules may be covered by the agreement to arbitrate, given the appropriate wording, as presupposed in RT. 1996.443 NSC, BRICON V. P&O and RT. 2000.1312 NSC, MARITIME WELL V. WELLTEC.

3. If the claim is between the original parties to the contract and the dispute is *prima facie* connected with that contract the claim is presumed to be within the agreement to arbitrate. The party contesting the applicability of the arbitration agreement must prove his point. In RT. NSC, NORSK LUFTAMBULANCE V. ARNULF & VA CONSULTING, RT. 1994.1489 NSC, M/T LAVENDER, RT. 1994.433 NSC, BRICON V. P&O, NIELSEN V. GJENSIDIGE, CA (LB-1995-02066), LIMPOX V. SAMHALL, CA (LB-1995-01689), LILLEHAMMER V. MOELVEN, CA (LE-1994-02647), BLANCK V. WISLØF & AASLAND, CA (LE-1993-00892), ICELANDAIR V. SAS, CA (LE-1992-02674) the party contesting the arbitration clause failed, however in WIIG V. BEKKE, CA (LB-1999-03103) the challenge to the arbitration agreement was successful.

4. If the claim is based upon the breach of mandatory law rather than upon the contractual relationship as such, the party wishing to invoke the arbitration agreement must show that the clause applies to the case, as seen in RT. 2000.1312 NSC, MARITIME WELL V. WELLTEC, and supported by the Danish case U 2000. 897 DSC, THE CHANGING MAT.

These rules of thumb take the arbitration agreement on face value except for in exceptional cases. The Norwegian Court's interpretation of arbitration agreements is thus by no means rigid.

Still, looking at the issue from the perspective of the requirements set out in the Norwegian Code of Procedure, one might conclude, that a party who has signed an agreement to arbitrate, or has entered into an arbitration agreement in one of the other ways, accepted and specified by Norwegian legislators, will be bound to arbitrate disputes that are prima facie within that agreement, unless very good reasons to the contrary are shown to exist.

6. The merit of the present regulation of arbitration agreements under Norwegian law

It has been said above in point 2.2.4 that the requirements for writing as presented in the Norwegian case law under the Norwegian Code of Procedure sec. 452 is too strict to cater for the needs of the professional players in the market. However, given that the formal requirements of sec. 452 have been met, the Norwegian Courts are likely to attach a wide scope of application to the arbitration agreement. Thus, the Norwegian case law on the interpretation of arbitration agreements and clauses generally favours the party who has alleged the wider interpretation. Once the threshold of sec. 452, sub-sec. 2, 1st sentence has been crossed, the Courts are willing to interpret an arbitration agreement thus formed to encompass disputes that do not come within the wording of the arbitration agreement, as long as the dispute is reasonably within the agreement. In this way the position under Norwegian law aids a structured approach to the arbitration agreement. The parties entering into an arbitration agreement have only needed to concentrate upon one provision of the Norwegian Code of Procedure to assess whether they are in fact obliged to arbitrate, and thus unnecessary preliminary cases before the Courts or the tribunal disputing the forum's competence have undoubtedly been avoided. Even so – the threshold provided by sec. 452 is too high.

The use of arbitration as a means of dispute resolution becomes increasingly common. Time and the developments in (international) trade and commerce has simply run out for an approach to arbitration that regards it with as much rigor as does the Norwegian Code of Procedure sec. 452. The fact that the Norwegian Courts do not interpret the arbitration agreement narrowly once the test of sec. 452 has been passed does not change this.

The recognition of this, following not only the TINE case[387] but also certain unsatisfactory arbitration awards on the tribunal's own competence,[388] was one of the sparks that has lead to the proposal of a new Norwegian Arbitration Act.

7. The regulation of the proposed Norwegian Arbitration Act

7.1. The first draft

Presently, a committee is preparing a Norwegian Arbitration Act. As a part of the preparation of the new Act the Committee held an expert seminar on arbitration.[389] At the seminar the formal requirements for arbitration agreements were discussed.[390] According to the minutes there was some feeling that the present regulation was too rigid, for example in the cases of arbitration agreements in union's rules, but all the same a general consensus that some formal requirements were necessary prevailed.

After the seminar, the Committee gave a preliminary proposal.[391] The Committee saw no reason to depart from the requirement for a written arbitration agreement. However, the Committee emphasised that the demand for writing should be amended so as to suit the needs of the parties. As put by the Committee:

"… [The] demand for writing must not represent an obstacle to the practicalities of entering into an agreement nor should it hinder the use of modern forms of communication".[392]

---

[387] Rt. 1999.1532 NSC, TINE v. LØKEN.

[388] See for example the ruling of the tribunal mentioned by *Røsæg, (1999)*, p. 673. Unfortunately, contrary to what follows from Røsæg's footnote, in the end parties to the case decided it should not be published.

[389] The minutes of the seminar are published in:
http://www.tvistemalsutvalget.net/seminarreferat.htm.

[390] Minutes of the Arbitration Seminar held 7th and 8th of March 2001, point 2.

[391] Draft Arbitration Act of 14th June 2001.

[392] Memorandum on New Rules on Arbitration, given by the Committee on the Norwegian Code of Procedure, June 14th 2001, point 8.6.2, p. 27. Writer's translation.

Even if the Committee was generally in favour of adopting the UNCITRAL Model Law,[393] it was found that Art. 7(2) of the Model Law was not apt to cover all modern communication. At this point the Committee noted the ongoing negotiations with view to amending Art. 7(2). The Committee found it most useful to use the proposed draft Art. 7(2) as a guideline for a new regulation.[394]

1st Draft Norwegian Arbitration Act, sec. 2-2: *The arbitration agreement*[395]
1) The parties can agree to arbitration for disputes that have emerged and for all or certain disputes of law that may emerge out of a particular matter of law.
2) The arbitration agreement shall be in writing.
3) The requirement for writing is fulfilled if the arbitration agreement is included in a document, written or electronic, which forms a part of the parties' agreement.
4) A party cannot claim that the arbitration agreement has not been concluded or that the arbitration agreement does not fulfil the requirement for writing after that party has submitted himself to negotiations regarding the subject matter of the dispute before the arbitration tribunal without bringing the objection forward.
5) Unless the parties agree otherwise the arbitration agreement is transferred together with the transfer of the subject matter that the arbitration agreement encompasses.

However, to ensure a sufficient consumer protection, the Committee suggested a special rule, dealing with arbitration in relation to consumers.[396]

1st Draft new Norwegian Arbitration Act, sec. 2-3: *Consumer relations*
1) An arbitration agreement to which a consumer is a party is not binding upon the consumer if it has been concluded before the dispute arose.
2) An arbitration agreement to which a consumer is a party shall be included in a document, written or electronic, which is signed by both parties. This document cannot contain other agreements than the arbitration agreement. Section 2-2(4) only applies if a consumer submits himself to negotiations

---

[393] As were most of the participants at the arbitration expert seminar, see the Minutes of the Arbitration Seminar held 7-8 March 2001, point 1(a).

[394] Memorandum on new rules on arbitration, given by the Committee on the Norwegian Code of Procedure, 14 June 2001, point 8.6.2, p. 27.

[395] Draft as per 14 June 2001. Source: Memorandum on new rules on arbitration, given by the Committee on the Norwegian Code of Procedure, 14 June 2001, point 8.6.2, p. 58, writer's translation.

[396] Memorandum on new rules on arbitration, given by the Committee on the Norwegian Code of Procedure, 14 June 2001, point 8.5.4, p. 23 f, and point 8.6.2, p. 27.

before the arbitral tribunal after he has been made aware that the arbitration agreement is not binding for him.

By choosing to single out the situations where one (or more) of the parties to the arbitration agreement was a consumer, the Committee cleared the way for a less rigid formal requirement without risking that non-professionals got caught up in arbitration clauses they could not assess.

The first draft Norwegian Arbitration Act sec. 2-2(2) stated that the arbitration agreement should be in writing. There is not much difference between this and the present regulation in sec. 452, sub-sec. 2, 1st sentence, stating that the arbitration agreement must be concluded in writing. However, bearing in mind the expressed intentions of the Committee it was clear, that a real change was intended. The existing case law on what is "in writing" would thus be obsolete. Under the proposed wording it would suffice that the arbitration agreement existed in writing (or in an electronic form), even if the consent had not been given in writing (the agreement had not been signed). The draft Act specifically included electronic media in the definition of writing, see sec. 2-2(3). Any doubt as to the feasibility of entering into arbitration agreements by e-mail for example was thus ruled out.[397] Still, oral or implied arbitration agreements would remain invalid, and some future cases as to the extent of written information required for the arbitration agreement to be in writing were to be expected. As far as incorporation by reference was concerned, the first draft § 2-2(3) provided that the requirement for writing would be fulfilled if the arbitration agreement was entered into a written or electronic document, which formed a part of the parties' agreement. The provision in this way referred back to the general rules of contract (as does the English Arbitration Act 1996 sec. 6.2). The Committee sent the memorandum containing the first draft out for hearing amongst experts, and continued its work, enabling the second draft to be published on December 20th 2001.

7.2. The second draft – the rules and the reasoning
In the draft published in NOU 2001:33, the Committee has gone even further, and chosen to eliminate the requirement for writing all together, consumer relations apart.

---

[397] See ND 1999.322 NCA, DSI v. VOSTOKTRANSFLOT, discussed above in point 3.2.

2nd Draft Norwegian Arbitration Act, sec. 2-2 and 2-3[398]

Sec. 2-2: The arbitration agreement
1) The parties may agree to submit to arbitration disputes which have arisen, as well as all or certain dispute which may arise in respect of a defined legal relationship.
2) Unless otherwise agreed between the parties in the arbitration agreement, the arbitration agreement shall be deemed to be transferred together with any transfer of the legal relationship to which the arbitration agreement applies.
3) Arbitration is binding on a party unless such party objects to the arbitral tribunal having jurisdiction over the case pursuant to section 4-1(3).

Sec. 2-3: Consumer protection
1) An arbitration agreement to which a consumer is a party shall be confirmed by way of a document, which may be in an electronic format, signed by both parties. Such document shall not include other agreements than the arbitration agreement.
2) An arbitration agreement to which a consumer is a party shall not be binding on the consumer if entered into before the dispute [arose]. Section 2-2(3) shall only apply if the consumer participates in proceedings before the arbitral tribunal after having been made aware that the arbitration agreement is not binding on him.

Considering the consumer relations, sec. 2-3 of the second draft seems to provide no change of substance from sec. 2-3 of the first draft. Arbitration agreements entered into before the dispute arose are not binding upon the parties, thus generally invalidating arbitration clauses in standard agreements if a consumer is a party to such agreements. Furthermore, once a dispute has arisen, an arbitration agreement may only be validly concluded if it is contained in a separate document, containing no other provisions, which is signed by all parties to the arbitration agreement. Thus, consumers will not unknowingly end up as parties to arbitration agreements.

When no consumers are involved, there is no longer a requirement that arbitration agreements should be in writing. In its reasoning for abandoning the requirement for writing the Committee starts by turning the discussion of formal requirements for arbitration agreements under Norwegian law upside down. Generally, it has been taken for granted by Norwegian lawyers that arbitration agreement should be in writing so as to ensure that the parties to the agreement has chosen to bar themselves from the Courts, and so that the scope of the agreement should be clear. However, the general starting point of Norwegian law is that agreements need not be in writing. Assuming this as a point of departure, the topic for evaluation is whether there are reasons that precisely arbitration agreements should not adhere to this rule. As mentioned, the reasons generally given in defence of the requirement for writing are

[398] Translation taken from NOU 2001:33, p. 122.

reasons generally given in defence of the requirement for writing are that the arbitration agreement should be patent, the concern for clarity and the concern that the parties ought to have reflected properly upon whether arbitration is the best way of solving any potential disputes. The best way of ensuring that these concerns are met is to require that the arbitration agreement should be put in a separate document signed by both parties. Requiring that outside consumer relations is admitted by the Committee to be unrealistic.[399] However, the Committee continues, once one starts "watering down" the requirement for writing, one at the same way does away with its legitimacy.[400] For example, if one allows that arbitration agreements are concluded by incorporation of a standard document containing an arbitration clause, it is not guaranteed that the parties have considered the arbitration agreement. Taking the argument further, if one allows, as does the first draft sec. 2-2(3), that arbitration agreements may be effective even without incorporation (most likely in cases where agreed documents are deemed a part of the parties' agreement without the parties having referred to them), none of the concerns mentioned in support of the requirement for writing are satisfied.

Another argument generally presented in favour of maintaining a requirement for written arbitration agreement are the rules of the New York Convention. With Norway dispensing with the requirement for writing, the risk that Norwegian arbitration agreements and awards may not be recognised and enforced in other States parties to the New York Convention has increased. However, as pointed out by the Committee, the requirement for writing in the New York Convention already differs from sec. 452 of the Norwegian Code of Procedure. Furthermore, the New York Convention Art. II has shortcomings, so the Committee was not intending to produce a requirement for writing that was an exact match of the Convention's Art. II. The Committee feared, that a national requirement for writing might lull drafters of international arbitration agreements into a false sense of security, thinking that if national requirements were met then also the New York Convention's requirements would be satisfied. If there was no requirement for writing at all "… anyone working with international arbitration [would] know that there might be a difference [compared] to the requirements of the New York Convention. They will therefore have a reason to evaluate their own position and needs …".[401] Consequently, the Committee concluded that "neither the general arguments in favour of requiring that arbitration

---

[399] NOU 2001:33, p. 56.

[400] NOU 2001:33, p. 55 f.

[401] NOU 2001:33, p. 57, writer's translation. (English summary: NOU 2001:33, p. 132).

agreements be entered into in writing, nor concern for the New York Convention, are sufficient for requiring that arbitration agreements be entered into in writing".[402]

Given that the Draft Norwegian Arbitration Act is endorsed by the Norwegian Parliament in its present form, the requirements to the formation of arbitration agreements will no longer be a matter of arbitration law, but instead follow the general rules on the formation of contract. On this point, the Committee notes that, generally, arbitration agreements will still be concluded in writing, and that arbitration agreements not evidenced in writing may be hard to invoke. If the parties choose to make a written arbitration agreement this may be done directly, through an arbitration clause in the parties' main contract, or indirectly, through incorporation by reference. As examples of cases where an arbitration agreement may be accepted by the Courts even if it does not exist in writing in the parties' agreement, the Committee mentions practices followed or documents applied by the parties in earlier transactions, or arbitration clauses in agreed documents, which are generally utilised within a certain area of trade. However, the fact that arbitration is common within a specific trade will not in itself suffice so as to constitute an agreement to arbitrate under the new Act.[403]

7.3. The second draft – pros and cons

7.3.1. The theoretical point of view

In this writer's view, the proposed regulation provides one major breakthrough, provided, and at the same time strangely unnoticed, by the Committee. Outside consumer areas, the regulation put forward in the NOU 2001:33 introduces the arbitration agreement as just another agreement amongst others. It does away with the view that an arbitration clause is always an onus upon the parties, and therefore ought to be regarded with a healthy scepticism. This writer warmly welcomes this aspect of the proposal. This writer also agrees that it is not necessary, from a legal point of view, to uphold a requirement that arbitration agreements need to be in writing. Danish and – especially – Swedish law provide good examples of this. Indeed, Sweden seems to have used its lack of formal requirements as a means of attracting international arbitration. Also, as pointed out by the Committee, a national requirement for writing is not needed for the purpose of the New York Convention. It is already pointed out elsewhere in this work that drafters of arbitration agreements under English law might be erroneous in expecting that an arbitration agreement fulfilling the

---

[402] NOU 2001:33, p. 132 and p. 57.

[403] NOU 2001:33, p. 57. (English summary: NOU 2001:33, p. 132).

requirement for writing in English law will always be regarded as satisfactory under the New York Convention Art. II(2).[404] Thus, a national requirement for writing does not eliminate the need for an independent evaluation of the New York Convention's requirements.

Consequently, when looking solely at the substance of the law, there is no need for the arbitration agreement to be in writing. At a theoretical level, the need for and legitimacy of a requirement for writing evaporates when one decides that arbitration clauses and agreements are not a burden upon the parties. All the same, this writer has reservations towards the proposed rule. It must be emphasised, though, that those reservations are not directed at the theory behind the new rule. Indeed, the reservations are based on this writer's concern, that the chosen approach is not the most preferable according to what are the needs of the trade.

7.3.2. This writer's reservations

7.3.2.1. Introduction

This writer's reservations are based on three different arguments that seem to pull in the same direction, namely 1) the benefit of providing a focus on securing proof of the arbitration agreement, and thus avoiding unnecessary litigation on the question of competence, whilst at the same time providing for a more structured approach when establishing whether an agreement to arbitrate has indeed been entered into, 2) the question of the Act's user-friendliness, and 3) this writer's contention that in fact a real absence of a formal requirement is hardly intended; consequently, that the wording of the provision may lead the parties to rely on an informal agreement to arbitrate, only to find at a later stage that the agreement is rejected by the Courts. In the following those points will be elaborated in turn.

7.3.2.2. Focus and clarity of case law

Even a lax requirement for writing will impose an emphasis on the arbitration agreement, and thereby makes it more likely that the parties consider the formation of the arbitration agreement independently of the formation of the other provisions of the parties' agreement. In international arbitration the parties already need to do so, due to the requirement for writing in the New York Convention Art. II(2), however, if a lax requirement for writing is kept in the new Norwegian Arbitration Act, then

---

[404] See § 5, point 4.1.

this focus will also be put on domestic agreements to arbitrate. This is thought to be beneficial, as it will help to avoid unnecessary litigation on the existence of the arbitration agreement.

Furthermore, by the proposal published in NOU 2001:33, the Committee has moved the discussion of the conclusion of arbitration agreements from arbitration law to the law of contract.

The Committee states in the proposal, that the discussion of whether an arbitration clause has been accepted under the rules of contract law is independent from the discussion of whether any formal requirements have been met. It follows from that, that the issue of acceptance under the rules of contract is equally important whether or not one applies formal criteria under the rules of arbitration law. Accepting that line of reasoning, there is no rationale of practicality for the preservation of the formal requirement. One is simply cutting away the superfluous. However, this reasoning, being formally correct, appears less convincing when one regards the case law from the Norwegian Courts. Cases, where the Courts, after having discussed the formal criteria of the Norwegian Code of Procedure sec. 452, sub-sec. 2, 1ˢᵗ sentence, continues to either accept or reject the arbitration clause on grounds of general contract law are not that common. Examples that come to mind are cases such as SITAS V. HØGLUND and ØSTREM ET AL V. BYGGESERVICE, where it was clear that there was a signature from both parties on the main document, that the main document contained a written reference to the conditions in question, and that those conditions existed in writing.[405] In those cases, it was necessary to revert to principles of general contract law to decide whether or not the incorporation was effective. But these cases do not form the bulk of the case law. Generally, sec. 452, sub-sec. 2, 1ˢᵗ sentence as interpreted by case law has provided an "either/or". Given that the very strict formal criteria of sec. 452 have been fulfilled, then also the requirements of general contract law on the formation of contracts have been satisfied. Therefore, until now the discussion of the conclusion of arbitration agreements has revolved around one provision, and the relatively few leading cases interpreting it. This will change.

Obviously, new case law will emerge, qualifying what the requirements are, and the points offered in NOU 2001:33 might also provide a guideline, but the certainty and transparency caused by the very strict formal requirement has receded.

It is not hereby suggested, that one keeps the requirement for writing in the Norwegian Code of Procedure sec. 452, sub-sec. 2, 1ˢᵗ sentence, but it is suggested that

---

[405] See also ND 1991.287. In the case it could not be proven that the arbitration clause had been agreed under the general rules of contract law. Therefore, there was no reason for the Courts to entertain the question of whether the agreement had been concluded *in writing* under the Norwegian Code of Procedure sec. 452.

by establishing a lax requirement for writing, one will provide a starting point for the Courts being presented with the arbitration agreement, a starting point based in arbitration law rather than in the general rules on the law of contract.

7.3.2.3. The Act's user-friendliness

Posing the question why there should be a (lax) requirement in the new Act that arbitration agreements should be in writing, the Committee was able to come up with no convincing answers. As a consequence, the Committee decided that there should not. However, the Committee asked the question from the point of view of the Norwegian legal profession, skilled arbitrators and other experts. Such persons have no difficulties in dealing with arbitration agreements after the general Norwegian rules on the conclusion of contracts, as they are already familiar with those rules.

The mandate of the Committee stated explicitly that when making the new rules it should be ensured that the rules could also be used by persons, who were not part of the legal profession. Moving the decision of whether or not arbitration is agreed upon into the general rules of contract law makes the law more inaccessible, thus requiring a general knowledge of the Norwegian legal system and case law that may not be expected of laymen. One could note at this point that one of the reasons why the English legal profession and legislators saw the need for the English Arbitration Act 1996 was that many of the English rules on arbitration were found in case law. "The law on these topics lies almost entirely in the reported cases, beyond the reach of lay users of arbitration, and indeed of non-specialist foreign and English lawyers."[406] It was felt that if arbitration in England was to be maintained as a popular means of dispute resolution in international trade, then it would be beneficial to state the rules on arbitration and on the arbitration agreement rather exhaustively. There is no such expressed policy behind the drafting of the Norwegian Arbitration Act. However, the Committee has noted that the number of international commercial disputes must be expected to rise in the future, in keeping with the growth of international trade.[407] One should not overlook that especially within international maritime arbitration, Oslo is an often-used forum, due to both the considerable Norwegian shipping industry and the availability of extremely skilled maritime lawyers. Thus, also in the future foreign lawyers will need to assess the requirements of the Norwegian regulation on the formation of arbitration agreements.

---

[406] *Mustill-report*, para 103. See also *Rutherford/Sims (1996)*, on p. 10 and p. 7.

[407] NOU 2001:33, p. 23. (English summary, see NOU 2001:33 p. 131).

For the purpose of making the law accessible also for laymen and foreign lawyers, the requirement for writing in the first draft's sec. 2-2(2) and the guidelines as to what is "in writing" provided in the first draft's sec. 2-2(3) seem to be the better option. They provide a starting point for the drafter as well as directions for the persons who at a later stage need to assess whether Norwegian Courts will accept a certain arbitration clause or agreement. One could keep the second draft sec. 2(2) as it now stands, and then strongly suggest that drafters and other users of arbitration clauses and agreements make sure, that both parties have signed the arbitration agreement or the main agreement, in which case the arbitration agreement will certainly be validly formed (invalidity on the substance apart). However, if that turns out to be the de facto rule of practice, one has not achieved much.

7.3.2.4. Still a requirement for writing?

Comparing the first draft sec. 2-2(2) and 2-2(3) to the position of the law under the second draft sec. 2-2, there seem little difference as to which arbitration agreements should be accepted by the Norwegian Courts. In the proposal the Committee explains the existing rule of the conclusion of contracts – also being the only rule, governing the conclusion of arbitration agreements in the future. According to the Committee, arbitration agreements, and other important agreements, will normally have to be in writing and may be included in the main document or incorporated by reference. The Courts may only rarely be expected to accept arbitration agreements that are not in writing. The Courts may accept an arbitration agreement even if it has not been incorporated directly into the parties' agreement in two cases, namely in cases where agreed documents are considered to form a part of the law within the relevant trade, and where a firm practice between the relevant parties requires that any disputes be solved by arbitration.[408] If this is the de facto position of the law intended, this writer argues that that position should be made clearer in the Act itself. A provision implying that there are no formal requirements is likely to give the reader an untrue impression of what is the law.

The first draft sec. 2-2(3) states, that "[the] requirement for writing is fulfilled if the arbitration agreement is included in a document ... that forms a part of the parties' agreement". In conjunction with the first draft sec. 2-2(2) it is clear that arbitration agreements that do not somehow exist in the written form cannot be accepted, but those agreements are rare. There is no reason why an oral reference to a set of standard conditions, as Lloyd's Open Form, for example, should not suffice, nor is

[408] NOU 2001:33, p. 57.

200

there any reason why agreed documents, forming a part of the law on a certain area, or a general practice between the parties to perform their trade according to one of the parties' General Conditions should not be adequate for the effectiveness of any arbitration clauses in such agreed documents of General Conditions. The only de facto difference between the second draft and the first seems to be that under the first draft, arbitration agreements that do not exist in writing will *never* be accepted by the Courts, whereas under the second draft they *might, in rare cases*. Obviously the scope of what is permitted has thereby been enlarged. But not by much, and it seems to this writer that the effect of the enlargement is likely to be negligible.

7.3.3. Conclusion

This writer is generally sceptical towards the advisability of having no formal requirements for arbitration agreements. Admittedly, this may be due to the somewhat unsatisfactory experience of having broken down Danish case law on arbitration agreements in order to try to establish some basic, general rule, and not finding any. To an extent, though, that experience in itself gives an indication as to what Norwegian law might come to look like. Moving the discussion of the requirements for the conclusion of arbitration agreements into the general law of contract does not solve the relevant legal problems – it just moves them into another field of law. Still, if in the upcoming case law the Norwegian Courts will lay out good precedence, qualifying the arbitration agreement as any other agreement, and thus involving no special requirements, the approach of the second draft may turn out well. If, on the other hand, Norwegian Courts still hold reservations towards arbitration agreements and clauses, being as they might under some influence of earlier case law and doctrine, then the position of the law under the new Norwegian Arbitration Act will be quite uncertain. This writer must admit to find that the most realistic scenario is that the Norwegian Courts will accept the arbitration agreement as any other *potentially onerous* agreement amongst others. If this, admittedly somewhat pessimistic, forecast turns out to be precise, then the rulings of the Norwegian Courts are likely to attain an unpleasing similarity to present Danish case law.

§ 5. Précis and deductions regarding the formation of arbitration agreements in national law in Denmark, England and Norway

Danish law, presenting no formal requirements for the formation of arbitration agreements hold one generally applicable test, developed in case law, namely that there must be a *clear agreement to arbitrate* between the parties. Unfortunately, this phrase is rather void of real information. The lack of formal requirements makes a convincing structure of a discussion of the requirements for the conclusion of arbitration agreements under Danish law hard to conjure. Furthermore, under Danish law, the answer to the question whether an arbitration agreement has been entered into necessitates an excursion into various areas of contract law.[409] The Danish Courts' tradition for making an overall evaluation of whether the parties have agreed on a specific issue provides for a case law that pays little attention to the scholar's wish to keep the different issues apart. Still, conclusions may be reached as to how the requirement for a "clear agreement to arbitrate" may be satisfied. The focus will be on what the actual parties knew or ought to have known.[410] The arbitration agreement

---

[409] § 2, point 1.

[410] § 2, point 2.

may be incorporated by a one-layered general reference to a contract or standard document containing the arbitration clause, but a two-layered reference is not considered a sufficiently clear agreement to arbitrate.[411] Finally, a party, who succeeds in a contract, containing an arbitration clause will – as a rule – also succeed in the duty to arbitrate.[412]

As regards English law, it is required under the English Arbitration Act 1996 sec. 5, that the *arbitration agreement should be in writing,*[413] which should be understood as evidenced in writing or as being recorded by any means, thus presenting a very lax attitude to the formal prerequisites for the conclusion of an arbitration agreement. Indeed, it seems that de facto only purely oral arbitration agreements are exempted from the scope of sec. 5. However, such agreements may be recognised under the rules of common law, see the English Arbitration Act sec. 81(1)(b).[414] The formal criterion provides for a starting point for the discussion of arbitration agreements under English law, however, the criterion being so lax, and the possibility for recognising agreements that do not fulfil sec. 5 under common law rules, allows for a relatively brief discussion of the formal criteria as between the parties. Instead, it is the arbitration agreement's effect as against third parties that is at the centre of the discussion. Especially the possibility of incorporating arbitration agreements by reference is important. It is shown that under English law, a one-layered reference may be effective, provided either that the reference is made specifically to the arbitration agreement, or that the document referred to upon its wording is also applicable to disputes under the contract in which the reference is made.[415] A two-layered general reference seems to have been rejected as effective for incorporation,[416] but it cannot be shown from case law that a specific two-layered reference may not be accepted.

Under Norwegian law, the main issue is the correct interpretation of the Norwegian Code of Procedure sec. 452, sub-sec. 2, 1st sentence, requiring that the arbitration agreement should be in writing. It is concluded that under Norwegian law, not

---

[411] § 2, point 4.2.1.

[412] § 2, point 4.2.2.2.

[413] § 3, point 1.

[414] § 3, point 1.

[415] § 3, point 4.

[416] § 3, point 5.1.

the arbitration clause but the *consent to arbitration must be in writing.*[417] It also seems clear from case law that the validity of the arbitration agreement requires that both or all parties to the arbitration agreement have signed the agreement.[418] However, an arbitration agreement may be incorporated by a one-layered general reference,[419] and it also seems that parties who claim under a contract through succession or assignment must respect an arbitration agreement in that contract.[420] Apart from that the requirement for a reciprocal signature allows little room for allocating the arbitration agreement any legal effect towards parties, who have not succeeded in or been assigned the legal position of the original parties. Still, arbitration may be validly concluded under special rules such as the NMC sec. 311[421] and the Norwegian Company Act sec. 2-30.[422]

The differences in the legal framework in the three jurisdictions provide for three quite different chapters, and for different focus and different issues being discussed. As for the requirements for the arbitration agreement to be valid from the outset, the only common denominator is that in all jurisdictions an arbitration agreement contained directly in a document signed by all parties to the agreement will be effective, invalidity on the substance apart. However, there are still some rules that the three regulations seem to agree upon, namely that a party succeeding in the rights and obligations of one of the original parties must respect any valid arbitration agreement in the original parties' contract, that arbitration agreements may be incorporated by a one-layered reference even if some discrepancies exist regarding whether such incorporation needs to be specific or whether a general reference will suffice, and that a two-layered reference is unlikely to be accepted in any of the jurisdictions.

The pros and cons described and suggestions de lege ferenda made above regarding the different regulations should not be repeated here. Instead, one issue will be mentioned namely that all jurisdictions seem to lack sufficient appreciation of the need to accept arbitration agreements in contracts on back-to back terms. In TRYGG

---

[417] § 4, point 2.2.1.

[418] § 4, point 2.2.3.

[419] § 4, point 2.2.2.

[420] § 4, point 4.

[421] Chapter IV, § 2.

[422] § 4, point 4.

HANSA V. EQUITAS,[423] Trygg Hansa argued that an arbitration clause in the primary insurance contracts had been incorporated into first the excess of loss insurance and then into the reinsurance of the excess of loss insurance. Such a two-layered incorporation was not held to be ineffective under the English Arbitration Act 1996. Under Danish law, an attempt to achieve back-to-back conditions by incorporation was rejected in KLINTEMARKEN,[424] as the incorporation technique was that of a two-layered reference. The possibility of generally accepting arbitration agreements between different parties in the contract chain if the contract chain is on back-to-back terms has been accepted by some legal writers, but has been rejected de lege lata by this writer, except for situations where the arbitration agreement according to its wording applies to the whole contract chain.[425] Under Norwegian law, there does not seem to be any cases, where it has been argued that arbitration agreements should be valid between parties in the contract chain for the reason alone that the contracts are on back-to-back terms. It is suggested by this writer, that the very strict requirement for a mutual signature found under Norwegian law have dissuaded any would-be parties to such an "arbitration agreement" from taking the case to the Courts.

It is suggested, de lege ferenda, regarding all jurisdictions that the Courts in the future should pay more regard to the need for keeping a contracts on back-to-back terms effective, such as to facilitate recourse claims and the possibility of keeping a dispute before a single forum. This does not mean that back-to-back conditions should always be accepted as constituting an agreement to arbitrate between different parties in the contract chain. It is only suggested that in situations where contracting on back-to-back terms constitutes a trade practice and where the parties are professionals working within that trade, the presumption should be for accepting the arbitration agreement.

---

[423] [1998] 2 Lloyd's Law Reports 439 QBD, TRYGG HANSA V. EQUITAS. See § 3, point 4.1.

[424] U 1963.488 DSC, Klintemarken. See above § 2, point 4.2.1.

[425] See § 2, point 4.2.2.5.

§ 6. The New York Convention's requirement for arbitration agreements to be in writing

1. Introduction

The New York Convention 1958 was created in an attempt to improve the international regulation of arbitration given in the Geneva Protocol 1923[426] and the Geneva Convention 1927.[427] For the parties that have ratified the New York Convention, the Geneva regulations are thus replaced.[428] The Convention aims at aiding international arbitration by ensuring that the Courts of the Contracting States will recognise and enforce international arbitration agreements and awards, see Art. II(1) and III, 1st sentence. At the same time, the Contracting States must refrain from imposing more onerous requirements for the recognition and enforcement of international arbitration agreements and awards, than for domestic ones.[429] The New York Convention provides a minimum standard of regulation. Thus, the Contracting States may impose

---

[426] The Geneva Protocol on Arbitration Clauses of 1923.

[427] The Geneva Convention on the Execution of Foreign Arbitral Awards of 1927.

[428] The New York Convention Art. VII(2). See the English Arbitration Act 1996, sec. 99.

[429] The New York Convention Art. III, 2nd sentence.

less restrictive criteria in national law, see the so-called "more favourable rights-provision" in Art. VII(1).

The New York Convention is one of the most successful conventions within international private law, and has been acceded to by most States.[430] At the same time, the Convention is a general convention, and will, according to Art. VII(1) not affect other bi- or multilateral conventions that the Contracting States may enter into on special areas of law. The New York Convention has been incorporated into the English Arbitration Act 1996, Part III, secs. 99-104 and secs. 5 and 6(2). The incorporation into Danish law can be found in the Arbitration Regulation secs. 1-3, and in the Danish Arbitration Act sec. 1, sub-sec. 1. There is no verbatim incorporation of the New York Convention in Norwegian law, however, the Norwegian Code of Procedure sec. 36a and sec. 168, 2nd sentence and the Norwegian Enforcement Act sec. 4-1(f) allow for the recognition and enforcement of foreign arbitral awards. Foreign arbitration agreements will generally be accepted under the same preconditions as Norwegian ones, the most important provision thus being the Norwegian Code of Procedure sec. 452.

In the following, the focus will be on the provisions of the Convention that deal with arbitration agreements. Thus, a complete discussion of the whole convention will not be found here. Especially, for an in-depth discussion of the rules regarding the recognition and enforcement of arbitral awards one will have to consult other writers.

Instead, the emphasis will be on the formal requirements for arbitration agreements given in the New York Convention Art. II(2). However, before that discussion is entered into, a definition of the scope of application of the New York Convention is called for.

2. Scope of application

2.1. In general

The New York Convention applies equally to institutionalised and ad hoc arbitration.[431] It governs the situations where the arbitration agreement or award encounters the Courts. The arbitral procedure is only dealt with indirectly, e.g. in Art. V(1)(a) and V(1)(b), stating that the recognition and enforcement of an arbitral award may be refused if the award suffers from significant procedural flaws. Thus, the rules gov-

---

[430] As per 13 November 2001, the New York Convention was ratified or acceded to by 139 States.

[431] Art. I(2).

erning the arbitral procedure will have to be found in national law, in other conventions,[432] or in the relevant arbitration rules.[433] Even so, the New York Convention governs far from all the remaining questions of arbitration law. First and foremost, the Convention defines the extent of the Contracting States' obligation to recognise and enforce arbitration agreements and awards. Most questions of substantive law are referred to be dealt with in national law, but the New York Convention will tend to hold choice of law rules to the determination of *which* national law will determine a certain issue.[434]

The New York Convention Art. I(3) allows the Contracting States to make two reservations regarding the scope of application of the Convention. Firstly, a State may declare only to apply the Convention to awards made in the territory of another Contracting State, a common reservation, made also by Denmark, Norway and the United Kingdom, (the first reservation). A State may also reserve the right to only apply the Convention to commercial disputes, (the second reservation). Such a reservation has been made by Denmark. Thus, Danish Courts will not apply the Convention in consumer relations. Norway and the United Kingdom have not taken the second reservation. However, undesirable effects of applying the Convention to international disputes concerning consumers may be avoided by other means; see e.g. [1979] 1 Lloyd's Law Reports 244 CA, WILLCOCK V. PICKFORDS.[435]

---

[432] E.g. The European Convention on International Commercial Arbitration 1961.

[433] E.g. ICC Arbitration Rules (1998) or UNCITRAL Arbitration Rules (1976).

[434] See Art. V.

[435] In the case Mrs. Willcock had over the phone asked Pickfords Removals Ltd. for an estimate of the removal of her furniture from UK to New Zealand. Pickfords sent Mrs. Willcock a written estimate on a standard form contract referring to their General Conditions, which contained an arbitration clause. The English Court of Appeal found that as long as there was a dispute as to the existence of the arbitration agreement, no written arbitration agreement within the meaning of the Arbitration Act 1975 sec. 7(1) existed. A commercial shipper, having delivered his goods to a carrier after having received a written estimate including the reference to the carrier's general contracts of carriage, would probably not as easily have convinced the Courts that he had not agreed to arbitrate. Also, arbitration agreements in consumer contracts are covered by the "Unfair Terms in Consumer Contracts Regulation 1994", (see the English Arbitration Act 1996, secs. 89-91), invalidating arbitration agreements in disputes regarding small claims.

2.2. Arbitral awards

According to the New York Convention Art. I(1) the Convention applies to arbitral *awards* "… made in a territory of a State other that the State …" where the award is sought recognised and/or enforced. The Convention does not require, that the *dispute* is international, instead it is required that the *award* is *foreign*.[436] A seemingly domestic arbitration award, as when two English parties arbitrate their dispute in England, may thus turn out to fall within the scope of the New York Convention provided that one of the parties seek to enforce the award abroad. In this way the arbitration agreement becomes subject to the rules of the New York Convention. This may cause problems if the arbitration award is given under a regime that has a more lax requirement for the formation of arbitration agreements than the one found in the New York Convention, see ND 1999.322 NCA, DSI V. VOSTOKTRANSFLOT.[437]

In the case Vostoktransflot wished to enforce an arbitral award as against DSI. The award was given in England according to English law, and it was accepted by the Norwegian Court of Appeal that the conditions under English law for the conclusion of the arbitration agreement were fulfilled. However, since the way in which the arbitration agreement had been concluded did not fulfil the requirements of the New York Convention Art. II, the Norwegian Court of Appeal refused to enforce the award.

Furthermore, the Convention is applicable to arbitral awards that are not made abroad, but that are not considered domestic in the State where they are sought enforced either. Norwegian Courts may thus apply the New York Convention to arbitral awards made in Norway, if the award is considered foreign under Norwegian law, see explicitly the Norwegian Code of Procedure sec. 168, 2nd sentence.[438]

According to the English Arbitration Act sec. 100(1) and sec. 100(2)(b), a New York Convention award is an award given by a tribunal *seated*[439] in another Contracting State, provided that the Contracting State had ratified the Convention at the time[440] that recognition and/or enforcement is sought. The wording of the provision

---

[436] *van den Berg (1981)*, p. 17.

[437] Also mentioned above, § 4, point 3.2.

[438] See further *Pryles (1993)*, on p. 264.

[439] Regarding what constitutes a "seat", see 1996 Report on the Arbitration Bill para. 26.

[440] See [1984] 1 Lloyd's Law Reports 459 HL, GOVERNMENT OF KUWAIT V. SNOW. An arbitral award was given in Kuwait before Kuwait ratified the New York Convention. Six years later, the award was sought enforced in England. In the meantime Kuwait had ratified the Convention, and the arbitral award could thus be enforced under the English Arbitration Act 1975.

is a reaction to the decision of the House of Lords in [1991] 2 Lloyd's Law Reports 435 HL, HISCOX V. OUTWHITE.[441] In the case a dispute was to be settled by a single arbitrator. The arbitral procedure was to take place in London according to English law. However, the arbitral award was signed "Nov. 20, 1990, 12 Rue d. Astorg, 75008 Paris". House of Lords found that such an award was not domestic, and thus that the New York Convention's rules applied. This somewhat undesirable result lead to the drafting of the English Arbitration Act 1996 sec. 100(2)(b) according to which it is the seat of the arbitration tribunal, and not where the award may be signed, that decides where the award is made. Real doubts as to where a tribunal is seated must be rare, and the determination under English law of whether an arbitral award falls within the ambit of the New York Convention thus seems rather simple.

The definition in Danish law of the scope of application of the New York Convention is given in the Arbitration Regulation sec. 2, sub-sec. 1.

Danish Arbitration Regulation sec. 2, sub-sec. 1

Arbitral awards in disputes regarding commercial relations, *which are binding* in this Country, and *which are given in a State* that has acceded to the New York Convention of 10. July 1958 on recognition and enforcement of foreign arbitral awards may be enforced in this Country.[442]

It follows from the Arbitration Regulation sec. 1 that foreign arbitral awards have binding effect in Denmark if they concern a dispute that may be settled by arbitration and if the recognition is not clearly in conflict with the Danish legal order. Thus, foreign arbitral awards will be *recognised* as long as the subject matter of the dispute is arbitrable and the effects of the recognition is not in conflict with Danish ordre public. *Enforcement* of the award under the expedient rules of the Arbitration Regulation furthermore presupposes that the award is given in a State that is party to the New York Convention. There does not seem to be any further requirement that the dispute should be international.

The Arbitration Regulation does not define when an award is "given" in another State, so problems of the sort encountered in HISCOX V. OUTWHITE may occur. It is therefore recommended that also Danish Courts will look at the seat of the tribunal to decide where the award is given. However, according to the travaux préparatoires, it is not intended that the Danish incorporation of the New York Convention should only apply to awards given in another State. According to the Committee, an award given in Denmark may also be foreign if the parties and/or the arbitrators are foreign,

---

[441] See *van den Berg (1996)*, p. 401.

[442] Writer's translation and emphasis.

and if the tribunal has applied foreign law to the dispute. However, the Committee did not wish to provide a definition of what was a foreign award – that was seen as best taken care of in case law.[443]

Norwegian law does not contain a verbatim incorporation of the New York Convention as such, however, the Norwegian Code of Procedure sec. 168, 2nd sentence seems to provide that the rules of the New York Convention apply equally to arbitration agreements given abroad and to arbitration agreements that, for other reasons, are not considered domestic.

Norwegian Code of Procedure secs. 167 and 168 *in extract*
Sec. 167. By treaty with foreign States it may be agreed that decisions made by the Courts of those States regarding civil disputes ... shall be binding in this Country. ...
Sec. 168. The provisions of sec. 167 apply equally to legal decisions made by the administrative authorities of a foreign State ... Likewise; the provision *applies to arbitration awards that are not considered domestic (cf. chapter 32) and in all cases where the arbitration decision has been made abroad.*[444]

In summing up it may be said that in Denmark, England and Norway, the New York Convention will apply to arbitration awards that are given by a tribunal seated in a foreign Contracting State. It seems that Danish and Norwegian Courts might apply the Convention also to awards given within those Countries, if for some reason the award is best described as foreign. However, real guidance as to when an award is foreign is not given. Whether also English Courts will apply to New York Convention's rules to awards given in England, but international in nature, is not quite clear. One could expect that the strict rule in sec. 100(1), defining the seat of the arbitral tribunal as the decisive factor, may mean that this will not be the case.

2.3. Arbitration agreements
The New York Convention also applies to arbitration agreements, see especially Art. II. The Convention applies both to arbitration clauses, and arbitration agreements that are entered into after the dispute arose. A real delimitation of the scope of application of the Convention is not given in the Convention. Instead, conditions for the recognition of arbitration agreements are given, see below in point 3. According to Art. II, an arbitration agreement should be recognised if the agreement is valid on the substance and satisfies the formal criteria in Art. II(2). The determination of whether

[443] Danish Arbitration Act travaux préparatoires 1, p. 34. See also *Petersen (1935)*, p. 72.

[444] Writer's emphasis and translation.

these conditions are satisfied go far beyond what one would normally expect when determining the scope of application of a convention. According to *Gaja*,[445] Art. II does not delimit the scope of application. Instead, the Convention is applicable to all arbitration agreements that may lead to an arbitral award that is recognisable and/or enforceable under the Convention. Thus, the arbitration agreement must be capable of leading to an arbitration award within the meaning of the New York Convention Art. I. Indeed, it is generally accepted that arbitration agreements should have been mentioned in Art. I, regarding the Convention's scope of application, but were omitted due to rush at the diplomatic conference.[446]

It seems logical that the New York Convention's application to arbitration agreements should be parallel to its application to arbitration awards. This would entail that arbitration agreements prescribing the arbitral procedure to take place in a foreign State would fall within the Convention. Also, arbitration agreements that are for other reasons not considered domestic in the State confronted with the plea for recognition should be deemed encompassed by the Convention's rules. However, the ambit defined thus may be too narrow,[447] and simply referring to the fact that the scope of application should be parallel to the scope set out regarding the arbitration awards is too vague to offer real guidance. Many different arbitration agreements are capable of resulting in an arbitration award that falls within the New York Convention Art. I. As stated by the German Oberlandesgericht in Hamm: "Notwithstanding its narrow title, the Convention regulates ... *all agreements, which have resulted, could result or could have resulted* in a foreign award."[448] This writer adheres to this statement. Considering that an award is not only foreign if it is rendered abroad, but also if the award cannot be considered domestic due to some foreign feature of the award, it is proper to conclude that the agreement to arbitrate is covered by the Convention if the agreement to arbitrate is international. The agreement to arbitrate is international most prominently if the parties are domiciled in different Countries, but it might also be considered international due to the fact alone that the dispute concerns international transactions.

In conclusion may be said as a starting point the New York Convention applies to all arbitration agreements that are not purely domestic. To fall outside the New York Convention the arbitration agreement must be connected solely to the State in which

---

[445] *Gaja (1979)*, I.A.2, before footnote 6.

[446] *Gaja (1979)*, I.A.2, before footnote 5 and *van den Berg (1981)*, p. 56.

[447] *van den Berg (1981)*, p. 61 ff.

[448] (1997) XXII ICCA Yearbook 707, on p. 708, para. 8.

recognition is sought, alternatively, in States who have taken the first reservation, to a State not party to the New York Convention.

3. The formal requirements in the New York Convention Art. II

3.1. Introduction
It follows from the New York Convention's Art. II(1), that arbitration agreements should be in writing. The requirement is further specified in Art. II(2).

The New York Convention Art. II *in extract*:
1. Each Contracting State shall recognise an agreement in writing under which the parties undertake to submit to arbitration all or any differences which have arisen or which may arise between them ...
2. The term "agreement in writing" shall include an arbitral clause in a contract or an arbitration agreement, signed by the parties or contained in an exchange of letters or telegrams. ...

Establishing the real contents of this formal requirement gives rise to several problems. *Firstly,* it is not clear what impact national law in the Contracting States has upon the provision. *Secondly,* the wording of the provision allows for different interpretations. *Thirdly,* when wanting to interpret the provision in accordance with its aim, international law considerations will have to be made, and *fourthly* it is unclear what effect the technological and legal developments that have taken place in the world since 1958 should be given as regards the interpretation of Art. II(1) and II(2).

Below, those uncertainties will be deliberated upon, and – insofar as this is possible – eliminated. In point 3.2 it will be discussed whether the New York Convention should be subject to an autonomous interpretation. In point 3.3, the writer's view upon the correct interpretation of the provision will be given, and also the proposed declaration on the interpretation of the New York Convention Art. II(1) and II(2) seen in the light of the proposed new wording of the Model Law Art. 7 will be discussed. In point 3.4, the requirement for writing in the New York Convention Art. II(2) will be compared to the national legislations in Denmark, Norway and England and finally, in point 3.5, the writer's views *de lege ferenda* will be presented.

3.2. An autonomous interpretation?
Both legal theory and case law in the Contracting States vary as regards national law's impact upon the requirements set out in the New York Convention Art. II(2). In some case law an autonomous interpretation is adopted, finding its legitimacy in reasons of unification, in other case law it is presumed that in the end national law will settle what is a written agreement. The divide is also found in legal theory on the

subject. *Gaja*[449] and *van den Berg*[450] both prefer that Art. II(2) should be subject to an autonomous interpretation, however according to *van den Berg* this starting point can probably not be maintained, as an increasing part of national case law seems to have rejected the idea. *Glossner*[451] finds, quite pragmatically, that an autonomous interpretation would be preferable. However, he does not find the idea likely to be effected regarding a convention such as the New York Convention, which has been acceded to by a large number of States, governed by different national rules, and which has no forum that can settle doubts as to interpretation.

Above, in Chapter I, § 4, point 2.2, it has been shown that international conventions, even when viewed from a country that supports the theory of dualism, have an independent existence, which is distinct from national law. This entails that the concepts used in international conventions to an extent must have a meaning that is independent of similar concepts used in national law. In the following it will be investigated which contributions to the interpretation of the New York Convention Art. II(1) and II(2) can be attained from an independent interpretation of the article. The term "an independent interpretation" is chosen since a real autonomous interpretation may hardly be achieved. It seems to this writer that an autonomous interpretation in its real sense presupposes both that a clear objective for a rule can be pointed out and that a forum equipped with the power to authoritatively define the correct interpretation of the rule exists. Regarding the New York Convention, none of these requirements are satisfied.

In this light, attempting to define the "independent" contents of the New York Convention Art. II(1) and II(2) may seem pointless. Still, the necessity of making an independent interpretation of the provisions is upheld. This mainly for three reasons:

1. The requirement for writing is the most important parameter when establishing the obligations of the Contracting States to recognise arbitration agreements. A Contracting State may in its national law have stricter formal requirements for the conclusion of arbitration agreements than is the case under Danish and English law, present Norwegian law being used as the standard example of this in this thesis. For such states, it is important that the New York Convention's formal requirements replace and relax the national requirements. For the same reason, it is hardly surprising that it is the Courts in jurisdictions that present stringent formal requirements, which have been most likely to express themselves in support of an autonomous interpreta-

---

[449] *Gaja (1979)*, point I.B.3, before note 49.

[450] *van den Berg (1996)*, p. 421.

[451] *Glossner (1989)*, p. 277 f.

tion of the New York Convention. Generally, those statements have been made in connection to the question of the recognition of the arbitration agreement. To sanction the acceptance of an arbitration agreement that does not conform to the requirements of national law, the Courts have needed to establish authority in a source of law that is independent of national law. Thus, the Greek Supreme Court in plenum stated that "… Art. II(2) of the New York Convention … introduced a directly applicable substantive rule, which binds the States-Parties and does not allow the Court, in the field of application of the Convention, the possibility to resort to another rule of substantive or private law in order to confirm the validity of the form of the conclusion of the agreement to arbitrate".[452] Likewise, the Swiss Supreme Court stated, with reference to earlier theory and case law, that "… the New York Convention, where applicable, prevails over national law, thereby guaranteeing its uniform application by the Contracting States. Hence, the issue of (formal) validity is determined solely according to the Convention; the requirement of the written form according to Art. II of the New York Convention is to be interpreted independently, without the assistance of a national law."[453]

An international source of law applied thus by the Courts of the Contracting States should have a well-defined content and scope. As regards the formal requirements for arbitration agreements, the content is determined by Art. II(1) and II(2).

Conversely, it is normally the Courts in States with lax requirements to the form of arbitration agreements, that support the contention that the requirement for writing in the New York Convention Art. II(2) should be determined by national law. From the point of view of such Courts, this is reasonable due to the more favourable right-provision in the New York Convention Art. VII.

The New York Convention Art. VII in extract:
"… the … Convention shall not … deprive any interested party of any right he may have to avail himself of an arbitral award in the manner and to the extent allowed by the law … of the country where such award is sought relied upon".

Although this provision is worded with view to the arbitral award, it is generally accepted to apply equally to arbitration agreements.

Under that provision, the Contracting States are ad liberty to recognise and enforce arbitration agreements and awards to a greater extent than what follows from the Convention. Consequently, to Courts and tribunals in "arbitration agreement

---

[452] (1998) XXIII ICCA Yearbook 654, THE BYZANTINE EAGLE, on p. 655, para. 4.

[453] (1997) XXII ICCA Yearbook 800, p. 803, para. 9.

friendly" states, there seems very little reason to define the contents of Art. II(2). However, the Courts in such states should keep in mind that the acceptance under the more favourable rights provision in Art. VII is based on national law, and not on the Convention. The Courts should not express themselves regarding the interpretation of the New York Convention Art. II(2), when in effect recognising or enforcing an arbitration agreement under the more favourable right-provision in Art. VII. There is no logical reason why lax national requirements should have impact upon the interpretation of Art. II(2), but strict national requirements should not.

Thus, an independent interpretation of the New York Convention Art. II(1) and II(2) is necessary for the determination of the obligations of the Contracting States, as regards the recognition and enforcement of arbitration agreements. The need is especially obvious as regards the obligations of Contracting States with stringent requirements in national law. However, there is also the academic interest in being able to establish, whether the Courts and tribunals of Contracting States with lax requirements to the form of arbitration agreement have recognised or enforced an arbitration agreement with authority in the Convention's Art. II, or with authority in national law in accordance with the Convention's Art. VII.

2. Establishing the independent interpretation of the New York Convention Art. II(2) is of direct and practical interest for those wishing to draft arbitration agreements. The parties' need to ensure that their dispute, despite the arbitration agreement, does not end up being heard by the Courts of a Contracting State necessitates a determination of how the provision should be understood. Little consideration should be given to a party who in international trade relies upon an oral agreement to arbitrate, but in many other situations justifiable doubt may exist as to whether an agreement to arbitrate satisfies the requirements of Art. II(2). For a transport lawyer it is especially important whether arbitration agreements, which are contained in, or incorporated into, a transport document that has been unilaterally issued, will be accepted or not. For example: Can a carrier who issues a tramp bill of lading with a direct reference to the arbitration clause in the charter-party expect this reference to incorporate the arbitration clause into a dispute under the bill of lading?

Establishing the correct independent understanding of Art. II(2) is therefore a necessary prerequisite without which the parties to (potential) arbitration agreements cannot foresee their procedural position.

3. Finally, establishing the correct independent interpretation of the New York Convention Art. II(2)'s formal requirements pursues a theoretical, comparative aim: It is a necessary prerequisite for a meaningful discussion of the incorporation and use of the provision in national law. The independent interpretation of the provision is the only relevant point of reference when comparing national law incorporating the

Convention in the Contracting States, here in particular in Denmark, England and Norway.

3.3. The interpretation
3.3.1. The regards to be taken and their weight
When trying to establish the aim of the regulation in Art. II(1) and (2), one is faced with having to weigh different considerations against each other, considerations, which are partly counteractive.

One must pay attention to the general aim of the Convention, namely to facilitate the recognition and enforcement of international arbitration agreements and awards. That aim speaks for flexible and informal requirements, according to which any method of formation of the arbitration agreement that is generally recognised within the particular area of law should be accepted.

Opposing this is the distinct aim of the requirement for writing, namely to ensure sufficient proof that arbitration has been agreed between the parties. Here, the Courts are likely to demand that clear evidence of the arbitration agreement is present, the reason being, as already mentioned, that the parties by entering into an agreement to arbitrate bar themselves from taking their dispute to the Courts. Thus, the requirement for the formation of arbitration agreements might be stricter than the requirement for formation of agreements as such.

Both these considerations are weighty. However, to the extent that a Contracting State has restricted the Convention to apply only to international trade, the regard to the safeguard of proof cannot be quite as pressing as maybe otherwise assumed. Parties to international trade transactions tend to be professional players in the market, and ought to be aware that arbitration agreements are common within certain trades. Therefore, one could contend that in international trade an interpretation of Art. II(2) making it equivalent to the Brussels and Lugano Conventions Art. 17 would be apt. However, by doing so one overlooks that the requirement for writing has a further aim, namely to be the most significant parameter in determining the Contracting States' obligation to recognise and enforce arbitration agreements. One might reject that much consideration should be paid to this factor. However, this writer maintains that international law considerations are important when determining the correct independent interpretation of Art. II(2). For the Contracting States that prescribe stringent requirements for arbitration agreements under national law, it must be seen as imperative that international arbitration agreements have to fulfil certain defined formal criteria.

It seems that none of the regards here mentioned can outweigh the other. Instead, they must be kept balanced. This balancing is taken into account in the following when establishing the correct interpretation of Art. II(1) and II(2).

3.3.2. The wording

The wording of the New York Convention Art. II(2) does give occasion to doubt. It is not clear whether the words "… shall include …" in Art. II(2) provide for examples or provides for a closed list of ways in which the arbitration agreement can be concluded. Especially English writers have expressed themselves in support of the article providing only examples of when an agreement should be considered done in writing.[454] The authoritative texts vary on this point. According to the French, Spanish and Chinese texts, Art. II(2) is exhaustive, whereas the English and Russian texts imply that Art. II(2) only provides illustrations.[455]

It seems to this writer that the question of whether Art. II(2) is exhaustive is not an either/or. Article II(2) cannot be assumed to be totally exhaustive, so that an agreement to arbitrate is only concluded if either both parties have signed the agreement to arbitrate, or both parties send the communication including the agreement to arbitrate to and fro between themselves. It must be possible to combine the options mentioned in Art. II(2), so that for example one party sends a signed arbitration agreement to the other, who in turn confirms it by telegram. Furthermore, it would be against the general aim of the New York Convention to interpret article II(2) so as to exhaustively list the channels by which the agreement can be communicated. The technical terms of the provision ("letters and telegrams") should not be subject to a strict verbatim interpretation. Instead, the provision should be interpreted in observance of the development in communication technologies.[456]

However, this writer finds that Art. II(2) does not in every way provide examples, but instead that the core of the article delimits which agreements are written according to the Convention. If Art. II(2) should only be regarded as examples, Art. II(2) would have no separate meaning in comparison to Art. II(1). In that case, there would be no binding standard for the requirement for writing in the New York Convention. The presumption must, for a number of reasons, be against this approach.

---

[454] 1996 Report on the Arbitration Bill, para. 34.

[455] *Holtzmann/Neuhaus (1989)*, p. 262, footnote 25 with references. See also the 1996 Report on the Arbitration Bill, para. 34.

[456] See below, in point 3.3.3

For example, in the making of the Convention the Dutch delegation suggested that an arbitration agreement should be concluded when one party confirmed the existence of an agreement to arbitrate, and this "confirmation" was not challenged by the counter-party. This procedure was rejected at the conference, as the procedure was not seen to be sufficiently reciprocal.[457] If Art. II(2) only provided examples of ways in which the arbitration agreement could be entered into, then it would not have been necessary to draw the line and vote on the Dutch proposal. Also, maintaining that Art. II(2) of the New York Convention only provides examples would penetrate the theory that the requirement for written agreement in the New York Convention is in any way independent of national law, leaving the Courts of the Contracting States with no other option than to revert to the requirements (if any) for writing set out in national law. The argument that international conventions exists independently of national law in the Contracting States can be read above in Chapter I, § 4, point 2.2. Here it will only be mentioned that a conclusion that the requirement for writing in the New York Convention Art. II(1) and II(2) is the same as the requirement for writing in any applicable national law will frustrate the use of international arbitration as a means of dispute resolution. There will not be any level of predictability in the legal effects of arbitration agreements if the procedural rules of "arbitration agreement hostile" states might be applied. One might add that within international transport it is virtually impossible to foresee, before a dispute has materialised, which Courts, and hence which procedural rules, that might become applicable to such a would-be dispute. Thus, both the general aim of the Convention and the separate aims of Art. II(2) are best achieved if one regards the "core" of Art. II(2) as binding.

On this background it must be concluded that even if the New York Convention Art. II(2) should not be subjected to a strict verbatim interpretation, there is a "core" in the provision which remains obligatory.

When reading the provision, it seems to provide that an agreement to arbitrate is in writing if
- it follows from an arbitration clause in a contract which has been signed by both or all parties to the agreement, or
- it follows from an independent agreement to arbitrate which has been signed by both or all parties to the agreement, or
- it follows from a mutual exchange of letters and telegrams, in which case the signature of the parties is not necessary.[458]

---

[457] *Gaja (1979)*, I.B.3, *Kaplan (1996)*, p. 32 f.

[458] See likewise, *van den Berg (1996)*, p. 419.

All these modes presuppose a certain activity of all parties to the arbitration agreement. Also, that activity must have taken place through some written medium. The agreement has been concluded if, and only if, the parties have signed the agreement or have participated in the exchange of written communications in which the agreement is contained. The arbitration agreement cannot be concluded through "quasi-contract", tacitly, or orally. Neither is the conclusion through passivity an option. As put by *Gaja:* "Each party must express its consent to arbitration in writing ...".[459]

Thus, Art. II(2) requires that the parties' consent to arbitration is established through their active and written adoption of the agreement. When cut to the core, Art. II(2) requires that the agreement to arbitrate is *in a written medium* and that it has come to life through a *mutual* written process. In this way, the requirement for a written agreement to arbitrate under the New York Convention presupposes that information in a written medium that proves or confirms the arbitration agreement has been created by or exchanged between the parties.

3.3.3. The development in information technologies

Above in point 3.3.1 it has been shown that when interpreting Art. II(1) and II(2), the interpreter must take into consideration two aspects, which to a degree oppose each other: On one hand the general aim of the New York Convention, namely to facilitate the use of international arbitration as a means of dispute resolution, and on the other hand the specific aims of Art. II(2), namely to ensure that a consent to arbitration has been given, and to define the obligation of the Contracting States in respect of recognising and enforcing arbitration agreements. It has also been mentioned that in this writer's view the technological terms used in Art. II(2) are not subject to a verbatim interpretation, but should be seen in the light of the technological developments which have taken place since then. Thus, as early as in 1961 it was not considered problematic to include messages conveyed by "teleprinter" in the European Convention on International Commercial Arbitration.[460]

Still, the question remains, whether there is a line drawn by the demand for a "written" agreement, which rules out certain media.

This problem was thoroughly discussed at the drafting of the UNCITRAL Model Law on International Arbitration Art. 7. Obviously, the contents and *travaux préparatoires* of the Model Law cannot be used as conclusive aids in the interpretation

---

[459] *Gaja (1979)*, I.B.3, before footnotes 46.

[460] See The European Convention on International Commercial Arbitration Art. I(2)(a).

of the New York Convention Art. II(2). This partly for temporal reasons – the Model Law was drafted much later than the Convention – partly as the Model Law is not a legally binding document, partly as it has not been formally adopted by any of the States here discussed, and partly as the weight as a legal source of international *travaux préparatoires* is generally very much in doubt. Still, there are other reasons to pay attention to the Model Law at this point of the work. Firstly, the Model Law was negotiated by a broad selection of states parties to the New York Convention under consideration of the general trends in national law in these states. Secondly, when drafting the Model Law it was considered to be of utmost importance that the requirement for writing in the Model Law Art. 7(2) satisfied the requirement for writing as set out in the New York Convention Art. II(2).[461] It was considered imperative that an arbitration agreement concluded in accordance with the Model Law's provisions would be recognised under the New York Convention Art. II, and that an arbitral award based on such an agreement should be recognised and enforced under the New York Convention Art. III-VI.[462] Article 7 of the Model Law, including the provision's *travaux préparatoires,* is the closest one gets to a super-national source of law that interprets Art. II(2) in consideration of the developments of information technologies that have taken place since the drafting of the New York Convention. Finally, the states which have adopted the Model Law, will necessarily interpret Art. II(2) of the New York Convention in accordance with the Model Law Art. 7(2). Thus, the Model Law does in this way provide for uniformity within some states as to the requirement for written arbitration agreements under the New York Convention.

The UNCITRAL Model Law Art. 7(2) in extract:
2. The arbitration agreement shall be in writing. An agreement is in writing if it is contained in a document signed by the parties or in an exchange of letters, telex, telegrams or other means of telecommunication which provide a record of the agreement, or in an exchange of statements of claim and defence in which the existence of an agreement is alleged by one party and not denied by another. ...

---

[461] *Holtzmann/Neuhaus (1989)*, p. 260 f, *Kaplan (1996)*, p. 37, *van den Berg (1981)*, p. 421. See also: FIRST SECRETARIAT NOTE, POSSIBLE FEATURES OF A MODEL LAW, A/CN.9/207, of 14. May 1981, published in *Holtzmann/Neuhaus (1989)*, p. 269 ff, "... the model law should be based on the pertinent provisions of the 1958 New York Convention ...". Then the New York Convention Art. II(1), II(2) and V(1)(a) are cited. The Secretariat Note continues: "For the sake of consistency between major legal texts governing international arbitration practice, it would be desirable not to include provisions in the model law which would be in conflict with any of the above rules."

[462] *Holtzmann/Neuhaus (1989)*, p. 262.

The UNCITRAL Model Law Art. 7(2) accepts any means of telecommunication, which *provide a record of the agreement.* It was understood at the negotiations that this "record" should be in writing, but that it needed not be paper based. Data stored on a hard- or floppy disc, which provided for a print-out at a later stage was considered sufficient.[463] Indeed, it was considered to insert the words "in another visible and sufficiently permanent form", but this was rejected as being too vague.[464] As long as the means of communication may be described as either "... letters, telex, telegrams of other means of telecommunication which provide a record of the agreement ..." then one can safely assume to be within the techniques of communication approved by the New York Convention Art. II(2).

The wording of the Model Law, however, reflects the developments in information technology as they presented themselves in the late seventies and early eighties. Since then, information technologies have performed a quantum leap. As a consequence, in the present work on the revision of the Model Law, a further step away from a stringent look upon "writing" has been taken. For example, it has been suggested that the revised Art. 7(2) should be worded thus:

Article 7(2) of the Draft Revised Model Law[465]

2. The arbitration agreement shall be in writing. For the purpose of this Law, "writing" includes any form provided that the [text/content][466] of the arbitration agreement is accessible so as to be usable for subsequent reference, whether or not it is signed by the parties.

According to the Draft Report para. 5, the wording is based on Art. 2(1) and 6(1) of the UNCITRAL Model Law on Electronic Commerce, as that Model Law expressed the Commissions most recent view on electronic commerce, and as it was desirable to maintain harmony between the Model Laws. However, it was not intended hereby

---

[463] *Holtzmann/Neuhaus (1989),* p. 263 with references to SECOND WORKING GROUP REPORT A/CN.9/232 of 10th November 1982.

[464] See *Holtzmann/Neuhaus (1989),* p. 279 f.

[465] United Nations Commission on International Trade Law, Working Group on Arbitration, Thirty-third session, A/CN.9/WG.II/XXXIII/CRP.I/Add. 2 of 27 November 2000.

[466] United Nations Commission on International Trade Law, Working Group on Arbitration, Thirty-third session, A/CN.9/WG.II/XXXIII/CRP.I/Add. 2 of 27 November 2000, para. 2, point 6.

to introduce a regulation that differed in substance from what was already covered by the Model Law Art. 7(2).[467]

Recognising that it has been sought to keep up with the technological developments taken place over the decades, uncertainties still remain, the main area being arbitration agreements, which are in origin oral rather than written. Imagine that the parties record their contract negotiations on a tape recorder. Under those negotiations the parties agree to arbitrate any future disputes which might arise out of their contract. It is not possible to fit that situation into the wording of the New York Convention Art. II(2). In the nineteen fifties it would have been perfectly feasible for the parties to an arbitration agreement to record an oral agreement. Therefore, one cannot argue that the drafters of the Convention had not been able to foresee such a situation. This even more so in the nineteen eighties when the Model Law was drafted. Bearing in mind that the Model Law refers to "… letters, telex, telegrams or other means of telecommunication …" it is hard to fit a tape-recorded oral agreement within the Model Law Art. 7(2). Still, if the agreed wording of the new Draft Revised Model Law in the end opts for "content" rather than "text",[468] then the described method of recording the arbitration agreement would be covered by the provision.

This writer finds that the term "writing" rules out media, which are not in some way based on a written format. If an agreement is essentially written, then the medium with which the agreement is transmitted should be secondary. Also, an original lack of written media may at a later stage be remedied. Thus, if an oral agreement is recorded in writing, and then signed by the parties, then the requirement for writing should be satisfied. However, if the form is oral, and then stored or transmitted through a vocal medium, or a written medium that is not later signed or exchanged in a binding way between the parties, one is outside the scope of what is a written agreement to arbitrate in the New York Convention Art. II. This conclusion works against the regard to the facilitation of the use of arbitration as a means of international dispute resolution and it is not necessitated by the regard to ensure of (proof of) consent either. However, a vocal recording of an oral agreement simply extends beyond what can reasonably be fitted within the wording of Art. II(1) and (2).

---

[467] United Nations Commission on International Trade Law, Working Group on Arbitration, Thirty-third session, A/CN.9/WG.II/XXXIII/CRP.I/Add. 2 of 27 November 2000, para. 2, point 5.

[468] United Nations Commission on International Trade Law, Working Group on Arbitration, Thirty-third session, A/CN.9/WG.II/XXXIII/CRP.I/Add. 2 of 27 November 2000, para. 2, point 6.

3.3.4. The requirement for mutuality in the New York Convention Art. II(2) and trade practices

In international trade one will normally be able to establish that the provision on arbitration exists in a written form either in the parties' own contract or, for example, in a standard document referred to in that contract. Instead, the problem is often that the written agreement to arbitrate must come to life through the parties' bi- or multi-lateral written efforts. The problems occurring may be described as either:

1. The conclusion of the contract in which the provision on arbitration is found has taken place otherwise than in writing, or
2. The conclusion of the contract in which the provision on arbitration is found has been unilateral in certain aspects, or
3. Combinations of these.

As examples of everyday situations falling outside the requirements of the New York Convention one may mention the issuance of bills of lading,[469] and, generally, the situation where an oral agreement is made with reference to written general conditions. This, of course, is not satisfactory when regarded from the point of view of international trade. *Kaplan* presumes that the correct interpretation of the New York Convention requires mutuality and a written medium, however, he confronts Art. II(2):

"... [What] I have difficulty in seeing is why one party is sent a contract which includes an arbitration clause and that party acts on that contract and thus adopts it without any qualification, that party should be allowed to wash his hands of the arbitration clause but at the same time maintain an action for the price of the goods delivered or conversely sue for breach".

Kaplan finds that this position of the law is "absurd", even if he appreciates that it is a possible consequence of the doctrine of separability, a doctrine he does not attack.[470]

Having said that the Model Law Art. 7(2) is within what is acceptable under the New York Convention Art. II(2), one might wonder whether Art. 7(2) of the Model Law softens the New York Convention's requirements on this point. Parts of Art. 7(2) may be read so:

---

[469] See for example (1980) V ICCA Yearbook 150, JAUCH & HUBENER GMBH. V. SOC. DE NAVIGA-TION TRANSOCÉANIQUE AND SOC. S.I.A.T. In the case the Court de Cassation held that a reference in a bill of lading to a charter-party that contained an arbitration clause did not fulfil the requirement for written arbitration agreements as set out in the New York Convention Art. II.

[470] *Kaplan (1996)*, p. 29 f and 35.

The UNCITRAL Model Law Art. 7(2) in extract:
The reference in a contract to a document containing an arbitration clause constitutes an arbitration agreement provided that the contract is in writing an the reference is such as to make that clause part of the contract.

Reading this provision, one could assume that Art. 7(2) provides a general solution to the problems concerned with entering into an arbitration agreement via reference to standard conditions, as long as the technique of incorporation is accepted by the rules of the applicable *lex contractus*. However, the contract in which the reference is made should still comply with the requirement for writing as this is set out in the rest of the Model Law Art. 7(2) and the New York Convention Art. II(2). The condition that the consent to arbitration should be mutual and in writing is thus not deviated from in Art. 7(2) *in fine*. The provision governs, and recognises, situation where reference is made to e.g. the general conditions of one of the parties, but the agreement in which the reference is made should still have been signed by the parties or follows from a mutual exchange of written documentation. Art. 7(2) does not allow for unilateral processes. Especially, the unilateral incorporation of an arbitration clause through reference, as one would find it in a tramp bill of lading, is not sanctioned by the Model Law Art. 7(2). This is not due to a slip, or to this writer's too narrow interpretation. Conversely, under the negotiations leading up to the drafting of the Model Law it was repeatedly pointed out, by the English and Norwegian delegations in particular, that a provision which allowed for arbitration agreements to be concluded also through unilateral processes, especially through issuance of bills of lading, would be advantageous.[471] The impact of the New York Convention Art. II(2) on the documentation used in maritime transport will be discussed more thoroughly below in CHAPTER V, § 3. Here it will instead be shown that a consensus existed at the time, according to which the requirements set out in the New York Convention Art. II(1) and (2) could not be satisfied by unilateral processes such as the issuance of bills of lading. In the negotiations leading up to the drafting of the Model Law Art. 7(2) the following observations were made in this respect:

"Norway, while observing that paragraph (2) of this article suggests that an arbitration clause in a contract contained in a document signed by only one of the parties will not be recognised as binding, notes that arbitration clauses are frequently found in bills of lading which are usually not signed by

---

[471] *Kàplan (1996)*, 37-39, *Holtzmann/Neuhaus (1989)*, p. 261 with reference to SIXTH SECRETARIAT NOTE, ANALYTICAL COMPILATION OF GOVERNMENT COMMENTS, A/CN.9/263 of 19 March 1985 with appendices, here as cited by *Holtzmann/Neuhaus (1989)* on p. 286 ff.

the shipper. ... Norway proposes to add the following sentence at the end of paragraph (2): 'If a bill of lading or another document, signed by only one of the parties, gives sufficient evidence of a contract, an arbitration clause in the document, or a reference in the document to another document containing an arbitration clause, shall be considered to be an agreement in writing.' ... The representative of the United Kingdom had similar concerns: "Article 7(2), in requiring a document signed by the parties or an exchange of letters or telecommunication in a tangible form, is not sufficient to encompass trade practice. A number of valid arbitration agreements are evidenced in documents not signed by the parties. Perhaps the most important of these are bills of lading. The United Kingdom prefers the approach adopted in Article 17 of the [Brussels Convention], which refers to agreements which are 'in writing or, in international trade or commerce, in a form which accords with practices in that trade or commerce of which the parties are or ought to have been aware'."

The Commission rejected both proposals, even if the proposals had been met with quite some support. The reason for rejecting the English proposal was that the wording of Art. 17 of the Brussels Convention was too vague to ensure a uniform interpretation, and that parties who did not know of international trade usages might be (unpleasantly) surprised to find that they were bound by an arbitration agreement. The reason for rejecting the Norwegian proposal was slightly different: "... the Commission, after deliberation, did not adopt the additional wording because it appeared unlikely that many states would be prepared to accept the concept of an arbitration agreement which, although contained in a document, was not signed or at least consented to in writing by both parties. It was also pointed out that there might be difficulties with regard to the recognition and enforcement under the 1958 New York Convention of awards based on such agreements."

It seems quite clear that at the time of the drafting of the Model Law, there was a general consensus that the New York Convention Art. II(2) could not, and hence that the Model Law Art. 7(2) should not, be stretched to entail the same modes of conclusion of contract, as did the Brussels Convention Art. 17(2), and in particular, that the unilateral processes did not fall within the New York Convention Art. II(2). At the negotiations it was pointed out that the bill of lading problem could be solved by the adoption of the Hamburg Rules,[472] as it follows from the New York Convention Art. VII that special convention prevail over the New York Convention's general rules. However, it has since then become clear that a general acceptance of the Hamburg Rules has not taken place, and should not be expected either.

Considering that at the drafting of the Model Law it was attempted to soften the requirement for mutual written consent, and that the attempt failed, one is left with the starting point, namely that a mutual consent is required. Obviously, a precondition that compels all parties to the arbitration agreement to give a written communi-

---

[472] United Nations Convention on the Carriage of Goods by Sea, 1978.

cation in which the arbitration agreement is consented to is too inflexible to satisfy the needs of modern-day international commerce. In recent years, therefore, a different interpretation than the one here presented has been put forward, particularly in a judgment form the United States Court of Appeals, SPHERE DRAKE V. MARINE TOWING.[473]

(1995) XX ICCA YEARBOOK 937, SPHERE DRAKE V. MARINE TOWING

Marine Towing contacted insurance brokers Schade & Co. with view to obtaining a P&I insurance for Marine Towing's vessels. Schade & Co secured a policy from Sphere Drake Insurance. An insured vessel sank before the policy was delivered to Marine Towing, but in the period covered by the policy. Upon receiving the insurance policy, Marine Towing discovered that the policy contained a London arbitration clause.[474] The way in which the documentation had been exchanged in the case was this: Marine Towing's insurance broker, Schade & Co. made a written offer to Sphere Drake. The offer requested coverage under a certain Sphere Drake policy, SD 350, Class 1. The policy contained an arbitration clause. Sphere Drake accepted the offer by stamping it with Sphere Drake's seal and then delivered the signed policy to Schade & Co.[475]

Marine Towing argued before the United States District Court that Marine Towing was not bound by the arbitration provision as is was unknown to them when the dispute on the subject matter arose.[476] The District Court found that an arbitration agreement needed not be signed, but it had to be in writing.[477] The Court found that the slips submitted by Marine Towing's insurance broker satisfied the requirement for a written agreement. Consequently, the arbitration provision in the insurance policy was an arbitration agreement "contained in an exchange of letters and telexes" and qualified as an agreement in writing.[478] The District Court found for Sphere Drake's motion and ordered arbitration.[479]

Marine Towing appealed this decision to the United States Court of Appeals, Fifth Circuit. The Court of Appeals stated:

"Marine Towing contends that, because it did not sign the insurance contract, the policy cannot provide the agreement in writing. Marine Towing would define an 'agreement in writing' only as 1) a

---

[473] (1995) XX ICCA Yearbook 937, SPHERE DRAKE V. MARINE TOWING, p. 941, point 9 and 10.

[474] p. 937.

[475] See (1994) XIV ICCA Yearbook 792, SPHERE DRAKE V. MARINE TOWING ET AL, United States District Court, para. 5.

[476] Ibid. para. 6.

[477] Ibid. para. 12.

[478] Ibid. para. 13.

[479] Ibid. para. 13.

contract or other written agreement signed by the parties or 2) an exchange of correspondence between the parties demonstrating consent to arbitrate. We disagree with this interpretation of the Convention. We would outline the Convention definition of 'agreement in writing' to include either

    (1) an arbitration clause in a contract or

    (2) an arbitration agreement

    (a) signed by the parties or

    (b) contained in an exchange of letters or telegrams.

The insurance contract indisputably contains an arbitral clause. Because what is at issue here is an arbitral clause in a contract, the qualifications applicable to arbitration agreements do not apply. A signature is therefore not required."

The conclusion in that judgment has been followed in later judgments from United States District Courts. The verbatim interpretation applied by the Court of Appeals is in one of these cases explained thus:

"... [The Court of Appeals] ... explicitly rejected a reading that defined 'agreement in writing' only as '(1) a contract or other written agreement signed by the parties or (2) an exchange of correspondence between the parties demonstrating consent to arbitrate' ... The court instead found that the phrase followed by the comma – 'signed by the parties or contained in an exchange of letters or telegrams' – modified only 'arbitration agreement' and not 'arbitration clause in a contract'".[480]

An agreement to arbitrate need not be signed to fulfil the writing-requirement of the New York Convention Art. II(1) and (2). This writer concurs to that part of the Court of Appeals' conclusion. However, this writer finds that it is open to doubt whether the way in which the insurance agreement was concluded entailed sufficient reciprocity so as to satisfy that part of the writing-requirement in Art. II(2). Even so, the interpretation applied by the United States Court of Appeals is defendable when considering the wording of the New York Convention Art. II(2), although, as shown, it is not within the general consensus on the interpretation. And; the interpretation applied is helpful as it puts an end to many of the problems caused in international arbitration by Art. II(2)'s written requirement. In SPHERE DRAKE V. MARINE TOWING, the Court eliminates the requirement for mutuality in cases where an arbitration clause is contained in a (standard form of) agreement that has been agreed between the parties according to the general principles on the formation of contracts. However, considering the other factors of interpretation of the New York Convention Art. II(2), the United States Court of Appeals' interpretation is hardly in accordance with the Convention as it now stands.

---

[480] (1998) XXIII ICCA Yearbook 1029, RONALD BORSACK V. CHALK & VERMILION, United States District Court, Southern District of New York, on p. 1032, para.4. See also (1998) XXIII ICCA Yearbook 1038, on p. 1043, para. 13

This does not entail that the conclusion in the case (accepting Sphere Drake's argument that there was an agreement to arbitrate between the parties) was wrong, but it may be that the conclusion should not have been based on the Convention. Instead, the conclusion would have been better based upon national law in accordance with the more favourable right-provision in Art. VII. However, due to the way in which the national rules in the United States are drafted, this was not possible in the case. According to U.S. legislation on arbitration, the United States' Courts shall enforce foreign arbitration agreements and awards falling within the New York Convention. There is no independent provision defining a requirement for writing under national law that can be applied to international arbitration agreements falling within the Convention. Therefore, to accept the arbitration agreement, the United States' Courts had to find that the requirements of the Convention were complied with.[481] On this background it must be suggested that States, wishing to impose a more lax requirement than the one following from the New York Convention Art. II(2) make distinct provisions in national law so that it is no longer necessary to rely on Art. II(2). In this way, such Contracting States will remain able to recognise international arbitration agreements that are within what is acceptable under the national rules that would otherwise have applied.

3.3.5. The proposed declaration on the correct interpretation of the New York Convention Art. II(2)

The New York Convention Art. II(2) provides consensus amongst the Courts of the Contracting States that arbitration agreements which fulfil the criteria set by a stringent interpretation of the provision will be accepted by the same Courts. Apart from this, uniformity as regards the formal requirements for international arbitration agreements is only conjured. The Contracting States continue to develop the criteria set by Art. II(2), and especially the criteria for mutuality in the process of concluding the arbitration agreement, under the more favourable right-provision in the New York Convention Art. VII.

This they must do, as developments are necessary. Focus was put on that issue at the New York Convention day on June 10, 1998. In deciding which route to take in this respect, the UNCTAD Working Group on Arbitration feared that proposing a revised version of the New York Convention, or making a protocol to the same convention, would be detrimental to the existing level of international uniformity. At present there is only one generally applicable Convention to take into consideration.

---

[481] See 9. United States Code, Chapter 2 – Convention on the Recognition and Enforcement of Foreign Arbitral Awards, sec. 201 and 202, 1st sentence.

Experience from other international conventions shows that the fear is well founded. Transport lawyers need only think of the convention-jungle governing the liability rules regarding international civil aviation, normally named the Warsaw System,[482] and the position within maritime transport is not much better, considering that there one is faced with both Hague,[483] Hague-Visby[484] and Hamburg[485] States, as well as States who are formally tied to one Convention but have made national regulations which adhere to one of the others. As a consequence, the UNCTAD Working Group on Arbitration has suggested that a declaration on the interpretation of the New York Convention Art. II(2) be issued. Thus, one maintains the base in the existing convention, but attempts to push the development of the interpretation in a certain direction.

A declaration issued by UNCTAD as to the interpretation of Art. II(2) is not legally binding under international law. Therefore, the initiative must be regarded as rather controversial. However, the desired effect might be achieved by it. It is generally accepted that the New York Convention's requirements are too stringent to provide the flexible solution that international trade needs. A declaration on the correct interpretation of the New York Convention Art. II(2) might therefore provide a means by which the party claiming that a valid arbitration agreement has been entered into may persuade the Court or tribunal to accept this argument.

Drafting such a declaration is not an easy task. If one only ensures that the New York Convention Art. II(2) is interpreted with view to the *technological* developments that have taken place since 1958, the Courts of the Contracting States should not have difficulties in accepting the declaration on interpretation. This view is already accepted by many. The request for a *mutual, written consent* is more problematic. In this respect the drafter must tread a tightrope. On the one hand, one needs to be within what can reasonably be considered to be the scope of the New York Convention Art. II(2). On the other hand, if one is not progressive, little is achieved by the effort.

---

[482] Convention for the Unification of Certain Rules Relating to International Carriage by Air, 1929, with protocols. (Mainly The Montreal Additional Protocol no. 1, 1975, The Hague Protocol 1955, and The Guadalajara Supplementary Convention, 1961).

[483] International Convention for the Unification of Certain Rules Relating to Bills of Lading, Brussels 1924.

[484] Protocol to Amend the International Convention for the Unification of Certain Rules Relating to Bills of Lading, signed at Brussels on 25 August 1924, Brussels 1968.

[485] United Nations Convention on the Carriage of Goods by Sea, 1978.

In that case, the declaration might even have the detrimental effect of freezing the developments taking place in Contracting States with no, or lax, formal criteria in national law. Hence, the Working Group is faced with the undesirable task of drafting an instrument which is both stringent enough so as to satisfy the demands of Contracting States that have stringent formal requirements in national law, and flexible enough to create a new temporal platform for the recognition and enforcement of arbitration agreements in today's international trade. If the Working Group does not achieve both these objectives, the instrument of interpretation is likely to be disregarded by Contracting States that have stringent formal requirements in national law, and thus not aid uniformity at all. At the Working Group's thirty-third session it was suggested that the instrument should provide that the New York Convention Art. II(2) should be interpreted so as to be at one with the Revised Model Law Art. 7. In the latest draft available to this writer, the Revised Model Law Art. 7 is worded thus:

The Draft Revised Model Law Art. 7[486]
(1) "Arbitration agreement" is an agreement by the parties to submit to arbitration all or certain disputes which have arisen or which may arise between them in respect of a defined legal relationship, whether contractual or not. An arbitration agreement may be in the form of an arbitration clause in a contract or in the form of a separate agreement.
(2) The arbitration agreement shall be in writing. For the purpose of this Law, "writing" includes any form, provided that the [text/content] of the arbitration agreement is accessible so as to be usable for subsequent reference, whether or not it is signed by the parties.
(3) An arbitration agreement meets the requirements in paragraph (2) if:
   (a) it is contained in a document established jointly by the parties;
   (b) it is made by an exchange of written communications;
   (c) it is contained in one party's written offer or counter-offer, provided that the contract has been [validly] concluded by acceptance, or an act constituting acceptance such as performance or a failure to object, by the other party;
   (d) it is contained in a contract confirmation, provided that the terms of the contract confirmation have been [validly] accepted by the other party, either [expressly/by express reference to the confirmation or its terms] or, to the extent provided by law or usage, by a failure to object;
   (e) it is contained in a written communication by a third party to both parties and the content of the communication is considered to be part of the contract;
   (f) it is contained in an exchange of statements [of claim and defence/on the substance of the dispute] in which the existence of an agreement is alleged by one party and not denied by the other;
   (g) [it is contained in a text to which reference is made in a contract concluded orally, provided [that such conclusion of the contract is customary / that arbitration agree-

---
[486] United Nations Commission on International Trade Law, Working Group on Arbitration, Thirty-third session, A/CN.9/WG.II/XXXIII/CRP.I/Add. 2 of 27 November 2000.

ments in such contracts are customary] and that the reference is such as to make that clause part of the contract.]

(4) The reference in a contract to a text containing an arbitration clause constitutes an arbitration agreement provided that the contract is in writing and the reference is such as to make that clause part of the contract.

As this is a preliminary draft, an in-depth discussion of the wording will not take place. However it will be noted that in the Draft Revised Model Law Art. 7(3)(c), 7(3)(d) and 7(3)(e), the requirement for mutual written consent has been departed from, and in 7(3)(g), contracts concluded orally with reference to written conditions are included in the concept of "writing". If eventually the Working Group does present an instrument of interpretation according to which the New York Convention Art. II(2) should be interpreted according to the Revised Model Law as the draft now stands, then one has exceeded what is, at least according to this writer, the scope of the New York Convention Art. II(2).

Instead, a more politically acceptable solution would probably be to endorse the interpretation made by the United States Court of Appeals in the above mentioned case, SPHERE DRAKE V. MARINE TOWING. As said above in point 3.3.4, the effect of that interpretation is to dispense with the requirement for mutuality as far as arbitration clauses in a contract are concerned. In the end, the effects of such an interpretation do not differ much from Art. 7(3) in the draft here mentioned, but there is a psychological difference, namely that the findings on interpretation of the Court of Appeals in that case is *within* a verbatim interpretation of Art. II(2). The draft of the Revised Model Law in its present form Art. 7(3) is so different from the wording of the New York Convention Art. II(2) that one must expect quite a few Contracting States to purely reject the instrument on interpretation as going far beyond the obligations of the same States under the Convention.

Summing up on the proposed declaration on the interpretation of the New York Convention Art. II(2), it can be said that it lacks basis in international law, that as it stands now it goes beyond what is encompassed in Art. II(2) of the Convention, and that it just might work. Maintaining arbitration as a good means of dispute resolution in international trade necessitates a new interpretation of the New York Convention Art. II(2). In many Contracting States there will therefore be a wish to find a way around the rigidity of Art. II(2), and a declaration like the proposed one, if drafted conscientiously, might just be it.

4. The New York Convention and the formal requirements in national law

4.1. The English Arbitration Act 1996, secs. 5 and 6(2)

The recognition and enforcement of New York Convention awards are governed by the English Arbitration Act 1996, Part III. According to sec. 100(2), the expression "agreement in writing" shall have the same meaning in Part III as it has in Part I. Thus, the concept of a written agreement to arbitrate as defined in sec. 5 of the Act also applies to arbitration agreements under the New York Convention. S. 5 has been discussed above in § 3, point 1, so here only a brief overview is intended.

The concept of a written agreement to arbitrate under the English Arbitration Act 1996 sec. 5 is very wide. Indeed, the English Arbitration Act sec. 5 is worded so as to accept many procedures as "written" which would not qualify under the New York Convention Art. II(2). Firstly, sec. 5 and sec. 6(2) to a large degree allow for the unilateral conclusion of arbitration agreements. There is no requirement under sec. 5 and sec. 6(2) that both parties to the arbitration agreement need to have participated in the exchange of written documentation. A liner bill of lading, for example, can be accepted under sec. 5(2)(a) as being an "… agreement … made in writing," or under sec. 5(2)(c) as being an "… agreement … evidenced in writing." Tramp bills of lading, referring to arbitration clauses in the charter-party they have been issued under will be accepted under sec. 6(2), provided that they fulfil the conditions set out in case law (see above, Chapter II, § 3) even if they do not conform to the requirements in the New York Convention Art. II(2). Also, under sec. 5(3) references, including oral references, to written conditions satisfy the requirement for a written agreement to arbitrate. Thus, if Lloyd's Open Form is orally agreed between the parties to a salvage operation, then the arbitration clause in LOF will be accepted under sec. 5(3).[487] Finally, sec. 5(6) states that "in writing" includes "being recorded by any means". Some writers have interpreted this as including a tape-recording,[488] and nothing in the wording contradicts that assumption. As mentioned above in point 3.3.3, this writer finds that a tape recording of an oral conversation falls outside what is "in writing" under the New York Convention Art. II(2). Despite these discrepancies, the Committee behind the Arbitration Act 1996, and certain English writers maintain that sec. 5 is within what is acceptable under Art. II(2).[489] The argument is

---

[487] 1996 Report on the Arbitration Bill, para. 36. See regarding this method of incorporation and the New York Convention Art. II(2), *Cohen (1997).*

[488] *Harris (2000),* p. 74, point. 5F.

[489] 1996 Report on the Arbitration Bill, para. 34, *Merkin (1996)* p. 20.

mainly based upon the difference in the wordings of the authentic texts, mentioned above in point 3.2. In short, the issue is that the English and Russian texts do not state Art. II(2) to be exhaustive. As said in the Report:

"The non-exhaustive definition in the English text ('shall include') may differ in this respect from the French and Spanish texts, but the English text is equally authentic under Article XVI of the New York Convention itself, and also accords with the Russian authentic text ... It seems to us that English law as it stands more than justifies this wide meaning ...".[490]

In accordance with the conclusion reached above in point 3.3.2 the argument of the Committee on this point must be party rejected. Admittedly, Art. II(2) is not in every way exhaustive, but the core of the provision remains binding. That the 1996 Act sec. 5 and sec. 6(2) should be in accordance with the New York Convention Art. II(2) must in any case be seen as a bit of a rationalisation, as one of the reasons for not adopting the Model Law given in the *Mustill Report* was that the requirement for written agreement in Art. 7(2) was regarded as too strict by the Committee.[491] The Model Law Art. 7(2) is so tightly tied to the wording of the New York Convention Art. II(2) that one cannot argue that a provision that is constructed so as to be more lax than the Model Law Art. 7(2) should still be within the New York Convention Art. II(2). Thus, the parties to and drafters of arbitration agreements under English Law should remain aware that even if their agreement fulfils the requirements set by the Arbitration Act 1996 sec. 5 and sec. 6(2), the arbitration agreement might not be recognised and enforced by the Courts of all States that are parties to the New York Convention. The parties should not only ascertain that the requirements set by the Arbitration Act 1996 are met. They must also look to the New York Convention Art. II(2) and consider whether the arbitration agreement fits within a rather verbatim interpretation of that wording. If it does not, they should be aware that the Courts of some Contracting States might not accept the arbitration agreement.

4.2. Danish law
Danish law holds no generally applicable rule, that arbitration agreements should be in writing, nor does it hold a specific provision that arbitration agreements falling within the New York Convention should. Indeed, not much consideration was given to the formal requirements of the New York Convention Art. II(2) by the committees behind the Danish Arbitration Act 1972, and no specific provision on the arbitration

---

[490] 1996 Report on the Arbitration Bill, para. 34.

[491] *Mustill Report,* paras. 89-90.

agreements that are covered by the New York Convention is given.[492] All arbitration agreements, including international ones, are recognised under the main rule in the Arbitration Act 1972 sec. 1, sub-sec. 1. Still, as the Danish Courts require that the existence of a clear agreement to arbitrate is proved before the arbitration agreement is recognised, the de facto difference between which arbitration agreements may be recognised under the New York Convention Art. II(2) and which may be accepted in accordance with the case law developed under the Danish Arbitration Act 1972 sec. 1, sub-sec. 1 need not be vast.

Below in Chapter V, § 2, the requirements in Danish and Norwegian law for arbitration agreements in bills of lading in the Nordic Maritime Code secs. 311 and 310 will be discussed. Regarding bills of lading it is a requirement that the arbitration agreement is in writing, see sec. 311, sub-sec. 1, and arbitration agreements in charter-parties are only recognised in bills of lading issued under the charter-party if the bill of lading holds a direct reference to the arbitration clause in the charter-party. However, even if the parties fulfil these conditions it cannot be expected that the Courts of all Contracting States will accept the arbitration agreement, as it has not been concluded subsequent to a mutual exchange of written documentation.

As the Danish Arbitration Act 1972 offers no guidelines, the parties to international arbitration agreements must themselves ensure that the requirements given under international rules, and in particular under the New York Convention Art. II(2), are fulfilled. In doing this they must keep in focus that under the New York Convention, the provisions on arbitration should not only be agreed – they should be agreed through a written, mutual process.

4.3. The Norwegian Code of Procedure § 452

It follows from the Norwegian Code of Procedure sec. 36a that the Code only applies insofar as this does not conflict with Norway's obligations under international law. Thus, according to sec. 36a, the Norwegian Code of Procedure sec. 452, sub-sec. 2, 1st sentence should not be applied to the extent that its requirements are stricter than what follows from the New York Convention Art. II(2). The requirement for writing as developed in case law under sec. 452, sub-sec. 2, 1st sentence has been discussed at considerable length above in § 4, and should not be repeated here. For the purpose of this paragraph the reader will only be reminded that sec. 452 requires that the parties sign a document that either contains or refers to the arbitration agreement in

---

[492] In fact, the Committees do not seem to have mentioned the New York Convention Art. II(2) at all in the *travaux préparatoires*. The whole focus in the *travaux préparatoires* are on the access to recognition and enforcement of international arbitral awards.

question. Such a requirement is obviously more restrictive than what is permitted by the New York Convention Art. II(2). Nevertheless, as shown above in § 4, point 3, the Norwegian Courts seem to apply sec. 452, sub-sec. 2, 1ˢᵗ sentence to both domestic and international arbitration agreements.[493] The discussion of this should not be repeated here either. This writer will only recapitulate her view that the Norwegian Courts ought to take the Norwegian Code of Procedure sec. 36a at face value and recognise arbitration agreements that are in accordance with the New York Convention Art. II(2), even if they fall short of sec. 452, sub-sec. 2, 1ˢᵗ sentence.

4.4. De lege ferenda on Danish, English and Norwegian law incorporating the New York Convention

Neither the Danish nor the English conditions for the conclusion of arbitration agreements are in breach of the New York Convention Art. II(2), as the "more favourable right-provision" in Art. VII allow the Courts of the Contracting States accept arbitration agreements to a greater extent than what follows from the New York Convention. But Art. VII is in no way reciprocal. Even if the Courts and/or statutory regulation of a Contracting State recognises arbitration agreements that are not written or that have been created through a unilateral procedure, the Courts of other Contracting States are, under the New York Convention, under no obligation whatsoever to recognise such agreements.

Still, the lax requirements of Danish an English law should under no circumstances be changed, so that only arbitration agreements that are clearly within the New York Convention Art. II are accepted. The New York Convention Art. II is rigid and out of step with the requirements of modern-day international trade and transport. However, the drafters of arbitration agreements used in international commerce should widen their focus and take both national and international rules into consideration when drafting the arbitration agreement.

As regards Norwegian law, obviously this writer still suggests, as first mentioned in § 4, point 2.2.4 and point 6, that the Norwegian Courts will interpret the Norwegian Code of Procedure sec. 36a cf. sec. 452, sub-sec. 2, 1ˢᵗ sentence so as to allow any arbitration agreement that is in conformity with the New York Convention Art. II(2). However, in the Draft Norwegian Arbitration Act this step has already been taken, as in the proposed sec. 2-2 the requirement for a written agreement to arbitrate has been rejected altogether.[494] Thus, if the Draft Norwegian Arbitration Act is ac-

---

[493] See Rt. 1991.635 NSC, SITAS V. HØGLUND and HR-2000-01539 NSC, FLEKKEFJORD V. CATARPILLAR.

[494] See above § 4, point 7.2.

cepted by Parliament in its current form, then the issue as regards the New York Convention Art. II(2) will instead be that the parties have to ensure that not only the lax national requirement but also the requirement of Art. II(2) is complied with.

5. De lege ferenda on the New York Convention Art. II(1) and II(2)

When considering whether action should be taken to make the formal requirements in the New York Convention Art. II(2) more up-to-date, one should take into account the following facts, that speak in favour of *amending* the convention: At present, there is no *real* uniformity in the Court practice in the Contracting States as to what the requirement for writing means. Furthermore, there is a general consensus that the requirement of the New York Convention Art. II(2), if interpreted so as to demand that arbitration agreements need to be concluded through a mutual written process, is out of step with the needs of international trade.

In favour of *maintaining* the Convention as it now stands it must be said, firstly, that the Convention has been very successful, and that an *extent* of uniformity has been created by it. Secondly, experience from other fields of international law shows that creating new conventions or making protocols etc. to existing conventions is detrimental to international uniformity of law.

Neither of these points are so important that one can be shown to outweigh the other. Thus, in the end, it is a decision for the politicians to make. However, it is nowhere said that lawyers cannot be politicians.

It has already been shown that the present Convention text is appropriate so as to encompass the developments that have taken place in information technologies over the last five decades, but that the process for conclusion of contracts recognised in the Convention is inept to fit the needs of international trade. In many Contracting States this inadequacy is being dealt with by the Courts, interpreting the requirements of the Convention in a new, wider manner, or by the legislators, deciding that the national requirements are less stringent than the Convention's requirement. In this way, the Convention is being expanded both through new interpretations of Art. II(2) and through the more favourable right provision in Art. VII. This expansion, though, is unsystematic. Figuratively speaking, the New York Convention is at the moment reproducing itself by budding. To recover unity, the developments of the Convention need to be taken in a certain direction. For exactly that purpose the declaration on the interpretation of the New York Convention has been proposed. Above, in point 3.3.5, this writer has shown some enthusiasm towards the declaration. Here it will only be briefly repeated that a declaration as the one mentioned might be sufficient to repair the shortcomings of the Conventions as it now stands. Still, there are other options open.

237

Above in point 3.2 this writer has argued that a real autonomous interpretation of the formal requirement in Art. II(2) cannot be achieved as long as there is no international forum in which doubts as to the interpretation of the provision can be solved in a final and binding way. It follows from this contention that international unity might be achieved by setting up a tribunal with the mandate to give a binding purposive interpretation of the New York Convention. However, this writer finds that a protocol to the Convention, establishing such a tribunal, is unlikely to be accepted by a sufficiently substantial number of Contracting States. An international tribunal with such a mandate would require a derogation of competence from the Courts of the Contracting States, and may not be politically feasible. Furthermore, there is a risk that a "New York Convention Tribunal" might freeze the developments under the New York Convention Art. II(2).[495] Also for this reason, the idea of a "New York Convention Tribunal" must be rejected for the present.

This writer also has reservations as to whether maintaining the present Convention is the correct route to embark on. Indeed, it seems to me that a revised Convention would be preferable.

The revised Convention should adopt a distinction between the requirements that apply to consumers and the requirements that apply in international trade. Preferably, the new Convention or Protocol should only apply to international trade, leaving arbitration agreements entered into by consumers to be dealt with by the existing criteria in Art. II(2). When considering consumers, it is reasonable that the conclusion of international arbitration agreements presupposes a mutual written adoption of the agreement.

As regards arbitration agreements entered into in international trade, this writer contends that there is no reason why international arbitration agreements should be subject to a stricter regulation than are international jurisdiction agreements. One may therefore create a regulation ad modum the Brussels and Lugano Convention Art. 17, or maybe even better ad modum Art. 4(2) of the proposed Convention on Jurisdiction and Foreign Judgments in Civil and Commercial Matters, drafted under the Hague Conferences on Private International Law.[496] In the latest draft available to this writer, Art. 4(2) is worded thus:

---

[495] Under the Brussels Convention unsatisfactory case law on Art. 17 has over the years lead to this provision being amended. However, there is no effective legislative system that may easily change the wording of the New York Convention Art. II(2), in case dissatisfactory case law should emerge.

[496] The draft can be downloaded from http://www.hcch.net/e/conventions/draft36e.html.

Preliminary Draft Convention on Jurisdiction and Foreign Judgments in Civil and Commercial Matters, Art. 4(2)

4(2) An agreement within the meaning of paragraph 1 shall be valid as to form, if it was entered into or confirmed –

in writing;

by any other means of communication which renders information accessible so as to be usable for subsequent reference;

in accordance with a usage which is regularly observed by the parties;

in accordance with a usage of which the parties were or ought to have been aware and which is regularly observed by the parties to contracts of the same nature in the particular trade or commerce concerned.

Admittedly, proposing a regulation *ad modum* the Brussels Convention Art. 17 has been tried before. It failed then, but maybe now the time is right.

Furthermore, the more favourable right provision should, as far as arbitration agreements are concerned, be drafted so as to be reciprocal *ad modum* the European Convention on International Commercial Arbitration Art. I(2)(a). In that Article it is held that:

European Convention on International Commercial Arbitration, Art. I(2) in extract

(a) The term "arbitration agreement" shall mean either an arbitral clause in a contract or an arbitration agreement, the contract of arbitration agreement being signed by the parties, or contained in an exchange of letters, telegrams or in a communication by teleprinter *and, in relations between States whose laws do not require that an arbitration agreement be made in writing, any arbitration agreement concluded in the form authorised by these laws ...* [497]

The provision is, admittedly, slightly unclear, as it is not obvious what "… in relations between States whose laws do not require that an arbitration agreement be made in writing …" means. The Danish incorporation of the emphasised part of the

---

[497] Writer's emphasis. See the Danish Arbitration Regulation 1973, sec. 4, sub-sec. 2: En voldgiftsaftale skal være underskrevet af parterne eller fremgå af en udveksling af breve, telegrammer eller fjernskrivermeddelelser. Hvis der ikke kræves skriftlighed efter lovgivningen i de lande, i hvilke parterne har bopæl eller sæde, er aftalen dog bindende, hvis den er i overensstemmelse med forskrifterne i vedkommende landes lovgivning.

239

provision is worded: "If there is no requirement for writing according to the law of the states in which the parties are [domiciled], the agreement remains binding if it is in accordance with the requirements of the law of those states." Still, it is this writer's contention that an amended convention containing such provisions ought to be sufficiently flexible so as to develop with, rather than obstruct, the needs of international trade and commerce.

Chapter III. Agreements to arbitrate – the validity on the substance

§ 1. Introduction

The substantial validity of arbitration agreements is governed by the special regulation on arbitration, by the general rules on the validity of contracts, and by special rules applicable to specific contracts such as contracts of carriage. Furthermore, as will be shown below,[498] arbitration agreements may be subject to supra-national rules, dealing mainly with public law concerns, such as the European Convention on Human Rights. To be valid on the substance the agreement to arbitrate needs to fulfil any requirements that may be set out in those rules of law.

In this Chapter, the requirements that need to be met for arbitration agreements to be valid on the substance are discussed. The rules of arbitration law require mainly that the arbitration agreement is concerned with a defined legal relationship, and that the subject matter of the case is arbitrable. These rules will be discussed below in point 3. The general rules on the validity of contracts apply to the arbitration agreement as it does to agreements in general. Thus, an agreement to arbitrate may be invalid due to coercion, misrepresentation, frustration, or lack of consideration etc., dependent upon what are the rules on contractual validity in the applicable law. It is considered to be beyond the scope of this work to enter into a full discussion of the law of the validity of contracts under Danish, English and Norwegian law. Instead, the most problematic issues will be described. The relevant rules of contract law as well as the possibility of rendering arbitration agreements null and void if inconsistent with the European Convention on Human Rights Art. 6 are dealt with in point 4. The special rules, applicable to contracts of carriage will be dealt with as a special issue in Chapter V, § 1. Such rules may require that the parties cannot arbitrate their

---

[498] Point 4.

claim at all,[499] or that the parties to do so need to ensure that the arbitration agreement fulfils certain criteria as to its contents.[500]

However, before entering into a discussion of the regulation of the arbitration agreement's invalidity, the relationship between the invalidity of the parties' whole contract and the invalidity of the arbitration clause will be discussed. This discussion generally takes place under the heading of the doctrine of separability, concerned with whether – and if so to what extent – an arbitration agreement is affected by the invalidity of the main contract.

---

[499] COTIF-COM Art. 56, discussed below in Chapter V, § 1, point 6.1.

[500] CMR Art. 33, See below Chapter V, § 1, point 3.5.

§ 2. The doctrine of separability

1. Introduction

Arbitration agreements regarding a contractual relationship may be entered into separately before or after a dispute has arisen. More often, however, they are entered into via an arbitration clause in the parties' main contract. If the arbitration agreement is entered into independently of the main contract, it is hardly surprising that the questions regarding the validity of the agreement are answered independently of questions as to the validity of the main contract. This applies to invalidity, which arises over the course of time, and to initial invalidity. Vice versa, it is hardly surprising that, as a rule, the invalidity of the arbitration agreement, due to procedural faults for example, does not affect the invalidity of the parties' main agreement. However, as expressed by the English Court of Appeal, the question is

"... whether ... [if] ... the agreement ... [is] ... expressed in an *arbitration clause*, which clause is contained in a written contract, the clause can give jurisdiction to the arbitrators under that clause to determine a dispute over the *initial validity or invalidity* of the written contract, upon the assumption that upon its true construction the arbitration clause covers such a dispute and that the nature of the invalidity alleged does not attack the validity of the agreement expressed in the arbitration clause itself".[501]

---

[501] As per Gibson, LJ, in HARBOUR V. KANSA, (1995) XX ICCA Yearbook 771 CA, p. 773, sub-sec. 1. Writer's emphasis.

The discussion of whether the arbitration clause can survive the initial invalidity of the main contract is normally addressed under the heading the doctrine of separability. In theory, the question may be regarded as a special variety of the question of whether, and if so to what extent, the arbitral tribunal may rule upon its own jurisdiction.[502] However, when one considers the arbitral tribunal's jurisdiction from the point of view of the initial invalidity of the main contract, the question changes from being one of competence to being a question of the special features of the arbitration agreement, or – one might say – from being one of procedure to being one of substance.

The main principle of the doctrine of separability is that an arbitration clause in a written agreement as a point of departure continues to bind the parties to the arbitration agreement, even if the main contract between them is invalid ab initio. That the arbitration agreement should be regarded as separable agreement is not always self-evident. *Samuel* correctly points out that "... the arbitration clause is not in any real sense a separate contract. It is commercially part of the overall bargain and sometimes will be a central part of it containing as it commonly does an express choice of law to govern the substantive agreement."[503]

Still, in commercial arbitration (and maritime arbitration in particular) where the arbitration clause, rather than the independent arbitration agreement, is the absolute rule, the doctrine is necessary. On the word of *Park,*[504] "... the separability doctrine permits arbitrators to invalidate the main contract (e.g., for illegality or fraud in the inducement) without the risk that their decision will call into question the validity of the arbitration clause from which they derive their power". In other words: If the doctrine of separability is not accepted, an award rendering the parties main contract void, is void with it. *Park* continues: "... the separability doctrine gives arbitrators the tool with which to do their job, by examining fully the parties' agreement". The acceptance of the doctrine thus supports the effectiveness of arbitration agreements.

2. International law on the doctrine of separability

Although the aim of the New York Convention is to ensure the effectiveness of arbitration agreements, the Convention does not hold rules on the separability of the arbitration agreement. It is implied by Art. V(1)(a) that an arbitration agreement may be

---

[502] Also described Kompetenz-Kompetenz, see below, Chapter IV.

[503] *Samuel (2000)*, p. 43.

[504] *Park (2000)*, p. 27 f.

governed by a different law than the main agreement, but the doctrine is not specifically touched upon.[505] The European Convention on International Commercial Arbitration Art. V(3) presupposes that the arbitration agreement may be valid even if the main contract is not, when allowing the arbitrator to rule on the existence or validity of both the main contract and the arbitration agreement.

European Convention on International Commercial Arbitration, Art. V

(3) Subject to any subsequent judicial control provided for under the lex fori, the arbitrator whose jurisdiction is called into question shall be entitled to proceed with the arbitration, to rule on his own jurisdiction and to *decide upon the existence or the validity* of the arbitration agreement or of the contract of which the agreement forms part.[506]

The UNCITRAL Model Law explicitly states that the arbitration clause shall be seen as an independent agreement when deciding the competence of the tribunal.

UNCITRAL Model Law Art. 16 in extract

(1) The arbitral tribunal may rule on its own jurisdiction, including any objections with respect to the existence or validity of the arbitration agreement. For that purpose, an arbitration clause which forms part of a contract shall be treated as an agreement independent of the other terms of the contract. A decision by the arbitral tribunal that the contract is null and void shall not entail ipso jure the invalidity of the arbitration clause.

However, in both the European Convention on International Commercial Arbitration and in the UNCITRAL Model Law the doctrine of separability is seen in the light of the effective application of the principle of Kompetenz-Kompetenz – the principle, that the tribunal may rule on its own jurisdiction. However, developments are taking the doctrine of separability even further. The ICC Arbitration Rules 1998 version Art. 6(4) holds the following provision under the heading "Effect of the Arbitration Agreement".

4. Unless otherwise agreed, the Arbitral Tribunal shall not cease to have jurisdiction by reason of any claim that the contract is null and void or allegation that it is non-existent, provided that the Arbitral Tribunal upholds the validity of the arbitration agreement. *The Arbitral Tribunal shall continue to have jurisdiction to determine the respective rights of the parties and to adjudicate their claims and pleas even though the contract itself may be non-existent or null and void.*[507]

---

[505] *van den Berg (1981)*, p. 146.

[506] Writer's emphasis.

[507] Writer's emphasis.

In this way, the doctrine of separability is stepping out of the shadow of the principle of Kompetenz-Kompetenz, and is being recognised as a special feature of the arbitration agreement, rather than a necessary requisite for the tribunal to have the competence to decide its own jurisdiction. This view is also displayed in some newer arbitration acts. Thus in the new Swedish[508] and English Arbitration Acts[509] the principle has been allotted a special provision in connection with the definition of what is an arbitration agreement, rather than being discussed in connection with the tribunal's competence. The Draft Norwegian Arbitration Act presents the principle in connection with the regulation of the tribunal's competence – very much in keeping with the UNCITRAL Model Law Art. 16(1).[510] However, in Denmark, as well as in the present Norwegian regulation of arbitration agreements in the Norwegian Code of Procedure chapter 32, no statutory regulation exists, leaving the doctrine of separability to develop in case law.

It follows that the doctrine of separability is still rooted in national law, even if generally recognised. Consequently, a national point of departure will be assumed in the following.

3. The doctrine of separability under Danish law

The doctrine of separability has been accepted in Danish legal literature.[511] As put by *Hjejle:* "… when the parties enter into an agreement, which contains an arbitration clause, they do not enter into one but two agreements – one on the subject matter of their relationship and one on the process regarding dispute on the subject matter".[512] The arbitration agreement may of course be invalid, but the fact that the arbitration agreement is a clause in a larger contract does not tie the lifespan of the arbitration agreement to the lifespan of that contract.

Also, the Danish Arbitration Act of 1972 sec 2, sub-sec. 1, and the Arbitration Regulation of 1973 sec. 10, sub-sec. 1, 1st sentence, which incorporate the European Convention on International Commercial Arbitration Art. V(3), presuppose that the

---

[508] Swedish Arbitration Act 1999, sec. 3.

[509] English Arbitration Act 1996, s. 7.

[510] See likewise the Tenth Book of the German Code of Civil Procedure s. 1040(1) 2nd sentence.

[511] *Gomard (1979)*, p. 26 simply seems to presuppose that this is the case.

[512] *Hjejle (1987)*, p. 20. My translation.

arbitration tribunal may rule upon its own jurisdiction irrespectively of the reasons for the challenge of jurisdiction.[513] The wording of those provisions thus cover situations where the arbitration clause is alleged to be invalid *ab initio*, even if the principle has not been put in specific words. The doctrine of separability has also been confirmed by case law.

U 1987.945 MCCC A v. B.

A and B agreed that A should procure B's project to the authorities of a "non-European" country. B obtained the intended contract. However, B claimed that the agreement was unlawful and thus invalid, and refused to pay A the agreed fee. The agreement held an arbitration clause according to which disputes were to be settled by ICC-arbitration in Geneva, Swiss law to apply. A initiated arbitral proceedings but decided to terminate them, as he would not accept the proposed settlement offered by the tribunal.

Before the Court, the parties were in agreement that the main contract was invalid as being contrary to Christian V's Danish Law 1683 s. 5-1-2.[514] A claimed that despite this he was entitled to a "customary international fee" of DKK 45 mill.

The Maritime and Commercial Court of Copenhagen based its decision upon the following: *That* A had initiated arbitral proceedings in accordance with the provisions of the agreement after he had become aware of the circumstances which rendered the main agreement void, *that* the main agreement *was* null and void, *that* the dispute had arisen out of the main agreement and was within the ambit of the arbitration clause, and *that* there was no basis for any criticism of the proceedings before the arbitral tribunal. Bearing this in mind the Court held: "The fact that the provisions of substantive law of a contract must be considered invalid does not, *neither according to Swiss nor Danish law*, in itself bring about the invalidity of the same contract's provisions as to choice of law and arbitration. On the contrary, as a starting point *it must be presumed that the parties – regardless of the general validity of the contract – have wished to maintain the validity of those provisions.*"[515]

[513] See below, Chapter IV, § 2, point 3.

[514] The principle that agreements are not binding if they are contrary to law or morality.

[515] "Den omstændighed, at en kontrakts materieltretlige bestemmelser må anses for at være ugyldige, findes hverken efter schweizisk eller dansk ret i sig selv at bevirke, at kontraktens bestemmelser om lovvalg og voldgift er ugyldige. Tværtimod må det som udgangspunkt antages, at parterne – uanset kontraktens gyldighed i øvrigt – har næret ønske om at fastholde disse bestemmelsers gyldighed." Writer's translation. Since the arbitration agreement constituted that Swiss law applied, the Court had to investigate the matter regarding both Danish and Swiss law. Had Swiss law had another point of view as to the contents of the doctrine of separability, it might have been impossible for A to in fact carry out the arbitration procedure. In that case the Courts could have disregarded the arbitration agreement under the New York Convention Art. II(3), and heard the case. (The New York Convention Art. II(3) has not been incorporated verbatim into the Danish Arbitration Act 1972 or the Danish Arbitration Regulation 1973. However, its contents are assumed to follow from general unwritten principles of Danish arbitration law).

Furthermore, A had previously regarded himself as bound by the arbitration agreement. At least in regard of those circumstances A was, both under Swiss and Danish law, considered to be bound by the arbitration agreement, and the case was dismissed from the Courts.

The findings of the Court, that as a starting point the arbitration agreement maintained its validity, form a part of the Court's ratio decidendi. U 1987.945 MCCC may therefore be regarded as authority that the Courts have embraced the doctrine of separability.

The Maritime and Commercial Court of Copenhagen accepts as a point of departure that parties in general wish to maintain the validity of provisions on choice of law and arbitration even if the main contract is null and void. Thus, the Court takes into consideration what would *generally* be considered to be the parties' intentions. Making a hypothetical average upon the parties' intentions, if they did in fact have any, as a standard of interpretation is somewhat unorthodox under Danish law. It is suggested though, that what the Maritime and Commercial Court did in fact carry out a purposive interpretation.[516] It would generally fit best with the purpose of the arbitration clause – to ensure that disputes regarding the main contract were dealt with by arbitration – that the arbitration clause maintained its validity even if the main contract's validity was challenged.

The Maritime and Commercial Court resolved the issue under the general rules on the interpretation of contracts rather than on principles of arbitration law. Thus, they needed not evaluate what is the question of principle under arbitration law, namely whether the arbitration agreement is per se an independent agreement. Regarding the issue as a matter of the correct interpretation of the arbitration agreement, it is also clear that the doctrine of separability will not be applied if the proper interpretation of the arbitration agreement contradicts it, or if it, for other reasons, can be shown that in the particular case the parties did in fact *not* intend the arbitral tribunal to be competent if the initial validity of the main contract is disputed.

4. The doctrine of separability under English law
For a long time it was uncertain to what extent the English Courts would accept the doctrine of separability. That arbitration agreements were independent had long been accepted,[517] but whether that independence was sufficient so as to make the arbitra-

---

[516] It is generally accepted as a principle of Danish contract law that contracts and agreements should be interpreted in accordance with their aim or purpose, see *Andersen/Madsen (2001)*, p. 376 (see footnote 43 for reference to case law) and *Andersen (1998)*, p. 243 f.

[517] See HEYMAN V. DARWINS, (1942) 72 Lloyd's List Law Reports 65 HL. Also published in [1942] A. C. 356.

tion clause in a written contract survive the allegation of initial invalidity of the main contract was unsure. However, in HARBOUR V. KANSA,[518] the Court of Appeal took a leap towards the full acceptance of the doctrine. In the case, the parties had entered into a reinsurance contract containing an arbitration clause. When a dispute arose out of the main contract, Harbour (the plaintiff) initiated proceedings before the Court, claiming that the contract was void mainly, but not only, due to the fact that the defendants were neither registered nor approved to carry out insurance business in the United Kingdom. Kansa relied upon the arbitration clause in the contract and applied for a stay under the English Arbitration Act 1975 sec. 1. The High Court found in favour of the plaintiff. According to the Judge, the scope of the autonomy of the arbitration agreement under common law, had not been extended so far as to include cases where it was alleged that the main contract was invalid *ab initio*. On appeal to the Court of Appeal, the Court found that *the initial invalidity of the parties' main contract only rendered the arbitration agreement null and void if the illegality had a direct effect upon the arbitration agreement.* In the case before the Court that was not so. Furthermore, the wording of the arbitration agreement was wide enough to encompass disputes regarding the main contract's validity. The arbitration agreement was thus valid and binding, and a stay was granted.

In HARBOUR V. KANSA the main contract was alleged illegal – it had not (yet) been deemed illegal.[519] Thus, the Court of Appeal's ruling only provided authority that the *alleged* illegality of the main contract did not per se render the arbitration agreement inapplicable. The general statements in the case regarding the arbitration agreement being separable also in the case of de facto illegality of the main contract were, strictly speaking, obiter dicta.[520]

Now, however, the position of the law has been clarified as the rule laid down in HARBOUR V. KANSA, *including* its obiter, has been incorporated into the English Arbitration Act 1996, s. 7:[521]

7. Unless otherwise agreed by the parties, an arbitration agreement which forms or was intended to form part of another agreement (whether or not in writing)[522] shall not be regarded as invalid, non-

---

[518] (1995) XX ICCA Yearbook 771 CA, HARBOUR V. KANSA ET AL.

[519] According to *Samuel (2000),* p. 43, the contract was not illegal at all.

[520] See in the same direction *Samuel (2000)*, p. 43.

[521] 1996 Report on the Arbitration Bill, para. 43.

[522] The main contract need not be in writing. However, the normal formal requirements as to the arbitration agreement apply.

existent or ineffective because that other agreement is invalid, or did not come into existence or has become ineffective, and it shall for that purpose be treated as a distinct agreement.

Also situations where the main contract is in fact illegal are covered by this provision. In this way, the position under sec. 7 of the 1996 Act corresponds to Art. 16(1), 2nd and 3rd sentence of the UNCITRAL Model Law on Arbitration. The UNCITRAL Model law was borne in mind when drafting,[523] and the results are in effect identical, however, as expressed by the Committee: "… it seems to us that the doctrine of separability is quite distinct from the question of the degree to which the tribunal is entitled to rule on its own jurisdiction …", and consequently the issue has been detached from the question of Kompetenz-Kompetenz.

The English Arbitration Act 1996 sec. 7 is declaratory. The parties may agree otherwise. They may specifically agree that the tribunal will not be competent in case of initial invalidity, or more often, they might simply have worded the arbitration agreement in a way that does not cover disputes as to the initial invalidity of the contract. Also, the doctrine does not render the arbitration agreement beyond reproach. The fact that causes the invalidity of the main contract may also render the arbitration agreement null and void. But for that to happen, the arbitration agreement in itself must be affected by the invalidity.

5. The doctrine of separability under Norwegian law

In the same way as the Danish Arbitration Act 1972, the Norwegian Code of Procedure chapter 32 does not contain any provisions on the arbitration agreement's separability from the parties' main agreement, but the principle has been accepted both in theory[524] and, in later years, by the Norwegian Supreme Court. However, until recently the Norwegian Courts have simply expressed themselves in terms of the interpretation of the arbitration agreement. In RT. 1924.216 NSC, DET NORSKE DAMP-TRAWLER-SELSKAB V. KALDNES, an arbitration clause provided that any dispute arising out of the contract or out of the carrying out of the work (shipbuilding) was to be settled in a final and binding way by the permanent technical arbitration tribunal of Kristiania.[525] The Norwegian Supreme Court confirmed the ruling of the Court of Appeal that such a provision encompassed the dispute as to whether the contract was

---

[523] 1996 Report on the Arbitration Bill, para. 44.

[524] See *Mæland (1988)*, p. 82 f.

[525] Now Oslo.

invalid ab initio due to inducement. Therefore the dispute as to the validity of the contract had rightfully been dealt with by the tribunal. Likewise, the minority in Rt. 1996.443 NSC, BRICON V. P&O held that the basis of the parties' dispute was whether the contract was invalid ab initio due to misrepresentation. The minority found that the parties' agreement to arbitrate was not worded so as to include this dispute and the Courts could hear the case.[526] Dealing with the question of whether the (alleged) invalidity of the main contract also invalidates the arbitration agreement as a matter of the scope of the arbitration agreement presupposes the acceptance of the doctrine of separability, which is why Norwegian writers tend to point at Rt. 1924.216 NSC, DET NORSKE DAMPTRAWLERSELSKAB V. KALDNES, when claiming that the doctrine is well established under Norwegian law. Lately, the doctrine has also been spelt out verbatim by the Norwegian Supreme Court. In Rt. 1998.1224 NSC SUNDBRYGGEN V. EEG-HENRIKSEN, Supreme Court embraced the doctrine of separability, stating, that "... the [main] contract and the arbitration agreement shall be seen as two independent agreements, even if the arbitration agreement is inserted into the [main] contract".[527] In the case before the Court, the alleged invalidity was in fact not invalidity ab initio but invalidity that had arisen during the cause of the contractual relationship. Therefore, the issue was to be dealt with by the arbitral tribunal and not the Courts.[528] It is noteworthy that unlike the Maritime and Commercial Court of Copenhagen, the Norwegian Supreme Court did not find it necessary to indulge in what were the general expectations of the parties. The Supreme Court simply stated the principle: That there were two separate agreements.

The Committee behind the Draft Norwegian Arbitration Act has suggested that the new Act should contain a provision stating the principle that the arbitration agreement is separable from the main agreement. The Committee seems to introduce this as a novelty to Norwegian arbitration law, without reference to existing Norwegian case law.[529] Obviously, an explicit statutory regulation is a novelty, but introducing the principle as such as a novelty seems somewhat imprecise.

---

[526] The majority found that the real dispute between the parties was whether the terms of the contract had been breached. Such a dispute was covered by the arbitration clause, and the case was consequently dismissed from the Courts.

[527] Rt. 1998.1224 NSC on p. 1226.

[528] The case was in any event outside the scope of the Norwegian Code of Procedure sec. 458, allowing the Court, under certain specified circumstances, to rule on whether the arbitration agreement has lapsed.

[529] Norwegian travaux préparatoires, point 8.7.3.

The provision is placed in chapter 4 of the draft, a chapter that deals with the tribunal's competence. The draft sec. 4-1(2) is a more or less verbatim copy of the Model Law's Art. 16(1), 2nd and 3rd sentence.[530] Thus, under the draft, the doctrine of separability is discussed in the context of Kompetenz-Kompetenz rather than as a feature of the arbitration agreement, as is the case under English[531] (and Swedish)[532] law. This is obviously a perfectly workable solution, however this writer finds the English approach more appealing as it points out the doctrine of separability as a special feature of the arbitration agreement rather than as a necessary requisite for the effectiveness of Kompetenz-Kompetenz. This even more so, as Norwegian law already at present seems to accept the doctrine as a principle that is distinct from Kompetenz-Kompetenz. One might argue that in this respect the Committee behind the Draft Norwegian Arbitration Act has been too true to the template – the UNCITRAL Model Law.

6. Choice of law and the doctrine of separability

It has already been shown that no real international consensus exists as to the existence and basis of the doctrine of separability.[533] Thus, even if the doctrine is becoming increasingly accepted, the choice of law rule applicable to the doctrine needs to be determined. In this respect one must keep in mind, that the real nature of the doctrine is still disputed. One's view on what is the proper choice of law rule for the doctrine might differ depending on whether one regards the doctrine of separability as a necessary prerequisite for the effective exercise of a tribunal's Kompetenz-Kompetenz – and therefore in effect as a matter of procedure – or one regards the

---

[530] **Draft Norwegian Arbitration Act, sec. 4-1 in extract:**
   (1) The arbitral tribunal shall rule on its own jurisdiction, including any objections with respect to the existence or validity of the arbitration agreement.
   (2) An arbitration agreement which forms part of a contract, shall for purposes of this provision be treated as an agreement independent of the other terms of the contract. A decision by the arbitral tribunal that the contract is invalid shall not in itself entail the invalidity of the arbitration agreement.
   (3) ...

[531] English Arbitration Act 1996, s. 7.

[532] Swedish Arbitration Act 1999, sec. 3.

[533] In point 2.2.

separability as a special feature of the arbitration agreement, and as such a matter of substance.

van den Berg[534] points out three possible starting points as to what the choice of law rule might be, namely the law of the main contract, the law of the arbitration clause and the lex fori. He further points out that some of these laws may be cumulatively applicable, and chooses, for the sake of practicality and safety, the lex fori.

It is generally accepted that the parties may contract out of the doctrine of separability. Furthermore, there is no pressing public interest in the separability issue. It is merely the parties' own convenience and effective dispute resolution that is at stake. These points seem to contradict the use of a lex fori rule – firstly, as there is simply no reason to do so, and secondly the use of the lex fori rule is generally counterproductive to predictability in international arbitration. Finally, this writer maintains that the doctrine of separability is a matter of substance, as it describes one of the special features of the arbitration agreement itself. In keeping with this, the lex contractus and not the lex fori is the obvious starting point. The question remains then, whether it is the law of the main contract or the arbitration contract that should settle the matter, or whether – as suggested by van den Berg – these might be cumulative.

One could argue that the law applicable to the main contract should decide, whether a certain provision of the main contract may be taken out of context, and even survive the initial invalidity of the main contract. However, having first assumed as the starting point that the doctrine of separability is used to describe a specific feature of the arbitration agreement, namely that the arbitration agreement is a separate agreement even if it is printed as a clause amongst others, the answer to this question becomes quite straightforward. As the separability flows from the arbitration agreement itself, the law that applies to the arbitration agreement should be the one to determine, whether the doctrine applies or not. In that way a single law is pointed out, without the need to fulfil cumulative criteria in several laws, which allows the parties to determine and ascertain beforehand whether the doctrine applies to their arbitration clause or not. To this writer, that seems as the "safest and most practical solution".[535]

---

[534] *van den Berg (1981)*, p. 146.

[535] Cf. *van den Berg (1981)*, p. 146.

7. Summing up and comparison

For practical purposes, the doctrine of separability seems to be accepted to more or less the same degree in Danish, English and Norwegian law. When considering the invalidity of the arbitration agreement that agreement should be regarded as *a separate agreement in its own right*, even if the agreement is printed as a clause amongst other clauses in the parties' main contract. The invalidity of the main contract *need not* entail the invalidity of the arbitration clause, but it *might*. Certain reasons for invalidity go the root of the parties' whole contractual relationship thereby also invalidating the arbitration agreement. Examples of this could be that one of the parties' are under some sort of incapacity, or that the contract is obtained through coercion or by a forged signature, or, maybe, that a person purporting to enter into an arbitration agreement on behalf of someone else lacks the authority to do so. To the extent that the facts, which impeach the main agreement, also impeach the arbitration agreement, the doctrine of separability has exhausted its role. The question raised in such a situation is a question of Kompetenz-Kompetenz, or of the ability of the arbitral tribunal to rule upon its own jurisdiction. These are dealt with below in Chapter IV.

Both under Danish and English law, the parties may agree that the doctrine of separability shall not apply to their contract. The issue is not touched upon in the Norwegian Supreme Court's ruling in Rt. 1998.1224 NSC, SUNDBRYGGEN V. EEG-HENRIKSEN, however it must be assumed that the doctrine only applies insofar as the parties have not agreed otherwise. The doctrine of separability is neither a matter of procedure nor a matter of pressing public interest. Consequently, there seems no reason to restrict the parties from deciding themselves whether the doctrine should apply or not.

Having said that the de facto application of the principle within the three jurisdictions does not seem to differ much, it must be noted that the reasons for the rule do. Three different lines of reasoning are applied. Firstly, the doctrine of separability may be seen as a necessary requisite for the arbitral tribunal's exercise of its competence to deal with its own jurisdiction – its Kompetenz-Kompetenz. This is the reasoning in the UNCITRAL Model Law, and consequently, the reasoning behind the Norwegian Draft Arbitration Act sec. 4-1(2), 1st sentence. The reasoning applied by the Maritime and Commercial Court of Copenhagen on the other hand is not directly concerned with the effectiveness of the arbitral procedure. Instead, it is concerned with principles of the interpretation of contracts as such, namely to interpret the contract in accordance with what the general expectations of the parties must have been and the purpose of the same contract. Finally, the doctrine of separability can be based on an assumption of principle, namely that the arbitration agreement is distinct from the main agreement. The successfulness of the doctrine within the last decades is probably due to the fact that all reasons are valid. An agreement regarding the dispute resolution process is in many ways a distinct agreement. It is often governed not only by rules of substance, but also of rules on procedure, it may be governed by a different law than the main contract, and it is supposed to come into play when something goes wrong, rather than being a provision which set out the parties' rights and obligations when things go according to plan. Also, it must be presumed that the parties, had they thought about it, would have intended the agreement to persist, even if the main agreement was declared null and void. In general, it cannot be presumed that the parties intended that claims under the contract should be settled by arbitration, whereas the Courts should deal with claims that the contract was invalid. This is especially so as the same facts might give rise to both claims under the contract, and claims that the contract is invalid. And finally, for arbitration agreements to be effective, the arbitral tribunal must have the competence to decide its own jurisdiction. The doctrine of separability is necessary if one wishes to ensure Kompetenz-Kompetenz irrespectively of the basis for the challenge to the tribunal's jurisdiction.

In summing up, it can be said that the doctrine of separability is accepted under Danish, English and Norwegian law – in practice to more or less the same degree. Thus, the doctrine, when coupled with the principle of Kompetenz-Kompetenz, aids ensuring the effectiveness of arbitration agreements in the three jurisdictions.

§ 3. Arbitration agreements' substantial validity – the requirements of arbitration law

1. Introduction: International consensus

According to the New York Convention Art. II, arbitration agreements shall be recognised by the Courts of the contracting states insofar as the arbitration agreement is in writing and is worded so as to contain an undertaking that the parties "submit to arbitration all or any differences which have arisen or which may arise between them in respect of a defined legal relationship … concerning a subject matter capable of settlement by arbitration". However, the Courts of the Contracting States need not refer the parties to arbitration if they find that the "… agreement is null and void, inoperative or incapable of being performed". These basic requirements are generally accepted in international law and will also be found in most national regulations of the validity of arbitration agreements, including Danish, English and Norwegian law. In the following, therefore, the regulations will be presented together using Danish, English and Norwegian case law as examples. But before doing that, a brief overview of the relevant provisions in the Danish and English Arbitration Acts, as well as in the Norwegian Code of Procedure chapter 32, will be given.

2. The provisions

The validity of arbitration agreements is dealt with in the Danish Arbitration Act 1972, sec. 1, sub-sec. 2, which applies to both domestic and international disputes. The provision reads:

"An agreement to arbitrate is invalid if the dispute according to its nature cannot be determined by arbitration, or the agreement prescribes a composition of the arbitral tribunal or an arbitral procedure, which is not reassuring for the parties or for one of the parties."[536]

The provision is reflected in the Danish Arbitration Act 1972 sec. 7, no. 1, stating that an arbitral award is invalid in its entirety or part if the arbitration agreement on which it is based is invalid. The specific reasons for the invalidity are not stated, but generally here one must refer oneself to the rules of contract law or the law of procedure that may apply. The New York Convention Art. II(3) has not been incorporated verbatim into the Danish Arbitration Act. Thus, there is no explicit provision in Danish law stating that an arbitration agreement may not be relied upon if it is "inoperative or incapable of being performed". This principle is however considered to follow from basic principles of Danish law. Given that an arbitration agreement that could not be carried out would still bar the parties from using the Danish Courts, the parties would be deprived of access to justice – a result that would be in breach of both basic Danish principles of justice and the European Convention on Human Rights Art. 6(1).[537] Also, the fact that an arbitration agreement will not be accepted by the Courts if the agreement is inoperative has been affirmed on several occasions by the Danish Courts.[538] Thus – the principles expressed in the New York Convention Art. II(3) are a part of Danish law, even if they are not explicitly stated in a statutory regulation.

According to the English Arbitration Act 1996 sec. 9(4) the Courts shall grant a stay of proceedings if the parties have entered into an arbitration agreement regarding the subject matter of the dispute, unless it is proven that the arbitration agreement is null and void, inoperative, or incapable of being performed. One may recognise the wording of the New York Convention Art. II(3), which is incorporated here, but the New York Convention Art. II(1) has not been subject to a verbatim incorporation. Still, the principles apply under English law. The requirement for arbitrability is recognised by the Committee behind the Act,[539] and the possibility of declaring a subject matter inarbitrable under Common Law is expressly preserved in sec. 81(1)(a) of the English Arbitration Act. Also, it is generally accepted in theory and

---

[536] Writer's translation.

[537] See U 1994.953 DSC, HUMMER V. BYGGEFORENINGEN CENTRUM.

[538] See e.g. U 1973.601 DCA, U 1983.442 DCA and U 1995.343 DCA.

[539] 1996 Report on the Arbitration Bill, para. 19.

case law that the terms of the arbitration agreement must be certain for the agreement to be valid.[540] A general undertaking to refrain from seeking the Courts' assistance in all time to come and for whatever reason would not be held valid by the English Courts.

If the arbitration agreement falls short of the requirements set out in sec. 9(4), the English Courts may refuse to enforce an arbitral award based on it under sec. 66(3). It follows from the sec. 66(3) that an award shall not be enforced if the tribunal lacked substantial jurisdiction. The invalidity of the arbitration agreement itself will always render the tribunal without jurisdiction.

Initially it was intended to introduce a special regime for domestic arbitration in the English Arbitration Act 1996 Part II. It follows from Part II, sec. 86, that in domestic arbitration, a stay could be refused not only if the agreement was "null and void, inoperable or incapable of being performed", but also if there were "other sufficient grounds for not requiring the parties to abide by the arbitration agreement". Thus, it was intended in domestic arbitration that there should be an "open-ended list" of reasons for the refusal of a stay. The idea of bringing Part II into force has been abandoned,[541] and with it the idea of an open-ended list. Instead, sec. 9(4) exhaustively lists the reasons why the English Courts may refuse a stay, in domestic and international arbitration alike. Especially English lawyers should note that it follows from the exhaustive list in s. 9(4) that the opportunity granted by the Arbitration Act 1975, sec. 1(1) to refuse a stay if there was "… not in fact any dispute between the parties …" no longer exists.

According to the Norwegian Court of Procedure sec. 452, sub-sec. 1, the parties may agree to have a legal dispute determined by arbitration when they are free to dispose with the subject matter of the dispute. Similarly, the parties may agree that future disputes that may arise out of a certain legal matter shall be settled by arbitration. The provision explicitly requires that the subject matter should be arbitrable and that the agreement should regard a defined legal relationship. The inoperability of the arbitration agreement is not dealt with in sec. 452, but instead in sec. 458, providing for a summary procedure before the Court in case of the lapse of the arbitration agreement. The summary procedure is only available if the arbitration agreement has ceased to have effect due to difficulties in the appointment of the arbitrators. Other challenges to the arbitration agreement require a normal Court procedure, see Rt. 1998.1224 NSC on p. 1227.

---

[540] *Russell (1997), para. 2-002.*

[541] *Russell (1997), para. 7-003.*

The Norwegian Code of Procedure sec. 452, sub-sec. 1 corresponds to sec. 467, no. 1, stating that an arbitral award will be declared invalid by the Courts – ex officio – if the subject matter of the dispute is not arbitrable. Other reasons for the invalidity of the arbitration agreement are dealt with in sec. 468, stating that the arbitral award may be declared invalid upon the request of one of the parties if e.g. the arbitration agreement is invalid.[542]

Hence, the substantial requirements of the New York Convention Art. II either exist as specific provisions in the Danish, English and Norwegian general statutory regulation of arbitration, or are accepted as reigning principles of arbitration law. Below these requirements will be considered in turn. In point 2, the requirement that the subject matter should be capable of settlement by arbitration will be considered, whereas the requirements that the arbitration agreement should regard a defined legal relationship, and that it should not be inoperative or incapable of being performed are discussed in point 3.

3. Is the subject matter capable of settlement by arbitration?

3.1. Introduction

The term "arbitrability" is here used to describe the question of which disputes may be settled by means of arbitration and which may not[543] – so-called objective arbitrability.[544]

Rules and regulations dealing with objective arbitrability have two characteristic features.

1) They govern whether, and to what extent, a certain dispute may be settled by arbitration.

2) They *may* be applied by the Courts according to a choice of law rule to the benefit of the lex fori.

Nevertheless, the question of which disputes are arbitrable and which are not is easy to put but difficult to answer. Firstly, no authoritative definition of what is arbi-

---

[542] Norwegian Code of Procedure sec. 468, sub-sec. 1, no. 1. According to the Draft Norwegian Arbitration Act sec. 8-2(1) an arbitration award may be declared invalid if the arbitration agreement is invalid under the law to which the parties have subjected it.

[543] See likewise *Russell (1997)*, p. 15, paragraph 1-027. In Anglo-American law the term is sometimes used to describe the scope of the arbitration agreement, see *Merkin (1991)*, p. 433 ff.

[544] *Blessing (1996)*, p.191.

trability exists. There are no formal characteristics that point out arbitrability rules. A regulation of arbitrability may be unwritten, founded in a basic conception that, for example, administrative law issues, which require that public law interests are taken into consideration, should not be settled in a final and binding way by an arbitrator. Or a regulation of arbitrability may be a written rule stating that (only) the Courts or another specified forum should deal with a certain dispute.

Secondly, the discussion of arbitrability presupposes a merger between the discussion of public law interests in the (potentially applicable) national laws and the general discussion of choice of applicable law and mandatory rules. It is not always obvious when a regulation is so overall important that a dispute falling within the scope of the regulation should not be settled by arbitration.

Finally, certain aspects of the choice of law regarding the arbitrability issue remain unsettled.[545] As mentioned, restrictions on arbitration in national law may generally be applied *ex officio* by the Court presented with the dispute,[546] however, the arbitrability issue may arise at an earlier state. Assuming that the arbitral tribunal's competence is being challenged on grounds of lack of arbitrability it must be established which law's rules on arbitrability affect the tribunal's competence. In this thesis, the arbitrability of transport disputes is specifically deliberated upon in chapter V, § 1. Therefore, in the following, a general presentation of the notion of arbitrability will be provided, allowing the specific transport law related problems to be dealt with later.

3.2. The legislators' approach to arbitrability

Generally speaking, the areas excluded from arbitrability are areas of law where the parties themselves need to be protected, where the rights of obligations of third parties are concerned, or where matters according to mandatory rules have to be dealt with by a certain authority or entity. When wanting to give examples of what cannot be arbitrated, normally issues of a non-economical nature within family law (e.g. paternity),[547] administrative law,[548] or criminal law topics are mentioned.[549] Also, it is

---

[545] See e.g. *Blessing (1996), Hanotiau (1996),* and *Arfazadeh (2001).*

[546] Norwegian Code of Procedure sec. 467, no. 1.

[547] Economical issues within family law are generally arbitrable – at least to an extent, see LE-1993-02236, A v. B.

[548] See U 1999.829 DSC.

[549] *Merkin, (1991),* para. 2.14.

not an area of law where the legislators have seen the need to make a dense regulation in the Arbitration Acts. According to the committee behind the Danish Arbitration Act 1972, "[there] is hardly any need to regulate via statute here. Such questions [the question of arbitrability] seem never to have caused any difficulties in practice. By interpreting the relevant provisions [of the relevant statutes] it can without difficulty be established if, and to what extent, disputes may be referred to arbitration. To express this in a general provision in an arbitration act seems superfluous."[550]

The Departmental Advisory Committee behind the English Arbitration Act 1996 did not find it necessary to include general provisions on arbitrability either. In fact, the question was largely ignored by the Committee, and only briefly touched upon when discussing the extent of the party autonomy.

"In some cases, of course, the public interest will make inroads on complete party autonomy, in much the same way as there are limitations on freedom of contract. Some matters are simply not susceptible of this form of dispute resolution (*e.g.* certain cases concerning status or many family matters) while other considerations (such as customer protection) may require the imposition on different rights and obligations."[551]

The need to legislate is indeed ignorable. For example, in Scandinavian legislation, different wordings in the national statutes do not provide for much information, and do for practical purposes provide the same results when applied in case law.

Also, attempts to govern the issue under a more extensive provision do not always provide more real information, as may be seen when reading for example the German Code of Civil Procedure.[552]

---

[550] Danish Arbitration Act 1972 travaux préparatoires, p. 24. My translation.

[551] 1996 Report on the Arbitration bill, para. 19.

[552] Danish Arbitration Act 1972, sec 1: "En voldgiftsaftale er ugyldig, såfremt tvisten efter sin art ikke kan afgøres ved voldgift ...". Finnish Arbitration Act 1992, sec. 2: "A dispute of private nature which the parties have the right to settle between themselves, can be submitted to be finally settled in arbitration between the parties ...". Norwegian Code of Procedure, sec. 452: "Parterne kan enes om at la en retstvist avgjøres ved voldgift, naar de har fri raadighet over det, som er gjenstand for tvisten." See retarding when the parties may dispose over the subject matter of a dispute, *Skoghøy (2001)*, p. 450 ff. Swedish Arbitration Act 1999, sec. 1: "Tvister i frågor som parterna kan träffa förlikning om får genom avtal lämnas till avgörande av en eller flera skiljemän. ...". [Lag (1999:116) om skiljeförfarande.]

German Code of Civil Procedure,[553] sec. 1030, "Arbitrability"[554]

1. Any claim involving an economic interest[555] can be subject of an arbitration agreement. An arbitration agreement concerning claims not involving an economic interest shall have legal effect to the extent that the parties are entitled to conclude a settlement on the issue in dispute.

2. An arbitration agreement relating to disputes on the existence of a lease of residential accommodation within Germany shall be null and void. ...

3. Statutory provisions outside this Book by virtue of which certain disputes may not be submitted to arbitration, or may be submitted to arbitration only under certain conditions,[556] shall remain unaffected.

The only de facto information provided by the German Code of Civil Procedure sec. 1030 which is not also provided by the Danish and Norwegian wording or the travaux préparatoires of the English Arbitration Act 1996, is that sec. 1030(3), emphasises that a provision under which disputes may only be submitted to arbitration under certain conditions is also a provision on arbitrability. However, it is submitted that in that way the German Code of Civil Procedure allows a wider scope for the discussion of the notion of arbitrability than does its Scandinavian and English counterparts. Generally, the notion of conditional arbitration has not been introduced as a principle in English or Scandinavian law.[557]

The focus regarding arbitrability issue is outside the areas of law where the party autonomy normally prevails. Therefore, there has only been a limited discussion of arbitrability within areas of law relevant to international transport and commerce. What is arbitrable and what is not has simply been thought a more or less settled issue,[558] and the only real discussion between the scholars in later years has concerned

---

[553] Zivilprozeßordnung (10th book).

[554] Source of English translation:
http://www.uni-muenster.de/Jura.iwr/english/berger/resear/10zpoe.html.

[555] "Vermögensrechtlicher Anspruch".

[556] Refer to this, when saying that "arbitrable if" is a provision on arbitrability, Chapter III, point 1.

[557] See *Moss (1999)*, p. 370 and *Skoghøy (2001)*, p. 457.

[558] *Dillén (1933)*, p. 68 ff; *Gomard (1979)*, p. 13 ff; *Kurkela/ Uoti (1994)*, p. 5 f; *Merkin (1991)*, para. 2.14; *Mæland, (1988)* p. 41 ff; *Russell (1997)*, para. 1-026 – 1-030.

the choice of law regarding arbitrability[559] and whether competition law issues are arbitrable.[560]

3.3. Rules on arbitrability – a version of ordre public?

Under Scandinavian and English law, the notion of ordre public is normally understood to denote ordre public in the negative sense, allowing the Courts of a fori to refuse to enforce foreign law if the effects of that foreign law are such as to be in conflict with the basic notions of justice within the Court's jurisdiction.[561] International conventions will often expressly provide, that the rules of the convention need not be adhered to by the Contracting States, if doing so would be contrary to ordre public within that jurisdiction, thus allowing for a "negative" ordre public escape clause. E.g. under the New York Convention Art. V(II)(b) the Courts of a State may refuse to recognise and enforce arbitration awards if doing so would be contrary to the public policy of that State.

Ordre public also exist in a positive sense, allowing the Courts of a jurisdiction to apply the rules of the fori to a foreign dispute, materialised before that fori.[562] Rules amounting to positive ordre public may be worded as internationally mandatory rules. Internationally mandatory rules are mandatory rules, applied according to a unilateral choice of law rule to the benefit of the lex fori.[563] However, the principle of positive ordre public also allows the Courts of a fori a discretion to apply the rules of the fori, that are not worded to be thus internationally mandatory to a dispute, even if the applicable law is not the law of the fori. In this way, the principle of positive ordre public allows certain rules of the fori to be internationally mandatory on an ad hoc basis. Rules on arbitrability are examples of such rules. The New York Convention Art. V(II)(a) allows the Courts of the Contracting States to refuse the recognition

---

[559] *Moss (1999)*, p. 366 ff, *Blessing (1996)* and *Hanotiau (1996)*.

[560] See *Rogers (1994), Dalhuisen (1995)* and *Moss (1999)*, p. 368 f. See regarding the arbitrability of intellectual property disputes, *Blessing (1996)*. It follows from the Swedish Arbitration Act 1999 sec. 1, sub-sec. 3 that the private law effects of competition rules may be dealt with by arbitration. This is also the solution proposed in the Draft Norwegian Arbitration Act sec. 2-1(2).

[561] See *Philip (1976)*, p. 65, *Nielsen (1997)*, p. 62, *Mæland (1988)*, p. 243, and *Skoghøy (2001)*, p. 47.

[562] *Hartley (1997)*, p. 351 ff., *Moss (1999)*, p. 135 ff.

[563] *Hartley (1997)*, p. 346 ff.

and/or enforcement of an arbitration agreement if the subject matter of the dispute is not capable of settlement by arbitration under the law of the fori.[564] On the word of *van den Berg,*[565] the question of the non-arbitrable subject matter is therefore a part of the general concept of *ordre public,* and as such superfluous – strictly speaking. The requirement for the subject matter to be arbitrable is simply mirroring the concept of ordre public. This writer supports that rules on arbitrability are rules of ordre public, even if it is ordre public in its positive sense. Therefore, restrictions on arbitrability should only be imposed if not doing so conflicts with basic notions of justice prevailing within the Court's jurisdiction. In certain cases, the use of dispute resolution by arbitration may do just that.

3.4. Arbitrability and mandatory rules – an overview

3.4.1. Introduction

In the following a brief overview of mandatory rules' impact upon whether a subject matter is arbitrable will be given. It is sought to outline what impact mandatory rules have upon the arbitrability of various disputes. Case law will only be used as examples.

3.4.2. Mandatory rules, which govern public interests

This heading mainly governs the areas of criminal law, public law and administrative law in the wider sense, including e.g. the law of social benefits. Within these areas of law the public interest is vast, and disputes may, as a rule, not be settled by voluntary arbitration. The reasons for not allowing arbitration within these areas of law differ, dependent upon what the specific subject matter may be, but outlines may be given.

Firstly, generally one cannot always expect arbitrators to take into account and evaluate public law interests in the same way as the Courts would. The tribunal's responsibility is mainly to settle the dispute between the parties in the particular case, and the evaluation of the decision's general consequences and impact upon society as such is likely to pay a less significant role. Thus in U 1999.829 DSC, THE DANISH PHARMACISTS' UNION V. SVOBODA, an arbitration award which in effect concerned whether Svoboda had acted in breach of the Pharmacist Act was not capable of settlement by arbitration, as that regulation was a part of the general public law

---

[564] Incorporated almost verbatim into the Danish Arbitration Regulation sec. 1 and the English Arbitration Act 1996 sec. 103(3).

[565] *van den Berg (1981),* p. 368 f.

regulation of pharmacies in Denmark. The decision as to whether such a regulation, *which took care of the general interests of the public,* had been complied with *could not be settled by arbitration.*[566] However, if it is only the economic assessment of the consequences of a public law regulation that is in dispute, arbitration may not be ruled out.[567]

Secondly, the State through its Courts holds the monopoly on the dispensing of justice within e.g. criminal law cases. Alternative dispute resolution procedures may be allowed, but they will be allowed only as permitted by the law, and the competence of the Courts cannot be ousted by the parties' agreement alone.

Finally, in disputes regarding mandatory rules that govern public interests, often one of the parties to the dispute is the State or at least a public authority. Therefore, the parties are likely to be on an unequal footing. That mismatch of powers is generally considered best met by the Courts.

---

[566] U 1999.829 DSC, THE DANISH PHARMACISTS' UNION V. SVOBODA. In that case a dispute arose between the pharmacist Svoboda and the Danish Pharmacists' Union. The Union alleged, that Svoboda had acted in breach of the Pharmacist Act sec. 44, and thereby in breach of the Union's rules. The Union initiated proceedings before the Union's tribunal, and the tribunal gave an award requiring Svoboda to pay a fine to the Union of DKK 40,000 as well as the Union's costs of DKK 20,000.The Supreme Court found that the real issue before the tribunal had been whether Svoboda had acted in conflict with the regulation on prices for medical products, issued under the Pharmacist Act sec. 44. As that subject matter was not capable of settlement by arbitration, the award rendered was null and void under the Danish Arbitration Act sec. 7, no. 3. See regarding the Court of Appeal's finding in the case below, point 4.

[567] See U 2002.870 DCA. In the case, a dispute regarding the economic assessment of the milk quota could be arbitrated.

3.4.3. Mandatory rules, which govern private interests

Under this heading fall a variety of cases and very different rationale may apply. Economical issues within family law and inheritance law matters are generally arbitrable, see e.g. BØDSTRUP HOVEDGAARD,[568] and RE Q'S ESTATE.[569] The mandatory rules governing the economical features of family law and inheritance law matters are subject to waiver, and thus, the protection offered by them does not bar the use of arbitration as a means of dispute resolution. However, even if arbitration is an accepted means of dispute resolution, the arbitration award rendered may not have the same legal effects as an arbitration award within other areas of law. Especially the finality of the arbitration agreement may be restricted, see LE-1993-02236, A V. B. Non-economical disputes within family law are not arbitrable. Disputes regarding e.g. the status of children[570] or the validity of a marriage[571] cannot be settled by arbitration.

Some mandatory rules governing private interests aim at the protection of a significantly weaker party, e.g. at the regulation of the relationship between the landlord and the tenant. Thus, according to the German Code of Civil Procedure sec. 1030, sub-sec. 2, disputes regarding the existence of a lease of residential accommodation within Germany cannot be arbitrated. The same is the case under Danish and Norwegian law, see the Danish Landlord and Tenants Act sec. 107,[572] the Norwegian Landlord and Tenants Act secs. 51-53[573] and U 2001.1935 DCA, A V. GRØNNEGÅRDEN.

U 2001.1935 DCA, A V. GRØNNEGÅRDEN.

A was a member of the housing company Grønnegården. The members of the company were entitled to use the company's flats in return for a fee. In connection with A moving out of his flat in the housing company, a dispute arose regarding the payment for the replacement of some tiles in the flat. A

---

[568] U 1984.1045 DCA, BØDSTRUP HOVEDGAARD.

[569] [1999] 1 Lloyds Law Reports 931 QBD.

[570] See e.g. the Danish Childrens' Act secs. 7 ff (Lovbekendtgørelse nr. 293 af 2.5.1995 om børns retsstilling som ændret ved lov nr. 389 af 14.6 1995 og lov nr. 966 af 20.12.1999).

[571] See e.g. the Danish Marriage Act I, secs. 23 ff (Lovbekendtgørelse nr. 147 af 9.3.1999 om ægteskabets indgåelse og opløsning).

[572] Lovbekendtgørelse nr. 347 af 14.5.2001 om leje som ændret ved lov nr. 447 af 7.6.2001.

[573] Lov om husleie av 16 juni, nr. 6, 1939.

initiated proceedings before the Tenant's board, claiming mainly that the legal relationship between the parties should be settled by arbitration, and that an arbitration clause in Grønnegården's rules was invalid. Grønnegården claimed that the rules of the Tenants Act were inapplicable to the case, as A was not in fact a tenant, but a part owner of Grønnegården. Therefore there was not the same conflict of interest between the parties, as one would normally expect between a landlord and a tenant. The arbitration clause was thus not conflicting with the Danish Arbitration Act 1972, sec. 1, sub-sec. 2, and the case should be dismissed from the Courts. The Copenhagen Court of First Instance found for the housing company. According to the mandatory rule of the Tenants Act sec. 107, seb-sec. 1 disputes between a landlord and a tenant regarding the lease were to be settled by the Tenant's board if the substance of the dispute was within the statutory rules on leases. Taking all the circumstances into consideration, the Court of Appeal found that A's influence on the company influence was negligible, and that the legal position of the parties had to be described as that of a normal tenancy. As a consequence of this, as well as the fact that the composition of the arbitral tribunals described in Grønnegården's rules seemed to be biased, the arbitration clause was found to be invalid under the Danish Arbitration Act sec. 1, sub-sec. 2.

Mandatory rules governing private interests, may also be given to the protection of a third party. Such rules might restrict the arbitrability of a certain subject matter. However, generally the party autonomy will not extend to impose rights and obligations upon a third party and thus, the parties cannot agree to arbitrate the legal position of a third party either. Sometimes, the parties will, by arbitrating their own position of law create direct effects upon a third party's legal position. This may be the case in e.g. bankruptcy, and also the receiver's position under a contract of carriage may be affected by the carrier's and sender's agreement to arbitrate their claim. Still, as long as the original parties deal within the boundaries of their party autonomy, a third-party can generally not question the original parties' right to arbitrate. However, the parties should be aware that in the interest of protecting the third party, an arbitration agreement validly entered into might turn out to be ineffective.[574]

Finally, certain mandatory rules dealing with private interests are given to protect the parties themselves. These rules may be found within the areas of contract, obligation, tort and property law. Claims within those areas of law are generally arbitrable. The reasoning applied is this: Within the areas of contract, obligation, tort and property law, the parties' relationship is generally governed by party autonomy. The parties may at the outset have rights that are protected by mandatory regulation, but these rights are subject to waiver. The parties themselves choose whether they will

---

[574] See regarding insolvency the English Insolvency Act 1986, sec. 285(1) and *Russell (1997)*, para. 3-021 and 3-022. It is generally accepted in Danish and Norwegian law that an arbitration agreement entered into by the debtor has to be respected by the debtor's estate, see *Hjejle (1987)*, p. 72 f, *Mæland (1988)*, s. 88. As regards the position of the receiver under a contract of carriage see e.g. the NMC sec. 311 and the Hague Visby Rules Art. 3(8).

take a claim to the Courts. When before the Courts they themselves choose which points to make. An even after a favourable judgment, the party winning the case may choose not to enforce it after all. Thus, even mandatory rules within contract, obligation, tort and property law tend only to be mandatory if the party protected by them so chooses. As a consequence, disputes within this area of law may generally be settled by arbitration.

3.4.4. The arbitrability of transport law disputes

As a rule, the legal problems faced when dealing with transport law fall within the law of contract, obligation, tort or property. Hence, the dispute will arise within the areas of law that are generally considered arbitrable. However, some areas of transport law bear the mark of a public law regulation[575] and the need to protect the weaker[576] and/or third party to the contract[577] may also arise. As mentioned, the issues arising due to this will be dealt with below in Chapter V, § 1.

3.5. The choice of law and the question of arbitrability

3.5.1. Introduction

The question of whether the arbitration agreement is valid may attract the attention of the Courts either when dealing with the recognition of the arbitral agreement[578] or when dealing with the recognition or enforcement of an arbitral award.[579] The same applies to the discussion of arbitrability.[580] In both cases, the effect of non-compliance with the rules will result in the arbitral agreement being invalid, and in both cases this lack of validity will lead to the Courts refusing to do whatever they

---

[575] The COTIF regulations should generally be considered to hold a public-law regulation, even if disputes under the rules tend to be of a private law nature.

[576] See the Hague-Visby Rules Art. 3(8).

[577] See the Nordic Maritime Code sec. 310, sub-sec. 3, cf. sec. 311, sub-sec. 2. (Here in the Norwegian version).

[578] New York Convention Art. II(3).

[579] New York Convention Art. V(1)(a).

[580] New York Convention Art. II(1) and Art. V(2)(a).

were asked to do by the party claiming the validity of the agreement. The difference between the two issues is the choice of law rules, which apply.

The Courts may, according to the New York Convention Art. II(3), refuse to recognise an arbitration agreement if it is found that the agreement is null and void. Art. II(3) does not contain an explicit choice of law rule. Instead, such a rule can be found in Art. V(1)(a) of the same convention. According to this provision, the Courts may refuse to recognise or enforce an arbitral award, given that the arbitration agreement, on which the award rests, is not valid under the law the parties have subjected it to.

If no choice of law has been made, the proper law of the contract, the contract in this case being the arbitration agreement, solves the question of contractual validity. This may be the law that governs the contractual relationship as a whole, but it is not necessarily so. For example, in the lack of special provisions in the contract, the localisation of the arbitral tribunal may be found to be the deciding factor regarding the validity of the arbitration clause, whereas the proper law of the main contract may be the law of the seller's principal place of business.[581]

It must be assumed that the choice of law regarding the substantial validity of the arbitration agreement should be the same, regardless of whether it is the arbitral award or the arbitration agreement that is sought recognised or enforced. As a starting point it will thus be possible for the parties to decide beforehand, which law(s) should govern the validity of the arbitration agreement. One should note, however, that even if the parties do make a specific choice of law provision, they may discover that the arbitrators find themselves bound by mandatory rules regarding contractual validity and/or arbitrability in force at the place of the seat of the arbitral tribunal. Not all arbitrators,[582] or indeed legislators,[583] are as yet convinced of the existence of such a thing as delocalised arbitration! Even so, the parties are free to determine the place, or optional places, of the seat of the arbitral tribunal in advance and hence this crinkle may be ironed out at a preliminary stage. In this way, the parties can ensure that they do in fact have a valid arbitration agreement in force between them.

This picture changes when dealing with the arbitrability issue. Firstly, the Court seized with the case is ad liberty to refuse recognition and/or enforcement if the rules in the lex fori regarding arbitrability are not satisfied.[584] Naturally, the parties may

[581] See the Rome Convention on applicable law, Art. 4(2).

[582] See for the comment of one of them *Brækhus, (1998)* p. 328 ff.

[583] Delocalised arbitration is not recognised under English law, see 1996 Report on the Arbitration Bill, para. 27.

[584] New York Convention Art. V(2)(a).

not need to consult a Court regarding the arbitration agreement, but they often will, especially when wanting to enforce the arbitration award. It is not possible to foresee in advance which Courts may be confronted with e.g. a request for execution. This is especially the case in international transport where the assets of the carrier by their very nature keep changing their geographical location. Neither is it possible at the time of the drafting of the arbitral agreement to foresee where one of the parties at a later stage, possibly in breach of the arbitration agreement, should choose to sue the other before the ordinary Courts. Secondly, it may be that the preconditions for arbitrability of other laws than the law of the fori needs to be satisfied for the agreement to be valid. In that way, the arbitrability rules of one jurisdiction may be recognised as reasons for invalidity in another. Therefore, it must be determined, which law governs whether a certain subject matter is arbitrable.

3.5.2. The approaches

When considering the issue of the choice of law regarding arbitrability, two principles present themselves as logical starting points for the discussion. The first principle being that rules of procedure, including regulation of the Court's competence, are governed by the *lex fori*, the second that the validity of contracts generally are governed by the *lex contractus*. Which principle provides the obvious place to start the investigation, depends on in which way, and for which forum, the issue has presented itself.[585]

If the question of arbitrability arises before the ordinary Courts in a case where the Court is met by a claim for dismissal due to an – alleged – agreement to arbitrate, then it will be natural for the Court first to ascertain that the subject matter of the case is arbitrable under the law of the *fori*.

If, instead, the issue of arbitrability is first entertained by the arbitral tribunal when the tribunal is determining its own competence, the tribunal might take its starting point in the rules of arbitrability in the law applicable to the subject matter of the parties' dispute as well as the law applicable to the arbitration agreement if that law differs from the law applicable to the subject matter. However, the arbitral tribunal is also likely to examine whether the case is arbitrable under the law applicable in the jurisdiction where the arbitral tribunal is seated.

Apart from these possibilities, legal theory has suggested e.g. the law of the fori of the Court that would have been competent if the parties had not entered into an

---

[585] *Hanotiau (1996),* p. 391 ff.

271

agreement to arbitrate, and the law of the place where an arbitral award based on the case is most likely to be enforced.[586]

Conceptually, three different approaches reign. The *choice of law approach* acknowledges the laws potentially applicable and attempts to make a reasonable choice between them.[587] The approach is problematic, as it does not provide a general rule to decide *which* law(s) will determine the issue of arbitrability. Instead, the choice of law approach must be applied to the facts of the specific case, and even then it might not come out with a clear answer.[588] As a consequence some Courts and legislators have applied a *substantive approach*. According to a substantive approach the Courts and arbitral tribunals seated within a certain jurisdiction shall apply the rules on arbitrability of that forum, regardless of any applicable foreign law.[589] Finally, an *anational approach* has been suggested according to which the arbitrability of international disputes should be determined with reference to internationally accepted principles of arbitrability – and thus without reference to any national law.[590]

The substantive approach purports to iron out the difficulties encountered when applying the choice of law approach to arbitrability.[591] To the extent that the substantive rules applies to the Courts and arbitral tribunals within the jurisdiction alike, this might be achieved; however, there is no general consensus as to what impact the rules of the jurisdiction where the arbitral tribunal is seated has upon that tribunal. According to *Goode*,[592] the law of the place of the arbitration should be allocated considerable importance, whereas both *Hanotiau* and *Kirry*[593] hold that the arbitral tribunal has no forum (and thus no lex loci arbitrii).[594] If the arbitrator regards him-

---

[586] *Blessing (1996)*, p. 192.

[587] See e.g. *Moss (1999)*, p. 371 ff.

[588] *Kirry (1996)*, p. 379 f.

[589] See *Kirry (1996)* with reference to the Swiss Private International Law Act 1988 Art. 177 and the ruling of the French Cour de Cassation in the *Dalico* case (Ruling of 20 December 1993).

[590] *Hanotiau (1996)*, p. 403 and *Blessing (1996)*, p. 192.

[591] See *Kirry (1996)*, p. 383 for reference to Swiss law.

[592] *Goode (2001)*, p. 39.

[593] *Kirry (1996)*, p. 379.

[594] *Hanotiau (1996)*, p. 396.

self as delocalised, or if the substantive rule only applies to the Courts, the substantive approach seems not to provide for any real predictability. Besides, it is feared by this writer that a automatic application of the substantive approach might lead the Courts of the fori to apply limitations of national law in situations where it is not called for. In any case, the substantive approach faces the same problem as the choice of law approach does as regards arbitrability at the enforcement stage. Under the New York Convention Art. V(I)(a) the Contracting States are still ad liberty to impose their own restrictions on arbitrability, despite the substantial approach being applied at the outset.

Considering the suggestion that in international arbitration restrictions to arbitrability should only be accepted according to an anational rule, the suggestion seems a little fanciful – at least at present. The rule would have the advantage of allowing for an extensive scope of arbitrability within most areas of law relevant to international trade and commerce. Even subject matters such as competition law issues and patent's law would be considered arbitrable under that rule, as no consensus that those subjects are *not* arbitrable may be shown to exist. Also, due to the ordre public nature of arbitrability rules, the restrictions on arbitrability changes over time. It will not be easy to determine which rules are in fact covered by the anational approach, and therefore the approach must be rejected as not providing a solution to the problems encountered.

It seems to this writer, that the most realistic approach to establishing which law governs arbitrability, is the choice of law approach. The approach has been accused of not providing clear conclusions. However, it is suggested, that one of the reasons for the discussion of the choice of law regarding the arbitrability issue being so chaotic is, that writers tend to mix two different issues, namely: 1) which law is theoretically the better to govern arbitrability and 2) how to best deal with the actual problems occurring when trying to predict which jurisdictions' rules on arbitrability may in the end be applied to a certain dispute. Therefore, below these two discussions will be split, allowing this writer to deal with the issue of which law would be best fit to govern the arbitrability of a subject matter in point 3.5.3, and then to face the practicalities of the issue under the present legal circumstances in point 3.5.4.

3.5.3. May one law be suggested to apply in al relations when deciding the arbitrability of a certain subject matter?
It is unlikely that the national States will ever give up their right to refuse recognition and enforcement of the arbitration *award* if doing so would be contrary to the basic notions of justice prevailing within that State. It is not suggested that they should either. Thus, total predictability regarding whether the enforcement of an award will be

273

refused due to lack of arbitrability, may never be achieved. But a universal rule applying to the recognition and enforcement of the arbitration *agreement* may still be realised.

When deciding what this rule should be, two issues should be taken into consideration. Firstly, although often suggested that the law of the arbitration agreement should decide the question of arbitrability, the focus regarding arbitrability must be on the subject matter. The question to ask is not whether an *arbitration agreement* regarding a certain subject matter is valid, but whether a certain *subject matter* is such that it is perceptible to settlement by arbitration. Arbitrability is not a matter of the legal effects and effectiveness of the arbitration agreement, to be solved by the law that applies to that agreement,[595] but a matter of the substance of the dispute, to be dealt with by the law that governs that matter. Secondly, regarding the issue from the point of view of jurisdictions generally allowing arbitrability would be erroneous. It has already been shown that arbitrability rules are rules of positive ordre public. This feature fits badly with a rule stating that "all subject matters are arbitrable". Such a rule carries none of the features of a regulation of ordre public. Instead, the regulations relevant to this discussion are regulations disallowing or giving preconditions for the arbitrability of a certain dispute. These rules tend to be of a public law or protective nature, see above, and are generally aimed at domestic relation, but may apply to disputes eventually sought settled by (international) arbitration. These two points urge this writer to suggest one law to settle the dispute of which subject matter may be arbitrable, namely the law *to which a subject matter is the most closely related*. Such a rule makes the discussion of the application of internationally mandatory or ordre public rules of other fora superfluous when determining the validity of the arbitration *agreement*, and it is suggested that most policy considerations will also be taken care of. It will not be often that the mandatory rules restricting arbitrability of a jurisdiction to which the dispute is *not* the most closely connected are so essential that they should be applied to the dispute nonetheless. Also, choosing the law to which the subject matter is most closely connected instead of the applicable law, rules out the possibility that the parties – by making a choice of law provision – drag the question of the arbitrability of the dispute out of the scope of application of the (internationally) mandatory rules of the jurisdiction to which the dispute has its most real connection.[596]

---

[595] As is e.g. the doctrine of separability, see above in § 2, point 2.6

[596] E.g. Leases of real property situated in Germany may not be arbitrated in Germany. Leases of real property situated in Denmark may not be arbitrated there either. But real property situated in Denmark may out of principle be arbitrated in Germany according to German law. Applying the law to which the dispute is the most closely connected will ensure that the Danish prohibition of arbitrability

This writer concedes that it may not always be obvious, to which law a subject matter is the most closely connected, and therefore, that suggesting this law as the law governing arbitrability is adverse to achieving predictability in international trade and commerce. However, considering the whole nature of the arbitrability issue, one must shift focus from the ongoing quest for ensuring predictability to the regard to ensuring the protective features generally prevailing in rules restricting arbitrability.[597] Also, one must keep in mind that often restrictions on arbitrability are not applicable to international trade and commerce.

3.5.4. Navigating within the present legal framework

This writer suggests that the arbitrability of a subject matter is most aptly determined by the law to which the subject matter is the most closely connected. However, considering the wording of the New York Convention, this rule is not realistic at present. Therefore, guidelines on how to best navigate within the present legal framework will be given.

3.5.4.1. The drafters of arbitration clauses

As the parties to an international arbitration agreement cannot be sure which Courts will ultimately entertain the issue of the subject matter's arbitrability, applying much effort in investigating the rules on arbitrability in potential enforcing jurisdictions seems a rather wasted effort for the drafter of arbitration agreements. Instead, the drafter's focus should be on ensuring that the arbitral tribunal will not consider itself incompetent due to lack of arbitrability, and that the potential Courts will not consider the arbitration agreement null and void under the applicable law, whichever that may be. Regarding the potential deficiency in arbitrability as a reason for the arbitration agreement being null and void, has the advantage of providing the drafter with a choice of law rule. Art. V(1)(a) of the New York Convention provides that the Courts may refuse to recognise the arbitration award on the action of a party if the arbitration agreement is invalid under the law to which the parties have subjected it –

is respected by the German Courts and arbitral tribunals (as a reason for the invalidity of the arbitration agreement) even if the parties should have decided to arbitrate the matter in Germany according to German law.

[597] See *Brækhus (1998)*, p. 39. Although being generally sceptical to the application of "the individualising method" in international maritime law, he admits that the method is suitable in disputes where it is imperative that one of the parties may avail themselves of a specific legal regulation. Such is exactly the case within the choice of law for arbitrability, due to the restrictions' generally public and/or protective character.

alternatively under the law in which the award was made. It is generally accepted that this choice of law rule also applies to the arbitration agreement. Thus, the drafter should ensure that the subject matter is arbitrable under the law applicable to the arbitration agreement. However, due to the lack of consensus on the matter, the drafter should not stop there. The drafter must ensure that there are no applicable restrictions in the lex loci arbitrii, and also that the subject matter is arbitrable under the law that governs the subject matter in case that law differs from the law applicable to the arbitration agreement. Finally, it ought to be considered whether the law to which the subject matter is the most closely connected have any applicable restrictions on arbitrability. If the restrictions of those four laws are satisfied, then the drafter should be able to rest assured that the arbitration agreement will not be rejected as null and void by either the arbitral tribunal or the Courts. This may seem a cumbersome task, but it is perfectly feasible by an appropriate choice of law provision in the parties' contract to ensure that the law of the arbitration agreement and the law of the subject matter is the same law. Thus, by choosing the law to which the subject matter is the most closely connected as the applicable law, both as regards the arbitration agreement and the subject matter of the dispute, the drafter needs only ensure that the arbitrability criteria of that law of the lex loci arbitrii are fulfilled. The drafter would in any case need to investigate the regulation on arbitration in that jurisdiction, to ensure that no unwanted substantive rules of that jurisdiction will be applied.

3.5.4.2. The Courts

According to the New York Convention Art. V(2)(a) the Contracting States are ad liberty to refuse the recognition and enforcement of the arbitral *award* if the subject matter of the dispute is not capable of settlement by arbitration under the lex fori. The provision may be applied ex officio by the Courts, but notably it is an option of the fori. The Courts have a discretion as to whether national restrictions on arbitrability should bar the recognition and enforcement of the award. As already said, it is not suggested that the Courts of the fori should give up this right, but it is suggested that the Court should exercise the right in keeping with the positive ordre public nature of arbitrability restrictions. Consequently the refusal of recognition and enforcement of the award should only take place if not doing so would be contrary to the basic principles of justice within the jurisdiction, in the same way as under the negative ordre public reservation of Art. V(2)(b).

The refusal of the recognition and enforcement of the arbitration *agreement* under the New York Convention Art. II(1) in fine is not equipped with a choice of law provisions such as is Art. V(2)(a).

Both *Gaja*[598] and *van den Berg*[599] hold that for the sake of the internal consistency of the Convention, the choice of law provided in Art. V(2)(a) should be applied under Art. II(1) as well, thus making the arbitrability of a subject matter an issue to be determined by lex fori. The writer has already shown that an approach to arbitrability on the agreement stage, which is totally devoid of regard to the lex causae is not desirable. Thus, writer must refuse the general application of a lex fori approach to arbitrability on the agreement stage, both as providing for insufficient predictability and as potentially providing for substantially undesirable results. But then, it cannot be assumed that the rule in the New York Convention was in all respects intended for general applicability. The New York Convention deals with the relationship between the arbitration award or agreement and the Courts, it does not deal with the arbitration tribunal as such, nor does it offer general rules on arbitration procedure. Therefore the New York Convention needs only provide a choice of law for the Courts, confronted with the arbitration agreement or award. It needs not consider whether that choice of law is fit to govern in all aspects of the matter. Still, considering the interpretation of the Convention text, the Courts of a fori may wish to imploy their prerogative to impose that fori's arbitrability restrictions. Once more, it is suggested that the Courts of the fori should only apply any restrictions on arbitrability if not doing so would be in breach of the jurisdiction's basic principles of justice. Thus, it is suggested that the Court of the fori may apply arbitration restrictions if the interest sought protected by the rule is considerable, and the dispute has such a close connection to the forum that the application of the rule is proper.[600] Regarding the applicability of the rules on arbitrability in other jurisdictions than the fori, it is suggested that the Courts apply the choice of law rule of Art. V(1)(a), and take their starting point in the law to which the parties have subjected the arbitration agreement to, alternatively the lex loci arbitrii.

---

[598] *Gaja (1979),* para. B.2.

[599] *van den Berg (1981),* p. 152.

[600] See for the application of Danish mandatory law due to the subject matter's strong connection to Denmark e.g. U 1972.138 DCA. In the case the question of whether a German retention of title clause was valid so as to give the German seller the right to the retention of the goods as against the Danish buyer's estate in bankruptcy was found to be so closely connected to Danish law that the Danish rules on retention of title clauses should be applied.

3. The requirement for a defined legal relationship

When entering into an agreement to arbitrate, the parties bar themselves from a basic right, namely the right to have their differences settled by the Courts. For the Courts to accept such an agreement, the agreement must have a limited scope. A party cannot validly commit himself to refrain from dispute resolution before the Courts in any matter whatsoever that may arise in the future, as a party cannot foresee the potential effect of such a commitment. However, the requirement does not often give rise to trouble. Firstly, in the cases where the arbitration agreement is entered into after the parties' dispute has arisen, both parties will be able to foresee the extent of their obligation to arbitrate. Secondly, if the arbitration agreement is entered into in advance, most often through an arbitration clause in the parties' main contract, then the scope of that main contract will generally define the scope of the arbitration agreement, and the issue will not arise either.[601] Finally, even when the point might be put, often the party contesting the arbitration agreement does not challenge the validity of the agreement to arbitrate, but instead argues that the dispute is outside the scope of the arbitration agreement.[602] In that case the Courts will express themselves in the terms relevant to the interpretation of the arbitration agreement and not in terms of the validity of the same; or the party contesting the arbitration agreement may argue instead that the purported arbitration clause is too vague as to be binding.[603]

What is required for an arbitration agreement to concern "a defined legal relationship" is a matter for national law to decide. The issue is not fit to be exhaustively regulated in statutory law, as the question will in the end depend on the proper interpretation of the arbitration clause. However, as shown, the Courts are unlikely to encounter the issue in its real form.

---

[601] Cases here generally regard the reciprocal problem, namely whether a claim is *encompassed* by the arbitration clause, and not how to restrict the scope of the arbitration agreement sufficiently for it to be valid, see e.g. [1988] 2 Lloyd's Law Reports 63 QBD, OVERSEAS UNION INSCE. V. AA MUTUAL and [1990] 1 Lloyd's Law Reports 86 QBD, ETHIOPIAN OILSEEDS V. RIO DEL MAR.

[602] See e.g. ND 1989.76 MCCC, UNIVERSAL AFRICA LINES.

[603] In LE-1992-02814 MOLKTE-HANSEN V. MOLTKE-HANSEN, there was an arbitration clause, according to which the parties were bound arbitrate disputes within the contract as well as disputes arising out of situations "that the contract do not encompass and which cannot be solved amicably". The point was put that the arbitration clause was invalid – seemingly under the Norwegian Contracts Act sec. 36, but with reference to its imprecise wording. However, for the Court of Appeal to reach its conclusion it needed not express an opinion on that matter, so no ruling on the wording of the arbitration clause was given.

4. The agreement to arbitrate is inoperative

The term "inoperative" generally covers the situations where there is nothing "wrong" with the arbitration agreement as such, but where, due to the surrounding circumstances, one or more of the parties may no longer invoke the agreement to arbitrate. Thus, the arbitration agreement originally existed, and was upon its correct interpretation worded so as to cover the parties' dispute, but it has ceased to have effect for one reason or other.

The arbitration agreement will cease to have effect if the parties agree to terminate it. Due to the doctrine of separability, if the arbitration agreement is in the form of an arbitration clause in the parties' main contract, one must consider in the individual case whether the parties have intended to end the arbitration agreement or whether it is only the main contract as such that has been terminated. The presumption in those cases should be that the parties have intended the arbitration agreement to remain in effect, at least as far as any dispute resulting from the agreement to terminate the main agreement is concerned. One should keep in mind that the agreement to terminate the arbitration agreement often will be made implicitly, either by the parties' specific agreement to use another forum, or by one of the parties being sued before the Courts without contesting the Court's competence.

An agreement to arbitrate may also become inoperative due to waiver, thus barring a party who has once waived his rights under the agreement to invoke it at a later stage. In such cases, the arbitration agreement becomes inoperative in the other party's option. Obviously, there is a grey zone between what is waiver and what is an implied agreement to terminate the arbitration agreement. Fortunately, however, there is no real need to distinguish the two situations as they carry the same legal effects. Generally, one of most common – and manifest – ways of waiving the arbitration agreement is to initiate proceedings before the Courts. However, initiating proceedings before the Courts might not be seen as waiver if the action is qualified, and based on other rationale than the wish to employ the dispute resolution capacities of the Courts. This was accepted by the Danish Supreme Court in U 1977.975 DSC, MERCANAUT.

U 1977.975 DSC, MERCANAUT
The charterers of Mercanaut directed a claim in recourse against the owners of Mercanaut, (a Danish company) for the amount of £ 22,208 – an amount that the charterers had had to pay in damages to

the cargo owners. In the booking note it was agreed that any dispute between the owners and the charterers should be settled by arbitration in London according to English law.[604]

The charterers were anxious that their claim would be time barred if the arbitral tribunal in London should find that it was not competent. On 10 December 1976 they therefore initiated both proceedings before the Maritime and Commercial Court of Copenhagen (the venue of the defendant owner) and proceedings before the arbitration tribunal by appointing an arbitrator and advising the owner to do the same.

After quite a few preliminary hearings, the Maritime and Commercial Court tried the procedural issues. The charterer requested that the case be stayed pending the outcome of the arbitral proceedings, whereas the owner requested that the Court heard the case. According to the owner, as the charterer had commenced proceedings before the Maritime and Commercial Court without reservation, the charterer could not invoke the arbitration clause.

The Maritime and Commercial Court found that as a starting point the charterer's right to arbitrate the dispute had *not* ceased by initiating proceedings before the Court, given that the action had been taken solely to prevent the dispute from being time-barred. At the same time, considering that not appointing an arbitrator might adversely affect the owner's legal position towards the charterer, the owner had not by the appointment consented to having the case heard by the London arbitral tribunal.

In the end the Court found that *as* the charterers had not reserved the writ of summons, by stating that they did in fact prefer to arbitrate the claim, *as* the owner had entered his own pleas on the substance before the Court, and *as* the arbitration procedure in London had not been expeditiously progressed, the case could proceed before the Courts. On appeal the Danish Supreme Court upheld the Maritime and Commercial Court's ruling on the grounds.

If one of the parties initiate proceedings before the Courts without wishing to abandon the arbitration agreement, e.g. to ensure that his claim is not time-barred, that party must ensure that this is clear from the writ. Also, the party must be seen to have exercised proper efforts to ensue the dispute's settlement by arbitration. Conversely, if the party participates actively in the Court proceedings, most significantly by entering a plea on the substance, that party will be considered to have waived his rights to pursue dispute resolution by arbitration.

Under Danish law, if a defendant wishes to dispute the competence of the Danish Courts, a plea for the dismissal of the case must be made before the defence on the substance. Otherwise, the defendant will be considered to have consented to the Court hearing the case, see the Danish Code of Procedure sec. 248. Similarly, under English law, the defendant must dispute the competence of the Court in accordance with the English Arbitration Act 1996 sec. 9(3), thus making the challenge after having acknowledged the proceedings against him, but *before* making submissions on the substance. Much of the case law dealing with whether the arbitration agreement

---

[604] The liner bills of lading contained a "principal place of business of carrier" jurisdiction clause. However, it was not disputed between the parties that in the internal relationship the booking note governed the dispute.

is inoperative is concerned with situations where the defendant disputes the Court's competence to hear the case too late in the proceedings.[605]

Finally, if one party acts in breach of the positive obligations arising out of the arbitration agreement, the other party has the option of taking the dispute to the Courts. The positive obligations under an agreement to arbitrate will not materialise before the arbitral proceedings have been initiated, so the other party may opt for the continuance of those proceedings. However, if the party in breach has shown to be exceedingly averse, then the other party may opt for dispute resolution before the Courts, even if this means that the proceedings will have to start anew.

---

[605] Danish cases that might be mentioned are e.g. U 1995.343 DCA and U 1973.601 DCA. In U 1995.343 DCA, a dispute arose under an insurance contract regarding water damage. The insured party had commenced proceedings before the Court of Appeal by writ of summons of 27 August 1993. The insurance company entered its defence on 19 October, claiming the dismissal of the *claim*. The insurance company's defence also contained detailed comments regarding a prospective survey. At a court hearing on November 2nd, the insured filed a reply on the substance of the case. The insurance company then claimed that the *case* should be dismissed from the Courts due to an arbitration clause in the insurance policy. Found by the Court of appeal that considering that the insurance company had been aware of the proceedings since August 1993, and especially that the company in its defence had entered a plea regarding the matter of the case, the insurance company was regarded as having waived the arbitration agreement and the case could proceed before the Courts.

5. The agreement to arbitrate is incapable of being performed

Out of principle there is little reason to distinguish between the different reasons for the arbitration agreement's ineffectiveness given in the New York Convention Art. II(3), as reflected in the domestic laws here discussed. However, if a distinction should be maintained, this heading should encompass situations where the arbitration agreement as such does not suffer from any legal shortcomings, but where, for certain reasons of practicality the arbitration agreement cannot lead to an arbitration award.[606] Also, those practical reasons must stem from something outside the direct control of the parties. If not, the parties are in breach of the arbitration agreement and the situation should be regarded as a matter of the arbitration agreement being inoperable, see above.

Generally, one party's lack of funds will not release that party from performing his obligations under a contract. This principle also applies to arbitration agreements, as was shown in PACZY V. HAENDLER.

[1981] 1 LLOYD'S LAW REPORTS 302 CA, PACZY V. HAENDLER[607]

Dispute arose between Paczy and Haendler regarding a licensing agreement. The licensing agreement held an arbitration clause referring disputes between the parties to be settled by ICC arbitration. Paczy initiated proceedings before the Courts, having obtained a legal aid certificate. Haendler argued that the case be stayed due to the arbitration agreement. Paczy argued, that he would be unable to provide the funds necessary to pay the tribunal's deposit, without which the proceedings would not be commenced, and hence that the arbitration agreement was incapable of being performed. It was held by the High Court that "... in the circumstances and as a matter of common sense, the arbitration agreement was incapable of being performed". On appeal, the Court of Appeal overruled the finding of the High Court. As per Lord Justice Buckley: "The incapacity of one party to that agreement to implement his obligations under the agreement does not ... render the agreement one which is incapable of being performed ... The agreement only becomes incapable of performance in my view if the circumstances are such that it could no longer be performed, even if both parties were ready, able and willing to perform it. Impecuniosity is not, I think, a circumstance of this kind".[608] Thus, the High Court had been erroneous in lifting the stay, and the parties were referred to arbitration.

---

[606] *van den Berg* seems to include situations where the arbitration agreement is to vague or contradictive to be binding under this heading. To me it seems more appropriate to deal with these situations from the point of view that an agreement to arbitrate has never been concluded, however, this is just a matter of taste. The end result – that the Courts are not under an obligation to recognise and enforce the arbitration agreement – remains the same in both situations.

[607] The position of the law under the English Arbitration Act 1996, sec. 9(4) is the same as under the Arbitration Act 1975, sec. 1(1). Case law under the 1975 Act is therefore still relevant.

[608] See p. 307, col. 2.

In the case, Paczy's own lack of funds did not relieve him of his duty to arbitrate the dispute with Haendler. The Court of Appeal maintained this conclusion even if it would most probably have the effect of *de facto* barring Paczy from access to justice. On this background it is proper to suggest, that had the case been argued today, after the entry into force of the Human Rights Act 1998, Paczy's counsel might have tried to invoke the European Convention on Human Rights Art. 6. The argument of the counsel would have been that by entering into the arbitration agreement, Paczy might have waived his right to a public Court hearing, but that Paczy had not intended to waive his right to any sort of justice, see below, in § 4, point 3.

Contrary, if Paczy had been the "defendant" in the case, his want for funds to pay his part of the tribunal's deposit would probably have amounted to breach of his positive obligations under the arbitration agreement. This would have rendered the agreement inoperative, and Haendler could have chosen to proceed with the case before the Courts.

The counter-party's deficiency in funds to satisfy a prospective arbitral award is neither a breach of the arbitration agreement as such, nor does it render the arbitration agreement incapable of being performed, as was seen in the RENA K.

[1978] 1 LLOYD'S LAW REPORTS 545 QBD, THE RENA K
The Rena K was fixed on a voyage charter-party, to carry sugar from Mauritius to England. The charter-party contained an arbitration clause according to which any disputes under the charter-party were to be settled by arbitration in London. Two bills of lading were issued for the cargo. The bills of lading purported to incorporate the arbitration clause in the charter-party by explicit reference. During the voyage, a part of the cargo was damaged by seawater and jettisoned. In the subsequent dispute between the consignees and the owner, the consignees claimed that the dispute should not be settled by arbitration, firstly as no agreement to arbitrate had been concluded,[609] secondly as the arbitration agreement was "incapable of being performed" due to the owners lack of funds. Even if the arbitral tribunal found for the consignees, they would not be able to enforce the award as against the owner. Found by the Court that as the notion of "incapable of being performed" in Art. II(3) concerned the recognition and enforcement of the arbitration *agreement*, the only issue the Court should consider was whether it would be possible to obtain an arbitral award on the matter. Whether the parties were capable of perform such an award was not relevant, and the Court found for the owner.[610]

---

[609] See regarding this part of the judgment, above in Chapter II, § 3, point 2.3.1.

[610] Indeed, in the case the consignees' claim that the award would not be satisfied was unconvincing, as it seemed that the relevant P&I club was going to meet any claim awarded the consignees, see p. 554, col. 1.

Having regarded the two cases, it seems quite clear that the arbitration agreement's incapability of being performed should be considered a narrow escape clause. It might encompass situations where a named arbitrator is unable or unwilling to participate, or where war or civil unrest at the place designated for arbitration makes the carrying out of arbitral procedures practically impossible, but apart from that the provision is not likely to be used very often.

§ 4. Validity on the substance under other rules of law – selected issues

1. Introduction and delimitation

As all other agreements, arbitration agreements are subject to the general rules on the validity of contracts as found in contract law. Also, the validity of arbitration agreements may be affected, directly or indirectly, by other rules of general applicability. The focus of this work is upon the regulation of the formation of the arbitration agreement, found in arbitration law or in special rules dealing with arbitration. To the extent that the regulation of the formation of arbitration agreements is found in other statutory rules or in case law, those sources of law must be discussed as well. A good example of this is the discussion of Danish Law as regards the formation of arbitration agreements found above in Chapter II, § 2. However, the starting point of the thesis must be maintained. In keeping with this it is found to be far beyond the scope of this work to indulge in a thorough analysis of the general rules on contractual validity on the substance. Equally, a complete presentation of any regulation that might in the end affect the validity of the arbitration agreement will not be found here. Instead, following a brief presentation of the invalidity of arbitration agreements under the general rules of contract law, it has been chosen to discuss the application of the European Convention on Human Rights Art. 6 on arbitration agreements. This discussion may seem remote. However, it is found that lawyers seeking advise on how general rules of contractual validity affect arbitration agreements can seek enlightenment in special works on contract law, whereas here the focus should be upon the rules that give rise to uncertainty due to the special features of the arbitration agreement.

2. The application of the traditional rules of contract law

Generally, the specific rules of the arbitration agreement's validity on the substance found in arbitration law, will suffice so as to encompass most of the situations where the validity of the arbitration agreement, seen separately from the main agreement, must be determined. The general rules of contract law tend to have a secondary importance. Typically, those rules will only be applied to the arbitration agreement as a reflex of the attempt to invoke the rules on the main agreement in which the parties' agreement to arbitrate is found.

In keeping with the discussion of the doctrine of separability presented above in point § 2, for an agreement to arbitrate to be invalid on the substance, the reason for invalidity must taint the arbitration agreement itself. The arbitration agreement must be seen as a separate agreement and thus, the arbitration clause will not always fall with the invalidity of the (main) contract in which the arbitration clause is found. Ultimately, it will be a matter for the Courts to decide whether, in a specific case, the reason alleged or proven to invalidate the parties' main agreement will also affect the parties' agreement to arbitrate, but rules of thumb do exist. In this respect the distinction used in Danish and Norwegian law between "strong" and "weak" reasons for invalidity is useful.[611] The distinction is not applied in English law, thus it is not so that all reasons for invalidity under English law may automatically be placed under either of the heading, still the line of thought behind the Danish and Norwegian distinction may be applied.

The strong reasons for invalidity encompass the reasons for invalidity where (one of) the parties did not intend to or was not capable of being bound by the contract. Thus, the term would encompass physical coercion, forgery, lack of mandate,[612] and lack of capacity to contract. In these cases the contract is invalid even if the counterparty neither knew nor ought to have known of the reason for the invalidity when the contract was formed. As a rule, if the main contract is tainted with a strong reason for invalidity, then the arbitration agreement will fall with it.

"Weak" reasons for invalidity encompass e.g. situations where a known precondition for the agreement has failed to present itself, situations where the agreement is seemingly within a person's mandate to act, but outside that person's authorisation to act, and most importantly fraud and misrepresentation. Generally, the reasoning behind the "weak" reasons for invalidity are that the party now claiming the invalidity

---

[611] See regarding the distinction between strong and weak reasons for invalidity *Andersen (1998)*, p. 289 ff, *Andersen/Madsen (2001)*, p. 120 ff, *Hov (1998)*, p. 189 f, and *Woxholth (2001)*, p. 304.

[612] See as illustration KFE 2002.11 VBA.

of the contract did intend to contract but not on the terms given, or the (real) facts (now) prevailing. In these cases the contract's validity will depend upon what the party claiming the validity of the contract knew or ought to have known, and thus a party in good faith will generally be able to enforce the contract against the party claiming the invalidity. Still, if the party now claiming the validity of the contract knew or ought to have known of the reason for the invalidity of the contract, the contract will be void ab initio. Thus, it must be decided whether the arbitration agreement is void with it. The starting point is, that "weak" reasons for the invalidity of the main contract will not affect the arbitration agreement. The weak reasons for invalidity do not necessarily "go to the root of the contract". Since the weak reasons for invalidity presuppose the existence of a will to make a contract, just not *this particular contract,* it would be wrong to say that there was never any contract at all, and thus never any agreement to arbitrate.

The traditional reasons for invalidity apart, it is possible that the Courts will consider the arbitration agreement an unfair term. Under the Danish Contracts Act sec. 36 an agreement that is found to be unreasonable or contra bones mores may be amended or deemed null and void in whole or in part. In considering whether to apply the provision, the Courts may take into account both the circumstances surrounding the formation of the agreement, the contents of the agreement and circumstances that have occurred later. The Norwegian Contract Act[613] sec. 36[614] is of a similar wording. In principle the provisions apply to both consumer contracts and contracts between professionals, however the protection offered by the specific consumer rules in the Danish Contracts Act secs. 38 a-38 d[615] and the Norwegian Contracts Act sec. 37 may be more favourable towards the consumer[616] and sec. 36 will therefore tend to only be applied between professionals. Even if English law does not hold a general clause on the validity of contracts ad modum the Danish and Norwegian Contract Acts sec. 36, English law recognises that the arbitration agreement may be an unfair term in consumer relations. This is especially provided for in the English Arbitration Act 1996, secs. 89-91.[617] Sec. 89 extends the application of the Unfair Terms

---

[613] Law of 31st May 1918 no. 4.

[614] See in general regarding the Norwegian Contracts Act sec. 36 e.g. *Hov (1998),* chapter 12.

[615] In KFE 2001.193 VBA, the Danish Contracts Act sec. 38 b was thus used so as to interpret an agreement so that the agreement did not provide for the settlement of disputes by arbitration.

[616] The provisions incorporate the Unfair Terms in Consumer Contracts Directive 1993.

[617] *Mustill (2000),* p. 171 ff.

in Consumer Contracts Regulation of 1994 (now 1999)[618] to arbitration agreements. Especially it is provided in sec. 91(1) that arbitration is always an unfair term if the pecuniary value of the dispute is less than a specified amount. At present, this amount is fixed at £ 5,000.[619] However, consumer relations apart, there seem very little room for de facto applying the Danish and Norwegian Contract Acts sec. 36 to arbitration agreements. Firstly, the threshold in the provision is very high – the unreasonableness must be apparent before the provision will be invoked.[620] Secondly, the special arbitration law rules on invalidity allow for undesirable arbitration agreements to be declared null and void, e.g. due to the lack of arbitrability. Finally, in professional commercial relationships, which are at the core of sec. 36 after the incorporation of the EC Directive on Unfair Terms in Consumer Contracts, the Courts are unlikely to find that a provision that the parties' dispute should be arbitrated is *unreasonable.*[621] Consequently, sec. 36 has only been pleaded as a reason for setting aside an agreement to arbitrate in very few cases, and, to this writer's knowledge, in none of those cases the plea has been successful.[622]

---

[618] See Statutory Instrument 1999 No. 2083, The Unfair Terms in Consumer Contracts Regulations 1999.

[619] See Statutory Instrument 1999 No. 2167, The Unfair Arbitration Agreement (Specified Amount) Order 1999, sec. 3.

[620] *Woxholth (2001),* p. 370.

[621] See in the same direction *Möller (1996),* p. 461.

[622] E.g. in U 2002. 870 DCA, the Western Court of Appeal did not, in its ruling, make any reference to the claimant's plea, that the arbitration agreement was invalid under the Danish Contracts Act sec. 36.

4. The arbitration agreement and the European Convention on Human Rights Art. 6

4.1. Introduction

The European Convention on Human Rights[623] Art. 6(1) reads:[624]

"In the determination of his civil rights and obligations or of any criminal charge against him, everyone is entitled to a fair and public hearing within a reasonable time by an independent and impartial tribunal established by law."

Thus, the provision requires that the Contracting States ensure that a person covered by the convention has access to justice, and in particular access to a fair trial in the determination of his civil rights and obligations. International commercial disputes are well within the scope of "civil rights and obligations".[625] Thus, the question arises what effect, if any, the European Convention on Human Rights has upon arbitration procedures and agreements. The legal writers do not agree on this subject. According to *Clayton/Tomlinson* voluntary arbitration agreements and procedures are beyond the scope of Art. 6 altogether, but the Convention applies to arbitration insofar as the arbitral procedure has been prescribed by law, and therefore is the only access to justice.[626] *Ambrose*,[627] on the other hand, refers to the arbitrator's implied duty to apply the law, including the Human Rights Act 1998,[628] and argues that Art. 6 binds the arbitral tribunal.

---

[623] Convention for the Protection of Human Rights and Fundamental Freedoms, as amended by Protocol No. 11 of 1998, done in Rome, November 4th 1950.

[624] See in general regarding Art. 6 also *Lorenzen/Rehof/Trier (1994)*, p. 136 ff.

[625] See *Harris/O'Boyle/Warbrick (1995)*, p. 177 ff.

[626] See *Clayton/Tomlinson (2000)*, para. 11.187 and para. 11.317B.

[627] *Ambrose (2000)*, p. 493.

[628] Containing the English incorporation of the European Convention on Human Rights.

4.2. Agreeing to arbitrate – a waiver of the protection under Art. 6?

Conceptually, the first question that arises is whether, and if so to what extent, the parties waive their rights under Art. 6 by entering into an agreement to arbitrate. In MOUSAKA V. GOLDEN SEAGUL,[629] Justice Steel held that "The parties have agreed to arbitrate their disputes. They have thereby largely renounced (in the interests of privacy and finality) the application of Art. 6 …". As Steel, J. notes, the parties have chosen to arbitrate "in the interest of privacy and finality". Thus, they have renounced the use of the Courts, a public hearing and – generally – the possibility of appeal.[630] However, some features of Art. 6 still remain – especially the right to an impartial tribunal and the right to have a hearing within a reasonable time. *Clayton/Tomlinson* suggest that the rights under the European Convention on Human Rights can only validly be waived if the waiver is clear and unequivocal and made in the absence of constraint and with full knowledge of the nature and extent of the right in question.[631] In any case, a waiver of a fundamental right should be construed narrowly. Thus, the presumption should be against that a party by entering into an agreement to arbitrate intended to waive the rights to a fair hearing, encompassing the right to an impartial tribunal and the right to equality of arms.[632] It is suggested that neither the right to a hearing within reasonable time, nor the right to an impartial tribunal may be validly waived. Even if it is permissible under the European Convention on Human Rights to waive the right to an impartial tribunal, such waiver would be contrary to what must be considered international ordre public,[633] at least in Western societies.

4.3. The impact of Art. 6 in different relations

4.3.1. Introduction

Having established that some features of Art. 6 remain even if the parties have agreed to arbitrate, it must be determined which effects this has upon the arbitration agreement and/or procedure. This would depend upon the context in which the ques-

---

[629] [2001] 2 Lloyd's Law Reports 657 QBD.

[630] The right to appeal is not protected by the European Convention on Human Rights, see *Dijk/Hoof (1990)*, p. 305.

[631] *Clayton/Tomlinson (2000)*, para. 6.161.

[632] See in the same direction *Ambrose (2000)*, p. 484 f.

[633] Otherwise on this point perhaps, *Ambrose (2000)*, p. 485 with footnote 91.

tion presents itself. The impact of Art. 6 may vary depending on whether it is the Courts or an arbitral tribunal that entertains the issue. Below, case law discussing these issues will be subject to a brief evaluation.

4.3.2. Court proceedings regarding arbitration

4.3.2.1. Point of departure

It must be so that the Court of a Contracting State is bound by Art. 6(1) as long as the subject matter before the Court regards a party's civil rights and obligations or a criminal charge. Therefore, fair trial standard must be maintained when the Courts settle disputes regarding arbitration agreements and awards. Those disputes are civil disputes, and thus well within the ambit of Art. 6.[634] This has also been accepted in recent English case law. As put by (a slightly irritated?) Justice Steel in MOUSAKA V. GOLDEN SEAGUL:

"The tentacles of the Human Rights Act, 1998 reach into some unexpected places. The Commercial Court, even when exercising its supervisory role as regards arbitration, is not immune. A corporate body is a person with rights protected by the Act and thus, for instance, can invoke Art. 6 where it may be the victim of action incompatible with its right to a fair trial."[635]

Consequently, it must be concluded that the Courts of a Contracting State are bound to ensure that the rights of Art. 6 are bestowed upon parties to Court proceedings regarding arbitration, as they are upon parties to other disputes within the scope of Art. 6.

---

[634] See *Danelius (2002)*, p. 129 with reference TO STAN GREEK REFINERIES & STRATIS ANDREADIS V. GREECE, Publications of the European Court of Human Rights, Series B, no. 301, 09.12.1994.

[635] [2001] 2 Lloyd's Law Reports 657 QBD, MOUSAKA V. GOLDEN SEAGULL, on p. 658, para. 1. The dispute before Justice Steel in the case was whether he was bound to give reasons for a refusal of leave to appeal on a point of law under the English Arbitration Act sec. 69. Mousaka required that full reasons for the Judge's refusal of the leave to appeal be given considering "... (1) the right to a fair hearing as provided by Art. 6. of the European Convention on Human Rights; (2) the general duty on a Court to give reasons for its decisions and (3) principles of fairness and natural justice". After a lengthy discussion of the European Court of Human Rights' decisions on the subject, the Judge found that the refusal of giving reasons was not inconsistent with Art. 6(1).

4.3.2.2. The Courts on Art. 6 as a reason for setting aside the arbitral award

The Danish Court of Appeal has found the European Convention on Human Rights Art. 6 applicable to the arbitral procedure. In U 1999.829 DSC, THE DANISH PHARMACIST'S UNION V. SVOBODA the Court of Appeal found that as 5 of 6 members of the arbitral tribunal were members of The Danish Pharmacist's Union, the tribunal by its composition had not provided the necessary reassurance against bias. This was found to be especially problematic in the case as the claims of the Danish Pharmacist's union, if accepted by the tribunal, would affect Svoboda's livelihood as well as require him to pay a substantial fine. The Court of Appeal therefore found that the arbitration award was null and void under the Danish Arbitration Act 1972, sec. 7, no. 2, cf. sec. 1, sub-sec. 2, cf. the European Convention on Human Rights Art. 6(1).[636]

It should be noted that the Danish Court of Appeal found that Art. 6(1) applied to the arbitral procedure itself. Thus, the Court of Appeal did not, contrary to *Clayton/Tomlinson*,[637] find that by agreeing to arbitrate, the parties had waived the protection offered them under Art. 6.

4.3.2.3. The Courts on Art. 6 as a reason to disregard the arbitration agreement

There seem to be no clear cases under Danish, English or Norwegian law where an arbitration agreement has been set aside or invalidated with direct reference to the European Convention on Human Rights Art. 6(1). However, in U 1994.953 DSC, HUMMER V. BYGGEFORENINGEN, Art. 6 was used as part of the reasoning for allowing a party, seemingly bound by an arbitration agreement, to pursue his claim before the Courts.

Hummer was an employee of Byggeforeningen. In 1991, Hummer was dismissed from his position with Byggeforeningen with immediate effect. Hummer claimed three months salary for the period of notice before the Courts. Byggeforeningen claimed that the case be dismissed from the Courts, due to an arbitration agreement in the covenant between Byggeforeningen and the relevant trade union. The dismissal had – arguably – taken place according to the trade union's rules. Disputes regarding the interpretation of trade unions' rules were to be dealt with by the Labour

---

[636] On appeal to the Danish Supreme Court, the Supreme Court found that the case was not arbitrable (see above point 3.4.2). Consequently, it was not necessary for the Court to express an opinion upon the application of the European Convention on Human Rights Art. 6(1), see U 1999.829 DSC on p. 893, col. 1.

[637] *Clayton/Tomlinson (2000)*, para. 11.187 and para 11.317B,

Tribunal, in a case initiated by the trade union. In Hummer's case, however, the trade union had declined to initiate such proceedings. The Town Court and the Danish Court of Appeal found for Byggeforeningen. The Danish Supreme Court, on the contrary, found for Hummer. The Supreme Court held that reading together the Labour Tribunal Act sec. 11, sub-sec. 2, and the European Convention on Human Rights Art. 6(1), the Labour Tribunal Act sec. 11, sub-sec. 2 had to be interpreted so that it did not bar an employee from taking a dispute to the Courts in cases where the relevant trade union had refused to initiate arbitral proceedings. Thus, the arbitration clause in the covenant did not bar Hummer from taking his case to the Court, and the case was referred to the Town Court for a ruling on the subject matter. This position of the Danish Supreme Court has been confirmed in a parallel case, U 2002.2060 H. In the case a trade union had attempted to have a dispute for salary regarding one of its members tried in the labour dispute arbitration system. However, in the trade union's rules the possibility of having disputes regarding the individual employees' salaries tried by the Labour Tribunal had been restricted, and the Tribunal dismissed the case. It was held by the Danish Supreme Court that in a case such as this, where the trade union had generally restricted its access to act for its members in the labour dispute arbitration system, then the Labour Tribunal Act sec. 11, sub-sec. 2 should be interpreted with respect to the European Convention on Human Rights Art. 6. Hence, the provision should not be seen so as to disallow a claim before the Courts.

In both cases the Danish Supreme Court interpreted the law so as to make an arbitration agreement that would otherwise have been in conflict with Art. 6 inoperative. Considering that the Supreme Court only uttered an opinion on the interpretation of the law, the ruling of the Supreme Court cannot be seen as a direct example of the Courts applying Art. 6 to the arbitration agreement. However, given firstly that the Court found it necessary to refer not only to the Labour Tribunal sec. 11, but also to Art. 6, and considering that the Danish Court of Appeal already has found Art. 6 to be applicable to the arbitral procedure (see above) there seems no reason out of principle why Art. 6 may not be applied directly to the arbitration agreement in the future, if it is clear that the agreement in itself is so as to bar a party from the protection in Art. 6 that has not been waived.

4.3.3. Is the arbitral tribunal bound by Art. 6?

It is disputed to what extent the European Convention on Human Rights has direct effect between private parties – so-called Drittwirkung.[638] However, even at to-day's

---

[638] See *Rehoff/Trier (1990)*, p.134 f.

status of that discussion, as long as the Courts apply the Convention to the arbitral award, as did the Danish Court of Appeal, the Convention is one to be reckoned with, also before the arbitral tribunal. If indeed Strasbourg case law to come establishes that the Convention has Drittwirkung, the importance of the Convention in international arbitration will increase. In that case, the tribunal will be under a direct obligation to ensure that the protection offered by Art. 6(1) is carried out. Arguably, they already are, as it can be maintained that most of what is "left" of Art. 6(1) when the parties have agreed to arbitrate, namely the right to an impartial tribunal and a hearing within reasonable time, is already imposed as an obligation upon the tribunal. Also, the right to an impartial tribunal – as indeed any other basic principle of a fair hearing – is already a part of international ordre public, and as such binding also upon an arbitral tribunal. The English Arbitration Act 1996 provides as a general principle that the object of arbitration is "to obtain the fair resolution of disputes by an impartial tribunal without unnecessary delay or expense." Thus, the remains of Art. 6 are already recognised as basic, indispensable features of arbitration. In conclusion this writer will settle for the argument of *Ambrose* that the tribunal is under an implied duty to apply the law, and that this argument seems to be supported by at least the Danish Court's willingness to scrutinise the arbitral procedure and the law concerning the arbitration agreement to ensure that those basic principles are respected.

Chapter IV. The tribunals competence to decide its own competence

§ 1. The notion of Kompetenz-Kompetenz

1. What is Kompetenz-Kompetenz?

The question of whether the arbitration tribunal is competent to deal with the question of its own jurisdiction is normally addressed under the term Kompetenz-Kompetenz. The German expression is quite descriptive, as it highlights the circularity[639] of the argument, that the arbitration tribunal should itself deal with whether or not it is competent to deal with the subject matter put before it.

The doctrine of separability breaks some of the circularity. To the extent that it is accepted that the arbitration agreement and the main agreement are two distinct agreements, it is not beyond reason that the arbitration agreement can bestow upon the arbitral tribunal the competence to deal with whether a dispute regarding the main agreement is within the agreement to arbitrate. However, the notion of Kompetenz-Kompetenz reaches further than that. It also encompasses situations where the challenge to the jurisdiction of the arbitrators regards the existence and validity of the arbitration agreement. Kompetenz-Kompetenz regards the objective criteria of the tribunal's jurisdiction. It includes any aspect of the arbitration agreement's existence and validity, whether they are based on the specific arbitration regulation or on more general rules on the law of contract. Also, it will embrace any question of arbitral procedure that may have an impact upon the tribunal's competence. Still, a distinction must be made to the question of the impartiality of the arbitrator. Whether or not an arbitrator has been appointed in accordance with the parties' agreement (the ob-

---

[639] *Gross (1992)* on p. 205-206: "The logical problem is that an examination by an arbitrator of his own jurisdiction in the event of challenge, involves an assumption that he has jurisdiction to make the investigation and, accordingly, an unsatisfactory element of circular reasoning."

jective criteria) is a question that falls within the scope of Kompetenz-Kompetenz. Whether or not the arbitrator is biased (the subjective criteria) falls outside the concept.

There is no internationally accepted level of Kompetenz-Kompetenz. The term Kompetenz-Kompetenz only describes a heading of a discussion. The extent to which the principle is accepted varies immensely.[640] In theory, two extremes exist. Total Kompetenz-Kompetenz effects the complete ousting of the Courts' competence already when the existence of an arbitration agreement is alleged. It brings about the incompetence of the Courts to deal with the questions of the existence, validity and scope of the arbitration agreement before, during and after the arbitral procedure. The other theoretical extreme is no Kompetenz-Kompetenz. No Kompetenz-Kompetenz brings the arbitration procedure to a halt as soon as the jurisdiction of the tribunal is challenged in any way. Potentially, the two extremes are equally damaging to the arbitration procedure, and thereby to arbitration as a workable means of dispute resolution. Therefore an in-between is normally chosen. This is also the case in Denmark, England and Norway. In the following, the concept of Kompetenz-Kompetenz as applied in Danish and English law will be discussed in quite some detail, and a short overview of Norwegian law at present and as proposed in the Draft Norwegian Arbitration Act will be given.

2. Why discuss Kompetenz-Kompetenz in this thesis?
In a thesis dealing with substantive rules regarding the conclusion of arbitration agreements, a chapter on Kompetenz-Kompetenz may be seen as somewhat out of place, as Kompetenz-Kompetenz is a matter of procedure, aiming at establishing who has the competence to decide the tribunal's competence. Still, the chapter is included mainly for two reasons. Firstly, above in Chapter III, § 2, the doctrine of separability is discussed. A thesis discussing the doctrine of separability without including at least a presentation of the notion of Kompetenz-Kompetenz would seem incomplete. Secondly, Kompetenz-Kompetenz is an effect of the arbitration agreement. A discussion of whether, and if so to what extent, the arbitration agreement may bestow the competence required upon the putative arbitral tribunal for it to decide its own competence seems to be within the parameters of what may be considered in a thesis dealing with the arbitration agreement.

---

[640] See *Schlosser (1992)* and *Park (2000)*.

§ 2. Kompetenz-Kompetenz under Danish law

1. Kompetenz-Kompetenz before the Danish Arbitration Act 1972

Before the Danish Arbitration Act of 1972 there was no statutory regulation of whether, and if so to what extent, the arbitral tribunal could rule upon its own competence. The tribunal was not barred from ruling on its jurisdiction, but if the parties did not accept the findings of the tribunal, they could take the jurisdictional matter to the Courts.[641] However, Danish law before the 1972 Act recognised that a certain extent of autonomy rested with the arbitral tribunal. Firstly, the Courts did not necessarily try all aspects of a dispute as to the tribunal's competence. For example, in U 1963.684 DCA the Court tried whether the subject matter of the dispute was within what was referred to arbitration. Having answered that in the affirmative, the Court left it to the arbitral tribunal to try a more trivial claim that the arbitral procedure could not be carried out because the time limit for the appointment of arbitrators had

---

[641] The question of the competence of the tribunal was addressed before the initiating of arbitral proceedings in U 1962.691 DCA. In U 1967.738 DCA the question whether disputes regarding audit were within the scope of an arbitration agreement in a partnership contract, regardless that one of the parties had requested arbitration regarding disputes concerning the partnership as such. See also U 1963.1051 DCA where the plaintiff claimed that the arbitration tribunal for trainees should hear the matter in a case concerning an illegal trainee-ship contract, although the arbitral tribunal had declared itself incompetent to hear the matter.

been exceeded. Secondly, in cases where the arbitration agreement had been worded so as to encompass also disputes as to the tribunal's jurisdiction, the Courts were seen to consider themselves incompetent to deal with disputes regarding the competence of the arbitral tribunal. Thus, in U 1972.665 DCA.

In the case, contract work was agreed on AB 1951 terms.[642] The terms contained an arbitration clause, § 24, according to which all disputes should be settled by arbitration, unless the dispute only concerned law. It also followed from the clause that *disagreement as to whether the dispute only concerned law was to be settled in a final and binding way by the arbitration tribunal.* The builder initiated proceedings before the Town Court regarding the balance of the account. The owner claimed that the case should be dismissed because of the arbitration clause, alternatively that the claim as to the substance of the case was dismissed. The jurisdictional matter was referred to Court of Appeal, the issue before that Court being whether the material dispute only concerned law. The Court of Appeal dismissed the case from the Courts on the grounds that according to the arbitration clause in AB 1951 § 24, the arbitral tribunal should deal with this dispute.

In U 1972.665 DCA the provision that the tribunal should have Kompetenz-Kompetenz regarded a specific issue, namely whether the dispute concerned a question of law. The findings of the Court of Appeal may thus not be seen to support that before the 1972 Act total Kompetenz-Kompetenz could be agreed upon between the parties. Neither do the findings of the Court of Appeal concern whether or not one of the parties may revert to the Courts anew after the jurisdictional decision of the tribunal. As said, generally, a party to the arbitration agreement could at any time revert to the Courts as regards the question of the validity and scope of the arbitration agreement. Often, the arbitration proceedings were stayed pending the outcome of that decision, obstructing the expeditious carrying out of the proceedings.[643] The committee behind the 1972 Act considered this to be a major problem.[644]

---

[642] The General Conditions of the Building and Construction Trades, 1951 version.

[643] See as an example U 1974.889 DSC. In a dispute regarding a trainee contract the arbitral tribunal for trainee disputes first tried its own competence. The jurisdictional question was then brought before the Court of Appeal, and finally decided by the Supreme Court. In the case the decision upon the tribunal's jurisdiction necessitated a thorough investigation into the subject matter of the case. Consequently, although the ruling of the tribunal on jurisdiction took place on September 3rd 1970, the ruling of the Supreme Court on the same matter could not be obtained until August 29th 1974. See also *Hjejle (1973),* p. 80 f.

[644] Danish Arbitration Act travaux préparatoires 1, p. 28.

2. Kompetenz-Kompetenz according to the Danish Arbitration Act 1972, sec. 2, sub-sec. 1

To prevent the prolonged arbitration procedures often occurring due to more or less legitimate jurisdictional disputes, the committee behind the Danish Arbitration Act suggested that the following provision be inserted into the new Act:

Danish Arbitration Act 1972, sec. 2, sub-sec. 1.

During proceedings initiated after the seating of the arbitral tribunal, the Courts may not decide whether dispute in whole or in part is within the competence of the tribunal. The provision ... only applies until the arbitral tribunal has made its ruling, and may be dispensed with if supported by vital grounds.[645]

The provision is in keeping with the general minimalist approach of the Danish legislators when legislating on arbitration. What has been done is simply that the Courts have been made incompetent to deal with a jurisdictional dispute if an arbitration tribunal is already seated with the matter. Once the tribunal is seated, the tribunal has first-word competence. The Danish Arbitration Act 1972, sec. 2, sub-sec. 1 in this way effectively puts an end to the prolongation of arbitral proceedings due to the fact that a party has taken a challenge of the tribunal's jurisdiction to the Courts. Unfortunately this does not mean that arbitration will always be a speedy means of dispute resolution. The possibility to take a jurisdictional dispute to the Courts before the arbitral tribunal is seated or to challenge the jurisdiction of the tribunal after the award[646] can bring the final settlement of the parties' dispute to take a very long time indeed.

The first-word rule of sec. 2, sub-sec. 1, is not absolute. In exceptional cases, the Courts have a discretionary competence to deal with the question of the tribunal's competence, even if the tribunal is already seated. It is suggested in the travaux préparatoires that the discretionary powers should only be employed if good reason for doing so exist. This may be the case if it is quite clear that there is no arbitration agreement between the parties, if the arbitral proceedings have been unduly delayed,

---

[645] Danish Arbitration Act, sec. 2, sub-sec. 1. "Under en retssag, der er anlagt efter, at tvisten er indbragt for voldgiftsret, kan domstolene ikke tage stilling til, om tvisten i sin helhed eller for en del hører under voldgiftsrettens kompetence. Bestemmelsen i 1. pkt. gælder kun, indtil voldgiftsretten har truffet sin afgørelse, og kan fraviges, hvis vægtige grunde taler derfor." Writer's translation.

[646] This may be done either in an law suit to that exact effect or as a defence against enforcement of the award.

or maybe, if the subject matter before the tribunal has an impact on one of the parties' personal welfare.[647]

Thus, who is competent to deal with the question of the tribunal's jurisdiction under Danish law depends on, on which stage of the arbitral procedure the question presents itself. From the time of the entering into the arbitration agreement until the initiating of arbitral proceedings, the competence is with the Courts. During the proceedings, from the time when the arbitral tribunal is seated until the tribunal either dismisses the case or grants an award on the subject matter, alternatively until the parties agree to terminate the proceedings, the competence rests with the tribunal.[648] After that time, the competence as regards the question of jurisdiction reverts to the Courts – the arbitration tribunal having already decided the matter in one way or the other. One should note that overlapping competence exists if the Courts have been seated with the jurisdictional issue and, subsequently, an arbitration procedure is initiated. In that case both the tribunal and the Courts are ad liberty to deal with the issue. Obviously either forum may choose to stay its proceedings pending the outcome of the other forum's decision,[649] but neither needs to do so.[650]

The Danish regulation of Kompetenz-Kompetenz may seem quite straightforward. The general picture is nevertheless blurred by the fact that instead of protesting the tribunal's jurisdiction, a party may simply initiate proceedings before the Courts regarding a subject matter, which is already being dealt with by an arbitral tribunal, leaving the counter-party to claim the case's dismissal from the Court.

Having investigated if there is an arbitration agreement between the parties, the Courts will either allow the case to proceed (if there is not) or dismiss the case all to-

---

[647] Danish Arbitration Act travaux préparatoires 1, p. 37. In U 2001.2392 CA, the fear of multiple proceedings, delay and incompatible (recourse) claims lead the Court of Appeal to investigate the matter of a tribunal's competence even if the tribunal was already seated with the claim.

[648] The competence of the arbitral tribunal has been tried by the tribunal on many occasions. E.g. the arbitral tribunal for the building and construction trade tried the jurisdiction issue and found itself competent to deal with the case in KFE 1982.10B VBA, KFE 1983.73 VBA, KFE 1994.145 VBA, KFE 1997.77 VBA and KFE 2002.27 VBA. On the other hand, the tribunal found in the negative regarding its competence in the cases KFE 1982.10A VBA, KFE 1982.311 VBA, KFE 1983.52 VBA, KFE 1984.202 VBA, KFE 1991.14 VBA, KFE 1992.60 VBA, KFE 1996.5 VBA, KFE 2001.17 VBA, KFE 2001.217 VBA, KFE 2001.193 VBA and KFE 2002.11 VBA. Consequently, those cases were dismissed from the tribunal.

[649] See Danish Code of Procedure sec. 345.

[650] See KFE 1986.122 VBA.

gether, in accordance with the Danish Arbitration Act sec. 1, sub-sec. 1. Obviously, to carry out that investigation the Court must deal with certain aspects of the tribunal's jurisdiction. A lawsuit as described may thus provoke a Court ruling on the tribunal's jurisdiction although the tribunal is already seated with the matter.

3. The interpretation of the Danish Arbitration Act 1972, sec. 2, sub-sec. 1

The real extent of Kompetenz-Kompetenz accepted under Danish law remains somewhat unclear even after the Danish Arbitration Act of 1972. Firstly, because doubts as to the scope of sec. 2, sub-sec. 1, exist and secondly, since it is unclear whether or not sec. 2, sub-sec. 1, provides a mandatory and exhaustive regulation of Kompetenz-Kompetenz under Danish law.

The terminology used in sec. 2, sub-sec. 1, regards whether a dispute is within the competence of the tribunal. According to *Hjejle*,[651] a distinction has to be made between challenge of the arbitrator's jurisdiction founded on disputes as to the validity and existence of the arbitration agreement, and a challenge of the arbitrator's jurisdiction based on whether the terms of reference have been exceeded. On the word of *Hjejle* the provision only regards the possible exceeding of terms of reference. He therefore maintains that, as it is not regulated, the question of the existence and validity of the arbitration agreement may be referred to the Courts at any time. *Hjejle's* viewpoint is obviously not inconsistent with a verbatim interpretation of the provision.[652] However, it is not the only possible interpretation. For an arbitral tribunal to be competent to decide a case on its merits, certain conditions must be satisfied. There must be a valid arbitration agreement between the parties. This agreement must encompass the parties' present dispute and the appointment of arbitrators and other matters of procedure must be in accordance with the parties' agreement. The decision of whether the dispute is within the competence of the tribunal (in whole or in part) may therefore include any or all of these problems. *Gomard* supports this wider understanding of the provision.[653]

The original committee behind the Danish Arbitration Act 1972 went so far as to propose a general rule according to which the Courts would have to dismiss all to-

---

[651] *Hjejle (1987)*, p. 65 and *Hjejle (1973)*, p. 58 f.

[652] See likewise the Danish Arbitration Act sec. 7, on the challenge to the award. In sec. 7, no. 3 the term competence is used in the context of the scope of the terms of reference.

[653] *Gomard (1979)*, p. 25 f.

gether both law suits regarding a subject matter referred to arbitration, and law suits regarding the validity of the arbitration agreement. In the final version this provision was abandoned. The then seated committee did not find it advisable to bar the Courts from trying the extent of the tribunal's jurisdiction until after the award.[654] However, it does not follow from this that the question of the validity of the arbitration agreement does not fall within the concept of Kompetenz-Kompetenz described in sec. 2, sub-sec. 1.

Also, the wider interpretation provides that the Kompetenz-Kompetenz left to the arbitral tribunal under Danish national law, corresponds to the Kompetenz-Kompetenz available to the tribunal under the European Convention on International Commercial Arbitration. According to the travaux préparatoires, sec. 2, sub-sec. 1, of the 1972 Act introduces into Danish law the regulation of the legal effects of Kompetenz-Kompetenz in Art. VI(3) of the European Convention.[655] It must therefore be assumed that the contents of the concept as understood in the European Convention was intended to be adopted.

The European Convention on International Commercial Arbitration, Art. V.
Plea as to Arbitral Jurisdiction
…
Subject to any subsequent judicial control provided for under the lex fori, the arbitrator whose jurisdiction is called in question shall be entitled to *proceed* with the arbitration, *to rule on his own jurisdiction* and to *decide upon the existence or the validity of the arbitration agreement* or of the contract of which the arbitration agreement forms part.[656]

It is not necessarily so that national Danish law is always consistent with the European Convention of 1961, but the committee refers specifically to the convention when discussing the question of Kompetenz-Kompetenz. If it was intended that only the question of the scope of the arbitration agreement should be covered by the Danish concept of Kompetenz-Kompetenz as described in the Arbitration Act 1972 sec. 2, sub-sec. 1, in contrast to the position under the European Convention 1961 Art. V, on could reasonably have expected the committee to say so.

Finally, the reason for making a provision on Kompetenz-Kompetenz in the 1972 Act, namely, to address the problem of undue delay of the arbitral process, is neces-

---

[654] Danish Arbitration Act travaux préparatoires 2, col. 902.

[655] Danish Arbitration Act travaux préparatoires 1, p. 37 and p. 28. Danish Arbitration Act travaux préparatoires 2, col. 903.

[656] The provision is incorporated into Danish Law in the Arbitration Regulation of 1973, sec. 10.

sary and legitimate regardless of whether the basis of the undue obstruction is the allegation of excess of jurisdiction. The allegations that the arbitration agreement is invalid or that the parties have not entered into an arbitration agreement at all are equally hindering to the progress of the proceedings.

The wider interpretation of the Danish Arbitration Act sec. 2, sub-sec. 1, according to which the level of Kompetenz-Kompetenz accepted is independent of the specific reason for the allegation of lack of jurisdiction, is supported by both the travaux préparatoires and the more general regards to the raison d'être of the rule. Therefore, the wider interpretation will be adapted in this work.

It remains to be discussed, whether the regulation of the Danish Arbitration Act sec. 2, sub-sec. 1, is a mandatory and exhaustive regulation of the autonomy of the tribunal as regards the tribunal's own competence. May the parties agree otherwise and if so to what extent?

The Danish Arbitration Act sec. 2, sub-sec. 1, simply prescribes that except for special circumstances, jurisdictional disputes cannot be taken to the Courts if the arbitral tribunal is already seated with the matter. The provision cannot be seen to alter other aspects of Danish arbitration law than just that. Therefore, the Courts will still have the last word[657] regarding the tribunal's jurisdiction, see here *Hjejle*[658] and the travaux préparatoires.[659] The parties may thus not validly agree that the tribunal should be able to give a final determination of whether or not it is competent to deal with a given case. The regard for legal protection of persons, who might not think themselves parties to an arbitration agreement, is thus well taken care of. This restriction of the autonomy of the tribunal must be viewed it in the light of Danish law's lack of formal requirements in respect of arbitration agreements.[660] As the existence of the arbitration agreement is not checked by stringent requirements to form, it seems reasonable that the last word on the competence of the arbitral tribunal rests with the Courts.

On the other hand, nothing in sec. 2, sub-sec. 1, bars the parties from agreeing that the tribunal should itself have the "first word" on the tribunal's own competence. The granting of the first word to the arbitral tribunal may of course leave one of the parties with no other option than to initiate arbitral proceedings, even if that party in-

---

[657] Terminology stolen from *Schlosser (1992)*, p. 199.

[658] *Hjejle (1987)*, p. 66.

[659] Danish Arbitration Act 1972 travaux préparatoires 1, p. 37.

[660] See above, CHAPTER II, § 2.

tends to challenge the jurisdiction of the tribunal. Admittedly, this may cause problems of an economic and/or practical nature. Still, under the assumption that the arbitral tribunal acts bona fide and that the award may be subsequently challenged before the Courts, there should not be any lack of legal protection of the party disputing the tribunal's competence. Also, reason has it that in the majority of cases where an arbitration agreement is claimed to exist between the parties, the dispute should in fact be decided by arbitration. Allowing the parties to grant the arbitral tribunal the first word, also in cases where the proceedings have not yet been initiated, does in general seem the better option. On that background it is suggested that the findings of the Danish Court of Appeal in U 1972.665 DCA might not have been different had the Courts decided the case today. Due to the lack of case law this is only a suggestion. The Courts might find differently. However, it is hoped that they do not, as giving the parties the possibility of agreeing that the first word lies with the tribunal seems the best alternative, both the lege lata and de lege ferenda.

§ 3. Kompetenz-Kompetenz under English law

1. The position of the law before the English Arbitration Act 1996

Before the English Arbitration Act 1996, Kompetenz-Kompetenz was regulated by case law. Although it seemed that in theory an arbitration agreement could be worded so that the question of the scope of the arbitration agreement fell within the arbitrator's jurisdiction,[661] generally an arbitration tribunal was not considered competent to rule on its own jurisdiction.[662]

However, a variation of Kompetenz-Kompetenz was known. The competence of the tribunal to deal with its own competence was seen as a necessary prerequisite of a practical nature, without which the initiating of the arbitral proceedings would be difficult. In CHRISTOPHER BROWN V. GENOSSENSCHAFT OESTERREICHISCHER, Devlin J thus held that "[the arbitrators] are entitled to inquire into the merits of the issue whether they have jurisdiction or not, not for the purpose of reaching any conclusion which will be binding upon the parties – because that they cannot do – but for the purpose of satisfying themselves as a preliminary matter whether they ought to go on with the arbitration or not ... They are entitled, in short, to make their own inquiries

---

[661] As seen in WILLESFORD V. WATSON (1873) L. R. 8 Ch. 473.

[662] See (1942) 72 Lloyd's List Law Reports. 65 (obiter) HEYMAN V. DARWINS, [1979] 1 Lloyd's Law Reports 244 CA, WILLCOCK V. PICKFORDS, and (1995) XX ICCA Yearbook 771 CA, HARBOUR V. KANSA, p. 778, para. 22.

in order to determine their own course of action, and the result of that inquiry has no effect whatsoever upon the rights of the parties ...".[663]

Thus, before the 1996 Act, a party disputing the jurisdiction of the tribunal could take his concerns to the Courts, subject to waiver.[664] However, as the arbitration tribunal could choose to continue the arbitral proceedings, the jurisdictional challenge would not necessarily bring the proceedings to a halt. Still, it often would, either because of the tribunal deciding that to be the best option or because of an injunction given by the Courts to stay the arbitral proceedings,[665] making the English position of the law more or less the same as the Danish law before the Danish Arbitration Act 1972. As was the case in Denmark, the legislator found the situation to be less than satisfactory.

2. Kompetenz-Kompetenz according to the English Arbitration Act 1996 s. 30

To address the issue of prolonged arbitral proceedings due to jurisdictional disputes, the Departmental Advisory Committee introduced sec. 30 of the Arbitration Act 1996. In sec. 30 an extensive Kompetenz-Kompetenz is allocated to the tribunal.

---

[663] [1954] 1 Q. B. 8, CHRISTOPHER BROWN V. GENOSSENSCHAFT OESTERREICHISCHER, p. 12 f.

[664] During the proceedings a party could either apply to the Courts for an injunction that the arbitral proceedings should not proceed due to the tribunal's lack of jurisdiction, or a party could apply for a declaration that the tribunal was incompetent. Obviously, showing the Courts that the prerequisite for an interlocutory injunction were present could be difficult. (To obtain an interlocutory injunction the applicant would have to show, firstly, that the stay of arbitral proceedings would not be unjust for the claimant in the arbitration, and secondly, that the continuance of the arbitral proceedings would be oppressive or vexatious to the applicant or an abuse of the process of the court. See Sellers, L.J, in [1966] 1 Lloyd's Law Reports 477 CA, THE ORANIE AND THE TUNISIE, p. 487, col. 1). However, to obtain a declaration that the subject matter in dispute is not within the jurisdiction of the arbitrator, the claimant would have to show only that. After the proceedings the party could instead use the lack of jurisdiction of the tribunal as a defence against either an action on the award or an action for a declaration on the award. Alternatively, the party could, both during and after the arbitral proceedings, bring the relevant subject matter to the Courts and resist a stay. See *Russell (1982)*, p. 99 ff. and 389 ff.

[665] See [1966] 1 Lloyd's List Law Reports 477 CA, THE ORANIE AND THE TUNISIE. See in particular the obiter of Salmon, L.J. p. 488, col. 2: "... [There] is jurisdiction to stay arbitration proceedings when the validity of the contract containing the arbitration clause is impeached ...".

The English Arbitration Act 1996, sec. 30.

(1) Unless otherwise agreed by the parties, the arbitral tribunal may rule on its own substantive jurisdiction, that is, as to

(a) whether there is a valid arbitration agreement

(b) whether the tribunal is properly constituted, and

(c) what matters have been submitted to arbitration in accordance with the arbitration agreement.

(2) Any such ruling may be challenged by any available arbitral process of appeal or review or in accordance with the provisions of this part.

According to sec. 30, the arbitral tribunal has the first word on the tribunal's own competence. The Courts should thus refuse to deal with the matter of the tribunal's jurisdiction until the tribunal itself has ruled on the matter.

The parties may agree that sec. 30 shall not apply, and after a dispute has arisen, the parties may under sec. 32 ask the Courts to determine whether the tribunal has substantial jurisdiction to deal with the parties' dispute. These, however, are exceptions. As a rule, the tribunal decides the question.

The tribunal's determination of its competence is binding in much the same way as an award on the merits. Thus, the findings of the tribunal may only be challenged if access to do so follows from the English Arbitration Act 1996, or from other applicable law or rules, such as the tribunal's own rules of procedure. The DAC introduces the provision thus:

"137. This Clause states what is called the doctrine of *kompetenz-kompetenz*. This is an internationally recognised doctrine, which is also recognised by our own law (*e.g. Christopher Brown* v. *Genossenschaft Oesterreichischer Waldbesitzer* [1954] 1 QB 8), though this has not always been the case.

138. The great advantage of this doctrine is that it avoids delays and difficulties when a question is raised as to the jurisdiction of the tribunal. Clearly, the tribunal cannot be the final arbiter of a question of jurisdiction, for this would provide a classic case of pulling oneself up by one's own bootstraps, but to deprive a tribunal of a power (subject to Court review) to rule on jurisdiction would mean that a recalcitrant party could delay valid arbitration proceedings indefinitely by making spurious challenges to its jurisdiction."[666]

It thus seems that sec. 30 has been introduced into the English Arbitration Act 1996 without much theoretical discussion. One could assume that this is due to the Committee's expressed view, namely that as Kompetenz-Kompetenz is already recognised by English law, no major change has occurred. However, comparing the concept of Kompetenz-Kompetenz as stated by Devlin J in CHRISTOPHER BROWN V.

---

[666] 1996 Report on the Arbitration Bill, para. 137-138.

GENOSSENSCHAFT OESTERREICHISCHER to the level of Kompetenz-Kompetenz accepted by the 1996 Act, this is clearly not the case. Firstly, the declaratory rule in sec. 30 does as a main rule place the first word with the arbitral tribunal. The Courts, if confronted with a dispute, may decide that the question of the competence of the tribunal is better tried by the tribunal itself. The party disputing the competence of the tribunal may therefore be forced to initiate arbitral proceedings.[667] Secondly, before the 1996 Act one could, at any time, take any question regarding the tribunal's competence to the Courts. Now, instead, the party may challenge the finding of the arbitral tribunal in accordance with Part I of the Arbitration Act. The scope and time-limits for challenge there prescribed is not on a par with the access to take jurisdictional challenges to the Courts that was available before the regulation in sec. 30 came into place.

3. Challenging the jurisdiction of the tribunal before the Courts

The extent of Kompetenz-Kompetenz de facto left to the tribunal obviously depends on the extent to which the tribunal's findings will be tried by the Courts.

As briefly mentioned above the tribunal may in fact not have the first word on the competence issue. The Courts may, upon application, determine a jurisdictional dispute under sec. 32. The application may be given either by the parties in unison or, in certain cases, by one of the parties with the tribunal's permission. Still, the provision is worded rather narrowly, in most cases consolidating the first word method of the English Arbitration Act 1996, sec. 30. Also, the parties may decide that sec. 30 is inapplicable.

If the tribunal has indeed given a ruling on the tribunal's substantial jurisdiction, this ruling may be challenged according to the relevant arbitration rules or the Arbitration Act 1996 Part I. Challenge of the tribunal's substantial jurisdiction is dealt with specifically in sec. 67. However, also the general rules on challenge due to serious irregularity and the possibility of appeal on a point of law in sec. 68-69 apply.

---

[667] [2000] 2 Lloyd's Law Reports 1 QBD, VALE DO RIO V. BAO STEEL. According to Thomas J, the Arbitration Act 1996 was not designed to allow a party asserting a valid arbitration agreement to seek the determination by declaration of the question whether an arbitration agreement existed. Instead, the correct procedure was for the claimant to appoint an arbitrator and to refer the question of jurisdiction to the tribunal under sec 30 of the Arbitration Act 1996. The matter could then be referred to the Court under sec. 32 of the 1996 Act for a preliminary ruling, or any award on the point could be subject to an appeal under sec. 67 of the 1996 Act. Although there was no absolute prohibition on an application for a declaration, the Court should generally not become involved. See paras. 43-60.

An in-depth discussion of sections 68-69 falls outside the scope of this work.[668] Here, instead, an overview of sec. 67 will be given.

Section 67 offers two main options. If the tribunal is challenged to its jurisdiction the tribunal may give a partial award settling the question of jurisdiction.[669] Such partial award may be challenged according to sec. 67(1)(a). The arbitral tribunal is at liberty to continue the proceedings on the merits even though a party has challenged the tribunal's jurisdiction, see sec. 67(2), thereby avoiding undue delay. If the tribunal does not give a partial award on its jurisdiction, but chooses to deal with the jurisdictional dispute under the final award, the disputing party may instead challenge that award according to sec. 67(1)(b). Notably, the access to challenge under sec. 67 may not be used to mend the fact that a party has abstained from challenging the jurisdiction of the tribunal before the tribunal. This follows directly from the English Arbitration Act 1996 sec. 73(1)(a). Once the right to the challenge of the tribunal's competence has been waived, sec. 67 cannot be applied.[670]

When faced with a claim that the tribunal has acted in excess of its competence, the Courts will evaluate all aspects of the matter.[671] Also, the challenge under s. 67

---

[668] For case law discussing the Arbitration Act 1996 ss. 68-69 see e.g. [1999] 1 Lloyd's Law Reports 862 QBD, EGMARTA V. MARCO, [2000] 1 Lloyd's Law Reports 480 QBD, SHANGHI V. TII, (discussing s. 68 and s. 69), [2000] 2 Lloyd's Law Reports 83 QBD, HUSSMAN V. AL AMEEN, [2000] 2 Lloyd's Law Reports 109 QBD, PACOL V. ROSSAKHAR, [2001] 2 Lloyd's Law Reports 348 QBD, THE PETRO RANGER, [2002] 1 Lloyd's Law Reports 128 QBD, KALMNEFT V. GLENCORE, (discussing s. 68), and [2002] Lloyd's Law Reports 305 QBD, AEK v. NBA, (discussing s. 69).

[669] See the English Arbitration Act 1996 s. 31(4) and e.g. [2002] 1 Lloyd's Law Reports 128 QBD, KALMNEFT V. GLENCORE.

[670] See e.g. [2002] 1 Lloyd's Law Reports 305 QBD, AEK v. NBA, para. 20 ff.

[671] See [2000] 2 Lloyd's Law Reports 550 QBD, ASTRA S.A. V. SPHERE DRAKE, and [2000] 2 Lloyd's Law Reports 83 QBD, HUSMANN V. AL AMEEN. In ASTRA S.A. V. SPHERE DRAKE the insurance company of the Romanian State, ADAS, ceased to exist by the end of 1990. Its assets were transferred to Astra. Sphere Drake had entered into several reinsurance agreements with ADAS, which contained arbitration clauses. Dispute arose. Astra brought proceedings to the Courts. Sphere Drake claimed that Astra was bound by the arbitration agreement and initiated arbitration. The arbitrator ruled on his jurisdiction and held in a partial award that he was competent to hear the case. This ruling was appealed to the Court under the Arbitration Act 1996, s. 67. Held by Steel, J. that according to Romanian law Astra had succeeded in the rights and obligations of ADAS. As a novation of the contract had taken place Astra was a party to the arbitration agreement. The arbitrator's findings that there was an arbitration agreement in force between the parties had thus been correct. The Court in this way tried every aspect of whether the arbitrator's ruling had been the correct one.

may be subject to a full hearing before the Courts, see e.g. [1999] 1 Lloyd's Law Reports 68 QBD, Azov v. Baltic shipping,[672] although a decision based on affidavit evidence may be obtained.

The possibility of having the Courts try the findings of the tribunal on the jurisdictional dispute is not restricted in the same way as is the access to try the tribunal's findings on the merits of the case. As put by *Merkin:* "[The] arbitrators cannot be allowed to have the final say as to whether or not they possess jurisdiction over a particular matter and thus whether they can alter the rights of a person under a procedure to which he has not agreed."[673] If indeed challenged, the Courts may try every aspect of the jurisdictional dispute. The Courts will not leave a margin for error or discretion with the tribunal in this respect. Thus, it is clear that s. 30 only gives *first word*-competence to the tribunal.

4. The interaction between s. 30 and s. 9

Other rules on arbitration law may, if applied, make inroads into the Kompetenz-Kompetenz of the tribunal. The most obvious example of this is that the regulation of Kompetenz-Kompetenz in the English Arbitration Act 1996 sec. 30 and the general regulation of the legal effects of arbitration agreements in sec. 9 overlap.[674] According to sec. 9, as a rule, the proceedings before the Courts are stayed if the parties have entered into an arbitration agreement regarding the present dispute. According

---

[672] [1999] 1 Lloyd's Law Reports 68 QBD, Azov v. Baltic Shipping. After the splitting up of the Soviet Union disputes had occurred between certain former USSR shipping companies regarding containers. Several companies entered into an arbitration agreement regarding the dispute. Dispute also arose between the plaintiff and the defendant. The defendant initiated arbitration proceedings. The plaintiff disputed the jurisdiction of the tribunal as he claimed not to be a party to the arbitration agreement. The tribunal in a full hearing tried its own jurisdiction under s. 30 of the 1996 Act. With uncertainty the arbitrator found that Azov was a party to the arbitration agreement, and thus, that the tribunal was competent to hear the case. Azov challenged the award under s. 67(1)(a) of the 1996 Act. Found by the Court that although it might cause some prejudice to the expeditious and economical disposal of the application, the justice of the case required that Azov's challenge was heard under the aid of oral evidence and cross-examination, in other words, a full hearing. The case is commented by *Davidson (2000)*, p. 233 f.

[673] *Merkin (2000)*, p. 75.

[674] The same is the case under Danish law. See above, point § 2, point 2, regarding the possibility that a party may provoke the Courts to deal with the jurisdictional issue, after the tribunal has been seated with the case, by initiating court-proceedings and leaving it to the counter-party to claim the case's dismissal from the Courts due to the arbitration agreement.

to sec. 9(4) the Courts shall grant a stay "unless satisfied that the arbitration agreement is null and void, inoperative or incapable of being performed." Obviously, ascertaining whether the arbitration agreements suffer from any of those deficiencies involves a decision upon the jurisdiction of any tribunal being composed following the agreement. The interaction between the provisions has already given rise to case law, see BIRSE CONSTRUCTION V. ST. DAVID LTD. [1999] BLR 194, followed by a seemingly unreported Court of Appeal ruling of November 5th 1999, and AL-NAIMI V. ISLAMIC PRESS, [2000] 1 Lloyd's Law Reports 522 CA, following the seemingly unreported ruling of Justice Lloyd in the High Court. The cases both regard arbitration agreements in standard conditions used in contract work. Here, the Court of Appeal's findings in AL-NAIMI V. ISLAMIC PRESS will be used as basis for the discussion, as this case conveniently sums up the previous cases, reported or not.

In AL-NAIMI V. ISLAMIC PRESS, the question was whether certain contract work was carried out as extra work governed by the parties' original contract, to which an arbitration clause applied, or whether the contract work was carried out under an independent oral agreement, in which case no arbitration agreement was entered into. Before the High Court the parties had urged Judge Bowsher to decide the jurisdictional question on the affidavit evidence before him. The Judge had declined to do so in accordance with the "first word" principle. He held that "[t]hose disputes [the jurisdictional disputes] are disputes which the parties have agreed shall be submitted to arbitration, and they are not therefore matters for me to decide".[675] The Judge consequently stayed the case pursuant to the Arbitration Act 1996, sec. 9.

On appeal the Court of Appeal engaged in a general discussion of what is the position of the law regarding the interaction of sec. 30 and sec. 9. In doing that the Court first referred to the statement of the law made by Lloyd, J, in BIRSE CONSTRUCTION V. ST. DAVID.[676] In his statement Judge Lloyd, QC, pointed out the following four options for the Court when met with a dispute as to an arbitral tribunal's jurisdiction:

"It is common ground that the following courses are open to me:
1. To determine, on the affidavit evidence that has been filed, that an arbitration agreement was made between the parties, in which case the proceedings will be stayed in accordance with section 9 of the 1996 Act ...
2. To stay the proceedings but on the basis that the arbitrator will decide the question of whether or not there is an arbitration agreement ... [due to] ... section 30 or the Arbitration Act ...
3. Not to decide the question immediately but to order an issue to be tried. ...

---

[675] As cited by Lord Justice Chadwick, p. 527, col. 2.

[676] C.A. Nov. 5, 1999, unreported. Appeal of [1999] BLR 194.

4. To decide that there is no arbitration agreement and to dismiss the application to stay."[677]

The Court of Appeal in AL-NAIMI V. ISLAMIC PRESS[678] then laid down which criteria should be applied when deciding which option to follow. Also, they gave guidelines as to the correct approach when applying s. 9 or s. 30 respectively.[679] The findings of the Court of Appeal may be summarised thus:

Situation A: The parties are in dispute whether or not there is an agreement to arbitrate. Contentions regarding that dispute may be dealt with by the Courts both under sec. 9 and sec. 30 of the 1996 Act. However, the Courts' general powers to hold parties to their agreement also encompass arbitration agreements. Accordingly, the Courts, apart from the authorities bestowed upon them by sec. 9 and sec. 30, hold an inherent jurisdiction to stay Court proceedings if they find that the parties are bound by an agreement not to take their dispute to the Courts.

The choice between the different options, when it is claimed that there is no agreement to arbitrate, should be carried out as follows:

If it is clear whether or not the agreement is in existence, the Courts should apply sec. 9 of the Arbitration Act. Thus, if the Court finds that there is in fact an arbitration agreement between the parties, the Court proceedings should be stayed. If not, the Court should refuse to grant a stay and let the case proceed before the Court. The role of sec. 9 is allocated to these clear-cut situations. As said by Waller, LJ:

"I would in fact accept that on a proper construction of sec. 9 it can be said with force that a Court should be satisfied (a) that there is an arbitration clause and (b) that the subject of the action is within that clause, before the Court can grant a stay under that section."[680]

If it is not clear whether or not there is an agreement to arbitrate between the parties, two main options exist.

The Court may find that the arbitration tribunal better deals with the question. In that case, the Court proceedings should be stayed. The *reasons* for the stay is to best carry out the regulation set out in sec. 30, but the *authority* to do so is to be found in

---

[677] As cited by Lord Justice Waller, in [2000] 1 Lloyd's Law Reports 522 CA, AL-NAIMI V. ISLAMIC PRESS, p. 524, col. 1 & 2.

[678] [2000] 1 Lloyd's Law Reports 522 CA. AL-NAIMI V. ISLAMIC PRESS.

[679] For a slightly critical comment to the Court of Appeal's findings in the case see [2000] ADRLJ 324, on p. 330.

[680] Per Lord Justice Waller, p. 525, col. 2.

the Court's inherent jurisdiction to keep parties to their agreement – the principle of pacta sunt servanda.

" ... [A] stay under the inherent jurisdiction may in fact be sensible in a situation where the Court cannot be sure of ... [whether there is an arbitration agreement between the parties or not] ... but can see that good sense makes it desirable for an arbitrator to consider the whole matter first."[681]

And as agreed by Lord Justice Chadwick: " ... [If] the Court decides that the proceedings should be stayed so that the issue can be referred to arbitration, the better view is that it is acting under the inherent jurisdiction rather than under s. 9 of the 1996 Act."[682]

Instead, the Court may find that it is best to have the jurisdictional dispute decided by the Courts. In that case two further options exist. The Court may choose to stay the current Court proceedings so that the question may be considered in a new hearing. Alternatively, the Court may choose to settle the issue immediately on affidavit evidence. However, the latter should normally only be done if the parties so agree, and the Court may decline to decide the matter on the affidavit evidence if it finds that oral evidence is necessary.[683]

Still, these are all starting points. In general, the option that best takes care the interests of the parties and the avoidance of unnecessary delay or expense should be chosen.[684]

Situation B: The parties agree that there is an agreement to arbitrate, but disagree as to whether or not that agreement covers the present dispute. In that case sec. 30 should generally be applied. Unless the parties have agreed to the contrary or applied to the Court to settle the dispute on the substantial jurisdiction of the tribunal under sec. 32, the Court should stay the Court proceedings under its inherent jurisdiction and refer the parties to put the dispute before the arbitrators.

5. The extent of Kompetenz-Kompetenz under the English Arbitration Act 1996 sec. 30

In theory, the first word-competence under sec. 30 provides a clear-cut point of departure. However, if the dispute on the tribunal's competence does make its way to

[681] Per Lord Justice Waller, p. 525, col. 2.

[682] Per Lord Justice Chadwick, p. 528, col. 1.

[683] Lord Justice Waller, p. 526, col. 1, Lord Justice Chadwick, p. 528, col. 1.

[684] Lord Justice Waller, p. 524, col. 2.

the Courts, the picture becomes less clear. The Court's exercise of the discretion as to whether the jurisdictional dispute should proceed before the Courts or be dealt with by the tribunal, may hardly be predicted in advance. However, as long as the discretion is carried out in accordance with the general principles of arbitration law set out in the English Arbitration Act 1996 sec. 1(a) and (b), in particular keeping the regards to avoidance of unnecessary delay and expense and party autonomy in mind, the parties' interests should in the end be taken well care of.

In the end, the real extent of the first word Kompetenz-Kompetenz depends on how a party, directly of indirectly presenting the dispute to the Courts, has worded his claim. If the party simply takes the subject matter of the parties' dispute to the Courts, leaving the counter-party to object, the first word-competence bestowed upon the tribunal under sec. 30 may be illusory. If, instead, the claiming party has worded the claim as a dispute regarding the tribunal's competence only, the first word approach will most probably be effected.

6. The parties have agreed that the provision should not apply

The English Arbitration Act 1996 sec. 30 states the declaratory background law. The parties may agree that the provision should not apply.[685] They may do so by either specifically stating that the tribunal should not be able to rule upon its own jurisdiction, or by stating that the Courts should settle any dispute as to the jurisdiction of the tribunal. Or, they parties may simply have worded the arbitration agreement in a way that does not cover jurisdictional disputes. Even in those cases the tribunal should establish prima facie whether it has got jurisdiction to hear the case. The tribunal should examine arbitration agreement's validity and scope, and also procedural questions should be ascertained, for example, that the parties have been correctly summoned or that the composition of the tribunal corresponds to the parties' agreement. Thus, the alleged existence of an arbitration agreement bestows upon the (putative) tribunal an inherent competence to satisfy itself that the alleged jurisdiction exists. However, any finding by the tribunal may at any time, and at the initiative of either party, be brought before the Courts. The tribunal's findings carry practical results, which may result in legal effects if the parties choose to adhere to the findings of the tribunal, but the findings in themselves are not legally binding. The position of the law when the parties have agreed "otherwise" than sec. 30 is thus the exact same as was the position under the law before the 1996 Act, as described in CHRISTOPHER BROWN V. GENOSSENSCHAFT OESTERREICHISCHER.[686]

---

[685] This is contrary to the position under the Model Law Art. 16(1) over which sec. 30 was modelled.

[686] [1954] 1 QB 8, CHRISTOPHER BROWN V. GENOSSENSCHAFT OESTERREICHISCHER.

§ 4. Kompetenz-Kompetenz under Norwegian law – an overview

The question of Kompetenz-Kompetenz is not specifically dealt with in the Norwegian Code of Procedure chapter 32. It is presumed in Norwegian legal theory and case law that the arbitral tribunal is competent to investigate its own jurisdiction,[687] however the question of the competence of the tribunal may always be brought to the Courts.[688] Proceedings may be brought to the tribunal irrespectively of proceedings brought before the Courts, as long as the Courts have not given a ruling that they are competent, which has become res judicata.[689] Thus, the challenge to the Court of the tribunal's jurisdiction need not bring the arbitral proceedings to a halt. Still, no real first word competence lies with the tribunal. In this way the position of Norwegian law approximates the position under English law before the English Arbitration Act 1996 was given. And in the same way as under earlier Danish and English law, an averse party to an arbitration agreement may obstruct the arbitral proceedings by making spurious challenges to the tribunal's jurisdiction. Recognising this, the com-

---

[687] *Schei (1998)*, p. 1165.

[688] *Mæland (1988)*, p. 128, presumed in Rt. 1998.1224 NSC, SUNDBRYGGEN V. EEG-HENRIKSEN. See also LE-1993-01981.

[689] *Schei (1998)*, p. 1165.

mittee behind the Draft Norwegian Arbitration Act felt that the new Arbitration Act ought to better promote the effectiveness of arbitration procedures by providing the tribunal with a first word-competence.[690] According to the committee it would be most opportune if the arbitral tribunal tried the question of its own competence before the question could be brought before to the Courts.[691] Thus, it seems that the tribunal in its general proposal envisaged a genuine first word-competence to lie with the arbitral tribunal. Unfortunately, in the ultimate proposal of the committee a real first-word competence seems not to have been achieved. It is stated as a mandatory rule in sec. 4-1(1) that the arbitral tribunal decides its own competence. The provision follows the UNCITRAL Model Law Art. 16 very closely.[692] Sec. 4-1(1) states that the tribunal has an extent of Kompetenz-Kompetenz, and that the parties cannot agree between them that disputes as to the jurisdiction of the arbitral tribunal may only be tried by the Courts, but the provision gives no indication as to the extent of the tribunal's Kompetenz-Kompetenz. That is governed in sec. 2-4 instead. It follows from sec. 2-4(1) that the Courts shall dismiss a lawsuit regarding a subject matter subjected to arbitration unless it finds that the arbitration agreement is null and void or that the arbitral procedure cannot be carried out. However, according to sec. 2-4(2), if arbitral proceedings have already been initiated, that is if the defendant has received a claim that the dispute be settled by arbitration,[693] then the Courts can only hear the case if it is *clear* that the arbitration agreement is invalid or that the arbitral procedure cannot be carried out. Thus, unlike the Danish Arbitration Act sec. 2, subsec. 1, the initiation of arbitral proceedings does not freeze the competence of the Courts, but simply shrinks the Courts' margin of appreciation in determining whether the arbitration agreement is null and void or whether there are other reasons why the arbitral procedure cannot be brought to its conclusion. Also, there does not seem to be a possibility for the Court to refer a dispute regarding the jurisdiction of the tribunal to be decided by the tribunal itself. That may have been the intention of the committee, but if it is, it needs to be spelt out more verbatim in either the Draft or the travaux préparatoires. Indeed, it seems that the de facto first word-competence of the Norwegian arbitral tribunal under the Draft Norwegian Arbitration Act is slighter than both its Danish and English equivalents.

---

[690] NOU 2001:36, p. 63 f.

[691] NOU 2001:33, p. 63.

[692] NOU 2001:33, p. 96.

[693] Draft Norwegian Arbitration Act sec. 5-4, NOU 2001:33, p. 99.

§ 5. The systems compared

The conceptual starting points applied by the Danish and English legislators when approaching the issue of Kompetenz-Kompetenz could hardly differ more. Under English law Kompetenz-Kompetenz is an intrinsic feature of the arbitration agreement. The Kompetenz-Kompetenz is triggered by the parties' agreement to arbitrate, and the parties must have agreed not to apply sec. 30 to avoid the first word-approach. The first word-competence remains with the tribunal throughout the life-span of the arbitration agreement, subject only to the exceptions provided for in the Act, or in any (other) applicable arbitration rules.

Instead, under Danish law, the autonomy of the tribunal to decide its own competence is a legal effect of the initiation of the arbitral proceedings. As long as no proceedings are commenced, generally, no (putative) competence lies with the tribunal. The Danish Courts will therefore not be able to refuse to deal with the jurisdictional issue, even if they should consider the issue better dealt with by the tribunal.[694] And conversely, unless exceptional circumstances exist, the Courts must refrain from dealing with the question of the tribunal's competence during the arbitral proceedings. The Danish concept of Kompetenz-Kompetenz is based on the mere practicality of avoiding delay, rather that on the issue of principle, namely the idea that Kom-

---

[694] This may be the case if deciding the jurisdictional issue involves extensive inquiry into the subject matter of the case.

petenz-Kompetenz derives from the party autonomy and therefore exists parallel to the arbitration agreement.

As already mentioned, the present Norwegian regulation of Kompetenz-Kompetenz is equivalent to the regulation found in English law before the English Arbitration Act 1996. Thus, the tribunal has the right to rule on its jurisdiction and to proceed with the arbitral procedure if it finds that it is competent to do so, however, the decision of the tribunal does not in any way bar the parties from taking the dispute to the Courts. Thus, the tribunal has a de facto competence to deal with its own jurisdiction, but this competence carries no direct legal effects. This may change if the new Arbitration Act goes through, however, it is not clear to this writer how the proposed provisions are intended to work. If the Courts shall refer the parties' dispute on the jurisdiction of the tribunal to be settled by the (putative) tribunal, then one will have a regulation very much ad modum the English one, with the extra feature that the initiation of arbitral proceedings narrows down the Courts margin of appreciation regarding the validity and effectiveness of the arbitration agreement. However, if it is not intended that the Courts should refer the parties to the tribunal for the decision on the jurisdictional issue then, even after the new Act, the first word-competence of tribunals seated under Norwegian law is negligible.

Reverting to English and Danish law, one might pose the question of which regulation is the better one. The clear-cut either/or of the Danish Arbitration Act sec. 2, sub-sec. 1, or the more intelligent regulation in the English Arbitration Act s. 30? The answer to this is not obvious. If what one wishes to achieve is mere efficiency and the avoidance of (unnecessary) disputes regarding arbitral jurisdiction before the Courts, the Danish regulation seems adequate. It might lead to unfortunate situations, in case the arbitral procedure drags on, however problems arising from this may be taken care of by the escape clause in sec. 2, sub-sec. 1 in fine, allowing the Courts in exceptional cases to rule on the jurisdiction of the tribunal also after the initiation of the arbitral procedure. On the other hand, if one wishes to ensure a first word-competence, this is more likely to be effected under the English regulation. The Courts may refer the parties to have their dispute settled by the arbitral tribunal itself, and generally the Courts will only deal with the issue after the tribunal has made its ruling, by a party challenging that decision under sec. 67 of the English Arbitration Act. Still, the system is imperfect due to the possibility of a party to initiate proceedings on the subject matter before the Court, and leaving it to the counter-party to object to the Court's jurisdiction. In that way the Courts may end up expressing the first word on the tribunal's jurisdiction under sec. 9, and it does seem that that possibility has generated quite some case law already.

Chapter V. Special issues concerning arbitration agreements in international transport

§ 1. The Arbitrability of Transport Disputes

1. Introduction – arbitrability in a transport law perspective

The general features of arbitrability are described above in Chapter III, § 3 point 3. In this Chapter, instead, the specific issues regarding the arbitrability of transport law disputes will be considered. The notion of arbitrability is a variant of the notion of ordre public. Thus, for a subject matter to be deemed inarbitrable, strong reasons must exist. Those reasons could be for example the regard to the protection of a weaker party or maybe the regard to securing that justice within the public law areas is dispensed by public authorities and not by arbitrators.

Above it has been said[695] that rules on arbitrability have no formal characteristics, and that the only two features, which may be shown to qualify a regulation on arbitration, are that the regulation deals with whether and/or to what extent dispute within a certain subject matter may be settled by arbitration, and that the regulation may be applied by the Courts of a fori, even if the law of the fori is not the applicable law. In this way, arbitrability becomes the unruly horse of the arbitration agreement, just as ordre public is the unruly horse of the arbitration award.[696] The parties to an international arbitration agreement simply cannot foresee at the time of the conclu-

---

[695] Chapter III, § 3 point 3.1.

[696] See *Harris/Meisel (1998)*.

sion of the agreement, which rules of arbitrability foreign Courts may potentially apply to the arbitration agreement.

The discussion of arbitrability tends not to take place within the law of contracts and obligations, as disputes within those areas of law are generally arbitrable. However, several of the transport conventions hold specific rules dealing with arbitration as a means of dispute resolution. It is the aim of the discussion in this Chapter to interpret those rules to establish, whether they are indeed rules on arbitrability, or whether they deal with contract law requirements to the arbitration agreement.[697]

Admittedly, the issue dealt with in this section is conceptually rather abstract, as there is a thin line between what is a regulation on arbitrability, and what is a regulation of contractual invalidity. The question I have asked myself to enable a distinction between the issues is whether it may be argued that a claim falling within a certain regulation may not be arbitrated – or that it may only be arbitrated under the compliance with certain requirements, lacking which, the arbitration agreement will fall. If these questions may be answered in the affirmative, I have considered the regulation to be a regulation of arbitrability. One could also argue, that any provision, which affects the validity of the arbitration agreement and which was applied according to a strict lex fori rule should be considered to hold a regulation of arbitrability. However, in this writer's view, if the arbitration agreement is "mended" so as to fulfil the requirements set out by the legislators, but left valid so that the parties are still bound to arbitrate their present dispute, then the boundaries of what is a regulation on arbitrability have been exceeded.

The aim of the discussion in this section is twofold. The first aim is to point out the situations were a Court may consider itself bound by a transport law regulation in national law in the same way as the Court would consider itself bound by – other – rules on arbitrability. Thereby, indications may be given as to when the Courts may strike through a choice of law – or a choice of applicable transport conventions – made by the parties, and apply (other) convention rules, or where the Courts may apply a stricter national incorporation of the conventions, and thus leave the arbitration agreement void. Thus, the aim of this section cannot be to achieve total predictability, as predictability and arbitrability are rather incompatible concepts, but the aim can be – and is – to identify the situations, where total certainty cannot be achieved. This will be done in point 3. Having established, which of the transport law regulations, if any, that hold rules on arbitrability, then the second aim may be achieved, namely to review those rules with regard to establishing whether imposing such requirement are legitimate within the particular type of dispute. This will take place in

---

[697] See for this distinction, the discussion above in Chapter III, point 3.4.2.

point 4, permitting a short conclusion as to the nature of arbitrability regulations within transport law to take place in point 5. First, however, an example from case law, showing the arbitrability-like features of the transport regulations of arbitration agreements will be given.

2. An example from case law: Bofors v. Skandia

Above it has been said that the only general features of rules on arbitrability are that they regulate the extent to which a certain subject matter may be dealt with by arbitration and that they are applied according to an indispensable choice of law rule to the benefit of the lex fori. Bearing this in mind, the regulation of forum agreements found in the international transport conventions does present itself as having features expected of a regulation of arbitrability.

An English case regarding the CMR Convention offers an example.

[1982] 1 Lloyd's Law Reports 410 QBD, BOFORS V. SKANDIA
A grinding machine was carried from Stockholm via Felixstowe to Sudbury. The machine was loaded unto a trailer in Stockholm and hauled to Gothenburg. In Gothenburg the trailer was loaded unto a Ro-Ro vessel and carried to Felixstowe. The first defendants, Skandia, carried out this part of the transport. In Felixstowe the trailer was allegedly unloaded from the vessel by the second defendants and taken to a depot. At the deport, allegedly, the machine was unloaded from the trailer and due to be loaded unto a truck in which the third defendants were to take the machine to Sudbury. In the course of loading or unloading the machine suffered extensive damage.

The manufacturers, the consignees and the ultimate receivers brought proceedings against all three defendants before the English Courts. Skandia sought the proceedings stayed under the Arbitration Act 1975 sec. 1, due to an arbitration clause in the contract of carriage between Skandia and the manufacturer, Bofors. (The other two defendants did not appear before the Court, neither were they otherwise represented there).

The arbitration clause was found in the "Nordic Conditions",[698] which were incorporated by reference into the waybill issued by Skandia to Bofors. The clause was ambiguous, and would probably not have been interpreted as providing for an exclusive choice of forum, had English law on construction of contracts applied. However, *it was clear that the proper law of the contract was Swedish law*.[699] According to the Swedish rules on the construction of contracts the arbitration clause did provide for arbitration to be the proper mode of dispute resolution between Bofors and Skandia.[700]

---

[698] NSAB, seemingly.

[699] See p. 412, col. 1.

[700] See p. 412, col. 2.

Accordingly, as starting point arbitration had been agreed upon between Bofors and Skandia.

However, the part of the transport, which was carried out under the waybill governing the relationship between Bofors and Skandia, was a CMR transport, clearly falling within the Ro-Ro provision in the CMR Convention Art. 2(1). It had to be decided whether the arbitration clause in the "Nordic Conditions" fulfilled the requirements set out in the CMR Convention Art. 33. In Bingham J's words:

"The second question accordingly arises: does cl. 30 [the arbitration clause], as construed, satisfy the C.M.R. Convention? The two most relevant clauses of the Convention, *as incorporated into English law* by the Schedule to the Carriage of Goods by Road Act, 1965, are Art. 33 and Art. 41. ... Now in approaching this question of interpretation *I am not, of course, applying Swedish law as the proper law of the contract but English law as the appropriate governing law for interpreting the Schedule to an English Act.*"[701]

The relevant part of the arbitration clause provided: "Disputes between the freight forwarder and the customer shall with the exclusion of Ordinary Courts of law be referred to arbitration in Stockholm according to the Swedish law on arbitrators and with the application of Swedish law ... ". It was quite clear that a Swedish arbitration tribunal would have applied the rules of the CMR Convention as incorporated into the Swedish International Carriage of Goods by Road Act 1969.[702] However, the judge did not find that sufficient to satisfy the requirement set out in Art. 33. Instead, he found that the criteria set out in Art. 33 required "... an express provision that the tribunal shall apply the Convention ...". Such a provision was lacking. Consequently, the arbitration agreement was null and void under Art. 41 and the application for a stay was refused.

The BOFORS V. SKANDIA case is normally used as authority that the fulfilment of the conditions of the CMR Convention Art. 33 requires that a specific provision, according to which the CMR Convention applies to the parties' dispute, is inserted into the arbitration clause. Here, instead, it is the choice of law applied by the Judge that will be deliberated on.

According to the CMR Convention Art. 33, "[the] contract of carriage may contain a clause conferring competence on an arbitration tribunal *if* the clause conferring competence on the tribunal provides that the tribunal shall apply this Convention". (Emphasis added). Thus, article 33 obviously regulates the conditions under which arbitration agreements are allowed within transports covered by the Convention. In the case, the Judge found that the criteria of the provision were not fulfilled, and he found the arbitration clause "bad under Art. 41 of the [CMR] Convention".[703]

---

[701] Emphasis added.

[702] Lag (1969:12) med anledning av Sveriges tillträde till konventionen den 19 maj 1956 om fraktavtalet vid internationell godsbefordran på väg.

[703] P. 413, col. 1. Article 41 of the CMR Convention governs the party autonomy within areas covered by the convention – by ousting party autonomy.

It follows that the Judge applied a rule of the fori to an arbitration agreement governed by Swedish law. He compared the arbitration clause to the conditions set out under English law, and found it wanting. Consequently, there was no arbitration agreement between the parties.

The exact same result would have been achieved in the more "traditional" arbitrability cases, where an arbitration agreement is in conflict with what may be arbitrated according to the lex fori. It seems that when within transport law, the general lex fori regime has the effect that rules, which may at first present themselves as rules on the contractual validity of arbitration agreements, may indeed govern the issue of arbitrability within a certain area of law.

Whether or not a provision excludes arbitration as a means of dispute resolution in certain disputes, depends on the proper construction of the provision. Below in point 3, the rules on forum in the transport conventions and in the Nordic Maritime Code chapter 13 will be construed, to enable a conclusion as to which of the rules on forum restrict the arbitrability of transport disputes and which do not.

3. The interpretation of the relevant provisions in international transport conventions and in domestic Scandinavian transport law

3.1. The COTIF-CIM Convention Art. 56
The COTIF-CIM Convention Art. 56 offers an example of a rule, which excludes arbitration as a means of solving a dispute between professionals regarding transport law.

COTIF-CIM Art. 56

Actions brought under the Uniform Rules may only be instituted in the competent court of the State having jurisdiction over the defendant railway, unless otherwise provided in agreements between States or in acts of concession … .

Unless special provisions have been made, the only forum for disputes under the Uniform Rules Concerning the Contract for International Carriage of Goods by Rail is the Courts. The provision does not explicitly mention arbitration, but the exclusivity used in the wording must be interpreted so that any other fora by which to solve the disputes are ruled out.

Although this provision is in a document, which mainly deals with issues of substance regarding the carrying out of international transport of goods by rail, the provision is a procedural rule. Procedural rules bind the Courts of the fori. Hence, the Courts in a State bound by the COTIF-CIM convention are bound by Art. 56. Since it is the Courts themselves who are bound, the question whether the parties may have waived their rights according to Art. 56 does not arise.

In this way, the COTIF-CIM Convention Art. 56 excludes the use of arbitration as a means of solving a dispute, and hence the article renders disputes within the scope of application of the COTIF-CIM inarbitrable. States bound by this provision will thus be ad liberty to refuse to recognise and/or enforce an arbitration agreement or arbitral award concerning matters, which fall within the material rules of the Convention.

This conclusion can also be reached by another route. The COTIF-CIM Art. 56 is not a typical rule within international transport. Public law interests govern the COTIF based conventions.[704] Public authorities, such as the Courts, best take care of those considerations, and Art. 56 should also for that reason be seen as a restriction on the arbitrability of disputes falling within the scope of application of COTIF-CIM.

3.2. The Hamburg Rules Art. 22

As a starting point, disputes regarding the subject matter falling within the Hamburg Rules[705] may be settled by arbitration. However, Art. 22 provides in paragraph 1 that certain requirements have to be met.

The article sets out to regulate arbitration clauses in transport documents rather than arbitration agreements in general. Thus, the article does not concern itself with procedural or material requirements regarding arbitration agreements entered into after the facts, which have lead to the dispute, have presented themselves.[706]

Hamburg Rules Art. 22 (in extract) [707]

1. Subject to the provisions of this article, parties may provide by agreement evidenced in writing that any dispute that may arise relating to carriage of goods under this Convention shall be referred to arbitration.

2. ...

3. The arbitration proceedings shall, at the option of the claimant, be instituted at one of the following places: ...

---

[704] This being a reflection of the fact that railways are either run by the States, or by private parties according to concessions given by the State.

[705] United Nations Convention on the Carriage of Goods by Sea, 1978.

[706] See paragraph 6.

[707] The Multimodal Convention 1980 Art. 27 contains the same rules.

4. The arbitrator or arbitration tribunal shall apply the rules of this Convention.

5. The provisions of paragraphs 3 and 4 of this article are deemed to be part of every arbitration clause of agreement, and any term of such clause or agreement which is inconsistent therewith, is null and void.

6. Nothing in this article affects the validity of an agreement relating to arbitration made by the parties after the claim under the contract of carriage by sea has arisen.

The article aims at protecting the cargo interests against arbitration clauses being used as a means of escaping or lessening the carrier's liability as set out in the Hamburg Rules. The lessening of the liability can be done directly by a combination of arbitration and choice of law clauses in the contract, or indirectly by simply causing the settlement of the dispute to be exceedingly difficult and/or expensive for the cargo interest.[708] To achieve this aim, Art. 22 regulates certain aspects of both form[709] and substance of the arbitration agreement. The material requirements are firstly, that the tribunal shall apply the rules of the Convention to the dispute. Secondly, the tribunal, at the option of the claimant, shall be seated either at the place provided for in the arbitration agreement, or in certain other jurisdictions, which are considered to have a close connection to the transport agreement and/or the carriage itself.

The mandatory choice of law, requiring that the arbitral tribunal use the Convention, is not worded as a provision on arbitrability. The paragraph may invalidate a choice of law provision in the arbitration agreement, or create such an agreement where none existed before, but the requirement does not seem to affect the possibility of arbitrating the matter, set out in paragraph 1. The requirement that the plaintiff shall have an option on the seat of the arbitral tribunal may seem a procedural one. This, however, would entail that the requirement only bound Courts in the Contracting states. Instead, by "einer Fiktion des Parteiwillens",[710] both requirements are deemed to be a part of the arbitration agreement. This is combined with a compulsory insertion of a Clause Paramount in the transport document, making the Ham-

---

[708] (Ad hoc) arbitration as a means of solving a dispute will often be unsuitable if the claim is comparatively small. Hence, in contracts of carriage regarding general cargo, setting up an arbitral tribunal may prove so costly that it makes pursuing the cargo claim economically impossible.

[709] Art. 22, paragraph 1 contains a requirement for arbitration agreements to be in writing, whereas Art. 22, paragraph 2 requires, that an explicit reference to an arbitration clause in a charter-party be done in a bill of lading issued under such charter-party, if the arbitration agreement is to have effect against third parties in good faith.

[710] *Asariotis (1998)*, p. 182.

burg Rules applicable to the contract of carriage.[711] If the Clause Paramount has in fact been inserted in the transport document, it is thus likely that Courts and arbitral tribunals in both Contracting and non-contracting States may find that the parties have agreed that the arbitration agreement should be interpreted so as to satisfy the conditions set out in Art. 22.

By choosing the approach of contractual modification, the legislators implementing the Hamburg Rules have at the same time barred themselves from refusing the recognition and/or enforcement of arbitration agreements and awards, which do not comply with the rules in the Convention on grounds of lack of arbitrability. Also, as Art. 22 does not deal with arbitrability, the Courts may only apply the provision when the case before the Court is in fact governed by the Convention.[712]

A different situation arises if the parties do not dispute the existence of the arbitration agreement, but instead its contents. Many countries have in their procedural law provisions enabling the Courts to decide certain disputes regarding the procedure of the arbitral tribunal including the seat of the arbitration and the choice of law of the subject matter. If the matter of the case according to the Hamburg Rules falls within the scope of application of those rules,[713] the Courts of a contracting State may apply Article 22 to the arbitration agreement in question. The Courts would be able to apply the provision in the face of the New York Convention, as that Convention does "not affect the validity of [other international conventions] concerning the recognition and enforcement of arbitral awards".[714] A party, claiming the contractual modifications of Article 22 may thus meet the Court's approval. Still, the arbitration agreement is not invalid and the material questions of the case should not be admitted to the Courts.

---

[711] Hamburg Rules Art. 23, paragraph 3. (Multimodal Convention 1980 Art. 27, paragraph 3).

[712] The protective qualities of the Hamburg Rules depend on their own application – a necessary, but somewhat circular feature of the rules.

[713] According to the Hamburg Rules Art. 2. For practical purposes, the Hamburg Rules are applicable to all contracts of carriage of goods by sea to or from Hamburg States, and to such transports governed by transport documents which are either issued in a Contracting State or which contain a Clause Paramount making the Hamburg Rules applicable.

[714] The New York Convention Art. VII(1).

3.3. The Scandinavian Maritime Codes sec. 311

The Maritime Codes of the Scandinavian States are Hague-Visby based. The Nordic Maritime Codes have a broad scope of application,[715] and contain a mandatory requirement that a Clause Paramount to the benefit of the Nordic Maritime Codes, or, in cross-trade, to the benefit of the Hague-Visby Rules as incorporated into another Hague-Visby State, be inserted in the transport document.[716] The aim of this is to enhance the applicability of the Nordic Maritime Codes.[717]

However, to the extent that the obligations under the Hague-Visby Rules do not forbid this, a regulation similar to the one found in the Hamburg Rules has been made. As the Hague-Visby Rules do not contain rules on jurisdiction or arbitration, provisions modelled over the Hamburg Rules Art. 21 and Art. 22 have been entered into the Codes. Below, in § 2, the general regulation of arbitration agreements under sec. 311 is discussed. Here, sec. 311 will be put into an arbitrability perspective.

3.3.1. The Finnish, Norwegian and Swedish Maritime Codes sec. 311 (sec. 13:61)

The Finnish, Norwegian and Swedish versions of sec. 311 are equivalent, although the Finnish and Swedish provisions are numbered differently (sec. 13:61). They hold the following regulation:[718]

Norwegian Maritime Code sec. 311[719]

Section 310[720] notwithstanding, the parties may agree in writing, that disputes shall be settled by arbitration. It shall be regarded as part of the arbitration agreement that arbitration proceedings can be instituted at the discretion of the plaintiff in one of the States where a place as mentioned in the first paragraph of Section 310 is located, and that the arbitration tribunal shall apply the provisions of the present chapter.

The second, third and sixth paragraphs of Section 310 shall apply correspondingly.

---

[715] Norwegian Maritime Code sec. 252.

[716] Norwegian Maritime Code sec. 254.

[717] See further on sec. 311 (sec. 13:61) of the Nordic Maritime Code, below in § 2.

[718] Here the Norwegian provision in translation. The Finnish and Swedish Maritime Codes have different numbering, but the same provision can be found in their sec. 13-61.

[719] Translation taken from *Bilton/Solvang/Røsæg (1997)*.

[720] Sec. 310 is similar to the provision in the Hamburg Rules Art. 21 on jurisdiction agreements.

The provisions of the first paragraph do not apply if neither the agreed place of receipt for carriage nor the agreed or actual place of delivery according to the third paragraph of Section 252 is in Norway, Denmark, Finland or Sweden.

In the same way as the Hamburg Rules Art. 22, the provision is worded as a provision on contractual interpretation and modification. The provision does not bar arbitration agreements in certain relations; it simply modifies them to the extent that the arbitration agreement does not adhere to the requirements of sec. 311.

Also, it would be against the verbatim interpretation of sec. 311 to regard it as a procedural rule, which would bind the Finnish, Norwegian and Swedish Courts. Indeed, if regarded as a rule of procedure the provision would not be applicable if the fori is that of a non-Scandinavian State.

In conclusion, the provision should not be seen as a provision regulating arbitrability. The Finnish, Norwegian and Swedish sec. 311 (sec. 13:61) governs the contractual validity of arbitration agreements, and should be regarded in the same way as the Hamburg Rules Art. 22. An arbitration agreement which conflicts with the requirements of sec. 311 is still valid, however, the Courts may modify its contents.

3.3.2. The Danish Maritime Code sec. 311

Danish Maritime Code sec. 311 in extract[721]
Sub-sec. 1. Regardless of the provision in section 310, subsection 1, the parties may make an agreement in writing that disputes shall be settled by arbitration, *if the dispute in the option of the plaintiff can be initiated in either of the jurisdictions* [mentioned in sec. 310, sub-sec. 1].
Sub-sec. 2. The arbitral tribunal *must apply* the provisions of this chapter. The provisions of sub-sec. 1 form a part of the arbitration agreement.
…

The Danish Maritime Code sec. 311, sub-sec. 1, seems to provide that arbitration agreements may be entered into *provided* that the claimant can choose the seat of the arbitration tribunal and that the seat may be either one of the jurisdictions mentioned in sec. 310, sub-sec. 1, or the seat provided for in the arbitration agreement.[722] Consequently, it seems that the mandatory option on the seat of the tribunal is a necessary prerequisite for the arbitrability of disputes regarding carriage of goods by sea in the container, general cargo and tramp trades under Danish law. Still, before one sat-

---

[721] Writer's translation and emphasis.

[722] See sec. 311, sub-sec. 3 in conjunction with sec. 310, sub-sec. 2, no. 1.

isfies oneself with such a far-reaching conclusion, one should consider whether that conclusion is supported by the other factors influencing the construction of the provision.

The travaux preparatoire's discussion of the rule does not offer much guidance, as no distinction between arbitrability and contractual invalidity is made. The travaux address the issue in terms of validity,[723] but since the legal effect of lack of arbitrability is invalidity that alone does not decide the issue.

The Danish Maritime Code chapter 13 is a piece of private law legislation, carried by private law considerations rather than public law concerns, as is the case regarding the COTIF-based regulation. Also, the scope of application and general regime of the Danish Maritime Code chapter 13 is somewhat less aggressive than is the case as regards, for example, the CMR Convention. The Danish Maritime Code chapter 13's regulation of the container, general cargo and tramp trades are Hague-Visby based and as such only mandatory to the protection of the cargo interest.[724] (Excluding maybe – this is open to question – the one-year limitation period for cargo claims).[725] Also, although the Danish Maritime Code sec. 252 prima facie provides for a very extensive application of the rules of chapter 13, it follows from sec. 311, sub-sec. 4 that the mandatory choice of law and the mandatory option on the seat of the arbitration only applies to transports to or from Denmark, Finland, Norway or Sweden.

Finally, there is no evidence that the committee behind the Danish Maritime Code 1994 intended to regulate the matter differently than the other Nordic States participating in the joint effort of making the Nordic Maritime Code 1994. Conversely it seems that the rules on forum were intended to be identical.[726] Certainly, the expressed intention of the committee was to introduce a Hamburg based regulation albeit with a less aggressive scope of application.[727] Bearing this in mind, the Danish Maritime Code sec. 311 should be interpreted to hold the exact same regulation, as its Scandinavian counterparts. Hence, in the following, both the Danish and the Finnish, Norwegian and Swedish provisions will be dealt with collectively, and it should

---

[723] Danish Maritime Code travaux préparatoires p. 96.

[724] DMC sec. 254, sub-sec. 1. Hague-Visby Rules Art. 3(8).

[725] DMC sec. 501, sub-sec. 1, no. 6 and no. 7. Hague-Visby Rules Art. 3(6), 3rd and 4th sentence.

[726] See explicitly the Danish Maritime Code travaux préparatoires p. 53 regarding the regulation on jurisdiction in the Danish Maritime Code sec. 310.

[727] Danish Maritime Code travaux préparatoires p. 54, and Swedish Maritime Code travaux préparatoires p. 264.

be concluded that they hold a regulation on contractual validity, as do their model, the Hamburg Rules Art. 22.

3.4. The Hague-Visby Rules Art. 3(8) and similar provisions

The Hague-Visby Rules do not hold a specific regulation on the forum for disputes to which the rules apply. Only a regulation of the extent of the party autonomy may be found.

Hague-Visby Rules Art. 3(8), *in extract*

Any clause, covenant, or agreement in a contract of carriage relieving the carrier or the ship from liability for loss or damage to, or in connection with, goods arising from negligence, fault or failure in the duties and obligations provided in this Article or lessening such liability otherwise than provided in this Convention, shall be null and void and of no effect. ...

The provision governs the validity of contracts and contractual stipulations. Considering that it is placed amongst the provisions regulating the liability of the carrier and that the Hague-Visby Rules in general are concerned only with substantial rules, it could be argued that Art. 3(8) only concerns the validity of agreements or contractual stipulations regarding the subject matter of the contract of carriage. Still, the rule encompasses "any" clause, covenant, or agreement, and case law exists applying the provision to choice of law clauses. Thus, in the MORVIKEN case a jurisdiction and choice of law provision in the contract of carriage that effected a lessening of the carrier's liability compared to what followed from the Hague-Visby Rules was deemed null and void according Art. 3(8).

[1983] 1 LLOYD'S LAW REPORTS 1 HL, The Morviken

Cargo carried under a bill of lading was damaged during discharge and the cargo owners brought an action in rem against the Morviken before the Admiralty Court. Morviken's owners claimed that the case should be stayed due to a forum agreement in the bill of lading according to which all actions should be brought before the Court of Amsterdam, applying the Hague Rules 1924 and Netherlands' Law. The maximum package limitation under those rules were Dfl. 1250. The bill of lading was issued in the United Kingdom, and the carriage had its starting point in a U.K. port. The Hague-Visby Rules were thus mandatory applicable law.

The House of Lords held that insofar that the provision of the bill of lading led to a liability for the carrier that was less than the liability prescribed by the Hague-Visby Rules, the provision was null and void. Article 3(8) embraced all provisions to that effect, including provisions on forum. It was clear that the forum and choice of law clause would effect a package limitation that was significantly lower than what was fixed by the Hague-Visby Rules. As a consequence, the forum and choice of law provision was null and void and the cargo interests were ad liberty to proceed with the action in rem before the Admiralty Court.

Considering that the English Courts saw fit to invalidate a jurisdiction and choice of law clause under the Hague-Visby Rules Art. 3(8), it must be assumed that the provision may be applied to arbitration agreements as well, if the arbitration agreement governs the relationship under the bill of lading. There are no Norwegian or Danish cases accepting this line of argument.[728] Indeed the argument seems to have been positively rejected by the Danish Supreme Court in ND 1987.112 DSC, TROPIC JADE. Considering the wording and substantive nature of the Hague-Visby Rules Art. 3(8), this writer supports the findings of the Danish Supreme Court. Obviously, in the face of the House of Lords' ruling in THE MORVIKEN, English Courts will be unlikely to follow this argument. Consequently, instead of attempting to argue against the applicability of the precedence of that case, it will be suggested that English Courts when faced with a situation parallel to the one encountered in THE MORVIKEN, choose to uphold the agreement to arbitrate, but instead render any choice of law provision, resulting in an outcome of the case, which is less favourable than Art. 3(8), null and void. This would be perfectly in keeping with Art. 3(8), as this provision is concerned with substantial results rather than with the method of dispute resolution. To this writer, considering Art 3(8) to provide for restrictions on the arbitrability of transport disputes is simply incompatible with the provision's wording, and also excessive, considering the provisions aim. (The stringent lex fori solution now adopted in the Nordic Maritime Codes 1994 chapter 13 will to an extent lead to similar results, although, strictly speaking, for different reasons).

3.5. The CMR Convention Art. 33

It follows from the CMR Convention Art. 33[729] that arbitration clauses may be introduced into contracts of carriage of goods by road, if, according to the arbitration clause, the tribunal shall apply the rules of the CMR Convention to the parties' dispute.

CMR Convention Art. 33.
The contract of carriage may contain a clause conferring competence on an arbitration tribunal if the clause conferring competence on the tribunal provides that the tribunal shall apply this Convention.

---

[728] See e.g. ND 1987.112 DSC, TROPIC JADE and ND 1989.208 NSC, VISHVA APURVA.

[729] Danish International Carriage of Goods by Road Act sec. 42 (Lovbekendtgørelse nr. 602 af 9.9. 1986 om internationale fragtaftaler), Norwegian Carriage of Goods by Road Act sec. 44. (Law of 20 December 1974 No. 68).

The wording of the text is quite absolute implying that the choice of the Convention as applicable law is a condition sine qua the arbitration agreement will be invalid. However, whether or not the provision is a provision on arbitrability cannot be determined on that basis alone. Other means of interpretation must be consulted.

The article has the following effect: If there is any chance that the Courts should find the CMR convention applicable to a contract of carriage, the parties will have to insert a specific provision,[730] making the CMR Convention applicable to their arbitration agreement. If they do not, they run the risk of the arbitration agreement being set aside by the Courts at a later stage. Such a choice of law will also bind an arbitral tribunal seated in a state not party to the CMR Convention. Also, it follows from both the New York Convention Art. V(1)(a), and from the national arbitration law in most states that an award may be set aside if the arbitration agreement was not valid according to the law the parties had subjected it to, alternatively that an award may be set aside if the tribunal has not respected the choice of law of the parties.[731] The CMR Convention Art. 33 thus effects a very expansive application of the substantive rules of the Convention.

An interpretation of Art. 33, which promotes the use of the CMR Convention to the largest possible degree is consistent with the general policy of application of the convention. Firstly, the CMR Convention applies to all transports by road to or from a contracting State, see Art. 1(1), except the special transports mentioned in Art. 1(4) and 1(5). The convention also applies to hucke-pack and Ro-Ro transports, see Art. 2(1). The rules as thus described are, potentially, mandatory applicable to a wide spectrum of contracts. Furthermore, the scope of application of the rules is widened by Art. 6(1)(k), according to which a consignment note has to contain a paramount clause to the effect that the carriage is subject to the CMR Convention. Out of principle, the provision for the insertion of a clause paramount does not trigger the mandatory application of the CMR Convention, as is the case with the Hamburg[732] or Hague-Visby Rules.[733] It only provides for a contractual agreement. However, it does mean that the CMR Convention will apply to the whole transport in road transport to or from contracting States, either by mandatory regulation or by contractual incorporation. Also, if a dispute is brought before a Court finding the CMR Conven-

---

[730] See [1982] 1 Lloyd's Law Reports 410 QBD, BOFORS V. SCANDIA.

[731] English Arbitration Act 1996 s. 68. Danish Arbitration Act 1972 sec. 7, sub-sec. 1, nos. 1 and 2.

[732] Hamburg Rules Art. 2(1)(e).

[733] Hague-Visby Rules Art. 10(1)(c), Danish Maritime Code sec. 252, sub-sec. 2, no. 5.

tion applicable to the case, a carrier not having inserted the required paramount clause into the consignment note shall be liable for all expense, loss and damage sustained by the cargo interest due to that omission, see Art. 7(3). A carrier will thus be wise – if not always likely – to insert the paramount clause just so that certainty may be achieved and the insurance cover adapted correspondingly. Finally, and probably most importantly, the CMR Convention provides for absolute mandatory regulation. According to the CMR Convention Art. 41(1), 1st sentence, any stipulation, which would directly or indirectly derogate from the provisions of the Convention, is null and void. Thus, neither agreements to the benefit nor agreements to the detriment of the legal position of the carrier are allowed.[734]

The regulation of the application and mandatory effects of the CMR Convention shows that a strict regime, only to be departed from when expressly provided for in the convention, is intended. To satisfy that intention, the requirement of substance in Art. 33 must be a condition for the arbitrability of disputes falling within the scope of that Convention.

Consequently, the Courts of a CMR State may refuse to recognise and enforce arbitration agreements or awards to the extent that the Court finds *that* the CMR Convention applies to the parties' dispute, and *that* the arbitration agreement does not expressly provide that the tribunal shall apply the CMR Convention.

3.6. The Warsaw Convention Art. 32

The Warsaw Convention Art. 23 holds the general regulation of party autonomy laid down by the Convention.

Warsaw Convention Art. 23

Any provision tending to relieve the carrier of liability or to fix a lower limit than that which is laid down by this Convention shall be null and void, but the nullity of any such provision does not involve the nullity of the whole contract, which shall remain subject to the provisions of this Convention.

The provision aims at situations where the attempt to lessen or limit the liability of the carrier is done by making provisions of substance in the contract of carriage; provisions, which are germane to the contract of carriage. Provisions attempting to lower the air carrier's liability by inserting choice of law or forum clauses in the contract of carriage are dealt with specifically in Art. 32.

---

[734] *Bull (2000)*, p. 33; *Clarke (1997)*, p. 348; *Loewe (1976)*, p. 593; *Regnarsen (1993)*, p. 25; Danish CMR travaux préparatoires p. 9.

Warsaw Convention Art. 32.

Any clause contained in the contract and all special agreements entered into *before* the damage occurred by which the parties purport to infringe the rules laid down by this Convention, whether by deciding the law to be applied, or by altering the rules as to jurisdiction, shall be null and void. *Nevertheless, for the carriage of goods arbitration clauses are allowed*, subject to this Convention, if the arbitration is to take place within one of the jurisdictions referred to in the first paragraph of Article 28.

The Warsaw Convention Art. 32 distinguishes between contracts for the carriage of passengers and contracts for the carriage of goods.

Dealing first with the carriage of *passengers*, the Warsaw Convention Art. 32 only governs agreements entered into before the damage in dispute occurred, as does the Hamburg Rules Art. 22. The regulation is hence aimed at arbitration and other *clauses* in the transport documents used in contracts of carriage by air. The transport customer, and especially the airline passenger, is to be protected against having (unforeseen) difficulties in obtaining damages from the air-carrier. Thus, forum or choice of law clauses entered into *after* the damage that caused the dispute arose, are not covered by Art. 32, but may, nonetheless, be invalid under the general rule in Art. 23.

Art. 32, 1st sentence provides the starting point. Any choice of law or forum clause, which may lead to a lessening of the air carrier's liability, is null and void. The provision should be read together with the Warsaw Convention Art. 28(1):

Warsaw Convention Art. 28(1)

An action for damages *must* be brought, at the option of the plaintiff, in the territory of one of the High Contracting Parties, either before the Court having jurisdiction where the carrier is ordinarily resident, or has his principal place of business, or has an establishment by which the contract has been made or before the Court having jurisdiction at the place of destination. [Emphasis added]. ...

The provision on jurisdiction in Art. 28(1) is absolute. Action must be brought before the Courts at the places specified. Seen in that context it is clear, that when it is provided in Art. 32, 1st sentence that clauses laying down another jurisdiction for damages than what follows from Art. 28 is null and void, that provision also invalidates arbitration clauses. The dispute, if concerned with damages at least, shall be dealt with by the Courts.

Regarding the contracts of carriage of *goods* by air, Art. 32, 2nd sentence states that arbitration clauses may be entered into regarding carriage of goods, given that certain preconditions are met. Art. 32, 2nd sentence provides an exception to the main rule and should be interpreted narrowly. The provision does not speak in terms of validity. It clearly states that arbitration clauses may be *allowed* under certain conditions thus indicating that it is the question of arbitrability, which is regulated.

Disputes regarding air carriage of goods *may* be arbitrable, even if the arbitration agreement has been entered into before the damage occurred, but it is a precondition for the arbitrability that the seat of the arbitral is within one of the jurisdictions mentioned in Art. 28(1). Also, the provision should be interpreted so that it is a precondition for the arbitrability that the rules of the Convention are applied to the parties' dispute. It is not totally clear whether it is required that the arbitration clause expressly provides that the Warsaw Convention shall apply to the dispute, as is the case with the CMR Convention Art. 33. The wording, at least, is less stringent. Probably, it will suffice that it is clear from the circumstances that the Warsaw Convention will de facto be applied when deciding the parties' dispute.

In conclusion may be said that disputes covered by the Warsaw Convention are arbitrable if *either* the arbitration agreement has been entered into after the damage which caused the dispute occurred, *or* the arbitration agreement has been entered into before the damage which caused the dispute occurred, and the dispute regards carriage of goods, and the arbitration agreement provides that the tribunal should be seated at one of the jurisdictions which are mentioned in Art. 28(1), and it is clear from the circumstances of the case that the rules of the Warsaw Convention will be applied to the dispute, all these criteria to be seen as cumulative.

In the Convention for the Unification of Certain Rules for International Carriage by Air, done in Montreal, 28 May 1999 (The Montreal Convention 1999) Art. 34, a step away from the arbitrability approach has been made.

Article 34 – Arbitration

1. Subject to the provisions of this Article, the parties to the contract of carriage for cargo may stipulate that any dispute relating to the liability of the carrier under this Convention shall be settled by arbitration. Such agreement shall be in writing.
2. The arbitration proceedings shall, at the option of the claimant, take place within one of the jurisdictions referred to in Article 33.
3. The arbitrator or arbitration tribunal shall apply the provisions of this Convention.
4. The provisions of paragraphs 2 and 3 of this Article shall be deemed to be part of every arbitration clause or agreement, and any term of such clause or agreement which is inconsistent therewith shall be null and void.

The regulation is very much ad modum the Hamburg Rules Art. 22. It is still required that the tribunal shall be seated within a jurisdiction that accords to Art. 33(1), and that the tribunal shall apply the provisions of the Montreal Convention 1999. However, in Art. 34(4) it is provided that those conditions shall be deemed incorporated into the arbitration agreement, invalidating any and all provisions to the contrary. Thus, the approach of contractual incorporation and modification has been opted for, barring, as is the case with the Hamburg Rules Art. 22 and the NMC § 311 (sec. 13:61), the Courts of the Contracting States from regarding the issue inarbitrable. On the other hand, the Montreal Convention 1999 Art. 34 seems to apply equally to arbitration agreements entered into before and after the damage.

Applying of the incorporation approach instead of the arbitrability approach will, as a starting point, favour the autonomy of the parties to the arbitration agreement compared to what follows from the present regime. However, seen in an overall perspective, the regulation is in fact more stringent than what follows from the Warsaw Convention 1929 Art. 32. Firstly, a requirement for the arbitration agreement to be in writing has been inserted. Secondly, it seems that Art. 34 of the Montreal Convention 1999 applies arbitration agreements irrespectively of when they are entered into. Consequently, the possibility of entering into any arbitration agreement of the parties' choice after the damage occurred, presently given in Art. 32 of the Warsaw Convention, is no longer at hand. And, finally, under the regime of the Warsaw Convention Art. 32, the parties may in advance pinpoint one of the jurisdictions mentioned in Art. 28(1). In the Montreal Convention Art. 34(2) the seat of the tribunal remains in the option of the claimant. The insecurities potentially arising from this construction are obvious. Therefore, it may be concluded that arbitration does not necessarily present itself as a better option for cargo claims under the Montreal Convention 1999 than it does under the Warsaw Convention 1929.

3.7. Conclusion – the arbitrability of transport disputes
The regulations of arbitration agreements found in the transport conventions and in the Nordic Maritime Code chapter 13 may be divided into three groups, according to whether they do, do to an extent, or do not affect the arbitrability of transport disputes.

3.7.1. Rules, which exclude dispute resolution by means of arbitration
These rules may be described as arbitrability rules in the traditional sense. They should therefore be founded in the need to protect a party or to support public law considerations. The Courts would probably have applied such rules in the lex fori even if the lex fori tendency of international transport law did not exist.

Such a rule is the COTIF-CIM Convention Art. 56. The rule provides an exclusive forum for disputes, namely,
the Courts. Also, it forms a part of a regulation, which is traditionally governed by public law considerations.

3.7.2. Rules that do not bar arbitration as a means of dispute resolution
This heading covers two different types of rules.

Firstly, it covers the rules, which govern arbitration agreements, but do not invalidate the parties' agreement to arbitrate. The rules may be applied so as to alter the details of the parties' agreement, but the Courts will accept that arbitration has been chosen as a means of dispute resolution. Consequently, the Courts should not deal with the subject matter of the parties' dispute. These rules include the Hamburg Rules Art. 22 and the NMC sec. 311 (sec. 13:61).

Secondly, rules ad modum the Hague-Visby Rules Art. 3(8) also fall within this heading. Art. 3(8) may in principle render the arbitration agreement void, meaning that the parties may not be able to arbitrate their dispute. Still, as it is this writer's view that Art. 3(8) deals with contractual validity rather than arbitrability, the Courts ought to restrict the application of the provision so as to apply to the choice of law part of the arbitration agreement, but not to the agreement as such.

3.7.3. Rules, which bar arbitration as a means of dispute resolution to an extent
These rules may be worded either as rules on jurisdiction or as rules on requirements for entering into arbitration agreements. These rules include the CMR Convention Art. 33, and the Warsaw Convention Art. 32. Neither the CMR Convention Art. 33 nor the Warsaw Convention Art. 32 govern arbitration agreements entered into after the damage that caused the dispute occurred. Here the general rules apply. Disputes within the scope of application of the conventions are thus arbitrable *if* the arbitration agreement has been entered into after the damage occurred.

Disputes entered into before the damage occurred, generally through arbitration clauses in the transport agreement, *may* be arbitrable, given that certain preconditions are fulfilled. These conditions have been discussed above. Here it suffices to say that under the Warsaw Convention disputes regarding the transport of passengers and luggage may not be arbitrated if the arbitration agreement has been entered into before the damage occurred. On the other hand, disputes regarding the transport of goods under the Warsaw Convention and the CMR Convention may to the extent that the arbitration agreement satisfies the above-mentioned requirements.

However, when these rules are applied according to a strict lex fori rule, the regulation provides all the characteristics of a regulation of arbitrability and should be regarded as such.

339

4. The matter of policy – the CMR Convention Art. 33 and the Warsaw Convention Art. 32

The CMR Convention Art. 33 and the Warsaw Convention Art. 32 deal with the extent to which disputes under the conventions may be settled by arbitration. The rules do in fact restrict the arbitrability of disputes under them. The rules apply according to a unilateral choice of law rule. This choice of law rule will by Danish, English and Norwegian Courts be interpreted so as to be to the benefit of the lex fori. In that way the lex fori will override what would otherwise be the applicable law.

Such a regulation is a regulation on arbitrability. There are no differences of principle separating these rules from other rules on arbitrability; consequently, there is no reason to regard them differently than other arbitrability rules. It must follow from this that there should be just as clear policy reasons supporting arbitrability rules within the transport regulation as there is when concerned with other areas of law that exclude arbitration as a means of dispute resolution. The regulations are only legitimate if such policy reasons may be shown to exist.

Barring arbitration as a means of dispute resolution regarding claims for air carriage of passengers and luggage in situations where the arbitration agreement has been entered into in advance – which is the de facto effect of the Warsaw Convention Art. 32 – is very much in keeping with general consumer protection tendencies in national and international law. There is a real need to protect a party, whom may just have lost the breadwinner of the family due to a plane crash from having to accept an arbitration agreement inserted into the small print of an airline ticket. Likewise, a person simply having lost his or her luggage during transit should hardly have to initiate an arbitration procedure to recover the claim. However, outside these areas the need for protection is less obvious.

In his commentary to the CMR Convention, *Loewe* describes and defends the ousting of party autonomy within the CMR Convention thus:

"Unlike other private transport law conventions which allow the carrier to offer to his clients better conditions than those provided for under the said convention, the provisions of CMR are peremptory for all parties. The reasons for this are first, that there was no way of knowing which party to a contract for the carriage of goods would be the strongest economically and therefore in a position to exercise pressure on the person with whom he has contracted and, secondly, that it seemed advisable to avoid undue competition between individual transport enterprises ...".[735]

Such considerations are not on a par with the considerations that has rendered certain disputes within mainly administrative, criminal and family law inarbitrable. When

---

[735] *Loewe (1976),* p. 401, para. 292.

introducing restrictions on arbitrability the legislator should not only be able to show that a reason of fact or policy for doing so exist. Conversely, the legislator must show that a real, indispensable need for barring the parties from arbitration exists. And the legislator should bear in mind that the arbitrability exception found in national and international arbitration law is a procedural pendant to the ordre public exception.[736]

Within transport of goods by road or air, such a need has not been shown to exist. Fortunately, this seems to have been recognised as far as air carriage is concerned, and the Montreal Convention 1999 has, as shown above, meant a shift towards the contractual modification technique. Remaining is the CMR Convention. One may only suggest, that in a future revision that provision too will be changed so that the arbitration agreement is upheld, and if need be modified rather than nullified.

5. Arbitrability of transport disputes – a relative term

Traditionally, arbitrability has been considered to be an either-or. A subject matter may be arbitrated or it may not. The transport regulation shows that this approach is over-simplified. Some subject matters are arbitrable *if* ...

It is hoped that the rather lengthy excursion into the arbitrability of transport disputes has not seemed totally fruitless to the reader. Instead, it is hoped, that the Chapter has helped pinpoint areas where the arbitration agreement might encounter vital problems, such as arbitration agreements entered into within the scope of application of the CMR Convention, from areas where arbitration agreements may survive the encounter with the Courts relatively untarnished.

Out of principle, this writer supports the party autonomy within international trade. The restrictions on arbitration as a means of dispute resolution in transport disputes do seem too many. However, if restrictions must be had, the modification approach, as seen in the Hamburg Rules, the Nordic Maritime Code chapter 13, and the new Montreal Convention 1999 are preferred. At least they let the parties arbitrate. Outside areas where consumer interests and/or personal injury is involved the strict preconditions, sine qua the matter may not be arbitrated at all, are unwarranted.

---

[736] *van den Berg (1981)*, p. 368.

§ 2. Arbitration agreements and the Nordic Maritime Codes Chapter 13

1. Introduction[737]

The Scandinavian States are Hague-Visby States. However, in the Nordic Maritime Codes 1994 (NMC 1994) chapter 13, the legal position of the cargo interests has been strengthened, compared to what one would generally expect from a Hague-Visby based regime. Obviously, strengthening the legal position of the cargo owners and interests provides for a greater onus upon the carriers. Therefore, it was feared that the carriers might simply opt out of the new rules, using appropriate forum- and choice of law clauses. To avoid this, the NMC 1994 sec. 252, sec. 310 and sec. 311[738] have been introduced, containing special legislation on such issues. The means employed by the legislators to uphold the liability regime are twofold. Firstly, rules are made to secure that the NMC 1994 chapter 13 is used as applicable law to the furthest extent possible when cargo claims are concerned. Secondly, rules are

---

[737] For other literature specifically on this subject see e.g. *Schelin (1995), Siig (1995), Tiberg (1995), Philip (1996),* and *Wetterstein* in *Honka (1997).*

[738] Swedish and Finnish sections 13:2, 13:60 and 13:61. Unfortunately, even if it was possible to agree on a whole new Maritime Code, it was not possible for the four Scandinavian legislative committees to agree on a common numbering of the sections. In the following, the Swedish and Finnish numbering will be presented in brackets.

given to avoid a cargo owner's claim under the NMC 1994 chapter 13 being obstructed, either by excessive costs caused by having to use a foreign Court or arbitration tribunal or by other fori applying other law.

The Hague-Visby Rules contain no explicit regulation of the forum for disputes arising under the rules; indeed, the rules presuppose that such rules exist in national law. Thus, the Scandinavian States are free to enact national legislation specifically dealing with the question of forum in disputes covered by the Rules. The means chosen has been to introduce a regulation very closely modelled on the Hamburg Rules Art. 21 and 22. Readers familiar with those rules will thus recognise much of the NMC 1994 secs. 310 and 311. The Hague-Visby Rules Art. 10 contains a provision on the applicability of the rules, which is to be understood as a unilateral choice of law rule.[739] Under the previous NMC, this provision was simply translated into the Codes. In the NMC 1994 the provision has been altered so that it provides for a rather strict *lex fori* regime – the fori being the Scandinavian states. Such a solution is clearly not required by the Hague-Visby Rules Art. 10, but Art. 10 does not forbid the insertion of a lex fori rule either. However, an in-depth discussion of the boundaries of the High Contracting Parties' obligations under the Hague-Visby Rules is not within the scope of this work.

The NMC sec. 311 governs the arbitration agreements and is the main topic for the discussion in the following. The provision is found in the NMC Chapter 13, dealing with the liner, general cargo and (to an extent) tramp trades. Especially in the liner and general cargo trades, arbitration agreements are rare, and instead the carriers are likely to insert a combined choice of law and jurisdiction clause into their standard documentation, normally in the form of a so-called "principal place of business of the carrier-clause". Those clauses are governed by the NMC secs. 252 and 310. However, to avoid that the carrier circumvents the regulation presented in those provisions by inserting an arbitration clause into his standard contracts, sec. 311 was inserted into the Code. Considering that sec. 311 is designed to ensure, that the regulation in sec. 252 and sec. 310 remains effective, it is considered proper to start this Chapter with a short presentation of those provisions. Also, for a part of the regulation in sec. 311, the legislator has simply made a reference to sec. 310. Those rules in sec. 310 must be specifically discussed, however, for a thorough analysis of sec. 310 other sources must be consulted.[740]

---

[739] *Clarke (1976)*, p. 14.

[740] See for example *Wetterstein* in *Honka (1997)*, p. 328 f; *Falkanger/Bull (1999)*, p. 14 f and 273 f; and *Siig (1998)*, p. 39 ff.

The regulation in sec. 311 presupposes the applicability of the Nordic Maritime Code chapter 13. Therefore, below in point 2, a short introduction to the scope of application of chapter 13 will be given, followed, in point 3, by a brief introduction to sec. 310. Point 4 provides a condensed overview of the regulation set out in sec. 311. The formal requirements of the regulation are dealt with more thoroughly under point 5, whereas the requirements of substance are discussed in point 6. The Courts', and, to an extent, the arbitral tribunals' application of sec. 311 are discussed in point 7. Both the interrelation between sec. 311 and international conventions on arbitration, and the use of sec. 311 when outside these conventions are considered. Finally, a summary and critical review is offered in point 8.

Above, in § 1, the arbitrability of transport disputes including the regulation in sec. 311 has been examined. Reference to that chapter will be made; and it will be attempted not to indulge in too much repetition, although, for the sake of readability and consistency, some areas already touched upon are repeated. Also, in § 1, point 3.3.2, it was concluded that the regulation of all the Nordic Maritime Codes sec. 311 (sec. 13:61) should be considered to contain the same regulation, even if the wording in the Danish Maritime Code sec. 311 might indicate otherwise. As a consequence, to avoid unnecessary inconsistencies, the wording in the Danish Maritime Code sec. 311 will not be used in the following. When need be, reference to the Norwegian text will be given.

2. The application of the Nordic Maritime Code sec. 311

2.1. The application of the Nordic Maritime Code chapter 13
The application of the NMC sec. 311 presupposes that the dispute falls within the NMC chapter 13. The scope of application of chapter 13 is defined in secs. 252 and 253. For chapter 13 to be applicable, it is required that two criteria present themselves, firstly that a certain (if sometimes weak) geographical connection exists and secondly, that the dispute regards a certain type of contract of carriage.

2.2. The geographical criterion in sec. 252
According to sec. 252, sub-sec. 1 (sec. 13:2, sub-sec. 1), the NMC chapter 13, including its mandatory liability regime and its provisions on forum and choice of law applies to all contracts of carriage in domestic trade in a Scandinavian Country as well as to inter-Scandinavian trade.

Outside Scandinavian trade the NMC chapter 13 also applies to contracts of carriage where the place of delivery of the goods to the carrier or his representative is within a Hague-Visby State, or

the actual or agreed place of delivery of the cargo to the receiver/consignee or his representative is within a Scandinavian Country, or

the document governing the carriage is issued in a Hague-Visby State, or

where, according to the contract of carriage, the carriage is subject to the Hague-Visby Rules, see sec. 252, sub-sec. 2.

If neither the place of delivery of the goods to the carrier nor the place of delivery of the goods to the receiver/consignee is within a Scandinavian Country (cross-trade), a choice of law agreement stipulating that the Hague-Visby based legislation of a specific and named Hague-Visby State shall apply to the contract of carriage will be accepted by the Scandinavian Courts, see sec. 252, sub-sec. 3.

A transport to or from Denmark, Finland, Norway or Sweden will thus always be subject to the NMC 1994 chapter 13. Furthermore, if the parties have not made a choice of law agreement according to which the Hague-Visby based regulation of a specific Hague-Visby state shall apply, also transports with no connecting factors pointing at Scandinavian may be subject to the NMC 1994 – given that there is the connection to *any* Hague-Visby stated in sec. 252, sub-sec. 2 and that jurisdiction may be established before a Scandinavian Court.

2.3. The contracts of carriage, sec. 253

The NMC chapter 13 contains what is the Scandinavian Hague-Visby regulation. The Hague-Visby Rules apply specifically to bills of lading and similar documents of title, but the Rules expressly provide that they may be applied to other contracts as well.[741] In keeping with this, the application of the NMC chapter 13 is not linked to the issuing of a bill of lading. Instead, the contract of carriage to which the regulation applies has been defined in the negative. Thus, in sec. 253 (sec. 13:3) sub-sec. 1, 1st sentence, it is provided that chapter 13 does not apply to charter-party trade unless a bill of lading is issued and the bill of lading governs the relationship between the carrier and the consignee. In this way, chapter 13 is governs the liner trade and other trades where the transport of cargo, rather than the hire of a vessel, is at the centre of the parties' agreement.

It follows from the NMC sec. 322, sub-sec. 1 and sec. 347, sub-sec. 1 that the rules on the liability of the carrier in chapter 13 apply as mandatory applicable law to voyage chartering within Scandinavia. However, the rules on forum are specifically

---

[741] Hague Visby Rules Art. 10(3).

omitted, and will thus only come into play if a bill of lading is issued and the bill of lading is transferred to a third party.

3. Agreements on jurisdiction – an overview of sec. 310

Sec. 310 (13:60) gives rules on jurisdiction regarding the liner, general cargo and tramp trades. It holds three distinct regulations.

Firstly, sec. 310 give rules on direct jurisdiction. It follows from sec. 310, sub-sec. 4, that the Scandinavian Courts may hear proceedings regarding a contract of carriage falling within the NMC chapter 13 if any of the places mentioned in sec. 310, sub-sec. 1 falls within the Court's jurisdiction. The places mentioned in sub-sec. 1 are: 1) The venue (principal place of business) of the defendant, 2) the place where the contract of carriage was entered into, provided that the defendant has a place of business or an agency there, 3) the agreed place for the delivery of the goods to the carrier and 4) the agreed or actual place of delivering the goods to the consignee or receiver.

Secondly, sec. 310 provides a mandatory option on Court jurisdiction. Thus, at the option of the claimant, a lawsuit may be brought before either the place designated for that purpose in the parties' contract, or at any of the places mentioned in sub-sec. 1.

Finally, sec. 310 holds rules on the incorporation of jurisdiction clauses from charter-parties into bills of lading. According to sec. 310, sub-sec. 3, the carrier may only invoke a jurisdiction clause in a charter-party, as against the holder of a bill of lading, if the jurisdiction clause has been incorporated by direct reference.

4. The basic features of sec. 311

The Nordic Maritime Codes sec. 311 (sec. 13:61) hold provisions on the validity of arbitration agreements entered into before the incident in dispute took place, governing primarily the validity of arbitration agreements in transports to or from a Scandinavian Country.

The Norwegian Maritime Code, sec. 311[742]

Section 310 notwithstanding, the parties may agree in writing that disputes shall be settled by arbitration. It shall be regarded as part of the arbitration agreement that arbitration proceedings can be instituted at the discretion of the plaintiff in one of the States where a place as mentioned in the first para-

---

[742] Translation taken from *Bilton/Røsæg/Solvang (1997)*.

graph of section 310 is located, and that the arbitration tribunal shall apply the provisions of the present Chapter.

The second, third and sixth paragraphs of Section 310 shall apply correspondingly.

The provisions of the first paragraph do not apply if neither the agreed place of receipt for carriage nor the agreed or actual place of delivery according to the third paragraph of Section 252 is in Norway, Denmark, Finland or Sweden.

As mentioned,[743] arbitration agreements are rare in documents originally designed for the liner trade. For practical purposes sec. 311 thus governs the validity of arbitration clauses in charter-parties, which have been incorporated into bills of lading.

Sec. 311 provides two formal criteria and two criteria of substance. The formal requirements are that the arbitration agreement should be in writing[744] and that an arbitration agreement in a charter-party must be incorporated by specific reference into the bill of lading, for the carrier to be able to invoke the clause against the bill of lading holder.[745] The criteria of substance are a mandatory option on the seat of the arbitral tribunal and a mandatory choice of law to the benefit of the NMC 1994.[746] Thus, to be accepted by the Scandinavian Courts, the arbitration agreement has to be in writing, it has to point out the Nordic Maritime Code 1994 chapter 13 as applicable law, and it has to leave it open to the claimant to initiate the arbitration procedure either at the place stated in the agreement, or at one of the places mentioned in sec. 310, sub-sec. 1. Especially the requirements of substance may be seen as problematic, since arbitration clauses meeting these requirements only seldom appear in the charter-parties. To avoid making all clauses that do not comply with the requirements null and void, thus leaving the parties to take their dispute to the Courts, the two latter requirements of the rule are worded as rules of incorporation. Generally, as long as a written arbitration agreement is found to exist between the parties, the mandatory choice of law and the mandatory option on the geographical seat of the arbitration tribunal will be regarded as forming a part of the agreement.[747] Stipula-

---

[743] See Chapter I, § 2.

[744] Sec. 311, sub-sec. 1.

[745] Sec. 311, sub-sec. 2, cf. sec. 310, sub-sec. 3.

[746] Sec. 311, sub-sec. 1.

[747] See further above, § 1, point 3.3.

tions to the contrary will be regarded as non-existent, and replaced by the wording of sec. 311, sub-sec. 1.[748]

The reason for regulating arbitration agreements in the NMC 1994 was to avoid evasion of the rule on jurisdiction in sec. 310. Considering the wording of the section, and especially the fact that sec. 311 also applies to arbitration agreements incorporated from a charter-party into a bill of lading, the term "evasion" should not be understood in the narrow sense of the word, as implying some sort of unlawful intentions on either of the parties. Instead, the aim of sec. 311 is to cover all situations where the insertion of an arbitration agreement into the contract of carriage effects a different geographical location or choice of law than if sec. 310 had been applied.

Importantly, the two most prominent features of sec. 311, namely the mandatory choice of law and the mandatory option on the seat of the arbitration tribunal, only apply to transports to or from a Scandinavian Country. In other transports, only the provision that an agreement should be in writing and the provision on the incorporation of arbitration agreements from charter-parties into bills of lading apply.

Below the different criteria will be considered in more detail.

5. The formal criteria

5.1. Agreements to be in writing

Requirements that arbitration agreements should be in writing are common in international trade.

In Finnish and Norwegian law,[749] the general regulation of arbitration agreements contains a requirement for arbitration agreements to be in writing, but in Danish and Swedish law no such requirement exists in the general law on arbitration.

From the discussion above in CHAPTER II, § 2, may bee seen that in Danish law the de facto rule as developed through case law is that arbitration agreements, which are not in writing are rarely recognised. Also, the documentation used in the trade already contains written arbitration agreements when relevant. Introducing the precondition that arbitration agreements in the liner, general cargo and tramp trades should be in writing was thus only a novelty to the Danish and Swedish academics.

What exactly is required for an arbitration agreement to be in writing does not follow from the provision. According to the Danish Maritime Code 1994 travaux préparatoires the arbitration agreement is to be "… confirmed in writing. Such an agreement may for example follow from a clause in the transport document or [the agree-

---

[748] For specific problems with the Danish version of sec 311, see below point 3.3.2.

[749] Norwegian Code of Procedure sec. 452, sub-sec. 2. See above, CHAPTER II, § 4.

agreement may be] entered into through correspondence or through the exchange of telex or fax messages."[750] Thus, under Danish law, the general requirement for writing should not be interpreted any stricter than that the agreement should be evidenced in writing.[751] This written evidence may be provided by any appropriate means, including by electronic means.

Sec. 311 does not provide an exhaustive regulation of the use of arbitration as a means of dispute resolution within the ambit of the Nordic Maritime Code chapter 13, but should, when relevant, be supplemented with the general rules of arbitration law. Above, CHAPTER II, § 4, the requirement under Norwegian law that arbitration agreements should be signed has been discussed and, to an extent, criticised. The question is, whether the Norwegian Court might apply this requirement to arbitration agreements in disputes falling within the scope of the Nordic Maritime Code chapter 13. This writer maintains that the case law on what is in writing under the Norwegian Code of Procedure sec. 452, sub-sec. 2, 1st sentence should not be applied under the Norwegian Maritime Code sec. 311, sub-sec. 1. Firstly, a bill of lading or a sea waybill is issued unilaterally by or for the carrier and is only signed by the carrier's representative. Thus, the reciprocal signature necessary under sec. 452, sub-sec. 2, 1st sentence is not present. It follows, that if the case law under sec. 452, sub-sec. 2, 1st sentence is applied, any arbitration agreement in a bill of lading or sea waybill to which Norwegian law applies is invalid. Secondly, accepting the general Norwegian doctrine would leave the provision for the incorporation of arbitration agreements in sec. 310, sub-sec. 3, as referred to in sec. 311, sub-sec. 3, (see below) devoid of any meaning. The carrier would not be able to invoke the arbitration agreement even if incorporated according to that provision, since the bill of lading, in which the explicit reference to the charter-party's arbitration clause is found, is not signed by both parties. Finally, if the approach under the Norwegian Code of Procedure is applied also under the Norwegian Maritime Code, the whole regulation of sec. 311 would only apply if a bi- or multilateral transport agreements had been signed by all parties involved. When within the container, general cargo and tramp-trades such situations are not the norm. It was surely not the intention of the legislators to regulate in this way.

Instead, the Nordic Maritime Code sec. 311 should be regarded as lex specialis, exhaustively regulating which preconditions of form should be satisfied when entering into arbitration agreements within the scope of the Nordic Maritime Code chapter

---

[750] Danish Maritime Code 1994 travaux préparatoires p. 96. Writer's translation.

[751] See for Finnish law see *Wetterstein* in *Honka (1997),* p. 337.

13. This approach would also best concur with the unification idea otherwise adopted by the Scandinavian States when creating the Codes.

5.2. Incorporation of arbitration agreements from charter-parties into bills of lading

The NMC 1994 sec. 310, sub-sec. 3, governs the incorporation of forum agreements from charter-parties into bills of lading. It specifically applies to jurisdiction clauses, but according to the reference in sec. 311, sub-sec. 2 it applies equally to arbitration agreements. As mentioned above, in CHAPTER I, § 2, jurisdiction agreements are rare in charter-parties, arbitration agreements being the preferred forum agreement within that trade. In effect, therefore, sec. 310, sub-sec. 3 aims at regulating arbitration agreements sought incorporated into tramp bills of lading issued under charter-parties.

The Norwegian Maritime Code 1994 sec. 310, sub-sec. 3
If a bill of lading has been issued under a charter-party containing provisions on the competent court or jurisdiction without the bill of lading expressly stating that these provisions are binding upon the holder of the bill of lading, the carrier may not invoke the provisions against a holder of the bill of lading who acquired it in good faith.

The provision requires that the arbitration agreement in the charter-party is "expressly stating" that the arbitration clause is "binding upon the holder of the bill of lading". The purpose of the provision is to avoid the situation where a holder of a bill of lading unknowingly ends up as a party to an arbitration (or indeed jurisdiction) agreement. As mentioned, the provision is a part of the strengthening of the cargo interests' position as towards the carrier that was carried out in the 1994 Codes. The travaux préparatoires are quite exhaustive on this point:

"If the Bill of Lading holds an explicit provision that the clause [in the charter-party] is binding upon the holder of the Bill of Lading, the holder has been *made aware* of the clause in such a way that it may be presumed that he *makes himself acquainted* with the clause. On the other hand, if the Bill of Lading lacks such an explicit provision and e.g. only contains a general reference to the charter-party, the jurisdiction or arbitration agreement is not binding upon the holder of the Bill of Lading."[752]

---

[752] The Finnish Maritime Code 1994 travaux préparatoires p. 57. Writer's translation and emphasis. See also the Danish Maritime Code 1994 travaux préparatoires p. 54 and the Swedish Maritime Code 1994 travaux préparatoires p. 263.

By requiring that the bill of lading shall "expressly state" that the arbitration clause in the charter-party applies to the legal relationship between the contracting carrier and the holder of the charter-party, it is ensured that the holder of the bill of lading by examining the bill of lading alone is notified that an arbitration agreement applies. If he or she considers the agreement important, further inquiries can be made.

One of the ways in which arbitration agreements may be incorporated from a charter-party into a bill of lading under English law is by specific reference, see above, Chapter II, § 3. Thus in THE RENA K and THE NERANO the English Courts accepted that the arbitration agreement in the charter-party had been incorporated into the bill of lading by these provisions:

In THE RENA K:[753]
"All terms, clauses, conditions and exceptions *including the Arbitration Clause* ... of the Charter-Party dated London 13 April 1977 are hereby incorporated ...".

In THE NERANO:[754]
"All terms and conditions, liberties, exceptions *and arbitration clause* of the Charter-party, dated as overleaf, are herewith incorporated ...".

It is required in sec. 311, sub-sec. 3 that the bill of lading should contain a statement according to which the arbitration clause in the charter-party is *binding* upon the holder of the bill of lading. However, it should be expected that the Danish or Norwegian Courts would accept incorporating clauses as the above stated as satisfactory. The incorporation of the stated provisions clearly signifies that these provisions are binding. Since most of the relevant transport documentation has been drafted to match the criteria set out by English law, one should not expect the requirement for specific reference to cause any unpredicted problems within the trade.

Above, CHAPTER II, § 3 point 3.3.2, the English case THE MERAK[755] is mentioned. In THE MERAK, the reference in the bill of lading to the charter-party said: "All terms, conditions, clauses and exceptions ... contained in the said charter-party apply to this Bill of Lading and are deemed to be incorporated herein." The arbitration clause in the charter-party read: "Any dispute arising out of this Charter or any Bill of Lading issued hereunder shall be referred to arbitration." As the arbitration clause was worded to also cover disputes arising under the bill of lading, the Court

---

[753] [1978] 1 Lloyd's Law Reports 545 QBD.

[754] [1996] 1 Lloyd's Law Reports 1 CA.

[755] [1964] 2 Lloyd's Law Reports 527 CA.

accepted the reference as sufficient to incorporate the clause into the bill. This mode of incorporation will not fulfil the conditions set out in sec. 310. Even if the general rules of interpretation of contracts would deem the arbitration clause to be incorporated, the holder of the bill of lading would not be made aware of the arbitration clause by studying the bill of lading text. In the interest of protecting the cargo owners and cargo interests an explicit reference to the arbitration clause must be made.

It follows from sec. 310, sub-sec. 3, as referred to in sec. 311, sub-sec. 3, that an explicit reference is only necessary if the carrier wants to invoke the arbitration clause as against a holder of the bill of lading in good faith. Thus, if the holder of the bill of lading is already aware of the arbitration clause, the requirement for explicit reference does not apply. As yet, no published case law has dealt with this point, and a definite determination of what is good faith in this respect is wanting. However, considering that the requirement has been inserted into the Nordic Maritime Codes 1994 as a part of the general strengthening of the cargo interests' position as towards the carrier, it is suggested that the holder of the bill of lading will be in good faith unless he or she has knowledge of the existence and applicability of the specific arbitration clause in the relevant charter-party. A general knowledge of the trade and the clauses and documentation normally used does not suffice. Unless the parties are long-term business partners, trading on the usual conditions or the holder of the bill of lading for other reasons ought to have been aware of the incorporation of the arbitration clause *in question*, a specific reference is indispensable.

Until the introduction of the NMC sec. 310, sub-sec. 3, as referred to in NMC sec. 311, sub-sec. 3, the position of the law regarding the incorporation of arbitration clauses from charter-parties into bills of lading was less than clear.[756] Under Norwegian law it seemed that the incorporation would never hold as against a holder of the bill of lading, who was not the charterer under the charter-party, see ND 1957.366 NCA, JALNA, and ND 1970.223 NSC, ARGO. Under Danish law no clear-cut cases existed. In U 1934.865 MCCC, OXELÖSUND, and in ND 1939.339 MCCC, NIRITOS, the issues in question were not strictly whether the carrier could invoke the arbitration agreement in the charter-party as against the bill of lading holder. However, in the latter case the MCCC stated, obiter, that the receivers under the bill of lading *probably* would be free to initiate proceedings before the ordinary Courts, due to their lack of knowledge of, and the unsatisfactory reference to, the arbitration clause. However, in the case it was the charterer who, after succession in the receivers' claim, was directing the claim as against the carrier. The charterer was bound by the arbitration clause even if the consignees *po ssibly* would not have been.

---

[756] See *Rasmussen (1984)*, p. 119 f.

6. The requirements of substance

It follows from the Norwegian Maritime Code sec. 311, that in transports to or from Scandinavia the parties will be deemed to have agreed that the tribunal shall apply the Norwegian Maritime Code chapter 13 to the parties' dispute. Also, the parties will be deemed to have agreed that the tribunal, at the option of the claimant, should be seated at either one of the places mentioned in sec. 310, sub-sec. 1, or at the place(s) actually designated for that purpose in the arbitration agreement. Those two requirements will be discussed here.

6.1. The mandatory choice of law

It follows from sec. 311, sub-sec. 1, that if one wishes to use arbitration as a means of dispute resolution in connection to a *transport to or from Scandinavia*, the dispute will be subject to the regulation of the Nordic Maritime Codes chapter 13. This will be the case even if the parties have entered into an explicit agreement to the contrary. This part of the sec. 311 aims to support the general regulation of the geographical scope of application for chapter 13, as provided in sec. 252. The strict application of the liability regime "in and out" is not unique to the Nordic Maritime Codes. For example, it follows from the Hamburg Rules Art. 2(1), 21 and 22, and from the CMR Convention Art. 1(1). Also the applicability of the US-COGSA is defined thus.[757]

In other contracts of carriage, the party autonomy is less restricted. The parties will be allowed to enter into choice of law agreements according to the rules set out in the NMC sec. 252 (sec. 13:2). It follows from the NMC sec. 252, sub-sec. 3, that in cross trade (trade, which is not destined to or from Denmark, Finland, Norway or Sweden) the parties may enter into an agreement that the Hague-Visby based regulation of another, specifically mentioned Hague-Visby state should apply. Finally, it follows from the NMC sec. 252, sub-sec. 2, *ex contrario*, that if the transport takes place from a port in a non-Hague-Visby state *and* if no transport document has been issued in a Hague-Visby state, *and* if the transport document in fact issued does not contain a paramount clause to the benefit of the Hague-Visby rules, the parties are outside the scope of the Nordic Maritime Codes chapter 13, and may thus enter into any choice of law agreement that may suit them. However, considering the factual situation of the trade, this possibility will seldom be used.

---

[757] 46 U.S.C. app § 1300 (1994). See also the INDUSSA case, 377 F. 2d 200 (2d Cir. 1967).

When discussing the legitimacy of sec. 311, one must keep its scope in mind. The provision only applies to transports to or from Denmark, Finland, Norway or Sweden, see sec. 311, sub-sec. 4. Even if the legal relationship between the parties is most closely connected to another state, there will still be a real connection to a Scandinavian State for the regulation to apply. Given that perspective, the deemed choice of the NMC 1994 is acceptable.

6.2. The mandatory option on the seat of the tribunal

In international arbitration the seat of the tribunal is normally considered to be an important, although out of principle not indispensable, feature of the arbitration agreement. The provision in the NMC sec. 311, sub-sec. 1, that the parties should have been deemed to agree that the claimant has a wide range of options as to the seat of the tribunal, does not concur with the approach of international arbitration law. However, the provision is not uncommon within transport conventions. Similar constructions may be found both in the Hamburg Rules 1978 Art. 22, para. 3, from where the regulation in sec. 311 has its inspiration, in the Multimodal Convention 1980 Art. 27, para. 2, and in the regulation of arbitration agreements found in the Warsaw system, see the Warsaw Convention Art. 32, 2nd sentence, and also the Guadalajara Convention 1961 art IX, para. 3, 2nd sentence. The newly drafted Montreal Convention on air transport of May 28, 1999 also provides an option on the seat of the arbitration tribunal in Art. 34, para. 2.

A mandatory provision that the parties have more options on the seat of the tribunal than what follows from the arbitration agreement cannot be defended from a strict arbitration law point of view. Providing an option on the seat of the arbitration does not correspond to the normal intentions of the parties when choosing (international) arbitration as a means of dispute resolution. The parties are barred from securing that a forum they might consider "neutral" or an international arbitration institution after their choice will in the end deal with the dispute. Also, multiple proceedings may occur if arbitration is initiated by one of the parties according to the mandatory option and by the other party at the seat of the tribunal as agreed in the arbitration agreement. Finally, as mentioned below in point 7, enforcing an award given at a different place and/or according to different rules than what follows from the parties' agreement may prove to be difficult.

The legislators drafting the NMC 1994 sec. 311, or indeed the conventions mentioned, did not set out to regulate arbitration law issues. They were concerned with regulating the liability of the carrier in the relevant transport liability systems. When seen in that perspective, the regulation set out in sec. 311 is less problematic.

Firstly, the documentation used in the contracts of carriage covered by the substantive rules of the NMC chapter 13, sec. 311 mainly governs arbitration clauses incorporated from charter-parties into bills of lading in the tramp trade. Unless the holder of the bill of lading is also one of the original parties to the charter-party, in which case sec. 311 is often inapplicable, he or she will not have taken any part in the negotiations under the charter-party, and thus he or she will not have any expectations as to the seat of the tribunal that may be dissatisfied by the application of sec. 311, sub-sec. 1.

Secondly, in all the cases mentioned, where an option on the seat of the arbitration is required or deemed to exist, including sec. 311, the regulation of arbitration agreements corresponds to a very strict regulation of jurisdiction agreements. If that regulation could be circumvented by the parties entering into an arbitration agreement instead, little would be achieved.

Thirdly, the stringent rules on jurisdiction and jurisdiction clauses reflect the fact that the carrier's liability may be illusory if the cargo interests cannot establish a forum at a convenient place. As put by the Norwegian committee:

"Exclusive jurisdiction clauses often render it difficult for the cargo owners to enforce the rights as towards the carrier that the transport contract and the law gives. One of the reasons being that much of the liner trade is carried out as "cross-trade", meaning that ships registered in states far away from where the transport is carried out, and [therefore, that] it may present practical difficulties to carry out a law suit against the carrier in a far away state. Another reason is that exclusive jurisdiction clauses often are combined with choice of law provisions stating that the law of the carrier's [domicile] shall apply, or which for other reasons may entail that the Hague-Visby Rules are not applied. Within the Hague-Visby trade, and other trades which are subject to mandatory statutory regulation in the states to which the carriage is connected, this combination has often lead to [a situation where] the cargo owner has had a [...] position as towards the carrier which was substantially less [beneficial] than that which follows from the Hague-Visby Rules or the Hague Rules."[758]

These concerns are of course real. The stricter liability regime introduced by the Danish, Finnish, Norwegian and Swedish legislators in the NMC 1994 chapter 13 will be illusive if it is not combined with rules on forum and choice of law. The NMC 1994 chapter 13 weighs the application of the national rules against international comity within international commercial arbitration and finds for the national rules. This, of course, is the prerogative of the legislators and should be accepted. However, the problems of an arbitration law nature described above still remain, as does the problems with the international conventions discussed below in point 7.

---

[758] Norwegian Maritime Code 1994 travaux préparatoires, p. 51. Writer's translation. See on the importance of the seat of the tribunal *Philip (1992),* on p. 125.

No case law has as yet been published concerning the NMC sec. 311. It remains to be seen how the Scandinavian Courts will approach the problems arising from it. On an international scale, players in the market, arbitrators and non-Scandinavian Courts may find some comfort in the fact that sec. 311 is a strictly national law rule, and that the most problematic features of the rule only apply in transports to or from a Scandinavian port.

7. Problems regarding the effective application of the NMC sec. 311

7.1. The NMC sec. 311 and International Conventions on Arbitration

Although the Hamburg Rules have inspired the regulation set out in sec. 311, its basis is not in convention, but in national law. The provision in the New York Convention Art. VII(1) and in the European Convention on International Commercial Arbitration Art. X(7), according to which special conventions prevail over the general provisions set out in those conventions, does therefore not apply to the Nordic Maritime Code sec. 311. Obviously it must be presumed that the obligations undertaken by the Scandinavian States under those conventions should still be satisfied. Denmark, Finland, Norway and Sweden have all ratified the New York Convention, and Denmark and Finland have ratified the European Convention on International Commercial Arbitration as well. When within the scope of application of these conventions, sec. 311 should not be applied by the Courts if doing so would lead to results incompatible with same conventions.[759]

The requirements that arbitration agreements should be in writing and that an arbitration agreement in a charter-party may only be incorporated into a bill of lading by specific reference do not clash with any of the conventions on arbitration entered into by the Scandinavian States. The requirement is more lax than that of the New York Convention Art. II. The reader will remember that the New York Convention Art. VII(1) holds a "more favourable right-provision", thus endorsing that any less stringent formal requirements in the national law of a High Contracting Party may be applied. The European Convention does not have a definite requirement for the arbitration agreement to be in writing.[760] Thus, the requirement of sec. 311 that the arbitration agreement should be in writing is not problematic. Instead, the problem-area is the mandatory choice of law and the mandatory option on the seat of the tribunal.

---

[759] See explicitly the Norwegian Code of Procedure sec. 36a.

[760] See the European Convention Art. I(2)(a).

It follows from the European Convention on International Commercial Arbitration Art. VII, that the parties to the arbitration agreement "shall be free to determine ... the law to be applied by the arbitrators to the substance of the dispute. Failing any indication by the parties as to the applicable law, the arbitrators shall apply the proper law under the rule of conflict that they deem applicable. In both cases the arbitrators shall take account of the terms of the contract and trade usage." The recognition of party autonomy forms an important part of the regulation in the European Convention. If the parties have entered into a choice of law agreement regarding the substance of the case, the mandatory choice of law in sec. 311 is not applicable. It is however probable that the mandatory choice of law may be applied in the absence of an explicit choice of law, if, according to the arbitrators, the rules of conflicts of law point at Scandinavian law. Also, according to the European Convention Art. IV(1), the parties to the arbitration agreement are free to submit their dispute to either institutionalised or ad hoc arbitration. It follows that the seat of the tribunal is clearly a matter for the parties to decide. Tribunals seated in Denmark or Finland should therefore not apply the mandatory option on the seat of the arbitration set out in sec. 311, nor should they apply the mandatory choice of law in the face of the parties' agreement to the contrary.

High Contracting Parties to the New York Convention undertake to recognise arbitration agreements in writing given that the agreement concerns a defined legal relationship and that the subject-matter of the dispute is capable of settlement by arbitration, see Art. II(1). As a consequence, the Courts of a contracting State will have to refer the parties to arbitration unless the Court finds that " ... the said agreement is null and void, inoperative or incapable of being performed." Art. II does not, as a rule, leave it open to the Courts to refuse to recognise an agreement to arbitrate solely due to the fact that mandatory rules in the lex fori have not been respected. Art. II of the New York Convention should generally be construed to apply the same choice of law principles as does Art.V on the recognition and enforcement of arbitral awards.[761] Article V holds an exhaustive list of situations in which the Courts of a contracting State may refuse the recognition and/or enforcement of an arbitral award. Here only the provisions relevant to the present discussion will be considered.

Article V (in extract)

1. Recognition and enforcement ... may be refused ...[if]
   a. The parties to the agreements referred to ... were, under the law applicable the them, under some incapacity, or the said agreement *is not valid under the law the which the*

---

[761] See above, CHAPTER II, point 2.3. and *Gaja (1984)*, para. C.2.

parties have subjected it or, failing any indication thereon, under *the law of the country where the award was made …* [762]

b. …

c. …

d. The composition of the arbitral authority or the arbitral procedure was not in accordance with the agreement of the parties, or, failing such agreement, was not in accordance with the law of the country where the arbitration took place …

e. …

2. Recognition and enforcement … may also be refused … [if] …

a. The recognition or enforcement of the award would be contrary to the public policy of *that country.* [763].

It follows that the Scandinavian Courts must accept a choice of law made in the arbitration agreement. The Courts may not alter this choice of law according to sec. 311, and they may not refuse to recognise the arbitral agreement or award solely due to the fact that the domestic rule of sec. 311 has not been applied.

The same applies to the mandatory option on the seat of the tribunal. According to Art. V(1)(d), recognition may be refused if " … the composition of the arbitral tribunal or the arbitral procedure was not in accordance with *the agreement of the parties*". [764] The New York Convention does not allow the Courts of the contracting States to refuse recognition and/or enforcement on the grounds that rules of the *lex fori* are not complied with, unless, of course, the parties have in fact chosen the law of the *fori*. The only remaining option for the Scandinavian Courts if wanting to refuse recognition and/or enforcement for non-compliance with sec. 311 is the *ordre public* provision in Art. V(2)(b). However, the reservation for *ordre public* in Art. V(2)(b) must be kept an ordre public-reservation in the traditional, restricted sense. It does not provide an opportunity for refusal of recognition or enforcement just because mandatory domestic law of the *lex fori* has not been applied. Instead, the provision allows the Courts of the Contracting States to refuse recognition if the effects of the arbitration agreement clash with basic principles of justice in the *lex fori*. [765] Thus, the Court may refuse recognition etc. if otherwise results would occur, which are not only contrary to the laws of the *fori,* but which also appear fundamentally

---

[762] Writer's emphasis.

[763] Writer's emphasis.

[764] Writer's emphasis.

[765] *van den Berg (1981),* p. 376, *Moss (1999),* p. 132, *Philip (1976),* p. 65, *Nielsen (1997),* p. 62.

unacceptable. The interests protected by sec. 311 are not so imperative as to warrant the use of the *ordre public* rule.

It may be concluded that the Scandinavian Courts must accept arbitration agreements fulfilling the criteria set out in the New York Convention and/or the European Convention as they stand. Also, foreign arbitral awards fulfilling those conventions' criteria should be recognised and enforced by the Scandinavian Courts.

At the same time, it is clear that foreign Courts may refuse to enforce the findings of an arbitral tribunal, which, despite the parties' clear choice of law to the contrary, has applied the mandatory choice of law in sec. 311. The same applies if the seat of the tribunal is not the one set out in the parties' agreement, but instead a seat pointed out according to the option in sec. 311, see the New York Convention Art. V(1)(d). Outside situations where the arbitration clause and/or procedure is in fact governed by sec. 311, the modifications provided by sec. 311 are contrary to the parties' agreement.

7.4. Applying sec. 311 outside the scope of application of international arbitration conventions

7.4.1. Applying sec. 311 to the arbitration agreement

When confronted with the question of recognition and/or enforcement of national or other arbitration agreements or awards outside the scope of the New York or other applicable international conventions, the Scandinavian Courts may apply sec. 311. Still, having chosen the route of contractual modification and incorporation, a claim that an arbitration agreement not corresponding to the provision is *invalid* should not be accepted. A lawsuit before the ordinary Courts concerning a subject matter covered by the arbitration agreement should still be dismissed.[766]

A party claiming that the arbitration agreement should be interpreted in accordance with sec. 311 may, however, expect the approval of the Courts. It is noteworthy that this modification will only have real effect if one of the fora referred to in sec. 311, sub-sec. 2, and sec. 310, sub-sec. 2, is within a Scandinavian State, and the arbitration subsequently is initiated there. Arbitral tribunals seated elsewhere may pay very little, if any, attention to a foreign Court stating that the seat or the choice of

---

[766] In Scandinavian law, the legal effect of a valid agreement to arbitrate is that disputes covered by the agreement will be dismissed from the Courts, see the Danish Arbitration Act sec. 1, sub-sec. 1; the Finnish Arbitration Act 1992 sec. 5(1) reg. arbitration, which is to be carried out in Finland and sec. 51(1) reg. arbitration, which is to be carried out abroad; the Swedish Arbitration Act 1999, sec. 4(1), which according to sec. 49 governs both Swedish and international arbitration and the Norwegian Code of Procedure sec. 452 (3) in conjunction with sec. 92. (Implied).

law of the arbitral tribunal should not be the one following from the arbitral agreement. Indeed, it is suggested that even arbitrators seated in the Scandinavian states, dependent on the circumstances, might choose to disregard the provision out of consideration paid to the party autonomy as established in international arbitration law and the possible difficulties of international enforcement of an award based on another law than the one originally chosen by the parties. This would seem an option to tribunals seated in Denmark, if the parties have agreed that the tribunal shall give its ruling according to equity/*ex bono et æqvo*,[767] however, tribunals seated in Norway may be less inclined to do so, according to Norwegian law's more stringent approach to the tribunal's obligation to apply the law as it stands.[768]

7.4.2. Sec. 311 and the arbitral award

As long as outside the scope of the New York or other international Conventions on arbitration, however limited that area might be, the Courts may refrain from enforcing an arbitral award according to any applicable provision in national law. Sec. 311 does not in itself provide for the setting aside of arbitral awards given in a different place or under different rules than what follows from the provision. It should be investigated whether the Danish, Finnish, Norwegian or Swedish general rules on arbitration law cater for the possibility of refusing recognition of "non-convention awards" regarding a subject-matter falling within the Nordic Maritime Code on the grounds that the choice of law or the seat of the arbitral tribunal is not in accordance with sec. 311.[769]

---

[767] *Hjejle (1987)*, p. 88 ff.

[768] *Mæland (1988)*, p. 198.

[769] Sec. 311 allows, through the reference to sec. 310, sub-sec. 1, that the arbitration be held the place designated for the arbitral tribunal in the arbitration agreement, regardless of where this place is situated. Real discrepancy between the optional places for the seat of the arbitral tribunal and an arbitration award given in accordance with the arbitral agreement can therefore hardly arise.

7.4.2.1. Finnish and Swedish law

The grounds set out for invalidating and hence refusing the recognition of an arbitral award in both the Swedish Arbitration Act sec. 33 and sec. 34[770] and the Finnish Arbitration Act s. 40 and 41[771] do not seem to provide for setting aside an award if the requirements of sec. 311 have not been satisfied.

[770] **33 §.** En skiljedom är ugiltig
1. om den innefattar prövning av en fråga som enligt svensk lag inte får avgöras av skiljemän,
2. om skiljedomen eller det sätt på vilket skiljedomen tillkommit är uppengart oförenligt med grunderna för rättsordningen i Sverige, eller
3. om skiljedomen inte uppfyller föreskrifterna om skriftlighet och undertecknande i 31 § förste stycket.

34 §. En skiljedom som inte kan angripas enligt 36 § skal efter klander helt eller delvis upphäves på talan av en part
1. om den inte omfattas av ett giltigt skiljeavtal mellan parterna,
2. om skiljemännen har meddelat dom efter utgången av den tid som parterna bestämt eller om de annars har överskridit sitt uppdrag,
3. om skiljeförfarande enligt 47 § into borde ha ägt rum i Sverige,
4. om en skiljeman har utsetts i strid med parternas överenskommelse eller denne lag,
5. om en skiljeman på grund av någon omständighet som anges i 7 eller 8 § har varit obehörig, eller
6. om det annars, utan partens vållande, i handläggingen har förekommit något gel som sannolikt har inverkat på utgången. ...

[771] **§ 40.** The arbitral award is null and void:
1. to the extent that the arbitrators have decided in an arbitral award a matter which cannot be settled by arbitration under the law of Finland;
2. to the extent that the arbitral award is to be considered to be in conflict with the public policy of Finland;
3. if the arbitral awards is so ambiguous or incomplete that it does not become clear therefrom what has been awarded in the matter; or
4. if the arbitral award has not been made in writing or it has not been signed by the arbitrators. ...

§ 41. The arbitral award may be reversed by the action of a party:
1. if the arbitrators have exceeded their authority;
2. if an arbitrator has not been appointed in due order;
3. if an arbitrator has been disqualified to act as an arbitrator according to section 10, but the challenge made in due order by a party has not been accepted prior to the rendering of the arbitral award, or it a party has learnt about the grounds for disqualification too late in order to be able to challenge the arbitrator prior to the rendering of the arbitral award; or
4. if the arbitrators have not reserved a party the necessary opportunity to plead his case. ...

The regulation of the Finnish Arbitration Act 1992 sec. 40 and 41 and the Swedish Arbitration Act 1999 sec. 33 and 34 are exhaustive.[772] It may hardly be argued that sec. 311 (sec.13:61) should be considered to contain a rule that amounts to public policy.[773] It cannot be claimed that the subject matter is not arbitrable.[774] Also, having chosen the approach of contractual modification it is hard to maintain that there is no valid agreement to arbitrate between the parties.[775] The only option for the party contesting the arbitration agreement seems to be the argument that the tribunal has acted in excess of its authority. Arguably, a tribunal, acting contrary to the requirements of sec. 311, has acted in excess of its jurisdiction. If this argument is not accepted, once an arbitral award is duly given in accordance with the parties' agreement, sec. 311 (sec. 13:61), even in national arbitration, seems to have concluded its role.

7.4.2.2. Danish and Norwegian law

7.4.2.2.1. The provisions
Under Norwegian law, arbitration awards may be set aside ex officio according to the Norwegian Code of Procedure sec. 467, or challenged according to the Norwegian Code of Procedure sec. 468.

According to sec. 467, no. 4 the arbitral award will be deemed null and *ex officio* if the contents of the award is contrary to law or morality. This is not interpreted as an *ordre public* exception; sec. 467(4) provides a much wider access to deem arbitral awards invalid. Although arbitration as a means of solving a dispute is recognised within areas governed by mandatory law, the provision binds the arbitral tribunal in national arbitration to the use of mandatory Norwegian rules.

---

[772] See *Kurkela/Uoti* p. 81; Swedish Arbitration Act 1999 travaux préparatoires, para 10.2.

[773] Finnish Arbitration Act, sec. 40, sub-sec. 1, no. 2 contains a public policy exception in the narrow sense, aiming at situations where the recognition and/or enforcement of the award would be contrary to fundamental principles of Finnish law, and not just at any situation where the result of the award is contrary to mandatory rules. (See Finnish Arbitration Act travaux préparatoires p. 24 f). The same applies as regards the Swedish Arbitration Act, sec. 33, sub-sec. 1, no. 2, see Swedish Arbitration Act travaux préparatoires, para. 10.2.

[774] Finnish Arbitration Act, sec. 40, sub-sec. 1, no. 1; Swedish Arbitration Act, sec. 33, sub-sec. 1, no. 1.

[775] See the Swedish Arbitration Act, sec. 34, sub-sec. 1, no. 1.

"When the Code of Procedure expresses that the award is invalid if it is contrary to law or morality, the aim is Norwegian mandatory law. Arbitration, namely, is also recognised in areas governed by mandatory law. But the arbitral tribunal has in such situations a duty to apply and follow the law in the same way as the ordinary Courts."[776]

According to *Mæland*[777] this even applies when the parties have agreed that the tribunal shall work as *amiables compositeurs,* making the real contents of that term fairly limited within Norwegian law. Also, sec. 467 is not exhaustive.[778] Provided that the transport falls within the scope of application of sec. 311, it is theoretically possible that the Norwegian Courts will refuse the recognition and enforcement of the award ex officio unless the arbitral tribunal has applied the material rules of the Norwegian Maritime Code chapter 13 to the case.[779]

Reasons for which an award may be challenged after sec. 468 – which is not exhaustive – include, that there is no valid arbitration agreement, that the arbitrators have exceeded their competence, or that statutory or specifically agreed instructions regarding the procedure have been ignored, and it is likely that the errors have influenced the outcome of the tribunal's decision.

It seems that the claim that an award should be set aside due to non-compliance with sec. 311 is best dealt with in the same way as these three examples. Therefore, non-compliance with sec. 311 should only be tried at the action of a party. Indeed, it is maintained that it would be contrary to the raison d'être and structure of sec. 311 if an award falling within the scope of application of sec. 311, but not satisfying its requirements, should be set aside ex officio. The requirement for an option on the seat of the arbitration and the mandatory choice of law in sec. 311 is concerned with arbitration clauses in contracts of carriage, or other arbitration agreements in carriage of goods by sea that have been entered into before the dispute has arisen. After the dispute, the parties may enter into any arbitration agreement of their choice. At the time of the enforcement of the award, the parties would thus be free to enter into a new arbitration agreement, pointing out a seat or a choice of law that differs from the

---

[776] *Mæland (1988)*, p. 197 f. Writer's translation.

[777] *Mæland (1988)*, p. 198.

[778] *Lindboe (1944)*, p. 169; *Schei (1998)*, p. 1183 and 1185.

[779] According to the Norwegian Code of Procedure § 468, arbitral awards may also be reversed by the action of a party in certain cases. However, the provision does not seem to cater for the reversal of arbitration agreements to a greater extent than § 467 when concerned with arbitral agreements under the NMC sec. 311, and will not be discussed in detail here.

regulation given in sec. 311. Consequently, there is no reason why the Court should apply ex officio competence to set aside an award not challenged by either party.

The Danish Arbitration Act 1972 sec. 7, sub-sec. 1, holds national Danish rules on the invalidity of arbitral awards.

The Danish Arbitration Act 1972 sec. 7[780]

An arbitral award is invalid in its entirety or in part, if
1) the arbitration agreement is invalid,
2) the composition of the arbitral tribunal or its handling of the case has not been appropriate for the parties or for one of these, or if it has not been in accordance with the rules applicable to the arbitral tribunal, and the discrepancy may have had substantial influence upon the decision,
3) the tribunal has exceeded its competence, or
4) the award is contrary to *ordre public*.

As a rule, sec. 7 is only applied at the action of a party. However, it is presupposed in the travaux préparatoires that the provision may be applied ex officio if issues of arbitrability or ordre public are involved. Obviously, the reasons set out immediately above why non-compliance with sec. 311 should not be tried ex officio, apply equally strongly to awards tried under the Danish Arbitration Act 1972 sec. 7. Consequently, sec. 7 should only be applied at the action of a party.

Despite the wording, sec. 7 is not exhaustive. The parties may challenge the award for reasons not specifically mentioned in sec. 7. For example it is suggested in the travaux préparatoires that the wording of sec. 7, no. 2 would encompass a situation where the legal basis for the award, including for example the choice of law, has been different from what follows from the parties' agreement.[781] Out of principle, therefore, also the Danish Courts may refuse to recognise and enforce arbitral awards concerning transport to or from a Scandinavian port, if the conditions in the NMC sec. 311 have not been met.

7.4.2.2.2. Summing up

The Courts may only consider rejecting an award on the grounds that the mandatory choice of law and the mandatory option on the seat of the tribunal in sec. 311 has not been complied with if those requirements actually apply to the award. Thus, unless the dispute considers carriage of goods to or from Scandinavia, the problem will not occur. Supposing that the dispute is indeed within the ambit of sec. 311, it must be

[780] Writer's translation.

[781] Danish Arbitration Act 1972 travaux préparatoires 2, col. 896.

considered what approach the Danish and Norwegian Courts should apply when deciding whether to uphold or refuse an arbitral award. It is contended that the Danish and Norwegian Courts should pay consideration to the raison d'être of sec. 311, to the technique applied in the provision and to the principle of *favour arbitrii*. Fortunately, in this case these components generally point in the same direction.

In the NMC sec. 311, the focus has been on effects rather than on criteria of form or substantial validity. The legislators have aspired to achieve the *de facto* application of the liability regime of the NMC chapter 13, rather that laying down stringent requirements *sine qua* the arbitration agreement is null and void. Therefore, the Courts should not focus on the arbitration agreement entered into by the parties, indeed it is suggested that that agreement will seldom comply with the sec. 311 requirements. Instead, it should be investigated if the award as presented to the Courts promotes the effects intended in sec. 311. If the tribunal has in fact applied the NMC chapter 13 to the dispute, a choice of law to the contrary in the arbitration agreement should be overlooked. This approach is most compatible with the modification technique chosen in the provision. However, if chapter 13 – or rules providing for a similar protection of the cargo interests, such as the Hamburg Rules – have not been applied, then it seems probable that the Norwegian and Danish Courts will render the award void.

More problematic is the requirement of optional seats. Obviously, if the seat of the tribunal has not been one of the seats accepted by sec. 311, recognition and/or enforcement may be refused. This would indeed follow from basic principles of arbitration law, as one of the seats accepted by sec. 311 is the seat set out in the arbitration agreement. The question arises though, what happens if the arbitration agreement has not provided for optional seats, but the seat actually used is one of the seats accepted by sec. 13, and subsequently one of the parties protests that he or she would have preferred that another seat had been used? Firstly, it should be considered whether the party's contention has been waived through the party's participation in the arbitral procedure. However, if the party has not participated or has participated but has protested the tribunal's jurisdiction, the effects of the non-compliance must be considered. As a starting point, an award, applying chapter 13 to the parties' dispute, which has been duly given by an arbitral tribunal seated at one of the places accepted by sec. 311, should be recognised and/or enforced by the Danish and Norwegian Courts. The protection of the cargo interests should be taken care of by the application of the liability regime set out in the NMC chapter 13. However, if the party manages to show, that the lack of options on the seat of the tribunal has *effected* a less beneficial position for the cargo interest than they would have had provided the optional seats, the Courts should consider not recognising/enforcing the award. Still, given that the liability regime has been the NMC chapter 13, this should only be done in extraordinary situations, where the seat of the tribunal has been so remote or obscure as to render the party unable to protect his or her interests or so as to make the claim of the cargo interests worthless due to excessive costs.

Thus, in conclusion may be said that the Courts should only refuse to recognise the award, if it may be shown that the non-compliance with sec. 311 has lead to the cargo interest having had a considerably less beneficial position than what would have been the case if the criteria of sec. 311 had been satisfied.

8. Evaluation

Above it has been said that the regulation provided in the Nordic Maritime Codes sec. 311 clashes with general principles of international arbitration law. This it does. But – as also mentioned above – sec. 311 should not be regarded as a piece of arbitration law. The *raison d'être* for sec. 311 is found in considerations, which are not relevant to arbitration as a means of dispute resolution in international commerce, but instead are relevant to the maintenance of a transport liability regime. The purpose of sec. 311 is to strengthen the position of the cargo interest by ensuring that the cargo interests are aware of any applicable arbitration clauses, and to put a plug in the loop-hole out of the liability regime, which might otherwise be provided by arbitration.

Having said that, the potential problems outlined above remain; the mandatory choice of law and the mandatory option on the seat of the tribunal still being at the forefront of these. In an arbitration law perspective, the best thing that may be said for these two mechanisms of sec. 311 is that they are *not* based in convention. Therefore, they will not override the rules of the general international conventions on arbitration. Especially, given the success of the New York Convention, the requirements will not play a significant role in international maritime disputes.

However, the requirements in sec. 311 that the arbitration agreement should be in writing and the provision that arbitration clauses in charter-parties may only be incorporated into bills of lading through specific reference are welcomed.

Firstly, establishing the common formal requirement that arbitration agreements should be in writing has created uniformity within Scandinavia in an area of law in which the general regulation has shown all colours of the spectrum, from the Danish and Swedish lack of formal requirements, through the Finnish liberal formal requirements, ending with the present Norwegian requirement that an arbitration agreement can only be entered into, if, at a certain stage in the process, the parties have signed a document containing, or referring to, the arbitration agreement.

Secondly, as regards the problem of incorporation, even the position of national law within the four jurisdictions has been uncertain.[782] Almost any regulation, creating an increased level of certainty would be appreciated. The route opted for by the Scandinavian legislators has been one that adheres to the practices already established within the documentation used in the trade. This seems as the correct and obvious route. The only complaint this writer can possibly think of, as regards the incorporation provision, is that it has not been drafted so as to apply bi-laterally. Indeed, only the situation where the carrier wishes to invoke the arbitration agreement as towards the holder of the bill of lading has been taken care of. This writer would have preferred if the provision had been worded so as to apply also if the holder of the bill of lading wished to invoke the arbitration agreement as against the carrier. Maybe the legislators assumed that the carrier would always be bound by his own clause, even if only a general incorporation of the provisions of the charter-party into the bill of lading had taken place. Still, the caution expressed by the MCCC in the OXELÖSUND[783] case, and the general caution used by the Norwegian Courts if concerned with the incorporation issue, does suggest that this may not always be so.

Summing up, the regulation of arbitration agreements found in the Nordic Maritime Codes 1994 chapter 13 has its pros and cons. The uniform regulation of the formal requirements and the incorporation problem is definitely a "pro", however, the requirement for a mandatory choice of law and most especially the mandatory seat of the arbitration are "cons". Still – as mentioned – they will probably not be applied very often, so the damage done will in all probability be negligible.

---

[782] E.g. U 1934.865 MCCC and ND 1956.366 CA. See regarding the discussion of what was the required under the former Nordic Maritime Code, *Rasmussen (1984)*, p. 120 ff.

[783] U 1934.865 MCCC.

§ 3. Maritime transport documentation and the New York Convention Art. II(2)

1. Approach

Above in CHAPTER II, § 6, the criteria of form in the New York Convention Art. II(2) have been presented. In this part, those criteria will be applied to the documentation and the arbitration clauses used in maritime transport.

Before commencing it seems convenient to recapitulate this writer's conclusion on the requirements of Art. II(2):[784] 1) The New York Convention Arts. II(1) and II(2) require that both or all parties to an arbitration agreement, actively and in writing, have consented to their dispute being dealt with by arbitration. 2) The requirement for writing may be satisfied by any means of communication which is written or which, by its nature, may be directly converted into writing. 3) The requirement for bi- or multilateral participation in the process of entering into the arbitration agreement may be satisfied either by the parties actually signing the arbitration agreement, or by the parties exchanging documentation – by a medium or in a form that complies with the requirement for writing as presented in no. 2 – that contains of refers to the arbitration agreement.

The requirements applicable to arbitration agreements covered by the New York Convention, as applied in Danish, English and Norwegian law on arbitration agreements, are dealt with elsewhere in this work.[785] However, to better present Art. II(2)

---

[784] See above, Chapter II, § 6, point 3.3.

[785] Chapter II, §§ 2-4.

in its context, short references to case-law and (statutory) regulation from those jurisdictions will be given in *petit* when appropriate.

2. Oral or implied contracts of carriage – with or without reference to general conditions

2.1. Oral or implied contracts of carriage and the New York Convention Art. II(2)

It follows from what has been said above[786] that arbitration agreements entered into by oral, quasi, or implied contracts of carriage do not conform to the requirements of the New York Convention Art. II(2) and thus need not be recognised and enforced by the Courts in States parties to the Convention. E.g. the handing over of goods to the carrier is not sufficient to establish a written agreement to arbitrate under Art. II(2), even if it will generally establish a quasi contract of carriage. Likewise, if a cargo owner calls up a general carrier, MTO or logistics company, and arranges for the company to carry out a transport of the cargo owner's goods according to the carrier's general conditions of carriage, an arbitration agreement in those general conditions does not fulfil the conditions set out in the New York Convention Art. II(2), as there is no reciprocal written confirmation of the agreement to arbitrate. This applies even if the carrier makes the conditions known to the cargo owner. One should keep in mind that this way of entering into contracts of carriage is customary within the container trade.

The carrier may ensure that the arbitration agreement is recognised under the New York Convention Art. II(2) by demanding a written confirmation of the standard conditions of carriage as a prerequisite for entering into the contract of carriage. Although in principle viable, this does not provide for a flexible formation of contract, and indeed, it does not match the informality of the trade. Instead, the carrier will probably have to satisfy him or herself with the fact that the Courts in jurisdictions with lax formal requirements for the formation of arbitration agreements might accept the arbitration clause, and that the conditions of carriage, which are germane to the contract of carriage will normally be considered as agreed, irrespectively of the jurisdiction's view upon arbitration clauses.

---

[786] Chapter II, § 6, point 3.3.

2.2. Arbitration agreements in oral or implied contracts of carriage under Danish, English and Norwegian law

Informal modes of contract formation are prevalent in the container transport. In liner transport of containers, the formation of the contract of carriage normally follows this pattern: The transport customer makes a telephone booking with either the line or the line's agent. The details discussed will be the quantity and type of the cargo to be transported, its destination and the freight. As a rule, no reference to general conditions of carriage will be made in this phone-call. The transport customer then provides the line or the agent with the details necessary for the issuance of the bill of lading (a bill of lading instruction) and upon shipment the bill of lading is issued. To the extent that this is a liner bill of lading, arbitration clauses will not occur, and consequently the situation falls outside the scope of the New York Convention. However, the said pattern repeats itself in multimodal transport. If cargo is transported by land before or after the shipment, the transport customer is likely to engage a logistics company. Within Scandinavia, the NSAB 2000 will generally apply to such transport in addition to mandatory rules. To the extent that Norwegian, Finnish or Swedish law applies, or alternatively, to the extent that the Norwegian, Finnish or Swedish Courts are faced with the issue, disputes will be settled by arbitration (see NSAB 2000 § 31). Dependent on the circumstances, an arbitration agreement may apply to disputes arising within the container trade. Above in § 2, point 5.1, the requirement in the Nordic Maritime Code sec. 311, sub-sec. 1, that arbitration agreements in the liner and tramp-trades should be in writing, has been construed so as to allow arbitration agreements which are evidenced in writing, such as the case when one makes an oral reference to a set of general conditions. Thus, as long as the standard form in question, as for example the NSAB 2000, is deemed to be a part of the parties' contract, an oral reference to the document should suffice so as to make the arbitration clause effective between the parties.[787]

If outside the Nordic Maritime Code sec. 311, the demand for a clear proof of the conclusion of an arbitration agreement found in Danish law makes it difficult to ascertain whether arbitration clauses found in general conditions of carriage that have been referred to orally will be considered as agreed.[788] The stringent rule under the

---

[787] Above in Chapter II, § 4 the requirement of the Norwegian Code of Procedure sec. 452 that arbitration agreements should be in writing has been described. Furthermore, above in Chapter V, § 2, point 5.1, this writer has maintained that the stringent requirements of sec. 452 should not be applied under the Nordic Maritime Code sec. 311. This position is maintained here.

[788] See above, Chapter II, § 2, point 4.2 and point 5.

Norwegian Code of Procedure sec. 452, sub-sec. 2, 1st sentence however renders it quite clear that an arbitration agreement will not be concluded.

Under the Arbitration Act 1996 sec. 5(3), if the parties make an oral agreement or other non-written agreement in which they refer to terms, which are in writing, the criterion for written agreement is fulfilled.[789] Thus, if the parties during the telephone booking-session do in fact agree on certain standard terms, as for example the NSAB, an arbitration agreement in those conditions might be concluded. This seems to collide with the English Court of Appeal's findings in [1979] 1 Lloyd's Law Reports 244 CA, WILLCOCK V. PICKFORDS. In the case, Mrs. Willcock made a telephone call, asking Pickfords Removals Ltd. for an estimate of the costs of moving her personal belongings from UK to New Zealand. Pickfords posted an estimate with reference to their printed general conditions. The Court of Appeal found against the contention that an arbitration agreement had been entered into. However, one must keep in mind, that Mrs. Willcock was a consumer, and that – arguably – the precedence may not apply in the face of the English Arbitration Act 1996. The Court of Appeal might not have reached the same solution if a professional cargo owner had called up for an estimate.

3. Bills of lading, sea waybills and multimodal contracts of carriage

As mentioned before, normally arbitration agreements only find their way into a bill of lading through a reference to (the arbitration clause in) a charter-party. In liner bills of lading, jurisdiction clauses are applied.

Bills of lading are issued unilaterally by or on behalf of the carrier. Therefore, if the bill of lading itself provides contract of carriage, an agreement to arbitrate provided in, or referred to in, the bill of lading will not meet the requirements set out in Art. II(2). The bill of lading is obviously a written document, but there is no reciprocity in the formation of the contract, as it is issued by or for the carrier only.

However, if it is not the bill of lading that governs the legal relationship between the carrier and the person entitled to the cargo, the issuance of the bill of lading in itself does not bring an already established arbitration agreement to an end. If, under a voyage charter-party or a contract of affreightment for example, the owner issues a bill of lading to the charterer, the arbitration clause in the charter-party still applies as between the owner and the charterer.[790] Likewise, if, in other trades, a transport

---

[789] See above, Chapter II, § 3, point 1.

[790] Regarding when a bill of lading does *not* govern the parties' relationship, see the U 1939.1130 MCCC.

agreement has been entered in another form, which satisfies Art. II(2), obviously the issuance of a bill of lading will not invalidate such agreement.

Sea waybills should in this respect be considered in the same way as bills of lading. Often, sea waybills are in form hardly distinguishable from a bill of lading. They are issued in the same way, unilaterally by or for the carrier,[791] and arbitration agreements are normally introduced through incorporation.[792]

Multimodal transport documents are generally drafted using the bill of lading as a template. They are laid out in much the same way, and they too are unilaterally signed by or for the carrier. Indeed, some of them even bear the heading: "Bill of Lading".[793] However, multimodal documents normally opt for jurisdiction clauses,[794] so the question of whether Art. II(2) of the New York Convention is abided with seldom arises. Multimodal transport documents are in that respect on a par with liner bills of lading and sea waybills.

An arbitration clause in a bill of lading (however impractical) fulfils the requirement for arbitration agreements entered into before the dispute to be in writing, set out in the NMC § 311, sub-sec. 1. It would also satisfy the general requirement for arbitration agreements to be in writing set out in the English Arbitration Act 1996 sec. 5.

4. Charter-parties

4.1. In general

Arbitration agreements are the absolute norm within the charter-party trade.

As a starting point, a charter-party deals with the legal relationship between the owner and the charterer and the charter-party is signed by these parties either in person or through representatives. When concerned with disputes within the relationship between the owner and the charterer, an arbitration clause in the charter-party should thus be considered binding under the New York Convention Art. II(2). Also, the agreements generally fulfil the requirements set out under Danish, English and Norwegian law. Still, arbitration agreements or clauses in the charter-party trade do raise certain issues. Firstly, it must be ensured that the dispute is between the original par-

---

[791] See e.g. Genwaybill; Maersk Line non-negotiable Sea Waybill; and P&O Containers Waybill.

[792] See e.g. Genwaybill, which is issued under the Gencon voyage charter party.

[793] See Wilhelmsen Lines "Bill of Lading for Combined Transport".

[794] See e.g. Combiconwaybill cl. 5; Combiconbill cl. 5; Multidoc 95 cl. 5; or Multiwaybill 95 cl. 5.

ties to the charter-party, or between persons, whom, according to the applicable law, are regarded to have succeeded in the position of these parties. Secondly, to the extent that bills of lading have been issued and transferred, it is likely that any dispute regarding the transport liability will arise out of the bill of lading and not out of the charter-party. As stated above, the bill of lading does not fulfil the requirement for reciprocity set out in the New York Convention Art. II(2). Therefore, to the extent that the dispute is under the bill of lading rather than under the charter-party, the arbitration agreement will not be accepted under Art. II(2). Below, different situations highlighting these issues will be considered.

4.2. Sub-chartering

If the Owner and the Charterer enter into an agreement on charter-party A, and the Charterer in turn enters into a charter-party with the Sub-charterer on charter-party B, normally difficulties will not arise. *(Diagram A)*. The Owner and the Charterer according to charter-party A are bound by any arbitration agreement in that document, and the Charterer and Sub-charterer will have to sort out any differences according to the arbitration agreement in charter-party B. However, according to the criteria for reciprocity in the New York Convention, there is no arbitration agreement in existence as between the Owner and the Sub-charterer.

Diagram A

Owner ——————▶ Charterer ——————▶ Sub-charterer
       C/P A   **C/P B**

If, instead, the Charterer chooses to refer, in charter-party B, to the conditions of carriage set out in charter-party A, the conditions in the New York Convention are still satisfied. The charter-parties are back-to-back, and the arbitration agreement in charter-party A is incorporated into charter-party B. *(Diagram B)*. Disputes between the Owner and the Charterer, respectively between the Charterer and the Sub-charterer should be settled by arbitration in the manner described in the arbitration agreement in charter-party A.

Still, a Sub-charterer wanting to direct a cargo claim against the Owner, may not be able to convince the Courts that such a claim should be arbitrated. The Owner is not a party to the Sub-charter-party, even if the conditions of carriage of that charter-party are the same as the conditions of carriage in the charter-party the Owner has entered into with the Charterer. The reciprocity criterion fails to be satisfied by this construction. This applies even if, according to the applicable law, the Owner and the Sub-charterer are considered to be in a contractual or quasi-contractual relationship.

To the extent that the arbitration agreement and/or the law applicable at the seat of the tribunal allow consolidation of arbitration procedures, this would certainly be a situation where it would be proper to apply such rules. However, no such option follows from the New York Convention as such, as indeed, no such general rule follows from the Danish, English and Norwegian statutory regulation of arbitration.

Diagram B

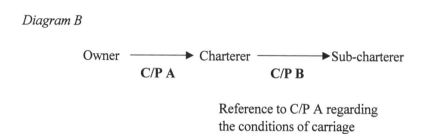

4.3. The impact of bills of lading
Above, point 4.1, it has been stated that when the parties' contractual relationship derives from the bill of lading and not the charter-party, the reciprocity criterion in the New York Convention Art. II(2) fails to be satisfied. One should keep in mind, that for the bill of lading to govern the parties' relationship, the bill should be issued or transferred to a third-party. Thus, as long as any bill of lading is on the hands of the charterer, the bill of lading is only a receipt. The charter-party governs the relationship between the Owner and the Charterer, and disputes arising out of the parties' contract of carriage should be dealt with by arbitration according to the charter-party's arbitration clause. *(Diagram C).*

Diagram C

$$\begin{array}{c} \text{C/P} \\ \text{Owner} \Longrightarrow \text{Charterer} \\ \text{(tramp) B/L} \end{array}$$

However, if the bill of lading has been transferred *(Diagram D)* or issued *(Diagram E)* to a third party, a different situation arises. The relationship between the owner and the holder of the bill of lading is now governed by the bill of lading. An arbitration agreement sought incorporated from the charter-party into the bill of lading does not fulfil the requirement of Art. II(2), and *could* thus be disregarded by the Courts. Still, as between the Owner and the Charterer, the arbitration clause applies.

Diagram D

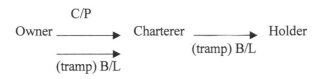

Diagram E

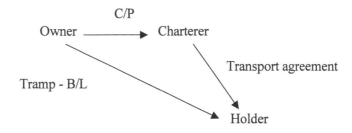

The problem illustrated in Diagram E may easily be varied. One of the more common variations is that the Owner issues a bill of lading to a sub-charterer, on behalf of the master. *(Diagram F)*. For the purposes of Art. II(2), the tramp bill of lading may simply be ignored, leaving two separate arbitration agreements in two separate charter-parties. Thus, under the New York Convention this situation does not differ from the situation discussed under Diagram A. The Owner and Charterer are bound by any arbitration clause in charter-party A, whereas the Charterer and the Sub-charterer must bring their disputes to arbitration according to the arbitration clause in charter-party B.

Diagram F

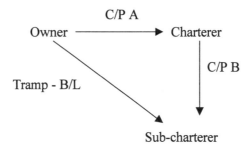

Danish and Norwegian law as regards the incorporation of arbitration clauses from charter-parties into bills of lading has been described above, in § 2. It follows from the Nordic Maritime Code sec. 310, sub-sec. 3, as referred to in sec. 311, sub-sec. 3, that an arbitration clause in a charter-party may be invoked as against a holder of the tramp bill of lading if it has been incorporated by specific reference. It follows from the English Arbitration Act 1996, sec. 6(2) that incorporation of arbitration agreements by reference is possible. As a rule, incorporation is best done by specific reference, but incorporation by general reference is also possible under certain preconditions, see above Chapter II, § 4, point 4.2.

5. Electronic documentation and communication

Above it has been concluded that the New York Convention Art. II(1) and II(2) approve of any form of communication which is in writing or may be directly converted into writing, regardless of how it is transmitted. Out of principle, there seem to be no reason why electronic media cannot fulfil the requirements for writing in Art. II. Consequently, a digital signature may be used to sign an arbitration agreement within the meaning of Art. II(2) and an arbitration agreement may be entered into by e.g. the parties' exchange of E-mail messages. However, throughout this process reciprocity must be maintained. A carrier who, after having entered into an oral contract of carriage, forwards his or her general conditions of carriage attached to an e-mail to the transport customer, whom, in turn, makes a print-out of these must be regarded to have the exact same legal position as does a carrier who sends the general conditions by post. Consequently, any arbitration clause in the general conditions will only be agreed, under the New York Convention Art. II(2), if the general conditions are accepted by the transport customer in a form of writing.

As is the case regarding other means of communication, it must ultimately depend upon an evaluation of the specific contractual technique applied in each case, whether the requirement for writing and reciprocity has been fulfilled. In the following, the Bolero bill of lading will be used an example of a form of electronic documentation applied in the maritime industry. It will be considered to what extent arbitration agreements in contracts of carriage fulfil the formal criteria set out in the New York Convention Art. II.

6. The Bolero bill of lading and the formal requirements

6.1. The modus operandi of the Bolero bill of lading – an overview

The Bolero System went into operation on September 27th 1999, and is therefore still a fairly new type of transport documentation. In the following section a short general presentation of the Bolero Bill of Lading (BBL) will be given. Readers already familiar with the system may wish to turn directly to point 6.2.

A BBL is, when cut to the core, simply binary data in a given format, stored in a database, which may be communicated to or from physical or legal persons via a server with certain legal effects as a consequence.

The Bolero System is based on party autonomy. All users of the services must be members of the Bolero Association Ltd. They have agreed to the rules laid down in the Bolero Rulebook (mainly governing the legal relationship between the users), the Operating Procedures (mainly regarding the more technical side of the operations), and the association agreement etc. governing the relationship between Bolero and the user. A BOLERO Bill of Lading can only exist within this system. When non-members need to have a B/L that has originated as a Bolero Bill of Lading, a shift to paper-documentation must take place, meaning that the bill of lading must be printed out, signed and then transferred in the usual way.

The BBL is created by the contracting carrier, as is a paper bill of lading. It consists of two main parts: A message header in a fixed EDI format (an E-mail), and an attached document, which may be in any format accepted by the Operational Rules.

The message header contains *inter alia* the relevant @bolero.net addresses, a code, describing the type of document attached, the identification of that document, the digital signature of the carrier and instructions for the Title Registry. The attached document contains the bill of lading text as such. This may, but need not, be similar to a scanned paper bill of lading, or to a CD-ROM based bill.

The contracting carrier (the originator of the BBL) provides this information and mails it to a server: THE CORE MESSAGING PLATFORM. The server checks that the message is in the correct format and that the digital signature corresponds to the stated carrier. The server also calculates hash-values for the message header and for the bill of lading document attached. A hash-value is an algorithm applied to the header and the attached document, which makes it possible to verify at a later stage that the header and the bill of lading text has not been altered. The server – THE CORE MESSAGING PLATFORM – then forwards the bill of lading to the addressee named in the message heading. At the same time THE CORE MESSAGING PLATFORM relays the contents of the carrier's mail to the TITLE REGISTRY. Any subsequent dealings with the BBL are carried out in a similar manner.

At the TITLE REGISTRY the transaction information concerning the Bill of Lading text is stored. The registry records, which users have rights and obligations relevant to the Bolero Bill of Lading. The users affected are each allocated a "role" in relation to the bill of lading. Thus, a person may be classified as a carrier or shipper, these terms bearing more or less their everyday, maritime meaning. Or a user may be a to order party, a holder or maybe a pledgee. To all these roles the Bolero RuleBook and the Operating Procedures prescribe a certain extent of competence as regards the Bolero Bill of Lading. The BBL may be transferred, sold or pledged according to those rules, but there is no possibility for a user to dispose of the BBL in a way not already defined by the rules.

Applying those rules, the status of the BBL is constantly up-dated in the Title Registry Records. At the same time, when a transaction takes place the TITLE REGISTRY automatically informs the users listed as having a relevant role towards the bill of lading about the transaction. Thus, a carrier (or other person in the Bill of lading "chain") may at any time ascertain the status of the BBL, and in any case, the carrier is automatically informed by the TITLE REGISTRY of who is entitled to the goods covered by the bill of lading.

One must note that a Bolero Bill of Lading does neither exist nor carry any legal relevance in its printed out, tangible form. Thus, the consignee at the port of discharge does not receive title to the goods by presenting a printout version of the BBL. Instead, he or she must identify himself to the carrier as being (representatives of) the legal person the TITLE REGISTRY points out as being receivers. Thus, in this respect the BBL resembles a sea waybill more than a traditional bill of lading. Obviously, if one wishes to achieve the position of law connected to the traditional bill of lading, where the presentation of one copy of the bill of lading at the port of discharge (or of the full set elsewhere than the port of discharge) entitles the holder to the goods, one may carry out a switch to paper routine. But having done that, the *Bolero* Bill of Lading no longer exists.

6.2. The Bolero Bill of Lading and the New York Convention Art. II(2)

6.2.1. The starting point

In the Bolero System, the parties may enter into an agreement via the reference to standard terms, including charter-parties.[795] The parties to the Bolero System accept that a reference made in a BBL to a set of standard conditions is equal to a reference made in a paper document. Thus, the questions concerning arbitration agreements including the question of incorporation is as a starting point no different inside the Bolero System than it is outside. Thus, the main issue is whether the BBL is issued in a way that complies with the reciprocity criteria of Art. II(2).

6.2.2. Issuing and transferring the BBL

Above it has been mentioned that the BBL is issued unilaterally by the contracting carrier. The BBL must contain a recognition of receipt of the goods for transport,[796] information to the identification of the BBL, a statement regarding who is the sender, information as to the transferability and/or negotiability of the BBL, and a statement as to who is the holder of the BBL.[797] As mentioned, this information is registered in the TITLE REGISTRY. The transport agreement as such is not a part of this information; instead it is attached to the BBL in a document format. A user, needing to see the transport agreement in full text may require the text from the TITLE REGISTRY. Finally, the contracting carrier signs the BBL, using a digital signature.

The procedure regarding transfer of the BBL follows from the Operating Procedures Rule 14. A transfer is effected by the holder of the BBL advising the TITLE REGISTRY to register a new holder. The transport documentation is attached to the message, and the existing holder signs it. The TITLE REGISTRY then informs the new holder of the registration. The new holder then has 24 hours within which he or she may refuse the transfer.[798] If refused, all the rights and obligations arising out of and/or connected to the BBL are returned to the preceding holder.

After the 24-hour interval, the new holder may not refuse the BBL, and all rights and obligations under the BBL are consequently transferred to the new holder with

---

[795] Bolero Rule Book, rule 3.2(1) and 3.2(2).

[796] Bolero Rule Book, 3.1.a.

[797] Bolero Operating Procedures, Rule 13.a.

[798] Bolero Rule Book, 3.5.2(1).

effect as of the original transfer, 24 hours earlier.[799] The same applies if, within the 24-hour time-span, the new holder either accepts the transfer or asserts his or her rights under the BBL.[800]

The basic legal effect of a transfer in the Bolero System is that of novation. Thus, after the 24 hours have elapsed, alternatively, after the transfer has been approved or the transferee has asserted rights under the BBL, the contract of carriage between the preceding holder and the carrier ceases to exist, and a new contract of carriage on exactly the same terms is established between the new holder and the carrier.[801] This new contract of carriage is on the conditions and terms that follow from the BBL, including any transport documents or conditions attached or referred to in the BBL.

There can be no doubt that a full transfer of all legal effects is intended. Hence, the new holder is regarded to have succeeded, through novation, in both the provisions of substance and the provisions of procedure etc. in the contract of carriage. However, it is open to question, whether the procedure here described satisfies the requirement for reciprocal exchange of written documentation set out in the New York Convention Art. II(2).

6.2.3. The compatibility of the BBL and the New York Convention Art. II(2)

The BBL operates between members of Bolero. Thus, the BBL is only issued to and transferred between parties, who by their signature have accepted the contractual structure of the Bolero System. This includes the rule that transfer of the BBL creates a novation of all the rights and obligations, which follow from the contract of carriage between the carrier and the transferor, so that they now apply in the relationship between the carrier and the transferee – the new holder. It must be assumed that the requirements of the applicable law[802] are hereby satisfied. However, the requirements of international arbitration law set out in the New York Convention Art. II(2) are not. The parties' using the same service provider do not satisfy the requisite that both parties have in writing acceded to the arbitration agreement. This is especially so as the service provider offers a whole range of facilities, of which the BBL is only one. The acceptance entailed when becoming a member and user of the Bolero system is much too general to provide an acceptance of an arbitration agreement which

[799] Bolero Rule Book, 3.5.2(2).

[800] Bolero Rule Book, 3.5.2(2) and 3.5.1(1)(a).

[801] Bolero Rule Book, 3.5.

[802] English law.

might be inserted or incorporated in a contract of carriage, entered into at a later stage. Instead, the prerequisites of the New York Convention must be met as regards the specific arbitration agreement. It must be ascertained whether the procedures for the issuance and transfer of the BBL as described above meet the requirements of Art. II(2).

The procedure for *issuing* a BBL seems equally one-sided as does the issuing of a paper bill of lading. The procedure is strictly unilateral. As a starting point, this is also the case as regards the *transfer*. The agreement structure only shows any written reciprocity if the holder, or the new holder in case of transfer, chooses to accept the BBL. If, instead, the holder of the bill of lading chooses not to revoke the issuance or transfer, or simply asserts his or her rights under the BBL, no active accession to the arbitration agreement in the contract of carriage has taken place. Indeed, the situation should be regarded as equal to any other passive accession or quasi-contractual act, thus not satisfying the conditions under Art. II(2).

6.3. Conclusion

The BBL does not provide a better tool for entering into arbitration agreements in international trade than does its traditional (paperbased) alternatives. An exception to this may be the situations where the new holder does in fact actively accept the BBL. This writer suggests that in those situations the conditions in Art. II(2) should be considered satisfied; firstly, since the contract structure is obviously both in written form and reciprocal; secondly, as all documentation may be downloaded from the TITLE REGISTRY and therefore, the arbitration clause and other relevant documentation is available for the holder; and thirdly, even if the acceptance of the Bolero System in itself may not create the sufficient acceptance of an arbitration agreement under Art. II(2), it does add further strength to the first two points. Outside these situations, one cannot expect that all Courts applying the New York Convention Art. II(2) will accept an arbitration agreement inserted in or referred to in Bolero Bills of Lading. One could suggest that Bolero changed their procedures so that all transactions must be accepted, thus facilitating acceptance by the Courts of arbitration agreements and other provisions, which might be considered onerous on one of the parties. Yet, although theoretically feasible in a net-based system, this writer cannot judge whether it is a practically viable solution.

Ultimately, the High Contracting Parties, which already accept arbitration agreements entered into in bills of lading under the more favourable rights provision in the New York Convention Art. VII should be expected still to do so even if the bill of lading presented to them is a BBL. Certain jurisdictions may find a need to legislate specifically as regards the contract law effects of agreements entered into via EDI,[803] but in general there does not seem to be a real need to do so.[804] The step from the fax-machine to the Internet is no greater than the step from the pen to the telegraph, which was easily accepted by the fathers of the New York Convention as they were already used to it.

The legislators in Denmark, England and Norway have not felt a need to make specific regulations on the contractual validity of EDI-contract and digital signatures. However, in connection to the EC-directive no. 1999/93/EC of 13th December 1999, the Electronic Communications Act 2000 has been enacted in England and the Act on Electronic Signatures, no. 417 or 31st May 2000 has been introduced in Denmark. However, neither the directive nor the Acts are concerned with the contract law issues arising.

Setting aside problems with the establishment of proof, there seems no reason in Danish, English and Norwegian law, why arbitration agreements entered into via digital documentation should not be treated in exactly the same way as arbitration agreements entered into by other means.

7. New York Convention Art. II(2) and transport documentation – a workable mix?

Obviously, the New York Convention does not cater for all the needs of the maritime transport industry, as the Convention does not recognise unilateral contract formation or contracts that are in any form except writing. The legal position of parties having purported to enter into an arbitration agreement using such documentation may be uncertain.

However, the question must be posed whether the de facto problems with the restrictive criteria of Art. II(2) are as numerous as the theoretical approach applied above might be taken to suggest?

Almost certainly not! Many of the potential problems are ironed out by the way in which the transport documentation is used.

The use of arbitration agreements and clauses in charter-parties comply with Art. II(2). Players in the money-heavy, professionals only charter-party trade may generally insert arbitration clauses into the charter-parties and rest assured that the clauses will be respected by the Courts of the High Contracting Parties to the New York Convention. The arbitration agreements in the charter-parties are normally drafted so as to provide for the seat of the tribunal to be within a jurisdiction which will uphold

---

[803] French law hold regulations on the evidentary effects of digital signatures in Droit de la preuve aux technologies de l'information et relatif á la signature électronique, of 29th February 1999.

[804] See *Røsæg (1999)*, p. 677 as regards Norwegian law.

not only the arbitration agreement as between the owner and the charterer, but also accept the incorporation of the clause into a charter-party. London arbitration clauses are a lucid example of this. Thus, the arbitration procedure may be initiated according to the agreement, and the agreement may be enforced at the place of the seat of the tribunal. This does not rule out the possibility of multiple proceedings for the same dispute, irreconcilable decisions and problems in enforcement, but it does increase the chance that the arbitration agreement will be effective in the end. Also, some of the general conditions, which may effect the introduction of the arbitration clause directly into the contract of carriage for goods in the liner trade such as the NSAB, are primarily regional. Consequently, they are adapted to the legal sphere in which they are most likely to operate.

These are not arguments that no attempt to improve the New York Convention by making the formal requirements more lax should be made. Neither is this an attempt to ignore the problems occurring when tramp bills of lading are issued in the bulk trade. Those problems are real. The above stated is simply an argument that although there is most definitely room for modernisation of the New York Convention,[805] the present situation when viewed from a maritime transport lawyer's perspective is not disastrous.

---

[805] See above, in Chapter II, § 6, point 5, regarding the writer's suggestions as regards the New York Convention Art. II(2).

Chapter VI. Summing up and conclusions

§ 1. Introduction

This thesis has entertained five questions – what is an arbitration agreement, what is required for the arbitration agreement to be validly concluded, what is required for it to be valid on the substance, who decides, whether these criteria are satisfied, and, finally, whether there are any special features that apply when the arbitration agreement is introduced into the contract of carriage. Alternatively, it may be said that the thesis has entertained one question, namely what is required for the derogatroy effects of arbitration agreements to be accepted by the Courts, in transport related and other disputes alike. In this Chapter, the conclusions reached in the thesis will be extracted and deliberated upon. First, it will be considered, whether any specific transport related problems have presented themselves in the thesis. In doing this, two issues will be reviewed, namely the conclusion of arbitration agreements within the transport chain, and the arbitrability of transport disputes. Then the general regulation will be evaluated. The evaluation will take place both from the point of view of the domestic specialist lawyer – the internal view – and from the point of view of the regulation's aptness as a tool for dispute resolution in international disputes, and indeed other disputes where domestic legal advise is not available – the external view. When approaching the regulations from the internal point of view, one is able to focus distinctly on the contents of the rules, thus allowing for a comparison of the rules and a conclusion as to which rules best cater for the recognition and enforcement of the arbitration agreement. Adopting this point of view presupposes the construction of the all-informed domestic lawyer. The reader will excuse the fiction. Considering then the situations where expert domestic legal advice is not available, it is not as much the substantial rules that are considered, as the way in which these rules present themselves. Finally, it will be evaluated, whether the fact that the regulation provides for a good regulation of arbitration agreements, when applying the internal view, necessarily leads to the conclusion, that the regulation also will be apt in the non-domestic sphere.

§ 2. The arbitration agreement in the contract of carriage

1. The conclusion of the arbitration agreement

The most common example of an arbitration agreement in the contract of carriage is that of an arbitration clause in the printed text of a charter-party. A charter-party is signed by the original parties to the charter-party. This form of conclusion of the arbitration agreement satisfies the requirements of all the regulations here considered. The insertion of an arbitration clause into a (standard form) charter-party does thus not lead to difficulties, unless the terms of the charter-party are later sought incorporated into another charter-party, alternatively into a tramp bill of lading.

Especially the latter situation does not provide for mutuality in the contract formation procedure, and will for that reason alone fail to meet the requirements of the New York Convention Art. II and the Norwegian Code of Procedure sec. 452, subsec. 2, 1st sentence. Nevertheless, the problems occurring in practice are slight. The standard form charter-parties have been worded so as to promote the effectiveness of the arbitration clauses. This has done both by adequate choice of law provisions, often to the benefit of US or English law, and by, particularly after the emerge of case law such as the RENA K,[806] ensuring that the arbitration agreement is incorporated by explicit reference, thus satisfying the requirements for the effective incorporation under English law.[807] This development in the standard documentation has

---

[806] [1978] 1 Lloyd's Law Reports 545 QBD, THE RENA K, discussed above in Chapter II, § 3, point 3.3.1.

[807] Discussed at length in Chapter II, § 3, point 3 and point 4.

then been introduced into legislation, such as the Hamburg Rules Arts. 21 and 22 and the Nordic Maritime Code secs. 310 and 311, and provides an example that case law in one jurisdiction may be absorbed by the standard documentation of the trade and end up being introduced into domestic or international legislation in other jurisdictions, due to it being perceived as the de facto regulation of the trade.

Introducing the NMC secs. 310 and 311 has solved the problem caused by the Norwegian Code of Procedure sec. 452, sub-sec. 2, 1st sentence, in the situation where the carrier wishes to invoke the provisions of the charter-party as against a holder of a tramp bill of lading.[808] Also, it has brought an end to the uncertainties previously reigning under Danish law.[809] Outside the scope of sec. 311, the uncertainties of the previous Danish regulation may still reign, but it is likely that the Danish Courts will apply sec. 310, sub-sec. 3, cf. sec. 311, sub-sec. 2, analogously, and generally accept the arbitration agreements in tramp bills of lading that are incorporated through direct reference. Under Norwegian law, the problems caused by the exceptionally stringent regulation in the Norwegian Code of Procedure sec. 452, sub-sec. 2, 1st sentence may still occur outside the regulation of the NMC sec. 310, sub-sec. 3, cf. sec- 311, sub-sec. 2. This is particularly problematic in international transport disputes, as the Norwegian Courts have shown a tendency to apply the criteria under sec. 452, which are considerably stricter than the criteria under the New York Convention Art. II, to disputes arguably falling well within the ambit of the New York Convention.[810] Thus, even if it may be shown that the agreement to arbitrate fulfils the requirement of the New York Convention, the Norwegian Courts may still decide to disregard it if the requirement for a mutual signature in the Norwegian Code of Procedure sec. 452, sub-sec. 2. 1st sentence is not complied with. It is noted, that this situation will change, if the Draft Norwegian Arbitration Act becomes a reality.

Reverting to the NMC sec. 311, the provision has provided Danish and Norwegian Courts with firm ground when wishing to enforce a foreign arbitration agreement under the more favourable rights provision of the New York Convention Art. VII, a firm ground, which under English law is provided by case law. Consequently, due to the more favourable rights-provision, the New York Convention Art. II does not cause significant problems to regarding transport disputes under Danish, English and Norwegian law. An amendment of the New York Convention should thus not take place for the aid in the tramp-bill of lading situations alone. By

---

[808] See in particular Chapter II, § 4, point 2.2.2 with reference to ND 1957.366 NCA, JALNA.

[809] See Chapter V, § 2, point 5.2. for reference to U 1934.865 MCCC, OXELÖSUND and ND 1939.339 MCCC NITRIOS.

[810] As shown in Chapter II, § 4, point 3.

and large the market has solved the problem on its own. Still, a revision of the New York Convention Art. II, especially by abandoning the requirement for a mutual written process seems to be called for.[811]

Generally, the relationship between the NMC sec. 311 and the New York Convention is strained. As sec. 311 is not based in convention, the rules of the New York Convention should prevail over sec. 311. Accordingly, the mandatory choice of law to the benefit of the NMC and the mandatory seat of the tribunal prescribed for by sec. 311, cannot be applied within the scope of application of the New York Convention, as the Convention clearly presupposes that in this respect the party autonomy must be acknowledged.[812] In this way, the New York Convention restricts the application of the more problematic features of the NMC sec. 311, and aids the conclusion that, at present, the formation of arbitration agreements in international transport is not faced with major problems.

2. The arbitrability of transport disputes

This work has shown that the question of the inarbitrable subject matter may also arise in disputes regarding the international contract of carriage.

Generally, rules on arbitrability should be seen as rules on the positive application of the principle of ordre public.[813] The doctrine of positive ordre public allows for the application of the rules of a jurisdiction to a dispute, even if the dispute is governed by other law, under the rationale, that *not* applying the rules would be contrary to basic notions of justice within the jurisdiction. The doctrine of positive ordre public thus allows the Courts of the jurisdiction to impose its rules *restricting* arbitrability in exceptional circumstances.

The problem of the inarbitrable subject matter also presents itself in another form. If it is shown, that the subject matter of the dispute is not arbitrable under the law that applies to it, then the arbitration agreement may be deemed invalid, and the recognition and/or enforcement of the arbitration agreement may be refused by Courts and arbitral jurisdictions alike.[814] Unfortunately, there is no international consensus on what choice of law rule applies when the substantial validity of the arbitration agreement is challenged on grounds of lack of arbitrability in a law other

---

[811] See Chapter II, § 6, point 5.

[812] See Chapter V, § 2, point 7.1.

[813] Chapter III, § 3, point 3.3.

[814] Chapter III, § 3, point 3.5.1.

than the law of the fori.[815] It is suggested in the thesis, that the law to which the subject matter is most closely connected is most apt to deal with whether the subject matter is arbitrable under other laws than the law of the fori,[816] however, it is appreciated that under the current regime, it may not be possible to introduce this rule.[817] The problem here described is partly created by the New York Convention's deficiency in dealing explicitly with many aspects of the arbitration agreement. Thus the Convention does not hold any special rules on the application of the Convention to arbitration agreements,[818] nor does it provide special provisions prescribing the choice of law rules applicable to the arbitration agreement before the arbitration agreement has resulted in an award.[819] These deficiencies seem to cause considerable difficulties, and it is suggested that a future revision of the Convention takes this into account.

Discussing the issue of arbitrability in a thesis mainly dealing with commercial disputes may be seen as somewhat disproportionate as, generally, disputes regarding the law of contracts and obligations are governed by the party autonomy and as such arbitrable.[820] Restrictions on the arbitrability of a subject matter are normally only imposed within public law, or, within private law, if it is required to the protection of a party, who is in a bargaining position that is radically weaker than the one of his counter-party.[821] The reason for the lengthy discussion in this thesis is, that the regulations on transport law within the jurisdictions investigated offer several examples of rules governing the validity of the arbitration agreement.[822] The restrictions imposed by these rules have generally not been seen as problematic, as they have been introduced to support the liability regime sought introduced in the rules concerned. The rules are often applied according to a unilateral choice of law rule to the benefit of the lex fori. This thesis has shown that in this way the rules on the validity or contents of the arbitration clause show the characteristic of a regula-

---

[815] Chapter III, § 3, point 3.5.2.

[816] Chapter III, § 3, point 3.5.3.

[817] Chapter III, § 3, point 3.5.4.

[818] Chapter II, § 6, point 2.3.

[819] See the New York Convention Art. V(I)(a).

[820] Chapter III, § 3, point 3.2.

[821] Chapter III, § 3, point 3.2 and 3.4.

[822] Chapter III, § 3, point 3.4.4. and Chapter V, § 1, point 3.

tion on arbitrability.[823] It has been concluded, that to the extent that the rules may invalidate the arbitration agreement, and leave the parties to take the dispute to the Courts, the rules should be considered as any other rules on arbitrability. Thus, the rules should only be applied if the doctrine of positive ordre public warrants it. Situations of this kind *are* found in international transport. Firstly, if the claim concerns personal injury or death of a passenger, the argument of the protection of the weaker party may call for restrictions on arbitrability. Such restrictions are found in the Warsaw Convention Art. 32.[824] Secondly, the COTIF-CIM Convention[825] was originally seen as a piece of international public law, and the use of arbitration as a means of dispute resolution is simply ruled out in Art. 56. Restrictions on arbitrability are also found in the CMR Convention, dealing with the international contract of carriage of goods by road. Thus, if it does not follow explicitly from the parties' agreement that the CMR Convention Art. 33. should apply to the dispute, then the arbitration agreement will be null and void. It is noteworthy, that although generally agreed that arbitrability should only be restricted in rare cases, it seems that this effect of the CMR Convention Art. 33 is acknowledged. In this writer's view, sufficient reasons for the restriction of the arbitrability of disputes concerning the carriage of goods by road have not been shown to exist. Still, de lege lata parties to international contracts of carrage of goods by road must take the provision at face value, otherwise they may find, that an arbitration agreement not explicitly stating that the CMR Convention should apply to the parties' dispute will not be accepted by the Courts. De lege ferenda, it is suggested that Art. 33 is changed ad modum the modification rules in the Hamburg Rules Art. 22 or the NMC sec. 311.[826]

Considering the above, one must conclude that the international and domestic regulations of the validity of the arbitration agreement in the contract of carriage are certainly to be reckoned with, but that transport disputes are generally arbitrable. As long as the Courts only apply the restrictions of arbitrability of the forum when this is called for due to a principle of positive ordre public, problems are unlikely to occur. Thus, the Courts should not apply resstrictions on arbitrability

---

[823] Chapter V, § 1, point 4.

[824] Convention for the Unification of certain Rules Relating to International Carriage by Air, Warsaw, 12th October 1929, see Chapter V, § 1, point 3.6 and point 4.

[825] The Convention Concerning International Carriage by Rail of 9 May 1980, Apppendix B, Uniform Rules Concerning the Contract for International Carriage of Goods by Rail, see Chapter V, § 1, point 3.1.

[826] Chapter V, § 1, point 5.

mechanically, simply because the Courts percieve the rules as applying according to a unilateral choice of law rule to the benefit of the lex fori.

§ 3. Evaluating the regulations considered

1. The internal point of view

1.1. Introduction

In Chapter I of this thesis it has been shown that arbitration as a means of dispute resolution needs to be regulated both on a national an an international level, if the effectiveness of arbitration is to be ensured.[827] This regulation must secure two things, namely that the Courts will assist the arbitration procedure if it grinds to a halt, and that the Courts will accept the arbitration agreement as having derogatory effect. This thesis, dealing with the arbitration agreement, has entertained the latter issue.

In this section it will be considered, whether the regulations investigated provide for a reasonable degree of acceptance of the arbitration agreement. As said above, this section will employ the internal point of view, and thus restrict itself to discuss the substance in the respective regulations.

1.2. Danish law

The Danish Courts will recognise an agreement to arbitrate, if "a clear agreement to arbitrate" the dispute at hand is shown to exist.[828] Generally, an agreement to arbitrate will be accepted as "clear" if it is proved that the party contesting the arbitration

---

[827] Chapter I, § 3, point 1.

[828] Chapter II, § 2, point 1.

agreement knew or ought to have known of the agreement.[829] As Danish law holds no formal requirements for the conclusion of arbitration agreements, the proof of this may be provided by any means, and the Courts will take into consideration all the facts of the case in its evaluation. Even so, guidelines may be provided. Firstly, the Courts will pay considerable attention to who had it in his control to ensure that the arbitration agreement was known to both parties.[830] Indeed, it is the argument of this writer, that the Courts' conclusions in quite a few cases may be explained by referring to a principle of risk allocation.[831] Secondly, the bulk of the Danish case law is concerned with whether or not the arbitration agreement or clause has become part of the parties' contract.[832] The Courts will tend to accept the arbitration agreement if the agreement is drafted specifically in the parties' contract, even if it has not been especially emphasised. Also, the Courts will accept the conclusion of the arbitration agreement if the agreement forms a part of a standard document, incorporated by reference into the parties' main agreement, provided that the incorporation has taken place by a "one-layered" reference.[833]

Under Danish law, arbitration agreements are subject to a strict verbatim interpretation.[834] The main contract or arbitration agreement may be modified as to parties, allowing for the succession in and transfer of rights and obligations under the arbitration agreement,[835] but the scope of the arbitration agreement will be stringently defined. Also, as the Danish Courts applies a free evaluation of proof and need not consider any formal requirements, the Courts will entertain all the facts of the case. As a consequence, uncertainties as to whether the arbitration agreement has been concluded may lead to the Courts applying an especially stringent interpretation. Still, no general rule, that arbitration agreements should be subject to a narrow interpretation

---

[829] Chapter II, § 2, point 2.

[830] Chapter II, § 2, point 3.

[831] Chapter II, § 2, point 3.3.

[832] Chapter II, § 2, point 4. 2.

[833] Chapter II, § 2, point 4.2.1.

[834] Chapter II, § 2, point 4.3.2.

[835] Chapter II, § 2, point 4.2.2.

(an interpretation, allowing for a lesser scope of the arbitration agreement than what a verbatim interpretation would suggest) may be shown to exist.[836]

This thesis has pointed out that the possibility of contracting on back-to-back terms in professional relationships is not sufficiently catered for in any of the laws considered. Apart from that, the lack of formal requirements and the focus upon the knowledge of the parties to the particular dispute seems to have allowed the Danish Courts to reach reasonable results in the specific cases. In this way, the Danish regulation seems fit to cater for most of the needs of parties, wishing to conclude international arbitration agreements. The Danish Courts will demand a "clear agreement to arbitrate", and do, overall, seem reasonably strict when determining whether such an agreement may be shown to exist, but if the parties have followed the normal procedures for the conclusion of agreements within their particular trade, the Danish Courts are likely to take the arbitration agreement at face value.

Assuming that an agreement to arbitrate has already been concluded, the Danish Courts will accept the doctrine of separability and the principle of Kompetenz-Kompetenz. Indeed, the Danish Courts seem willing to accept the doctrine of separability not only as regards arbitration agreements, but also as regards agreements regarding choice of law and jurisdiction. The doctrine of separability is thus not founded on a principle of arbitration law, but upon general rules on the interpretation of contracts. The doctrine of separability, as it is understood under Danish law, will generally entail, that the parties must arbitrate their dispute even if the contract in which the arbitration clause is found is invalid. However, certain types of invalidity will also affect the arbitration agreement – which is generally the case if the invalidity is one of the types of invalidity referred to as "strong reasons for invalidity" under Danish and Norwegian law. In that case, the arbitration agreement will fall. The Danish Arbitration Act sec. 2, sub-sec. 1 provides, that from the time when an arbitral tribunal is seated according to the (putative) arbitration agreement, until the arbitral tribunal has made a ruling on its jurisdiction, the Danish Courts are barred from entertaining a dispute regarding the tribunal's competence. In this way, Danish law ensures that the arbitration procedure is not unduly prolonged because of the challenge of the tribunal's jurisdiction. The provision does not necessarily ensure a first-word competence to the tribunal as the question of the tribunal's competence may be brought to the Courts before the tribunal is seated, but the provision does generally seem apt ensure that the arbitral procedure is not unduly delayed.

In conclusion it must be said, that from the point of view of a domestic lawyer, the Danish rules governing the arbitration agreement seem to provide for both flexibility and for a sufficient protection of the effectiveness of the arbitration agreement. Con-

---

[836] Chapter II, § 2, point 4.3.3.

sequently – from a domestic point of view – there is no real need to suggest a new regulation.

1.3. English law

The English Arbitration Act 1996, Part I, only applies to arbitration agreements that are in writing. Under the principle of pacta sunt servanda, the English Courts may also recognise arbitration agreements that are not written, but the framework established for the effective arbitration procedure in the 1996 Act, Part I, cannot be applied to such agreements. However, the requirement for writing under the 1996 Act sec. 5 is so lax as to cater for almost all the usual modes of formation of arbitration agreements in international commerce. The real restriction on the formation of arbitration agreements under English law lies not in the requirement for writing, but in the general rules of contract law, especially in the rules on the interpretation of contracts and in the rules on the incorporation by reference. The general standard of interpretation of contracts under English law is that of a strict verbatim interpretation, concerned primarily with the document allegedly containing the parties' agreement. Concentrating on the verbatim interpretation of the document itself puts less emphasis on e.g. preceding negotiations and other surrounding circumstances than one would find in Danish and English law. Also, the principle of a strict verbatim interpretation leads to problems when the arbitration agreement in the contract between A and B is sought incorporated by reference into a contract between B and C. However, English case law seem to have developed a firm rule for these situations, allowing for the incorporation of arbitration agreements by direct reference, alternatively allowing for the incorporation in cases where the arbitration agreement in A and B's contract clearly is worded so as to apply also to disputes between B and C.

Consequently, English law seems to offer a good regulation of the formation of arbitration agreements in international trade and commerce, this writer's reservation regarding the back-to-back situations apart. Introducing a requirement for writing, that in effect seems to be a requirement for the proof of the arbitration agreement in a reliable form, the contents of which may be certified later, seems to have provided regulation that balances the need for clarity as to the arbitration agreements and its terms and the need for a flexible formation of contract.

With the adoption of the English Arbitration Act 1996, English law has finally settled the discussion as to what extent the doctrine of separability and the principle of Kompetenz-Kompetcnz are accepted in national law. Firstly, the doctrine of separability is set out in the English Arbitration Act sec. 7. The arbitration clause will survive even if the main agreement is found invalid ab initio, unless the reason for invalidity is one that goes to the root of the parties' whole contractual relationship. Also, first word Kompetenz-Kompetenz is provided for in sec. 30 of the Act. The first word competence may be circumvented by the initiation of Courts proceedings, but the relationship between the first word competence given in sec. 30, and the Court's investigation of whether the matter is covered by an arbitration agreement under sec. 9 has already been discussed by Case law, and seems to be decided in favour of sec. 30 – or in favour arbitrii, one may say. In this way, English law provides for a good support of the effectiveness of arbitration agreements, once the arbitration agreement is shown to exist. Overall, this writer finds that the English regulation in the 1996 Act provides a recommendable regulation of the conclusion and effectiveness of the arbitration agreement.

1.4. Norwegian law

The requirement in the Norwegian Code of Procedure sec. 452, sub-sec. 2, 1st sentence, that the parties agreement to arbitrate must be in writing, has over the years been developed in case law. It seems that – at present – the requirement for writing may be described as a demand that all original parties to the arbitration agreement has signed the agreement, either directly or through reference. Taking into account the strict requirement, the Norwegian Courts seem to make allowances once it has been established that a signed agreement to arbitrate is in existence between the original parties to the contract. Thus, it is accepted that the arbitration agreement is transferred with the transfer of the legal relationship it concerns, and arbitration agreements are generally interpreted in rather a lax manner, allowing the arbitration agreement to encompass any claims which are reasonably within the contract, unless indications to the contrary are proved to exist.

The requirement for writing in sec. 452 is so strict as to disallow many of the modes of contract formation in international trade, and indeed, it is too strict as to take into consideration even the needs of domestic arbitration. Thus, even considering the somewhat less stringent Norwegian approach to the interpretation of the arbitration agreement, the threshold provided by the extremely stringent requirement for writing is not providing for an appropriate protection of the effective arbitration agreement.

In the Draft Norwegian Arbitration Act this has been recognised, and the committee has suggested that in the new Act there should be no requirement for the arbitration agreement to be in writing. In this way the committee has sought to distance itself even more from the position of the law as it is at present, than done in the committee's first suggestion – a suggestion providing a lax formal requirement. The rejection of a requirement that the arbitration agreement should be in writing will bring the Norwegian regulation on a par with the Danish regulation on this point, and one may expect a situation where, in the end, the test for the Courts is the knowledge of the parties. However, the travaux préparatoires seem to suggest that a clear proof of the arbitration agreement's conclusion will still be demanded, so a slight restriction from the Norwegian Courts, similar to the Danish Court's requirement for a "clear" agreement to arbitrate may be expected. Whether this will also entail that the Norwegian Courts under the new Act will apply a more stringent interpretation of the terms of the arbitration agreement remains to be seen.

The principle that an arbitration clause in the parties' main agreement may survive the initial invalidity of the main agreement, has for long been accepted by the Nowegian Courts, provided that the arbitration agreement has had the appropriate wording. Thus, the doctrine of separability has a long tradition and is also included in the Draft Norwegian Arbitration Act, even if, conceptually, tied to the tribunal's Kompetenz-Kompetenz. Under the present Norwegian regulation the latter principle is not explicitly mentioned. Indeed, it seems that on this point the position of Norwegian law is the exact same as the position of Danish and English law before the introduction of the 1972 and 1996 Acts, thus allowing the parties to take a dispute regarding the tribunal's jurisdiction to the Courts at any time. As shown, this position of the law works against arbitration as an expedient means of dispute resolution. This has been accepted by the committee, and in the Draft Arbitration Act, more real first word competence is allocated to the tribunal. However, it seems to this writer that the regulation suggested is less apt to ensure an expedient arbitral procedure than is both its Danish and English equivalents.

In conclusion it may be said, that neither the formal requirement in sec. 452, sub-sec. 2, 1st sentence, nor the Norwegian regulation of Kompetence-Kompetence seems satisfactory at present. It could be argued, that the very strict requirement for writing will make it evident whether or not the parties are bound by an arbitration agreement, thus making it less necessary to ensure a real Kompetenz-Kompetenz with the tribunal. Even so, the regulation of arbitration as a means of dispute resolution displayed in existing Norwegian law is not an example to be followed.

1.5. Conclusion

When regarding the regulation of the arbitration agreement from the point of view of the all-informed domestic lawyer, one reaches the conclusion that both the Danish and the English regulations seem adequate. However, the Norwegian regulation does not. Whether the conclusion is the same, when regarding the arbitration agreement from the external point of view will be seen below.

2. The external point of view

It has become apparent in this work that the choice of both domestic and international legislators as to whether there should be a formal requirement for arbitration agreements, and if so, how stringent this should be, has significant impact upon the developments of arbitration law within the relevant jurisdictions. Obviously, the formal requirements will be immensely important in the determination of whether an arbitration agreement has been concluded between the parties, as shown above, but the formal requirements, or lack of formal requirements, as the case may be, also carry a more general influence. Thus, the requirements affect the accessibility of the law on the conclusion of arbitration agreements and they dictate the focus and quantity of case law. Those issues will be considered here.

In this thesis it is apparent that the law lacking any formal requirements for the conclusion of arbitration agreements (Danish law) is the least accessible law. This is due to two different features of the regulation. Firstly, as there is no obvious starting point for the discussion of the formation of arbitration agreements, case law may approach the problem from many different angles. Secondly, the lack of a formal requirement invites lawsuits that might not have been initiated in the face of an indispensable requirement that there should be a written agreement to arbitrate between the parties. It seems to this writer that the diversity of the Danish case law is partly due to the fact that in many cases it has not been clear that there was *not* an effective agreement to arbitrate between the parties. Overall, the minimalist regulation in the Danish Arbitration Act provides non-specialists with very little information as to what are the real contents of the Danish regulation of arbitration and arbitration agreements. This may dissuade foreign parties to opt for arbitration under Danish law. Also, the allowance of much competence to the Courts may be of concern to users accustomed to a more positivistic regulation.

Under English law, the Arbitration Act 1996 sec. 5 and sec. 6(2) provide obvious starting points for a person wishing to establish what is English law on the conclusion of arbitration agreements. The sections cannot be regarded in isolation, and due to the lack of real contents in sec. 6(2) on the incorporation of arbitration clauses, much of the information as to the real contents of the law must still be found in case law. Thus, the lawyer, wishing to assess the position of the law within the field certainly needs to consult a considerable number of cases. However, the subjects of the discussions in English case law seem less diverse than the patchwork experienced under Danish law, and case law seems – at least for the present – to allow for reasonably firm conclusions, enhancing predictability. Overall, the predictability is also enhanced by a more positivistic approach, spelling much of the English law on arbitration out in black letter rules. The declared aim of the committee behind the English Arbitration Act was thereby to enhance the use of English arbitration, and it seems to this writer, that that effect may be achieved.

Of the three jurisdictions investigated, reigning Norwegian law offers the most transparent regulation. The real contents of the requirement of the Norwegian code of procedure sec. 452, sub-sec. 2, 1st sentence that the parties' agreement to arbitrate must be in writing must be extracted from case law, but a good picture of that case law may be obtained by reading a small number of cases. In this way, an overview of the general – harsh – requirement for writing may reasonably easily be obtained. Also, considering the requirement for a mutual signature to the arbitration agreement, case law generally seems to consider the relationship between the original parties to the contract. Unless a third party has succeeded directly in the position of one of the original parties to the contract, there simply seems little reason to engage in Court proceedings concerning the proposition that a third party should be bound by the provisions in the arbitration agreement. Cases on the incorporation of arbitration agreements by reference are found, but the incorporation is only accepted if the provision or standard document sought incorporated is one the parties ought to be familiar with the contents of. Considering the general regulation in the Norwegian Code of Procedure Chapter 32, it must be said that it does not provide for much information, and may for that be met with the same criticism as the Danish Arbitration Act. However, on the whole the rules of Norwegian law may relatively easily be established.

It has already been mentioned that if the Draft Norwegian Arbitration Act goes through in its present form, the requirement that arbitration agreements should be in writing will perish. Considering the formation of arbitration agreements, this will mean a shift of focus from the rules of arbitration law to the general rules of contract law. Thus, the case law on the conclusion of arbitration agreements might achieve some of the same features as Danish case law. However, setting up a Model Law inspired regulation will provide for more black letter rules, and therefore probably be more appealing to foreign and/or non-specialist users.

3. Conclusion

Splitting up the evaluation of the Danish, English and Norwegian regulation, and dealing with them from both an internal and an external point of view provides for a "two-layered" comparison and conclusion. Firstly, Danish and English law seem equally apt to ensure the effectiveness of arbitration agreements when viewed from the internal point of view. However, considering the regulations from the point of view of the outsider wishing to obtain information on the regulation, this picture changes. Danish law lacks transparency, and one must assume that Danish lawyers, wishing to introduce a clause, providing for arbitration in Denmark according to

Danish law, may experience problems, as the counter-party cannot easily establish what this will entail, and thus, cannot easily satisfy himself that the purported arbitration clause will indeed be effective.

Splitting up the discussion thus, also allows for the presentation of the good feature of Norwegian law, namely that its contents may easily be established. However, this is not enough to outweigh the burden of the excessively strict formal requirement.

Considering the above, if this writer was to pick one regulation as the better, it would be the regulation found in the English Arbitration Act 1996. However, the rationale for this would not primarily rest on regards to the contents of the regulation, instead, it is the higher degree of transparency that tips the balance.

§ 4. Afterword

When first writing this thesis, I used the catchphrases "arbitration agreement friendly" and "arbitration agreement hostile" as denominators for regulations with a lax or a strict formal requirement respectively. The reader will notice that those phrases have later been omitted. Indeed, if anything should be learned from this thesis, it is that the fact that a law provides no formal requirements for the conclusion of arbitration agreements does not mean that that law is necessarily "arbitration agreement friendly". The evaluation of whether a regulation is "friendly" towards arbitration agreements presupposes the evaluation of several factors, of which the formal requirements for the conclusion of the agreement is only one.

There is no rule of general validity that regulations on arbitration as a means of dispute resolution should always aim to cater (also) for the needs of international trade, as indeed, there is no divine law that the legislators of a jurisdiction should necessarily wish to attract international arbitration. English law has uttered such a wish, and consequently produced a new Arbitration Act. In doing that, the English committee took into account the UNCITRAL Model Law, but did not adopt it mechanically. Instead, English law was evaluated, and the parts of English law that seemed more appropriate than the rules of the Model Law were maintained. Also, even in cases where the substantive rule of the Model Law was preferred, systematic improvements were made. In this way, introducing a Model Law based regulation has been done as a part of the natural development of the domestic rules.

The Draft Norwegian Arbitration Act also introduces a Model Law inspired approach. However, it seems that in its eagerness to improve the present state of affairs, the Norwegian committee has not taken existing law into consideration as much as they might. Indeed, some of the provisions incorporating the Model Law are introduced as novelties, even if rules to the same effect are already fount in domestic Norwegian law. The wish of the committee to abandon the formal requirement all together is psychologically understandable. The stringent formal requirement was never introduced in the Norwegian Code of Procedure, but was developed by the Norwegian Courts over the years. The need to send a clear signal to the Courts that earlier case law should be abandoned seems real. Still, this writer maintains her slight worry that on this point the Norwegian committee may have gone too far. For the reasons already set out above, a lax formal requirement, on a par with the one found in the English Arbitration Act 1996 sec. 5, might be preferable.

So far, Danish legislators have not uttered a clear wish that Danish law should make itself attractive to international dispute resolution by arbitration.[837] If such a wish should emerge in the future, one must consider, which route to embark on. If a Model Law inspired approach is preferred, as one might expect, the English way of incorporation, taking into consideration already existing English law, seems the better option. Alternatively, one could suggest a separate regime, based more strictly on the Model Law, and setting out only to deal with international arbitration. It has already been shown, that from a distinctly domestic point of view, the Danish rules are quite appropriate. These could be maintained in domestic arbitration. However, this suggestion does not take into consideration the domestic non-specialist. Also laymen may need to consider Danish law on the arbitration agreement. For than purpose, rather exhaustive black letter rules, ad modum the English Arbitration Act 1996, seem the better option.

---

[837] However, recently practitioners have done so, e.g. on a seminar on arbitration held In Copenhagen on October 31st 2002, it was proposed to introduce a new Arbitration Act, based on the UNCITRAL Model Law.

Table of cases

English cases

Danish cases

Danish arbitration rulings

Norwegian cases

Other

Bibliography

Ambrose, C.
[Ambrose (2000)]

Arbitration and the Human Rights Act, [2000] LMCLQ 468.

Andenæs, J.
[Andenæs (2001)]

Statsforfatningen i Norge, 8. utg., Oslo 1998.

Andersen, L.; Madsen, P.
[Andersen/Madsen (2001)]

Aftaler og mellemmænd, 4. udg. København 2001.

Arfazadeh, H.
[Arfazadeh (2001)]

Arbitrability under the New York Convention: *Lex Fori* Revisited, (2001) 17 Arbitration International 73.

Asariotis, R.
[Asariotis (1998)]

Anwendungssystem und Zuständigkeitsvorschriften der Hamburger Regelen als Mittel zur Durchsetzung des Haftungregimes", ETL [1998], p. 161 ff.

Augdahl, P.
[Augdahl (1949)]

Rettskilder, Oslo 1949.

Bell, J.
[Bell (2000)]

Sources of law, in English Private Law, vol. I, p. 3-46, Oxford 2000.

van den Berg, A.
[van den Berg (1981)]

The New York Arbitration Convention of 1958. Towards a Uniform Judicial Interpretation, The Hague 1981.

van den Berg, A.
[van den Berg (1996)]

Court Decisions on the New York Convention 1958. Consolidated Commentary Vols. XX-XXI: Art. II (1) and (2), (1996), XXI ICCA Yearbook 398.

Bilton, P., Røsæg, E., Solvang, T.
[Bilton/Røsæg/Solvang (1997)]

The Norwegian Maritime Code of 24 June, 1994, No. 39, with later amendments up to and including Act of 2 August, 1996, No. 2. (Unofficial translation of the Norwegian Maritime Code 1994), Marius no. 236, Oslo 1997.

Bjarup, J.; Dalberg-Larsen J.
[Bjarup (1993)]

Retsbegreb, retsanvendelse og retsvidenskab. Indføring i Almindelig Retslære, Århus 1993.

Blessing, M.
[Blessing (1996)]

Arbitrability of Intellectual Property Disputes, (1996) 12 Arbitration International 191.

Blume, P.
[Blume (2001)]

Juridisk metodelære: En indføring i rettens og juraens verden, København 2001.

Boguslavskij, M.M.
[Boguslavskij (1965)]

Staatliche Immunität, Berlin 1965.

Boyd, S.C. m.fl.
[Scrutton (1996)]

Scrutton on Charterparties and Bills of Lading, 20th ed., London 1996.

Bull, H.J.
[Bull (2000)]

Innføring i veifraktrett, 2 utg., Oslo 2000.

Brækhus, S.
[Brækhus (1998)]

Sjørett, voldgift og lovvalg. Artikler 1979-1998, Oslo 1998.

Chitty on Contracts
[Chitty (1999)]

28th ed., Vol. 1, General Principles, London 1999.

Clayton, R.; Tomlinson, H.
[Clayton/Tomlinson (2000)]

The Law of Human Rights, Oxford 2000.

Clarke, M.A.
[Clarke (1976)]

Aspects of the Hague Rules, a comparative study in English and French law, Hague 1976.

Clarke, M. A.
[Clarke (1997)]

International Carriage of Goods by Road: CMR, London, 1997.

Cohen, M.
[Cohen (1997)]

Arbitration Agreements in Writing:Notes in the Margin of the Sixth Goff Lecture. (1997) 13 Arbitration International 237.

Cooke, J. m.fl.
(Cooke 1993)

Voyage Charters, London 1993.

D'Amato, A.
[D'Amato (1984)]

Jurisprudence. A Descriptive and Normative Analysis of Law, Dordrecht, 1984.

Dalhuisen, J.H.
[Dalhuisen (1995)]

The arbitrability of Competition Issues, (1995) 11 Arbitration International 151.

410

Danelius, H.
[Danelius (1997)]

Mänskliga rättigheter i europeisk praxis, Stockholm 1997.

Davidson, F.
[Davidson (2000)]

English arbitration law 1999, [2000] LMCLQ 230.

Dicey, A.W.; Morris, J.H.C.
[Dicey and Morris (2000)]

Dicey and Morris on the Conflict of Laws, 13th ed.; London 2000.

van Dijk, P.; van Hoof, G.J.H.
[Dijk/Hoof (1990)]

Theory and Practice of the European Convention on Human Rights, 2nd ed., Deventer, 1990.

Dillén, N.
[Dillén (1933)]

Bidrag til läran om skiljeavtalet, Stockholm 1933.

Eckhoff, T.
[Eckhoff (2001)]

Rettskildelære, 5. udg., Oslo 2001.

Ekelund, P.
[Ekelund (1997)]

Transportaftaler. En introduction til den almindelige transportjura, 2. udg., København 1997

von Eyben, W.E.
[von Eyben (1991)]

Juridisk grundbog 1, Retskilderne, 5. udg. København 1991.

Falkanger, T., Bull, H.J.
[Falkanger/Bull (1999)]

Innføring i sjørett, 5. utg., Oslo 1999.

Fleischer, C.A.
[Fleischer (1994)]

Folkerett, 6. Utg., 5. Oppl., Oslo 1998.

Fleischer, C. A.
[Fleischer (1998)]

Rettskilder og juridisk metode, Gjøvik 1998.

Franklin, K.
[Franklin (2000)]

Arbitration v. alternatives, [2000] ADRLJ 90.

Gaja, G.
[Gaja (1979)]

International commercial arbitration: New York Convention, compiled and edited by Giorgio Gaja, New York, Oceana Publications, 1979.

Germer, P.
[Germer (1996)]

Indledning til folkeretten, 2. udg., København 1996.

Giersing, P.; Madsen, L.
[Giersing/Madsen (2000)]

Voldgiftsklausuler og ulykkesforsikring, U 2000 B 481 ff.

411

Glossner, O.
[Glossner (1989)]

The New York Convention on the Recognition and Enforcement of Foreign Awards – Some Thoughts After 30 Years – 1985 – 1988, in *Sanders (1989)*, p. 275 ff.

Goode, R.
[Goode (2001)]

The Role of the Lex Loci Arbitri in International Commercial Arbitration, (2001) 17 Arbitration International 19.

Gulmann, C.; Bernhard, J.; Lehmann, T.
[Gulmann m.fl. (1989)]

Folkeret, København 1989.

Gomard, B.
[Gomard (1979)]

Voldgift i Danmark, Skrifter ved Det retsvidenskabelige Institut ved Københavns Universitet, København 1979.

Gomard, B.
[Gomard (1993)]

Obligationsret, 3. Del, 1, udg. København 1993.

Gomard, B.; Kistrup, M.; Petersen, L. L.; Lundum, J.
[Gomard (1997)]

Fogedret, 4. udg. 1. opl., København 1997.

Gross, P.
[Gross (1992)]

Competence of Competence: An English View , (1992) 8 Arbitration International 205.

Hanotiau, B.
[Hanotiau (1996)]

What Law Governs the Issue of Arbitrability?
(1996) 12 Arbitration International 391.

Harris, B.; Plantrose, R.;Tecks, J.
[Harris (1996)]

The Arbitration Act 1996 - a commentary, Oxford, 1996.

Harris, B.; Plantrose, R.;Tecks, J.
[Harris (2000)]

The Arbitration Act 1996 – a commentary, 2nd ed., Oxford 2000.

Harris, J., Meisel, F.
[Harris/Meisel (1998)]

Public policy an the enforcement of international arbitration awards: controlling the unruly horse, [1998] LMCLQ 568 ff.

Harris, D.J., O'Boyle, M., Warbrick, C.
[Harris/O'Boyle/Warbrick (1995)]

Law of the European Convention on Human Rights, London 1995.

Hartley, T.C.
[Hartley (1997)]

Mandatory Rules and International Contracts, 266 Collected Courses 1997, Den Haag 1997, p. 345-425.

Helmer Nielsen, B.
[Nielsen (1993)]

Fremmede staters jurisdiktionsimmunitet. En kommentar til ambassadør Tyge Lehmanns artikel i U 1993 B, p. 70-71, U 1993. B, 213-214.

Heumann, L.

Skiljemannarätt, Stockholm 1999.

Hjejle, B.
[Hjejle (1941)]

Foreningsvoldgift, studier over gyldigheden af selvdømmeklausuler i retlige fællesskabsforhold, København 1941.

Hjejle, B.
[Hjejle (1973)]

Frivillig voldgift, 2. rev. udg., København 1973.

Hjejle, B.
[Hjejle (1987)]

Voldgift, 3. rev. udg., København 1987.

Hoeck, H.
[Hoeck (1992)]

Fremmede staters jurisdiktionsimmunitet – en kommentar til U 1992. 453 HKK. U 1992. B, 427-432.

Holtzmann, H.M.; Neuhaus, J.E.
[Holtzmann/Neuhaus (1989)]

A Guide to the Uncitral Model Law on International Arbitration: Legislative History and Commentary, Deventer 1989.

Honka, H. (ed.)
[Honka (1997)]

New Carriage of Goods by Sea, The nordic approach including comparisons with some other jurisdictions, Åbo 1997.

Hov, J.
[Hov (1998)]

Avtaleslutning og ugyldighet, Oslo 1998.

Hurwitz, S.
[Hurwitz (1940)]

Om Begrebet »retlig« Interesse i Procesretten, i Festskrift til Vinding Kruse, Nyt Nordisk Forlag, København 1940, p. 107 ff.

James Jr., F.
[James (1965)]

Civil Procedure, Boston 1965. (This book exists in a 5th ed., published in New York 2001. Unfortunately I have not been able to obtain a copy of it).

Jensen, T.
[Jensen (1986)]

Retlig interesse i anerkendelsessøgsmål mod Forbrugerombudsmanden. U 1986 B, 409 ff.

Kaplan, N.
[Kaplan (1996)]

Is the Need for Writing as Expressed in the New York Convention and the Model Law Out of Step with Commercial Practice? (1996) 12 Arbitration International 27.

413

Kinander, M.
[Kinander (2000)]

Er det grunnlag ofr et normativt korrektiv til retten ut fra Eckhoffs rettsteori? TfR 2000.324.

Kirry, A.
[Kirry (1996)]

Arbitrability: Current trends in Europe, (1996) 12 Arbitration International 373.

Knoph, R.
[Knoph (1998)]

Knophs oversikt over Norges rett, 11. utg., Oslo 1998.

Kurkela, M.S., Uoti, P.
[Kurkela/Uoti (1994)]

Arbitration in Finland, Helsinki 1994.

Law Society (The)
[The Law Society]

Reform af voldgiftsloven, København 2003.

Lawson, F. H.
[Lawson (1980)]

Remedies of English Law, 2nd ed., London 1980.

Lehmann, T.
[Lehmann (1993)]

Fremmede staters jurisdiktionsimmunitet. En kommentar til U 1992.453 HKK samt til advokat Henrik Hoecks kommentar. U 1993. B, 70-71.

Lindboe, A.
[Lindboe (1944)]

Privat rettergang (Voldgiftsprosessen), Oslo 1944.

Lookofsky, J.M.
[Lookofsky (1985)]

Indsigelser mod voldgift, U 1985 B 404.

Lorenzen, P., Rehof, L.A., Trier, T.
[Lorenzen/Rehof/Trier (1994)]

Den europæiske menneskeretskonvention med kommentarer, 2. udg., København, 2003.

Malanczuk, P.
[Malanczuk (1997)]

Akehurst's Modern Introduction to International Law, 7th rev. ed., London 1997.

McClean, J.
[Morris (2000)]

Morris: The Conflict of Laws, 5th ed., London 2000.

Melchior, C.H.

Forvaltningens kontrol med domstolene under den tyske besættelse. U 1997. B, 169-170.

Merkin, R.
[Merkin (1991])

Arbitration Law, London 1991. (Looseleaf).

Merkin, R.
[Merkin, (1996)]

Arbitration Act 1996, an annotated guide, London, 1996.

414

Merkin, R.
[Merkin, (2000)]

Arbitration Act 1996, 2nd ed. London, 2000. (1st ed. is the abovementioned Arbitration Act 1996, an annotated guide, London, 1996)

Michelet, H.P.
[Michelet (1997)]

Håndbok i tidsbefraktning, Oslo 1997.

Mustill, M.J.; Boyd, S.C.
[Mustill/Boyd (1989)]

The Law and Practice of Commercial Arbitration in England, 2nd ed. London, 1989, with 2001 Companion Volume to the second edition, London 2001.

Mæland, H.J.
[Mæland, (1988)]

Voldgift, Bergen, 1988.

Möller, G.
[Möller (1996)]

Om jämkning av skiljeavtal, JFT 1996, 441.

Nielsen, P.A.
[Nielsen (1997)]

International privat- og procesret, København 1997.

Nielsen, R.
[Nielsen (1999)]

Retskilderne, 6. rev. udg., København 1999.

Nørgaard, S.B., Pedersen, P.V.
[Nørgaard/Pedersen (1995)]

Springende regres – kontraktsafhængigt retsbrudsansvar, U 1995 B, 385.

Park, W.
[Park (2000)]

Determining arbitral jurisdiction: allocation of tasks between courts and arbitrators. [2000] ADRLJ 19-30.

Pedersen, P.V.
[Pedersen (1999)]

Modern Regulation of International Unimodal and Multimodal Transport of Goods, Scandinavian Institute of Maritime Law Yearbook 1999, p. 53-109, Marlus no. 247.

Petersen, K.
[Petersen (1935)]

Nogle Bemærkninger om udenlandske Voldgiftskendelsers Anerkendelse og Eksekutionskraft, København 1935.

Philip, A.
[Philip (1976)]

Dansk International privat- og procesret, 3. udg., København 1976.

Philip, A.
[Philip (1992)]

Introduktion til international voldgift, U 1992 B 121.

Philip, A.
[Philip (1995)]

International voldgift i handelsforhold, U 1995 B 439.

Philip, A.
[Philip (1996)]

Scope of Application, Choice of Law and Jurisdiction in the New Nordic Law of Carriage of Goods by Sea, Il Dritto Marittimo, (1996) p. 309-324.

Pryles, M.
[Pryles (1993)]

Foreign Awards and the New York Convention, (1993) 9 Arbitration International p. 259 ff.

Rasch, J.
[Rasch (2000)]

Eksport af dansk retspleje. Festskrift i anledning af Den Danske Søretsforenings 100 års jubilæum, Den Danske Søretsforening 2000, p. 134-136.

Rasmussen, U.L.
[Rasmussen (1984)]

Jurisdiktionsklausuler og voldgiftsklausuler i søtransportkontrakter, Oslo 1984.

Regnarsen, K.
[Regnarsen (1993)]

Lov om fragtaftaler ved international vejtransport (CMR), 2 udg., Jurist- og Økonomforbundets Forlag 1993.

Rehoff, L.A., Trier, T.
[Rehoff/Trier (1990)]

Menneskeret, København 1990.

Rutherford, M.; Sims, J.
[Rutherford/Sims (1996)]

Arbitration Act 1996: A Practical Guide, London, 1996.

Rogers, A.
[Rogers (1994)]

Arbitrability, (1994) 10 Arbitration International 263.

Ross, A.
[Ross (1953)]

Om ret og retfærdighed. En indførelse i den analytiske retsfilosofi, København 1953.

Ross, A.
[Ross (1972)]

Lærebog i Folkeret, almindelig del, 4. udg., København 1972.

Røsæg, E.
[Røsæg (1999)]

IT, avtaleslutning og behovet for lovreform, i Festskrift till Gunnar Karnell: vid hans avgång från professuren i rättsvetenskap vid Handelshögskolan i Stockholm, våren 1999, av kolleger och vänner, Stockholm 1999.

Samuel, A.
[Samuel (2000)]

Separability of arbitration clauses – some awkward questions about the law on contracts, conflict of laws and the administration of justice, [2000] ADRLJ 36-45

Sanders, P.
[Sanders (1989)]

Arbitration In Settlement of International Commercial Disputes Involving the Far East and Arbitration in Combined Transportation, Deventer 1989.

Schei, T.
[Schei (1998)]

Tvistemålsloven med kommentarer av Tore Schei, 2. udg. Oslo 1998.

Schelin, J.
[Schelin (1995)]

Stykegodsbefordran enligt nya sjölagen – en replik, SvJT 1995.865.

Schlosser, P.
[Schlosser (1992)]

The Competence of Arbitrators and of Courts. (1992) 8 Arbitration International 189.

Siesby, E.
[Siesby (1965)]

Søretlige Lovkonflikter, Conflict of Laws in Maritime Matters, København 1965.

Siig, K.M.
[Siig (1995)]

Forum og lovvalg vedrørende transportansvaret, Marius nr. 215, Oslo 1995.

Siig, K.M.
[Siig (1998)]

Forum and choice of law in the linter and tramp trades, in Siig (ed.), Simply 1997, Scandinavian Institute of Maritime Law Yearbook 1997, Marius no. 240, Oslo 1998.

Sindballe, K.
[Sindballe (1917)]

Om Adgangen til at anlægge Anerkendelsessøgsmaal. U 1917 B, 145 ff.

Skoghøy, J.E.A.
[Skoghøy (1998)]

Tvistemål, Oslo 1998.

Skoghøy, J.E.A.
[Skoghøy (2001)]

Tvistemål, 2. utg., Oslo 2001.

Spera, K.
[Spera (1986)]

Internationales Eisenbahnfrachtrecht Kommentar, Wien 1986. (Looseleaf).

Sutton, D.St.J.; Kendal, J.; Gill. J.
[Russell (1997)]

Russell on Arbitration, 21st ed. London 1997.

Tiberg, H.
[Tiberg (1995)]

Styckegodsbefordran enligt nya sjölagen, SvJT 1995, p. 321.

417

Tweeddale, K.; Tweeddale, A.
[Tweeddale/Tweeddale (1999)]

A practical approach to Arbitration Law, London, 1999.

Ulfbeck, V.
[Ulfbeck (2000)]

Kontrakters relativitet: Det direkte ansvar i formueretten, Københanv 2000.

Vagner H.H.
[Vagner (2001)]

Entrepriseret, 3. udgave under medvirken af Torsten Iversen, København 2001.

Ventris, F.M.
[Ventris (1986)]

Tanker Voyage Charter Parties, London 1986.

Walton, A., Vitoria, M.
[Russell (1982)]

Russell on the Law of Arbitration, London 1982.

Wegener, M.
[Wegener (2000)]

Juridisk metode, 3. rev. udg., København 2000.

Windahl, J.
[Windahl (2001)]

Direkte krav og forumklausuler, U 2001 B, 242 ff.

Woxholth, G.
[Woxholth (2001)]

Avtaleinngåelse, ugyldighet og tolking, Oslo 2001.

Zweigert, K., Kötz, H.
[Zweigert (1998)]

An introdution to comparative law, 3rd ed., translated by Toni Weir, Oxford 1998.

Preparatory works etc.

Danish Arbitration Act 1972 negotiations

Folketingstidende 1971-1972 col. 947-950; col. 1982-1990; col. 5691; col. 5748.

Danish Arbitration Act 1972 travaux préparatoires 1

Betænkning nr. 414/1966 vedrørende lovgivning om voldgift. Afgivet af det af Justitsministeriet d. 3. februar 1962 nedsatte udvalg.

Danish Arbitration Act 1972 travaux préparatoires 2

Folketingstidende A, 1971-1972 col. 891-908.
Folketingstidende B, 1971-1972 col. 1089-1092.

Danish CMR travaux préparatoires 1	Betænkning nr. 319/1962 angående fragtaftaler vedrørende international godsbefordring ad landevej, afgivet af det ved Justitsministeriet skrivelse af 11. marts 1961 nedsatte udvalg.
Danish Maritime Code 1994 travaux préparatoires	Lovforslag nr. L 129, Folketinget 1993-94, incl. bemærkninger og betænkning nr. 1215 om befordring af gods, København 1994.
Finnish Arbitration Act 1992 travaux préparatoires	Regeringens proposition till Riksdagen med förslag till lag om skiljeförfarande samt vissa lagar som har samband med den, 1991 rd – RP 202.
Mustill report	Mustill, L. J.: A New Arbitration Act? The response of the Departmental Advisary Committee to the UN-CITRAL Model Law on International Commercial Arbitration, Department of Trade and Industry, Her Majesty's Stationary Office, London, 1989.
Scottish Advisory Committee on Arbitration Law	Report to the Lord Advocate on the UNCITRAL Model Law on International Commercial Arbitration, Edinburgh, Scottish Courts Administration, 1989.
Swedish Arbitration Act 1999 travaux préparatoires	Regeringens proposition 1998/99:35, Ny lag om skiljeförfarande. Prop. 1998/99:35.
Swedish Maritime Code 1994 travaux préparatoires	Prop. 1993/1994:195, Ny Sjölag, Stockholm, Riksdagen 1993/1994.
United Kingdom Department of Trade and Industry	United Kingdom Department of Trade and Industry Consultation Document on Proposed Clauses and Schedules for an Arbitration Bill, February 1994, published in [1994] 10 Arbitration International 189 ff.
1996 Report on the Arbitration Bill	United Kingdom Department of Trade and Industry: Departmental Advisory Committee on Arbitation Law, 1996 Report on the Arbitration Bill, July 1995. Published in [1997] 13 Arbitration International 275 ff.

Index

420

Index of statutory materials, conventions etc.

European Materials

International conventions

428